Great Aviation Collections of Britain

For
Don

Great Aviation Collections of Britain

The UK's national aeronautical treasures

Ken Ellis

Crécy Publishing Limited

Great Aviation Collections of Britain

First published in 2013 by Crécy Publishing Limited

A CIP record for this book is available from the British Library

ISBN 9 780859 791748

Printed in Malta by Gutenberg Press

Crécy Publishing Limited
1a Ringway Trading Estate, Shadowmoss Road, Manchester M22 5LH
www.crecy.co.uk

Vickers Varsity T.1 WL679 staging a run-by along Cosford's Runway 24 prior to make its, and the type's, last-ever flight to take its place in the RAF Museum, 27th July 1992. (See Chapter 6.) *RAF Museum*

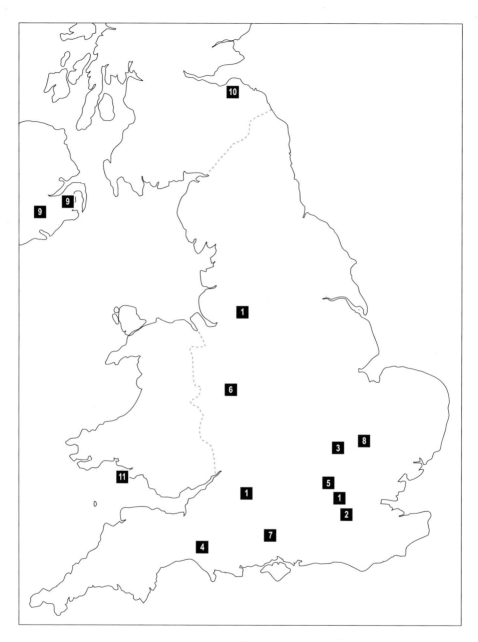

Key:

The numbers given correspond to the chapters within; eg 3 is
Chapter 3 on the Shuttleworth Collection.
© Pete West © 2013

Contents

Foreword
Dr Michael A Fopp

The development of aviation spans just over a century, encompassing a mere three generations. With the exception of the very earliest thinkers like Leonardo Da Vinci and aeronauts like the Montgolfier brothers those of us connected with aviation heritage, either as enthusiastic amateurs, or professionals privileged to work in the field we love, have actually been a part, either first, second or third hand, of virtually all the major milestones in the subject that we now seek to preserve. I always thought that this made people who worked in aviation museums, either professionally or as volunteers, very lucky (especially those of us who are more advanced in years) as we have had the opportunity to actually talk to, refer to, or even take part in, much of the history we looked after.

It also meant that, for the professionals, we could not ignore the fact it was also loved and researched by extremely knowledgeable enthusiasts worldwide. This meant that those of us who made our living preserving aviation history did so in full view of a host of critical onlookers; most of whom, in their own way, could be more knowledgeable about their specialist areas than we were. A perfect example of this was, and still is, Ken Ellis. For nearly 40 years Ken has been delivering quality research about everything to do with the preservation of aircraft. His series *Wrecks & Relics* is an archival gem charting the whole process of preservation (or lack of it!). His years as the editor of *FlyPast* magazine saw that publication grow in international, as well as national fame, and his legacy lives on with its excellent work to this day. His tour-de-force in 2011 was *Lost Aviation Collections of Britain* and it must have seemed impossible to cap such a wonderful piece of work. Now he is following that with an even greater achievement with *Great Aviation Collections of Britain*.

I was both proud and honoured to be asked to write the foreword for this seminal work, but more than that, I was also pleased to follow Ken's progress by reviewing every chapter as it came off his word processor. Each time a new chapter arrived I realised just how much work Ken was doing in order to ensure that everything was right – sorting out the intricacies of the museums covered in this volume must have been mind-bogglingly difficult. He has done it and I have learned a lot from his work.

Direct and tangible link

Two important points have really struck me in reading the manuscript. Firstly, in his descriptions of how the collections came together, there is a common thread of co-operation leading to something special being preserved. The interaction between private owners (eg Richard Nash), learned bodies (eg Royal Aeronautical Society), Departments of Government (eg Ministry of Defence) and museum directors has, in the main, been incredible. How else would so many gems have survived when, at the time, they were seen by many to be no more than scrap? From outside the profession there have occasionally been accusations of rivalry and competition between institutions, but Ken's listings show how aircraft have been gifted, loaned or swapped from one party to another for the benefit of all and, most importantly, to ensure the preservation of the aircraft.

Dr Michael Fopp, at the helm of a Meteor F.8 WH301 at Hendon on his retirement as Director of the Royal Air Force Museum, 2010. Michael's father flew Meteors and he has long had a fascination with the type. *Iain Duncan, RAF Museum*

Secondly, Ken has told the story of aviation museums during their most challenging time – in human terms, from their birth, through the toddling stage, pimply teenage years and now early adulthood – with experience behind them and an established future ahead. He has also covered a period of radical change as museums generally became, not just places to be visited by enthusiasts, but also leisure venues appealing to the masses; a period when they realised that their role was not just to preserve the past, but to look at the future and educate by entertaining. They fill the disposable time of their visitors and in so doing, are competitors in a huge industry which includes stately homes, theme parks, shopping malls, art galleries, and even television, radio and film.

Increases in disposable leisure time, coupled with more and more operators in the leisure industry, have made museums review the ways in which they attract audiences. Many have gone for the leisure attraction approach by offering the public the same type of synthetic thrill-seeking experience so eloquently pioneered by the Disney Corporation. I only subscribe to part of this notion. I believe museums should offer forms of interpretation and excitement which are comparable to their competitors but, most importantly, they should be centred around what can never be emulated by the theme park. I mean, of course, the uniqueness of museums in having *real* objects. This is their most powerful selling point; providing a direct and tangible link with the past because of their authenticity. Museums provide a rare and indisputable truth in a world of synthetic experience, social media, cold-calling, mis-selling, video games and other intangible falsehoods which define our daily lives.

Assumed authenticity

To provide this reality, museums must ensure that what they have is authentic and this book describes, in detail, examples of replicas and mis-marked aircraft. I believe those who make decisions in museums need to be conscious of the line between the real, the replica, the copy and the unreal. The public will not ask, nor will they assume that the museum's ethical stance on authenticity is in question. If the replica is good enough they will look at it and assume it is real because the word 'museum' gives authenticity to its contents. If the replica is bad the public will just think that the museum is poor.

It is important to understand that an object (aircraft or anything else) is in itself a document which can be read in the future. Some people will only need to look at the 'cover' (the external airframe) others may want to see the 'contents page' (flight deck), the 'index' (engineering panel) or even the 'bibliography' (the flight manual). There will always be people who want to devour the document from cover to cover. If they find pages missing or, worse still, dissimilar pages from another document, their understanding of the original will be compromised.

If the curator does his job, provision should be made for each type of 'reader' so that the object carries with it its *whole* story into the future. In the 'real world' pages fall out of documents, (they even get torn out) and others are inserted in their place. In the restoration of aircraft it is particularly important that the 'bookmarks' in the shape of restoration notes are comprehensively maintained to document these omissions.

When the museums catalogued so carefully by Ken in this volume were created things were different and record-keeping was primitive, if existing at all. All credit to him for following the 'travels' of so many airframes when, until relatively recently, even the museums had little idea of their past. This is the other great leap forward in recent years – the introduction of digital record-keeping and the ability to make information widely available via the internet. The cultural change embodied in this transition from paper to computer has never received the credit it deserves, but we should be grateful to the hundreds of curators and volunteers in museums who have ensured that not only is the airframe conserved, but also all other information about it.

Keeping it real

Ken's listings include aircraft which hold 'fake' identities. In a few rare cases this is necessary because the original provenance is not known or the airframe is built up from more than one machine. It may also be possible that it was given its 'alias' years ago and a simple lack of time or money have not yet put this right. But, in my opinion, there is no reason at all why a museum should restore an aircraft in misleading markings if it has a choice and knows the airframe's true history. There are a number of excuses for this behaviour: "it had no combat history so it's marked up in a famous scheme of an aircraft that didn't survive"; or "we wanted a British version, but could only get an American one"; and "it was only a target-tug, but was more famous as a fighter". These reasons are all specious because they fail to provide the authenticity which *only* museums can show. They are even more incredible when technology now makes it so easy to show the story of the aircraft in more than just two-dimensional ways. If your example served in the US Army Air Corps and also in the RAF and you can only find an USAAC version, what is the problem? You still have the aircraft, in all its glory, and you can explain its use by both air forces while, at the same time truthfully tell the audience its history. What they see is what they get – rare in this world of misleading information, bank misconduct, and fraud on a wide scale.

Museums are different – they tell the truth and the public can rely on them. Ken's book shows that honourable history comprehensively, and with a mixture of fact, detail and humour which I found compelling. I spent over 30 years working in museums and a lifetime as an aviation enthusiast. *Great Aviation Collections of Britain* is for me, a vindication of my generation's hard work in ensuring our aviation heritage is set fair for our children, grand children and those not yet weaned on machines that fly.

Introduction

To mark the fiftieth anniversary of the publication of the first edition of *Wrecks & Relics* in 2011, *Lost Aviation Collections of Britain* was written. It was a bit of a gamble, would readers be interested in the *history* of aircraft preservation? They were! So, what to do next? An examination of the heritage and legacy of the UK's fabulous spread of museums and collections seemed obvious. In 1977, I worked with Phil Butler on a book called *British Museum Aircraft*; the potted biographies of *all* of the 'front-of-house' airframes in *all* 39 venues then regularly open to the public. A quick bit of scribbling, revealed that a new version on those lines would be an *enormous* undertaking; such has been the expansion of the aviation heritage 'industry' in the last 36 years. Take a look at the Appendix, it lists 90 collections; add the 12 in the main section and we've exceeded the 'ton'!

"What about the nationals, then?" – came the author's naive cry. This was inspired by the knowledge that 2013 was the centenary of the first fully-fledged aeroplane to be gifted to a UK collection, an epoch that I think *very* worthwhile marking. (The Cody biplane offered and presciently accepted by the Science Museum – see Chapter 1.) National collections are the 'household' names which, by definition, hold the aeronautical 'crown jewels'. But what to call the book? Simples: *Great Aviation Collections of Britain*.

"But *we're* great!" I hear the team at Newark exclaim. And at Martlesham Heath, Weston-super-Mare, Speke Airport, Sunderland, Dumfries and Galloway, and all points in between. You get the picture... All over the UK there are museums with exhibits that directors of 'nationals' would love to drool over in their own galleries. There are also venues out there with collections that far surpass some of the 'nationals' in terms of the *number* of aircraft held. A look through this book will reveal how many 'non-great' museums have passed on exhibits to the 'big boys', or helped in crucial ways. So, there is greatness in *every* aviation museum and the word 'Great' in this title is not to belittle *any* collection.

What is a 'national' museum?

So, what *is* a 'national'? It's a museum that receives the majority of its annual revenue funding *directly* from a Government department, without an intermediary like the Arts Council or other funders. In the context of *Great Aviation Collections of Britain* these are: National Museums of Science and Industry (also known as the Science Museum Group), funded by the Department of Culture, Media and Sport (DCMS); Imperial War Museum, in this case South Lambeth and Duxford (also DCMS); National Museum of the Royal Navy – Fleet Air Arm Museum (Ministry of Defence – MoD); Royal Air Force Museum – Hendon and Cosford (MoD).

But, this is the *United* Kingdom; at least until the Scottish independence referendum is staged on 18th September 2014! It became clear that the constituent nations needed a look-in, so the following were added: National Museums of Northern Ireland – Ulster Folk and Transport Museum (funded by the Northern Ireland Government) and National Museums Scotland, in the form of the National Museum of Flight (Scottish Parliament). For Northern Ireland, I 'wobbled' the definitions, because I consider the Ulster Aviation Collection to be punching above its weight and deserving recognition as such. As will be seen from Chapter 11, Wales has nothing approaching the stature of a 'national' aeronautical collection, so the oldest Welsh aeroplane, the Watkins Monoplane was chosen, flying as it does inside the National Waterfront Museum.

Then two things started to nag at me. Not a 'national' by the above definition, but held in that esteem by many – the Shuttleworth Collection. This sincere regard and self-interest propelled Old Warden into the 'ranks'; it was very likely I'd be *lynched* if Shuttleworth was not included! Likewise the Museum of Army Flying at Middle Wallop. This is perhaps best defined as a 'Regimental' or 'Corps' museum. It is not a 'national' but it admirably flies the flag for a vital air arm.

What is and isn't covered

Having defined, and partially fudged, what a 'national' is here is a book devoted to the origins of each collection, the major waypoints in their existence and 'biographies' of a *selection* of their exhibits. Each chapter appears in the approximate order that the venues opened up to the public; followed by the 'provincial' museums. The emphasis is on *museums* and *aircraft*; if the reader is looking for a catalogue of the names of curators, director generals and the like, this is not for you. Equally, there are hundreds who have slaved over restoration projects but it would be impossible to name them all.

To keep the book within a reasonable size, the exhibit profiles (the aircraft 'biographies') *had* to be a selection to show the flavour and some of the highlights of each collection. The emphasis is unapologetically on British designed and built aircraft and I'm aware that trainers, communications types and helicopters are thinner on the ground than they deserve. The exhibit profiles do not attempt to list every oil change, service and re-spray in an exhibit's history. The aim is to explain *why* a particular airframe should be regarded as important, as a type or its particular career, and then *how* it came to be preserved. The assumption is that most readers will know the historical importance of most types, but rarer ones are given a deeper introduction. In general, I have not included composite recreations, cockpits, replicas or full-size replicas or unmanned devices in the 'biographies'.

Two tables are common to most of the chapters, one dealing with former exhibits, another with current ones. These are designed to provide an at-a-glance view of the extent of each collection, past and present. They are arranged by type and details including the year built and roughly (or occasionally precisely!) when it arrived are given. Regular *W&R* readers will have no problems with these and, if you seek more, then it is time to refer to your library of past editions! 'Ownership' or 'custodianship' of airframes in this book is not to be inferred as definitive.

Acknowledgements

As with *Lost Collections of Britain*, there are people in every edition of *Wrecks & Relics,* and each copy of *FlyPast*, who have contributed to my knowledge of UK aircraft preservation. The wealth of aeronautical heritage that the UK basks in is a tribute to a vast army of amateurs and professionals, all united by their enthusiasm for the subject.

Many thanks to the following for their considerable help during my researches: **Fleet Air Arm Museum**: Graham Mottram, Director; Dave Morris, Curator of Aircraft and Chief Engineer, Bob Turner Head of Corporate Services. **National Museums Scotland**: Louise Innes, Principal Curator of Transport. **Royal Air Force Museum**: Peter Elliott, Senior Keeper, Department of Research & Information Services; Ajay Srivastava, Public Relations Manager. **Science Museum**: Andrew Nahum, Senior Keeper; Rory Cook, Collections Information Officer. **Shuttleworth Collection**: John Benjamin, Hon Librarian and Archivist.

Alf Jenks and Terry Dann for access to their superb images; other photographers are credited with their work. Pete West provided the map. Roy Bonser and Peter Green supplied many of the 'archive' images.

Nigel Price of *FlyPast* checked through the draft and provided lots of encouragement. Peter Green also ploughed through the manuscript and was a constant font of information. Despite their efforts the responsibility for any mistakes is awl mein!

Dr Michael Fopp wrote the Foreword, but not content with this, he guided me through the heritage of the Royal Air Force Museum, the background to national museums and provided painstaking comments on the book as it evolved. I am indebted to him.

Rounds of applause go out to all of the team at Crécy Publishing, especially designer Rob Taylor and the ever-patient Gill Richardson. And to Pam and feline Rex for their respective brands of support during what turned out to be a mammoth project.

Ken Ellis
People's Republic of Rutland
May 2013

Myddle Cottage, 13 Mill Lane, Barrowden, Oakham, LE15 8EH
wrecksandrelics@kenavhist.wanadoo.co.uk

CHAPTER 1

From the 'Rocket' to DNA
Science Museum
South Kensington, London
www.sciencemuseum.org.uk

W ith the public long gone and the staff mostly departed, the duty officer did his rounds. Suddenly there was an almighty crack, followed by the sound of glass shattering. What was going on? This was not a scene from *Night at the Museum*; Ben Stiller could rest easy. This was 6th July 1986 in the Science Museum's Aeronautical Gallery and Mr Rhodes quickly discovered the source of the kerfuffle. Perched atop a substantial display cabinet, the Cody biplane had suffered a structural failure of its 'tail' skid. As the 74-year old flying machine settled, it had cracked the cabinet below it.

South Kensington's Andrew Nahum wrote the incident up: "The tail skid of this aircraft, which was partially bearing the weight of the machine, collapsed last Sunday... [It] rolled back off axle trestles [and the] broken stump penetrated the display case it was on. ...the area has been cordoned off." The Cody had been put into position 22 years previously. With his background in the Royal Aeronautical Establishment (RAE) Keeper of Aeronautics John Bagley set about an investigation that would have done the Air Accident Investigation Unit proud. "Examination of the fractured skid, which appears to be of ash, shows a relatively smooth fractured surface on the lower (tension) side. The deep discoloration here, perhaps caused by oil penetration, possibly indicates a limited facture when the aircraft was in service. There is some indication that this crack may, over the years, have propagated upwards progressively under structural load in the gallery."

Above: The 'Making of the Modern World' gallery at South Kensington. The Avro 504K and Lockheed 10 'fly' over other icons of technology, including a V-2 rocket in the background. *Ken Ellis*

I first met John Bagley in the early 1970s. His knowledge of history, from the agricultural revolution to the 'Cold War' was matched by an enthusiast's passion for aviation fused with experience of cutting-edge technology. Via National Service with the RAF he was posted to the RAE at Farnborough, Hampshire, where his degree in computational physics was snapped up by the Aerodynamics Department. He was encouraged to stay, becoming a Principal Scientific Officer in 1962. Much of his work was in supersonics; he devised the M-shaped wing, which to my delight is still known as the 'Bagley Wing' by present-day designers! His time at the RAE was not all research and his never-throw-it-away philosophy resulted in another structure with his name on it: 'Bagley's Barn'. Unofficially, the RAE Aero Club acted as a repository for airframes in need of a home. I first got to know John when he organised the loan of a Focke-Achgelis Fa 330 gyro-kite to the Merseyside Aviation Society; John had a couple stashed deep inside 'his' barn.

John was also Chief Handicapper for the Royal Aero Club's Records, Racing and Rallying Association (known as the '3Rs') from the 1950s into the 1990s. He took great delight in knowing which pilots were "pulling flankers", while having the flying skill to show others how they could shave valuable seconds off their lap times. At the '3Rs' Schneider commemorative race at Bembridge on the Isle of Wight in May 1988 John regaled me with the story of the Cody's strut fracture and took great satisfaction that the failure was more down to a flying accident in March 1913 than any slip in artefact husbandry at South Kensington! *FlyPast* magazine was sponsoring Terry Hiscock and his Beagle Pup at the time and, as one of the editorial perks, I served as his 'directional consultant'; we were delighted to come sixth around a very similar course to that was flown 57 years earlier by Flt Lt Boothman in one of the aircraft in John's custodianship – see below for the Supermarine S.6B.

In 1976 John became an Assistant Keeper at the Science Museum (ScM for here on), naturally looking after the aeronautical collection, and before long the word 'Assistant' was dropped. He was greatly involved in the Concorde display at Yeovilton, the Wroughton out-station and its Air Transport Collection, and the re-structuring of the 'Flight' gallery at South Kensington. Throughout all of this, mild-mannered and effortlessly 'laid-back' John put all these achievements down to his colleagues and friends.

John also led me to ponder what was *really* worth preserving and *why*. John had pioneered a 'listing' of significant airframes for the British Aircraft Preservation Council and his philosophies were ingrained in its National Aviation Heritage Register inaugurated in 1998. We both waxed lyrical about the centenary of the Cody being the first fully-fledged aeroplane to be gifted to a UK collection. John died in 2003 aged 74, much-missed by many from all walks of life. His influence and inspiration pops up in all sorts of places in this book and I am forever thankful to him for that.

I am, Sir, your obedient servant

So what were the circumstances that led to the Cody being given to a British museum? In the labyrinthine basement at South Kensington, the file for artefact inventory number 1913-136 records that on 6th September 1913, Major F Grant Ogilvie CB, ScM Director, had a letter from the War Office forwarded by a colleague from the British Museum: "I am commanded by the Army Council to acquaint you that No.304 Cody Biplane, without engine, is about to be disposed of, and to enquire whether the Museum authorities would care to accept it as an addition to their aviation section, seeing the machine is the last representative of a type of considerable historical interest. The aeroplane would be transferred free of charge, subject to Treasury sanction, but the Museum authorities would be expected to pay the cost of transport. I am, Sir, your obedient servant, R W Wade." (It is interesting to note that transfers today from the Ministry of Defence still ask for the caveat about costs, insurance etc – but probably involving much more paperwork!)

The 'historical' Cody had been handed over to the Royal Flying Corps (RFC) *less than nine months* before and wrecked in an accident at Farnborough on 31st March. Why 'target' the British Museum? It would not have been at all clear which collection would have domain over something as new-fangled as a flying machine.

ScM's response to the offer was to go and look and the results were recorded on 30th September 1913: "The biplane looks almost new, and I understand that it was overhauled and repaired quite recently. ...It appears to me impracticable to attempt to exhibit the biplane in the present buildings of the Science Museum and the question is whether the machine is worth storing with a view to its exhibition in the new museum. ...If we do not take the machine now, it will be broken up."

Perhaps the final line of the minute carried the day, because on 10th October 1913 the Director replied and accepted the War Office's offer. Within a card manila folder, tied with ribbon, South Kesington's bundle of documents on the Cody holds a Royal Aircraft Factory-headed 'flimsy' torn out of a duplicate book reading: "Advice Note No.8618, 26th November 1913. The following goods have been this day despatched to: Mr F Cowley, your representative: One Aeroplane." Britain's first whole aircraft exhibit had 'landed' and it celebrates its centenary with its custodian this year.

At this point it is as well to emphasize that ScM is tasked with all aspects of technology and science, so the modernity of the Cody was not of importance. Besides, in 1912 powered flight was only nine years old, *all* aircraft were youngsters! Readers should get used to the author straying off the subject... Among the telegrams that Charles Augustus Lindbergh received after arriving at Le Bourget, Paris, at the end of his solo transatlantic flight of 20-21st May 1927 was one from the exceptionally determined and visionary Paul Edward Garber of the Smithsonian Institution, asking 'Lindy' if he would hand over his Ryan NYP NX211 *Spirit of St Louis*! Persistence rewarded, the monoplane was presented to the museum on 30th April 1928. Garber, who became the first curator of the National Air Museum (later National Air and Space Museum) in 1946, carried out this 'pre-emptive strike' policy throughout his career. It's never too early to target potential exhibits!

I browsed in this wonderland

"Before long I discovered that by paying another penny excess fare I could go on to South Kensington. There was the Science Museum... Sir Hiram Maxim's machine dominated one hall, and Pilcher's glider hung suspended beside Stringfellow's model. ... For ten days I browsed in this wonderland with a mounting source

Cody's Military Biplane within the 'Flight' gallery. *Ken Ellis*

of guilt and lies building up that I seemed powerless to do anything about." This is Nevil Shute Norway, later to be part of the design staff of the R100 airship and founder of aircraft manufacturer Airspeed, writing of his days 'sagging off' from school at the tender age of eleven in 1910. These words appear in Shute's autobiography of 1953, *Slide Rule*, and provide a vivid image of the wonders a visitor could behold.

Young Nevil may have been a bit out with his recollections. I don't doubt he saw the Pilcher but, as Chapter 10 shows, it was at South Kensington for a brief exhibition in January and February 1913, in which case he was nearer to 14 than he was to 11. No matter. In 1896 Sir Hiram Maxim donated a "full-size steam engine, full-size screw propeller... together with several other items" to quote the Science Museum. A cache of relics from John Stringfellow's steam-powered model aeroplane of 1848, including the engine, boiler and propeller were presented in 1908. It is assumed that it was these that Nevil was writing about.

(To return briefly to the exhibition of January and February 1913, this was the first aviation-themed event held at the museum and centred on three borrowed gliders, the Pilcher, a Lilienthal and the Clarke Chanute. The Lilienthal was acquired from Germany by Oxford-based dentist T J Bennett and it arrived in the UK in March 1895. The following year it was on show at the grandly-titled 'International Exhibition of Motors and Their Appliances' at South Kensington. In 1897 it was given to Percy Pilcher and in 1920 was presented to the Royal Aeronautical Society, which in turn passed it on to ScM. It was removed from display in 1976 and replaced by the current replica. The other glider, the Clarke Chanute, is now with the RAF Museum Hendon – see Chapter 5.)

Wright stuff, wrong reason

Staged within the specially-built and awesome Crystal Palace, the Great Exhibition of 1851 highlighted in graphic terms the public's appetite for all things mechanical and scientific and gave rise to museums all over the nation. Packed with scientific, art and design items, the South Kensington Museum opened in 1857. In 1899 it was renamed the Victoria and Albert Museum and the scientific material had overflowed to temporary exhibitions on the site of the present-day Science Museum. In 1909 this separation was acknowledged and ScM was founded. Building of the East Block was started in 1914 and completed in 1918. The arrival of the Alcock and Brown Vickers Vimy (profiled below) in 1919 provided an obvious increase in footfall. A decade later one million visitors in a year was achieved and by 2012 that figure had tripled. It was not until 20th March 1928 that the East Block was formally opened by King George V and for the occasion the Avro company presented a brand-new Avian two-seat biplane on brief loan. Published in 1929, the handbook of the aviation artefacts, *Aeronautics*, made the first reference to South Kensington holding the National Aeronautical Collection. This was no idle boast as the museum was host to the most famous aircraft on the planet.

Aeronautics had the following to say about exhibit inventory number 1928-1866: "This was the first power-driven man-carrying aeroplane to make a free, controlled and sustained flight. It is the original aeroplane built by Wilbur and Orville Wright and flown by them on December 17, 1903, at Kitty Hawk, North Carolina, USA. ...Four flights were made ...in the presence of five witnesses. The first lasted 12 seconds and was made in a wind of about 22mph, the machine being piloted by Orville Wright. The last flight was one of 59 seconds, when the distance covered by 852ft; the machine was then overturned by a gust of wind, while left unattended, and the damage so caused prevented further experiments. ...Since the first

The author's copy of the Science Museum's *Aeronautics* may have suffered some damage in the last 84 years, but it is still a treasured part of his library.

flights were made the aeroplane has been preserved in the Wright Laboratory. Certain parts which were damaged have been replaced and the machine restored to its original condition by Mr Orville Wright." In 1916 the Flyer went on display at the Massachusetts Institute of Technology in Cambridge, Massachusetts, and statically at several air events elsewhere.

On the last day of January 1928 the 1903 Wright Flyer was shipped from the USA to Britain, on loan from Orville (brother Wilbur died on 30th May 1912) and displayed at ScM. Frederick Handley Page gave the 16th Wilbur Wright Memorial Lecture in May 1928 and afterwards an illuminated address was sent to Orville to commemorate the event. This concluded: "Further, we greatly appreciate the renewed evidence of your goodwill in sending this historic machine to England and not less the distinction you have thereby conferred on our renowned Science Museum where it is now exhibited for all the world to see."

Britain was basking in this loan and the great and the good of Britain had no doubts about its place in history. As the carefully-packed Wright biplane was crossing the Atlantic, it was leaving behind an almighty row that had severed relations between Orville and the Smithsonian Institution – which otherwise could have reasonably expected to have been showing off the Flyer 'for all the world to see'. While Orville was paying South Kensington an incredible compliment, the purpose of the loan was to deliver a massive snub to Washington. Much of the credit for Britain being chosen as the destination fell to balloon pioneer Griffith Brewer who became the Wright's first English passenger when Wilbur took him up at Le Mans in France in 1908. Brewer stuck up a lasting friendship with the Wrights, travelling to their home in Dayton, Ohio, on many occasions up to 1941.

So how did the 'exile' of the Flyer come about? A tandem-winged monoplane was catapult-launched from a houseboat moored on the Potomac near Quantico, Virginia, on 6th May 1896. Its single-cylinder steam engine of about 1hp drove twin pusher propellers, taking it for a flight of 3,300ft. This was Samuel Pierpoint Langley's Aerodrome No.5 and he had achieved the world's first successful sustained flight of an engine-driven heavier-than-air aircraft. Far-sighted as Langley was, he could never have envisaged that he had pre-empted by a century America's weapon of choice, the unmanned drone, or UAV. Langley had been the Secretary of the Smithsonian Institution since 1887 and the Aerodrome had been built on that organisation's premises. With a span of 13ft 8in and it could hardly be called a model; it carried no pilot but it was still an incredible achievement. Langley then scaled-up his machine and fitted a 52hp 5-cylinder radial, creating the man-carrying Aerodrome 'A' in 1903. With Charles Manly at the controls, the 'A' was launched from the same houseboat on 7th October 1903 and plummeted into the Potomac. On 8th December Manly was again on board as the 'A' broke up and nose-dived into the water. Nine days later the Wrights became world famous and Langley quit his aeronautical experimentation. (Langley's No.5 and the 'A' are today displayed at the Smithsonian, in downtown Washington DC and the massive Udvar-Hazy Center, close to Washington Dulles Airport, respectively.)

Charles Doolittle Walcott became Secretary of the Smithsonian in 1907, taking over after the death of his dear friend Langley the previous year. Walcott was also chairman of the National Advisory Committee for Aeronautics – the precursor of NASA – from 1919 to 1927; he was a man of influence. From 1911 the Wrights became embroiled in a bitter and costly series of law suits in which they attempted to protect their rights regarding others – principally Glenn Curtiss – using their control systems and design philosophies without financial settlement or licence. These legal wrangles had the effect of neutering the development of aviation in the USA, effectively wiping out America's lead.

The remains of Aerodrome 'A' were held by the Smithsonian and in January 1914 Secretary Walcott agreed to Curtiss borrowing it to help his legal battle. The aim was to prove that it *could* have flown in 1903 and it was Langley's influence that he and others were following, *not* the up-start Wrights. At his base at Hammondsport, New York, Curtiss set about radically rebuilding the 'A', installing a Curtiss control system, a new powerplant and putting it on floats – all very far removed from the machine of 1903. Walter Johnson flew it twice and it did achieve distances well in excess of the 1903 tumbles; but the rear wing collapsed on the second attempt, just as it had eleven years previously. Curtiss gave back the 'A' to the Smithsonian and it was rebuilt to its 1903 status and put on display in Washington in 1918. To add insult to injury, the new exhibit carried a label stating that Langley had constructed a machine *capable* of flight before the Wrights. Not content with this Walcott continued to deny the Wright's place in history. By way of response, Orville Wright decided upon his grand gesture.

In January 1928 Charles Greeley Abbot became Secretary of the Smithsonian, after Walcott had died. That same month the Wright biplane departed American shores and the new man was faced with a major problem: how could the rift be repaired? After many emissaries, including Charles Lindbergh, had probed what was needed to bring the Flyer westwards, Abbot published *The 1914 Tests of the Langley Aerodrome* in October 1942. Within was an unequivocal statement: "It is to be regretted that the Institution published statements repeatedly to the effect that these experiments of 1914 demonstrated that Langley's plane of 1903 *without essential modification* [author's emphasis] was the first heavier-than-air machine capable of maintaining human flight... If the publication of this paper should clear the way for Dr Wright to bring back to America the Kitty Hawk machine to which all the world awards first place, it will be a source of profound and enduring gratification to his countrymen everywhere. Should he decided to deposit the plane in the United States National Museum, it would be given the highest place of honor, which it is due."

The original agreement was that the iconic Wright biplane remain in the UK for five years, but its sojourn was extended. From October 1938, the Flyer was dismantled and stored within the basement complex at South Kensington, amid fears that London could be bombed. In April 1942 it was moved to a quarry in the West Country and to another subterranean location in February 1943. Secretary Abbot's manful statement of 1942 settled Orville's mind, but an Atlantic crossing during the war was out of the question and the biplane remained in the care of ScM. Orville died on 30th January 1948 and arrangements were put in hand for the Flyer's return to the USA. At Hatfield the de Havilland Aeronautical Technical School built a replica to take the place of the real thing. At a ceremony at South Kensington in October 1948 the US Air Attaché, Livingstone Satterthwaite, accepted the biplane on behalf of his country. (See Chapter 3 for details of 'his' Spitfire.) On the 44th anniversary of the Kitty Hawk flights, 17th December 1948, the Flyer was inaugurated into the Smithsonian – decades after it really should have been.

Rethinking and evolving

As with any collection, ScM has rethought what aircraft it holds, especially in terms of technological trends and ever-pressing space restrictions on occasions. With a span of 49ft 9in (6ft 9in more than the Cody) Curtiss Seagull *Eleanor III* donated by Dr Alexander Hamilton Rice in 1926 was relatively compact as biplane flying-boats go. From the spring of 1924 it had been used for a year-long survey of the upper reaches of Brazil's Amazon River, and had flown around 12,000 miles. When it arrived it was the first Seagull in the UK, and was to remain so. This was not of consequence, it had been a prestigious gift from an internationally-known explorer and represented all the attributes of a flying-boat of the mid-1920s. But by the 1960s, *Eleanor III* was less representative and it could be argued that the Schneider Trophy-winning S.6B (see the profile below) stood for marine aviation and the museum had its share of wooden-construction biplanes.

Having won the toss of a coin, Orville Wright took the honours on 17th December 1903, becoming the first man to fly a sustained, controlled, heavier-than-air powered flight. *US National Archives*

In 1965 South Kensington was approached by the National Aviation Museum of Canada (now the Canada Aviation Museum) about the Seagull. Several, including its military predecessor the MF, had served faithfully with Canadian 'bush' operators and it would be ideal for the nascent collection. After checking that no other UK museum was interested in the Seagull, it was despatched to Rockcliffe, Ontario, in May 1969, initially on loan. Inspection revealed that the flying-boat needed restoration and Rockcliffe was rightly not prepared to do this for an airframe it did not own. Recognising a round peg in a round hole, ScM agreed to give it to Canada in return for the former Royal Canadian Air Force Douglas Dakota cockpit that now graces the 'Flight' gallery. To some this may seem an iniquitous exchange, but the 'Dak' has proved to be a popular and compact 'walk-in' exhibit, providing a glimpse of a 1930s-era cockpit, an opportunity many members of the public just don't get.

Featured within 'Ones That Got Away' in the companion volume, *Lost Aviation Collections of Great Britain*, the fate of Cierva C.9 J8931 has been laid to rest. Built at Hamble in Hampshire by Avro, Roy Chadwick and his design team set about the lightweight C.9 under the designation Type 576, for the Air Ministry. It utilised a fuselage very similar to the prototype Avro Avian sporting biplane, with a four-bladed main rotor, a substantial undercarriage and small wings to take some of the lift in forward flight. Bert Hinkler first flew C.9 J8931, at Hamble in September 1927 and it was involved in rotor trials by May 1928. On the last day of July 1928, while being flown by Juan de la Cierva, the tailplane fittings fractured. Trials commenced with the Royal Aircraft Establishment at Farnborough on 18th September 1928. Its usefulness over, J8931 was gifted to ScM in January 1930.

In September 1935 the museum took on the retired de Havilland-built C.24 cabin autogyro G-ABLM from the manufacturers and this supplanted the earlier C.9. On the order of the Air Ministry, J8931 was broken up. By 1938, the Weir Group had handed on its W-2 prototype (see Chapter 10) and on 24th May 1946 the Avro-built Cierva C.30A AP507 – on display within the 'Flight' gallery – joined the collection. The W-2 eventually gravitated to the Museum of Flight at East Fortune and the C.24 was presented on loan to the de Havilland Aircraft Heritage Centre at London Colney.

Both the Imperial War Museum and ScM were quick off the mark exhibiting captured Luftwaffe aircraft in 1946. Between February and mid-May 1946 three were on display at South Kensington: Heinkel He 162A-2 120091 (Air Ministry number 66), Messerschmitt Me 163B 191912 (AM.208) and Messerschmitt Bf 109G-14 413601 (AM.229). All were on loan for the duration, the He 162 and Me 163 having previously been at the Royal Aircraft Establishment, Farnborough, while the Bf 109 had come from 6 Maintenance Unit, Brize Norton, Oxfordshire. The fate of all three beyond their time in London has not been confirmed.

On 12th June 1979, the MacCready Gossamer Albatross, powered *and* piloted by cyclist Bryan Allen, crossed the English Channel in 169 minutes. Seventy years previously Louis Blériot achieved this feat in 37 minutes, but he did have 25hp at his disposal! This man-powered aircraft (MPA) was presented on loan in 1982 and, with a wingspan of 96ft, took considerable thinking about how to display it, even if its empty weight was only 70lb. The museum had already accepted the two-man 139ft-span Newbury Manflier and

De Havilland-built Cierva C.24 G-ABLM at Hendon in 1951 for the *Daily Express* 'Fifty Years of Flying' event. *KEC*

this was destined to remain at Wroughton. By their very nature all MPAs – and the new generation of solar-powered devices – are exceptionally fragile, giving huge concerns about moving them *at all*, let alone exposing them to the sticky-fingered public. The Albatross was retired to the storage facility at Hayes after a brief spell at South Kensington and stayed there until it was shipped to the USA in 1994. Today it 'flies' within the enormous space afforded by the Smithsonian's Udvar-Hazy Center.

In 2002 an aircraft was retired from duty at South Kensington and placed into storage at Wroughton. This was Cessna F.150F G-AWAW which had been a central part of the 'FlightLab' 'hands-on' section since its opening on 16th June 1991. The Cessna was always intended to have a 'sell-by' date as it would take a goodly degree of punishment; with the onset of still more flight simulators at 'FlightLab', the time had come. It was not appreciated when it was acquired, but *Alpha-Whiskey* had been flown solo to Australia by Janette Schönburg in 1980. When the museum decided to dispose of the Cessna during 2010, Janette alerted the US-based Cessna 150-152 Club. That organisation acquired G-AWAW in June and it was shipped to Florida on 14th October that year.

Former Science Museum Aircraft

Type	Identity	Built	Arrived	Notes, *current status or fate*
Beagle 206 Srs 1	G-ATDD	1965	1975	Cockpit – *Bristol Aero Collection, stored*
Bristol Bulldog IIA	G-ABBB	1930	1938	To Bristol at Filton 1961 for restoration to flying condition. See Shuttleworth, Chapter 3. *RAF Museum Hendon* – Chapter 5
Cessna F.150F	G-AWAW	1966	1991	See narrative. *To the Cessna 150-152 Club, Florida, USA 14 Oct 2010*
Cierva C.9	J8931	1927	Jan 1930	See narrative – *scrapped circa 1935*
Curtiss Seagull	–	1924	1926	*Exchanged for Dakota cockpit; received by National Aviation Museum of Canada May 1968, on display at Rockcliffe, Ontario*
English Electric Wren	No.4	1923	1924	To English Electric, Preston 4 Feb 1926, used in restoration of G-EBNV for *Shuttleworth Collection* – see Chapter 3
English Electric Canberra B.5	VX185	1952	c1962	Cockpit – *Museum of Flight Scotland* – see Chapter 10
Gloster Meteor III	EE416	1945	1959	Cockpit – *Martin-Baker Aircraft, Chalgrove, Oxfordshire*
Hawker Hunter F.6	G-9-185	1957	c1966	Cockpit – *Within AirSpace at the IWM, Duxford*
HS Trident 1E	G-AVYE	1968	24 Apr 1981	(At Wroughton) *Fuselage to Hatfield for fire suppression trials 22 Jun 1989, scrapped there 2000*
MacCready Gossamer Albatross	–	1978	1982	See narrative – *Displayed at the Smithsonian's Udvar-Hazy Centre at Dulles, USA*
Pilcher Hawk replica	–	1934	12 Dec 1934	Disposed of 1994, later to *AirSpace at the IWM, Duxford*
Wallis WA-120	G-AYVO	1971	Jan 1977	On loan from K H Wallis; returned to him Sep 1985. *Stored in Norfolk*
Weir W-2	W-2	1934	1938	On loan from the Weir Group. To the *Museum of Flight* – see Chapter 10
Wright Flyer	–	1903	Jan 1928	On loan from Orville Wright – see narrative. Shipped to the USA Oct 1948 and *displayed at the Smithsonian Institution, Washington USA*

Note: This list does not include the Imperial War Museum airframes stored in the basement at South Kensington after the Crystal Palace exhibition closed in 1924. These were removed to Cardington, Bedfordshire, in the mid-1930s. Details of these are carried in Chapter 2.

The nose of Meteor III EE416 at South Kensington, complete with early 'bang seat'. Bernard Lynch made the first UK trial ejection from this machine on 24th July 1946. *KEC*

Airliners and an airfield

With well-known test pilot Brian Trubshaw at the controls, the prototype British-built Concorde G-BSST touched down at Yeovilton for the 438th and final time on 4th March 1976. As 002 taxied in, quite a few of the gathered press wondered just why this incredible airliner had been retired to a Fleet Air Arm base. As related in Chapter 4, much debate had gone on before G-BSST was destined for Yeovilton and the joint care of ScM and the Fleet Air Arm Museum (FAAM). Placed on a purpose-built ramp, Concorde was opened up to the public on 26th July 1976 and later gravitated to its own impressive display hall. Now, remodelled as the Leading Edge exhibition, in the author's opinion it is by far and away the best tribute to the supersonic airliner anywhere.

That 002 should be given to the National Aeronautical Collection was never in doubt, but South Kensington's capacity has always been challenged as aircraft increased their vital statistics. The availability of G-BSST helped to focus ScM minds on the need for its next large object store having a runway. At the same time, it was becoming clear that the UK needed a policy regarding the thorny issue of *how* its airliner legacy was to be preserved. With both of these in consideration, the museum formally took over Wroughton airfield in Wiltshire, along with six large hangars, out-buildings and offices on 1st May 1980. Just south of Swindon, easily accessible via the M4 from the capital, it was ideal for the ever-pressing need for space above and beyond its West London small object repository. By early 2013 the museum had at total of over six million artefacts, from ploughs and valves to the double-decker buses and the Apollo 10 command module; about a tenth of those holdings were on view, the rest awaiting their turn.

Wroughton was built with the storage and preparation of aircraft in mind; 15 Maintenance Unit (MU) opening on 1st April 1940. Indeed, Hurricane I L1592, now on show within the 'Flight' gallery, was stored by 15 MU between August 1941 and April 1942. With the proximity of industrial Swindon, it was bound to be on the receiving end of the Luftwaffe and it was bombed on 13th and 19th August 1940, with little damage. From June 1941 aircraft packing and despatch specialist 76 MU moved in and in March 1944 the grass landing ground was replaced by the present-day trio of concrete runways. By the end of the war the emphasis was on the decommissioning of airframes and 76 MU disbanded in September 1946. As related in Chapter 5, 15 MU took on a major role in taking receipt of airframes intended for 'retention' by the Air Historical Branch (AHB) of the RAF. This was a combination of aircraft singled out as being of particular value for museum purposes, or machines that could have a new life in travelling exhibitions and special events. A classic example of this is Lancaster I R5868 *S-for-Sugar* – now at Hendon – which was brought in by road in August 1945. In the mid-1950s, Wroughton took on still more AHB aircraft, in crates or dismantled, although by the late 1950s the bulk of these had moved on to storage at Fulbeck. On an operational level, 15 MU continued its work into the 1950s and 1960s, increasingly in a tri-service manner looking after Army, Navy and RAF helicopters. In April 1972 the MU closed and the Fleet Air Arm took over with a Royal Naval Aircraft Yard. The military storage facility finally closed on 3rd September 1992.

With the Navy in place, the FAAM used Wroughton as a store and it was via its good offices that ScM's first 'aerial delivery' took place ahead of formal occupation, when Dakota EI-AYO flew in from Shannon, Ireland, on 25th October 1978. It was not just aeroplanes destined for Wroughton, with farm machinery and transport vehicle collections arriving, among others. Indeed, the Czechoslovakian-built LET Cmelak crop-sprayer was acquired with its agricultural role more in mind. As mentioned at the beginning of this chapter, Keeper of Aeronautics John Bagley was very much involved in establishing Wroughton, embarking on an impressive fleet of airliners that became the Air Transport Collection as well as a range of light and sporting types. The Sandringham flying-boat *could* have come to Wiltshire, but a much more fitting venue was found at Southampton. This is another example of the active policy of placing exhibits with other venues when appropriate, short- or long-term – see the table 'Science Museum aircraft on loan elsewhere'.

Among the machines held at Wroughton is the Handley Page Gugnunc, which has been with the museum since June 1934. It was taken down from display in 1940 and since has been rarely shown off. As it served with the Royal Aircraft Establishment, this biplane could even provide great contrast among the 'Test Flight' hangars at the RAF Museum Cosford. Pioneered independently by Frederick Handley Page and German-born Gustav Victor Lachmann, leading edge wing slots greatly improved controllability at low speeds. A leading member of the team developing slots at HP was Geoffrey Hill (see his Pterodactyl profile below) and the mechanism became a very lucrative source of licence agreements worldwide. Lachmann joined HP in 1929, by which time the company had embarked on a biplane to have a crack at the Guggenheim Fund's 'Safe Aircraft Competition', to be held at Mitchel Field, Long Island, New York, later in the year.

Powered by a 150hp Armstrong Siddeley Mongoose radial within a Townend ring, with full-span slots on the upper wing and long-travel undercarriage, the HP.39 Guggenheim Competition Biplane', G-AACN, first flew on 30th April 1929. Quickly the aircraft was dubbed 'Gugnunc', one of a host of words created for the *Daily Mail's* children's strip-cartoon *Pip, Squeak and Wilfred* and at that very moment inspiring 11-year old Spike Milligan to the heights of surreal comic genius. Shipped to the USA in late September, only the Gugnunc and the Curtiss Tanager were in contention in the end. The competition was dominated not by flying prowess but by bitter legalities. Frederick Handley Page sued Curtiss for the full span slots on the Tanager which appeared to breach his patents and by Glenn Curtiss invoking a 1920 commerce act retrospectively preventing the importation of the Gugnunc. (Curtiss had waged a long courtroom battle with the Wrights – see the narrative above.) The Gugnunc entered service with the RAE at Farnborough on 16th October 1930, taking on the serial K1908 and was passed on to ScM four years later. The HP.39 appeared in the static at Hendon in 1951 for the *Daily Express* 'Fifty Years of Flying' celebration.

James Cordes showing off the Gugnunc's slow-flying ability, thanks to the full-span slots, at Cricklewood, summer 1929. *Rolls-Royce*

Take a look at the table 'Science Museum aircraft held at Wroughton' and the rapid pace of establishing the Air Transport Collection is evident: DC-3* 1978, Comet 4B* 1979, Trident 1E* and Dragon Rapide 1981, Boeing 247* and Lockheed 10* 1982 (now in the 'Making of the Modern World' at South Kensington), Dragon, Devon* (the military version of the Dove), Constellation and Piaggio P.166* in 1983. (Those marked with an asterisk flying in.) The Trident 1E was joined by a second example, stretched and take-off boosted Series 3B G-AWZM in February 1986. *Zulu-Mike* was equipped with the UK-developed Autoland system, thereby increasing its technological credentials. The earlier machine was disposed of in June 1989, going to Hatfield for life-saving fire suppression trials.

While the 'fleet' was assembling at Wroughton, I asked John Bagley what else was on his 'shopping list' and he said that a twin-turboprop, ideally powered by the incredible Rolls-Royce Dart, was very important. I noted that this would be a Manchester-born HS.748, but John replied that the type would have priority, but the Dutch Fokker F.27 Friendship would meet South Kensington's needs just as well. This chapter carries the table 'Britain's 'National Airliner Collection'' to illustrate airliners on public view in the UK and how ScM has widened an otherwise reasonably predictable 'menu'. It fell to the City of Norwich Aviation Museum to put an F.27 on show in August 2000, courtesy of local airline KLM UK. As will be seen from the table, an HS.748 has yet to gravitate to full-blown public view in a museum. (RAF Museum at Cosford – Chapter 6 – has an example of the military Andover.) In October 2011 the endeavours of North West-based individuals brought 1961-built HS.748 G-BEJD to the former Liverpool Airport at Speke, thanks to International Air Parts. In the hands of the innovative Speke Aerodrome Heritage Group, it is part of a growing airliner community 'fuelled' by enthusiasm and determination.

But to return to John Bagley's vision for Wroughton, pointing to the gap between the two main hangars in 1986 he mused that a Boeing 747 could be sited between them and "perhaps covered by a vast dome-like structure". By that time, regular open days were being held, the first taking place on 21st September 1980. Since then the buildings – museum pieces in their own right – started to dictate a different path. Over half a century old the hangars – never intended as long-term structures – are showing their age and visits to Wroughton are now no longer possible, pending a structural survey. (This does not affect access to the library and archives, which is possible on a prior appointment basis.) Hopes are still high for Wroughton as a multi-function out-station for South Kensington and as a potential airliner haven.

Trident 3B G-AWZM after arrival at Wroughton, having completed 22,956 flying hours with BEA and then British Airways. *Science Museum*

Britain's 'National Airliner Collection'

Type [Notes]	Total	Location
Airspeed Ambassador	1	Duxford Aviation Society
Armstrong Whitworth Argosy	2	East Midlands Aeropark, Midland Air Museum
Avro XIX [1]	1	Shuttleworth Collection
Avro York	1	Duxford Aviation Society
BAC One-Eleven	3	Brooklands Museum, Duxford Aviation Society, National Museum of Flight Scotland
BAC/Sud Concorde	5	Brooklands Museum, Duxford Aviation Society, National Museum of Flight Scotland, Runway Visitor Park Manchester, **Science Museum** (Yeovilton)
BAe Jetstream 31 [2]	2	National Museum of Flight Scotland
Boeing 247	1	**Wroughton**
Boeing 707	1	National Museum of Flight Scotland
Bristol Britannia [3]	2	Duxford Aviation Society, RAF Museum Cosford
Britten-Norman Islander	1	National Museum of Flight Scotland
De Havilland Dragon	2	National Museum of Flight Scotland, **Wroughton**
De Havilland Dragon Rapide [4]	2	De Havilland Heritage Centre, Museum of Science and Industry Manchester, **Wroughton**
De Havilland Dove [5]	8	De Havilland Heritage Centre, Duxford Aviation Society, East Midlands Aeropark, Midland Air Museum, National Museum of Flight Scotland, Newark Air Museum, North East Aircraft Museum, **Wroughton**
De Havilland Heron	2	De Havilland Heritage Centre, Newark Air Museum
De Havilland Comet [6]	4	Duxford Aviation Society, National Museum of Flight Scotland, RAF Museum Cosford, **Wroughton**
Douglas DC-3 [7]	2	South Yorkshire Aircraft Museum, **Wroughton**
Fokker Friendship	1	City of Norwich Aviation Museum
Handley Page Hermes	1	Duxford Aviation Society
Handley Page Herald	5	City of Norwich Aviation Museum, Dumfries and Galloway Aviation Museum, Duxford Aviation Society, Museum of Berkshire Aviation, Yorkshire Air Museum
Hawker Siddeley Trident	4	De Havilland Heritage Centre, North East Aircraft Museum, Runway Visitor Park Manchester, **Wroughton**
Hawker Siddeley HS.146 / BAe RJ	2	De Havilland Heritage Centre, Runway Visitor Park Manchester
Junkers Ju 52 [8]	1	RAF Museum Cosford
Lockheed 10	1	**Science Museum**
Lockheed Constellation	1	**Wroughton**
Piaggio P.166	1	**Wroughton**
Scottish Aviation Twin Pioneer	1	National Museum of Flight Scotland
Short Sandringham	1	**Science Museum** (Southampton)
Short 330	2	North East Aircraft Museum, Ulster Aviation Collection
Spartan Cruiser	1	National Museum of Flight Scotland
Sud Super Frelon	1	The Helicopter Museum
Vickers Viking	1	Brooklands Museum
Vickers Viscount	5	Brooklands Museum, Duxford Aviation Society, Midland Air Museum, Museum of Flight, North East Aircraft Museum
Vickers Vanguard [9]	1	Brooklands Museum
Vickers VC-10	2	Brooklands Museum, Duxford Aviation Society

At museums within Chapters 1 to 10 and those lists within the Appendix. Does not include airliner types flying with Classic Air Force, or 'statics' with that collection because of its state of flux at time of going to press. Includes airliners and larger-capacity 'corporate' types from DH Dragon and Dove size upwards and fuselages and substantial forward fuselages, but *not* cockpit sections. [1] Does not include Ansons built for RAF service. [2] Includes Handley Page-built, for airline purposes. [3] Cosford example is civilian, but in RAF guise. [4] Does not include examples in military guise, or airworthy. [5] Excludes Devons and Sea Devons, other than Wroughton example. [6] Mk.1XB at Cosford is essentially a civilian. [7] Not including examples in military guise, or airworthy. [8] CASA-built example at Cosford is in civilian guise, but a military example. See Chapter 8 for further comment. [9] In guise of a Merchantman freighter.

Science Museum aircraft held at Wroughton

Type	Identity	Built	Origin	With ScM since	Notes
Bede BD-5B Micro	G-BGLB	1979	USA	Nov 1993	–
Bensen B.7 gyroglider	–	c1974	USA	1981	–
Birdman Grasshopper hang-glider	–	1977	UK	1980	–
Boeing 247	N18E	1933	USA	3 Aug 1982	–
Cameron A-375 hot-air balloon	G-BBGN	1975	UK	1989	gondola
Chargus Midas powered h-glider	–	1978	USA	1981	–
Colt AS-105 hot-air airship	G-RBOS	1982	UK	Sep 1987	gondola
De Havilland Dragon	G-ACIT	1933	UK	Aug 1983	–
De Havilland Dragon Rapide	G-ALXT	1944	UK	Dec 1981	–
De Havilland Devon C.2/2	VP975	1949	UK	Feb 1986	–
De Havilland Comet 1A	G-ANAV	1952	UK	1955	cockpit
De Havilland Comet 4B	G-APYD	1960	UK	5 Nov 1979	–
Douglas DC-3A-197	EI-AYO	1936	USA	25 Dec 1978	–
Focke-Achgelis Fa 330A-1	100509	1943	Germany	Feb 1946	–
Folland Gnat T.1	XP505	1962	UK	18 Nov 1984	–
Handley Page Gugnunc	G-AACN	1929	UK	Jun 1934	–
Hartman Ornithopter	–	1959	UK	1993	–
Hawker Siddeley Trident 3B-101	G-AWZM	1971	UK	28 Feb 1986	–
Huntair Pathfinder II microlight	G-MMCB	1983	UK	Sep 1985	–
LET Z-37 Cmelak	G-AVZB	1967	Czech	25 Jun 1988	–
Lilienthal glider	–	1894	Germany	1920	see narrative
Lockheed L-749A Constellation	N7777G	1947	USA	12 Aug 1983	–
McBroom Cobra 88 hang-glider	–	1976	UK	Oct 1985	–
Newbury Manflier man-powered	–	1977	UK	Sep 1981	major elements
Piaggio P.166	G-APWY	1959	Italy	1 Jun 1983	–
Piccard gas balloon	OO-BFH	1932	Switz	c1937	gondola
Piccard hot-air balloon	G-ATTN	1966	Switz	c1978	–

Size matters

While ScM is a massive edifice, as noted above, large objects have always presented major problems within its confines. The Alcock and Brown transatlantic Vimy – profiled below – caused a surge in footfall when it was put on show in 1919. However, it could not be shown in its entirety; only when the Aeronautics Gallery opened in the early 1960s did the opportunity arise. Its vital statistics are: length of 43ft 6½in, height 15ft 7½in, wingspan 68ft 1in making it the largest airframe on show. Two examples of 'minimalism' are Blériot types that were accepted only as sections, or reduced to smaller dimensions upon receipt. In 1913 pioneer aviator and Royal Naval Air Service stalwart Sir Francis K McClean KBE donated his Blériot-based Universal Aviation Company Birdling, built at Brooklands in 1911. Science Museum inventory numbers 1913-443, -444 and -445 relate to sections of the Birdling which were on display in 1929 showing control functions. Some, or all, of these sections are *believed* to have gone to Hull Municipal Museum and were destroyed in a bombing raid on the city on 24th June 1943. McClean's claims to fame are many, the one that most stands out being his flight *under* the Thames bridges on 10th August 1912 on a sortie out of RNAS Eastchurch, Isle of Sheppey. He was flying a Short S.33 floatplane and later alighted near Westminster Bridge. In 1919 McClean handed on a float from the Thames S.33 to South Kensington.

In 1920 another Blériot was presented, this time by D S B Shannon. This is believed to have been the first aircraft to fly the Irish Sea; Denys Corbett Wilson taking 100 minutes to cross from Pembrokeshire to Enniscorthy, Ireland, on 22nd April 1912. Inventory number 1920-33, its centre section/cockpit of is in a display case today within the 'Flight' gallery, showing Louis Blériot's semisphere-like control 'base' (which he called the 'cloche') for his control column and the wire attachments for the wing warping and the tail 'feathers'. A decade later engine manufacturer John Alfred Prestwich gifted the Blériot-based JAP-Harding

Monoplane, built in 1910 and this is in the 'Flight' gallery in its entirety. (More of Mr Prestwich in the profile of the Roe Triplane, below.)

The 'Flight' gallery can be tackled in any order, but ideally the chronological 'path' is the best way to take it all in. Early in this 'journey' is a display case that contains the majority of the second Frost ornithopter which never ceases to draw the attention of visitors, young and old. It's a wing-flapping aircraft, the flying surfaces covered by thousands of artificial feathers, but it never got to emulate the birds that inspired its creator. Built by Edward Purkis Frost of West Wratting Hall, south of Newmarket, in 1902 it was powered by a 3hp BAT engine and presented to the museum in 1925 by Flt Lt H W Woollett DSO MC. Frost's Firth ornithopter, of circa 1900, was powered by a steam engine and all (or parts thereof) of this device were acquired by Richard Ormonde Shuttleworth – see Chapter 3. Frost also crops up in Chapter 10 as he was custodian of the Pilcher Hawk for a while.

The JAP-Harding Monoplane flying in 1910. When it arrived in 1930, it was the third Blériot-type airframe to be presented to the museum. *Science Museum*

After World War Two the National Aeronautical Collection was displayed in cramped conditions in galleries in the old Imperial Institute, just to the north of the Science Museum proper. Imperial College had plans to expand using that site and it was decided to complete the so-called 'Centre Block' and re-house the aircraft on its top floor. What is now the basement and ground floor of this building had been created for the Science Exhibition of the 1951 Festival of Britain. The Imperial Institute was cleared in 1961 and the new Aeronautics Gallery was opened in July 1963. The top floor was given the 'feel' of a hangar, airframes were suspended from its beams and an elevated walkway provided an entirely new dimension of access. Much emphasis was still placed on models, engines and cockpit sections, but the spacious 'sky' element allowed for more whole aircraft. An access door in the side of the gallery near where the HS.125 corporate jet is presently displayed allowed dismantled airframes to be craned up, or down, from the yard below. Throughout this time Margaret Weston (now Dame Margaret Weston) worked at the museum and in 1973 became Director, taking the museum into the Concorde era and pioneering Wroughton. Passionate about the aeronautical gallery, she helped to promote and expand the coverage of the subject; handing on the baton to Neil Cossons (later Sir Neil Cossons) in 1986. Neil was at the helm until 2000 (moving on to be Chairman of English Heritage) spearheading the redevelopment of the aeronautical gallery and the 'Making of the Modern World' exhibition.

Clearly a winning formula, the aeronautical gallery was substantially reworked in the early 1990s and opened, under the title 'Flight', on 17th October 1992. The opportunity was taken to remove all but the Dakota cockpit, bringing in the HS.125 and the P.1127. The side door was again used for exhibits arriving or leaving. The walkway was retained but among many changes the most striking – and utterly absorbing – were the engine 'stacks' allowing close inspection from several angles while *increasing* the number of powerplants on show, but *decreasing* the floor space previous occupied. The latest change within South

Kensington has been the extensive and impressive 'Making of the Modern World' hall which includes the Avro 504K, the Lockheed 10 from the Air Transport Collection at Wroughton – an iconic airliner with a moderate wing span – and the Rolls-Royce 'Flying Bedstead' and Short SC.1 vertical take-off pioneers.

When the Hawker P.1127 prototype was brought to South Kensington, it supplanted the Folland Gnat that had been in place since 18th November 1984. While the Gnat was used by the Royal Aircraft Establishment (RAE) in 1978 to investigate atmospheric turbulence at low altitudes, this 'science' application was a nice addition to its *primary* role at ScM: representing a modern swept-wing jet, with a very neat wing span of just 24ft. With RAE XP505 made 751 sorties; its last on 29th April 1983. Also of small span, the P.1127 could fulfil a dual role, showing off the vectored-thrust vertical take-off system *and* the features of a fast-jet. In a similar manner, the HS.125 executive jet provided most of the elements of a modern airliner within relatively small dimensions. Another clever use of space is the 1970-built Pitts S-1S aerobatic biplane which fits beautifully in a stairwell, providing a spectacular inverted image for visitors entering the gallery. That it was flown by test and display pilot legend Neil Williams to win the 1971 US National Championship, the 1974 European Championship and to gain fourth place in the World Aerobatic Championships of 1976 was well-planned icing on the cake!

Behind the P.1127 and the HS.125 and close to the Pitts, is an exhibit that is regarded with wonderment by many visitors. Wroughton may not (yet?) have a Boeing 747 'jumbo jet' but there is a 'slice' of one at South Kensington. Delivered to Japan Air Lines on 21st December 1973, upon retirement in 1992, the 747SR-46 was carefully cut up with a 2ft 6in section being taken out of the fuselage, complete with seat rows, windows and overhead baggage bays and cut-through freight containers in the belly.

Former Royal Aircraft Establishment Gnat T.1 XP505 after installation in the Aeronautical Galley in 1984. Below is a Rolls-Royce RB.211 turbofan and to the left the Supermarine S.6B. *Science Museum*

South Kensington covers the fields of science, technology, engineering, mathematics, medicine, transport, visual media and related arts, from Crick and Watson's original DNA model to Stephenson's *Rocket*, to John Logie Baird's original television apparatus and the forerunner of the Harrier. Under the title National Museums of Science and Industry (NMSI), it is the main component of a family that includes the National Railway Museum at York and Shildon, Durham, and the National Media Museum in Bradford. From early 2012, NMSI also welcomed the Museum of Science and Industry, Manchester, to the fold.

Careful use of space extended to the stair well at the rear of the 'Flight' gallery, perfect for the inverted Pitts Special. *Ken Ellis*

Avro 504K D7560
1918 | Two-seat primary trainer | One 130hp Clerget

South Kensington's Avro 504 'flies' within the 'Making of the Modern World' hall above Ford Model T PP7963 of 1916, the latter in Henry Ford's legendary "any colour you like, provided it's black". In many ways this is a gifted juxtaposition as both propelled their creators into massive industries and became world famous. Built at Newton Heath, Manchester, as part of an order for 300 Le Rhône-powered 504Ks placed in November 1917, ScM's example was issued to 3 Training Depot Station (TDS) at Lopcombe Corner, Salisbury, on 22nd March 1918. In July 1918 it was with the Aeroplane Repair Station, also at Lopcombe, and re-engined with a Clerget rotary. This was not a drastic piece of surgery, later production 504Ks having been fitted with a mounting plate easily adaptable to a variety of rotaries. After this, it was presumably re-issued to 3 TDS, later renamed as 3 Training Squadron. The trainer was retired on 8th April 1919 at 3 Aircraft Salvage Depot at Waddon, Croydon. On 22nd January 1920 it was presented to the museum, its acquisition file initially noting that it was: "Lent by the Disposal Board, Ministry of Munitions". The 504 was restored by Avro at its Bracebridge Heath plant just north of Waddington and was despatched to museum's storage site, 'Hangar 2' in West Byfleet, Surrey, on 29th September 1953. It was loaned to the Museum of Army Flying at Middle Wallop (Chapter 7) from October 1992, returning to take up its new position in the 'Making of the Modern World' in late 1999.

As the original is 95 years old, the condition of the original print can be forgiven! Avro 504K D7560 at Ensbury Park, Bournemouth, 1918. *Peter Green Collection*

Cierva C.30A AP507
1934 | Two-seat general purpose autogyro | One 140hp Armstrong Siddeley Genet Major IA

Built under licence from rotorcraft pioneer Spaniard Juan de la Cierva by Avro as a Type 671 at Newton Heath, Manchester, as G-ACWP and issued to the Cierva company's operations and sales centre at the London Air Park, Hanworth, by November 1934. It remained at Hanworth registered to a series of private owners, including the Autogiro Flying Club, until the spring of 1940. At that point, it and four others had been gathered by the Cierva Autogiro Company at Hendon, ready for impressment for military service on 1st June 1940. (One of the others was G-ACWM, which became AP506 and substantial wreckage of this survives with The Helicopter Museum at Weston-super-Mare.) Although allocated the serial AP507, G-ACWP was still in 'civvies' when it moved to its first assignment, at the Royal Aircraft Establishment, Farnborough. On 28th August 1940 the autogyro was issued to 5 Radio Maintenance Unit at Duxford, which became 5 Radio Servicing Section (RSS) 25 days later. For the bulk of AP507's service life the C.30A's slow-flying characteristics were used to calibrate radar installations. No.5 RSS became 74 Wing's Calibration Flight in February 1941 and a year later was retitled as 1448 Flight, still at Duxford. The unit moved to Halton on 2nd March 1942, taking AP507 with it. On 15th June 1943 the Flight became 529 Squadron and relocated to Crazies Hill at Henley-on-Thames in August 1944, by which time the autogyro was wearing the codes 'KX-H'. For five days in early October 1943 AP507 was loaned to the Fleet Air Arm for photographic work in conjunction with unspecified anti-submarine trials, operating from Sydenham, Belfast. No.529 Squadron was busy converting to Sikorsky Hoverfly I helicopters (see Chapter 6) in April 1945 and on 18th May AP507 was retired to 5 Maintenance Unit (MU) at Kemble. It was issued to ScM on 24th May 1946 and taken to 76 MU at Wroughton. There it was packed for long-term storage at the museum's site at Sydenham, close to Crystal Palace in South London. The autogyro did not see the light of day until 1961 when it was moved to an airfield it flew from 19 years previously; Halton. Here, the apprentices of 1 School of Technical Training prepared AP507 for exhibition, wearing the codes 'KX-H', in the new aviation gallery at South Kensington from 10th July 1963 and it has been there ever since.

Samuel Franklin Cody at the helm of the much-modified British Army Aircraft, 1909. *Peter Green Collection*

Cody Military Biplane 304
1912 | Two-four seat general purpose | One 120hp Austro-Daimler

Celebrating 100 years with ScM in 2013, refer to the narrative section of this chapter for more on this machine. It is impossible to profile the history of the oldest surviving UK military aircraft without highlighting its charismatic and pioneering creator, American-born Samuel Franklin Cody. He came to the UK while touring with his 'Wild West' show; though he is not to be confused with 'Buffalo Bill' Cody of greater fame in that form of entertainment. Samuel developed skills in building and flying large kites, initially as another spectacular for his shows. Eventually, these could lift a man aloft and the British Army became interested as a cheaper means of observation than gas balloons. Cody was appointed as Chief Kiting Instructor in April 1906 at the Balloon Factory, precursor of the Royal Aircraft Factory, at Farnborough. Cody was quickly involved in more than kites, taking a major hand in the creation of the 'car' that hung under the airship *Nulli Secundus* of 1907. (A replica of this is on show within Milestones of Flight at the RAF Museum Hendon – Chapter 5.) In his British Army Aircraft No.1 he made the first controlled, powered, heavier-than-air flight in the UK on 16th October 1908. Cody parted company with the Balloon Factory in April 1909 but remained at Farnborough, developing his flying machines, and that October he became a British citizen. A series of large biplanes followed, proving the practicality and robustness of his creations and Cody became a household name for his exploits.

As the War Office sought to standardise on a future type for the military, trials were to be held at Larkhill on Salisbury Plain during August 1912. The winning aircraft, and another example, would be purchased for the newly-formed Royal Flying Corps (RFC). The competition offered potentially rich pickings, with the prospect of large orders as military flying expanded. Cody came up with a monoplane but this was wrecked in July at Farnborough. With typical adaptability, he used as much of his previous biplane as possible which became competitor No.31 in the hotly-contested trials. On 27th August Cody was declared the winner and in late November it was handed over to the War Office at Farnborough. Referred to as the Military Trials Biplane, it was given the RFC serial number 301 and issued to 4 Squadron, which had formed at Farnborough on 16th September.

In late December Cody set about building the second example and, as 304, this was taken on charge by 4 Squadron on 20th February 1913. Four days later, Lt L C Rogers-Harrison was killed when 301 broke up in the air. On the last day of March, 304 was damaged in an accident and by 3rd April was in store in Cody's sheds on Laffan's Plain at Farnborough. It was repaired, but appears not to have flown again; its total 'air' time coming to no more than 2½ hours. By July Cody had created another large-proportioned biplane equipped with floats and called the Hydro-Biplane. During tests in landplane guise it broke up in the air, killing Cody and his passenger, W H B Evans. The death of Cody, and that of Rogers-Harrison in February, almost certainly convinced the War Office to not fly 304 and indeed to dispose of it. At the time of the Military Aeroplane Trials, the Royal Aircraft Factory's exceptional BE.2 designed by Geoffrey de Havilland, was ineligible for judging. Despite the Cody 'winning' it was BE.2 that was ordered in increasingly large numbers, setting the format for military aircraft for much of the war. As related at the beginning of this chapter, 304 went on to become the founder-member of Britain's preserved aircraft heritage. It was re-covered during refurbishment in 1976 and today 'flies' within the 'Flight' gallery.

A very fine replica of British Army Aircraft No.1 is displayed at the Farnborough Air Sciences Trust (FAST) just a matter of feet from where Cody set off for the historic flight of 16th October 1908. FAST plans a memorial to Cody at Farnborough to commemorate the centenary of his death.

De Havilland Moth G-AAAH
1928 | Two seat tourer/trainer | One 100hp DH Gipsy 1

One of the most famous light aircraft of all time, Gipsy Moth *Jason* was the fourth production example, incorporating additional fuel tankage to the order of William Laurence Hope of Air Taxis Ltd (see above for his King's Cup win). In September 1928 Hope flew G-AAAH from its birthplace at Stag Lane, Edgware, Middlesex, to Kisumu in Kenya and back. Just under a year later at Stag Lane, a vivacious young lady from Hull, Amy Johnson, was handed her 'A' Licence; a member of the London Aeroplane Club, she'd gone solo after 16 hours of tuition. Not content with her pilot's licence, she became the UK's first female licenced aircraft mechanic (No.1391, issued on 10th December 1929). Amy was determined to make a name for herself and by March 1930 she had developed the notion of a solo flight to Australia. In February 1928 Queensland-born Bert Hinkler had become the first person to fly solo from the UK to Australia, in Avro Avian prototype G-EBOV. (This is preserved at the Queensland Museum in South Brisbane.) With partial backing from oil magnate Lord Wakefield, she acquired G-AAAH and it was registered to her, care of the London Aeroplane Club, on 30th April 1930. The Moth was named *Jason* after the trademark of the Johnson family fishing business, founded in Hull in 1881 by Amy's Danish-born grandfather. The biplane cost £600, which would equate to about £33,000 in present-day spending values; the average salary in 1930 was just under £200.

Less than a year after her first solo, Amy set off from Croydon on 5th May 1930 and it was only as she got closer and closer to her objective that the press really took her seriously. By the time she had reached Calcutta on 12th May, the *Daily Mail* had pounced and secured an exclusive for the tidy sum of £2,000. Before her triumphant arrival in Darwin on the 24th after a gruelling 10,000 miles, the Mail had upped the ante with another £10,000 which included a UK tour on her return and purchase of *Jason*. Amy had become the first female to fly solo to Australia; she was awarded the CBE in June 1930 and instantly became an international personality. *Jason* was shipped back to the UK on the SS *Naldera* and after testing and re-assembly at Stag Lane, she flew it to Hull on 11th August for a civic reception. Amy and *Jason* started their contractual *Daily Mail* tour on the 26th, but it was clear that the entire adventure had taken a hefty physical and

Amy Johnson, a determined aviatrix who captured the heart of a nation. *KEC*

emotional toll on the 27-year old and on 4th September she made her last flight in G-AAAH, from Portsmouth to Stag Lane; the cavalcade was abandoned. The *Daily Mail* presented *Jason* to the nation, in the form of ScM, on 21st January 1931. Amy married well-known long-distance pilot Jim Mollison in 1932 and the pair had several aeronautical adventures before divorcing in 1938. Determined to 'do her bit' during the war, Amy joined the Air Transport Auxiliary, using her skills to ferry a wide range of types around the UK. While attached to the Hatfield-based 5 Ferry Pilots Pool, she was flying Airspeed Oxford I V3540 from Squires Gate, Blackpool, to Kidlington, Oxford, in atrocious weather on 5th January 1941. Way off course, the Oxford crashed in the Thames estuary and Amy was killed. The exact circumstances have never really been confirmed; claims that she was the victim of 'friendly fire' from Royal Navy Hunt-class Escort Destroyer HMS *Berkeley* returning from Channel convoy duties occasionally 'do the rounds' of the press.

Fokker E.III 210/16
1916 | Single-seat fighter | One 150hp Oberüsel

Genuine survivors from the Great War are very rare; figures vary but around 300 airframes is a reasonable figure for the world 'population'. Many people bemoan the absence of a Fokker Dr.I triplane – of 'Red Baron' fame – but the type's significance pales against ScM exhibit number 1918-210. (To discover why the world does not have a Dr.I, take a look at the profile of DH.9A F1010 in Chapter 5.) Shown in skeletal form, this is the world's only surviving Fokker E.III and without it, the Dr.I would have been toothless. Dutchman Anthony Herman Gerard Fokker was busy developing a series of monoplanes (German – eindecker) at his Fokker Flugzeugwerke at Schwerin, east of Hamburg, but had yet to attract major orders from Imperial Germany. On 1st April 1915 Frenchman Lt Roland Garros, piloting a Morane-Saulnier Type 'L' parasol monoplane cut to ribbons a German Albatros. After much trial and error, Garros had perfected a way of firing a machine-gun through the propeller arc. Using specially-shaped munitions and a crude deflector wedges that protected the propeller blade from being decimated by the hail of bullets, Garros had finally turned the aircraft into a predator. The shock effect of Garros's simple solution was all too fleeting. A single bullet from a German infantryman brought him down near Courtrai seventeen days after the deflector had proven itself. Sifting through the wreck, Germans noticed the wedges on the propeller and the placing of the machine-gun. The prop was sent overnight to Fokker at Schwerin. On 20th May, Fokker presented a pair of modified eindecker M.5s to amazed military officials. The wedge was present on the propeller, but only as 'insurance' against slow-discharging bullets. Fokker technicians had taken the concept from physics to mechanics, developing an interrupter (or synchronizer) gear that prevented a bullet firing in the split-second when a blade was in the way of its trajectory. Quickly the E.I, E.II then much-feared E.III followed and over the trenches in the autumn of 1915 the 'Fokker scourge' had begun.

Only around 150 E.IIIs were built, one of these was 210/16 which was involved in service acceptance flying at Schwerin on 26th March 1916. It was at Valenciennes, north east of Amiens on 1st April 1916 – a year to the day after Garros's debut – ready for delivery to an operational unit. Seven days later it fell to a humble Gefreiter (equivalent of an army private) of the 5th Feldfleiger Abteilung to take the new fighter to Wasquehal, to the west of Tournai. After a trial flight to familiarise himself, he set off in poor visibility. He made two precautionary landings to get his bearings, then the Oberüsel rotary engine – a German copy of the French Le Rhône – packed up. He landed near Renescure, near St Omer. It was a text-book dead-stick landing, except that the young pilot had well over-shot his intended destination and had crossed the lines; the Gefreiter was interrogated, the Fokker was lauded!

The black crosses were crudely painted out and the E.III was almost certainly flown in mock combat against a Morane-Saulnier Type 'N' monoplane. The war prize was taken to the Central Flying School at Upavon and thoroughly evaluated in May 1916. This proved valuable, but by this stage the 'fix' for the 'Fokker scourge' was well underway, that very month the Royal Flying Corps unleashed its own interrupter gear. Initially, designers worked on 'pusher' types that put the gun in the nose and the engine behind; for example de Havilland's DH.2 appeared in June 1915. Placing machine-guns on the top wing, firing above the arc of the prop was also an interim solution. Vickers fielded its Challenger interrupter gear for the first time on Bristol Scout C 5313 and Lt Albert Ball downed an Albatros on 15th May 1916. After all that needed to be known from the E.III had been extracted, its usefulness rapidly diminished. It joined the National Economy Exhibition, touring from city to city with trinkets of the war and a message of austerity. From mid-February 1917 the War Office had been allocating serials prefixed 'G' to captured aircraft and by the middle of the year a batch prefixed 'XG' was given to machines that had 'arrived' prior to that; Fokker E.III 210/16 was allocated XG4, but very likely never wore it.

On 18th July 1916 the War Office wrote to the Victoria and Albert Museum offering "a German aeroplane shot down in France by the RFC". This was forwarded to ScM along with a scribbled note that read: "Major Ogilvie, would you like it?" As related early, the Major was the museum's Director and he took up the offer. War Office allotment No.1263 granted the acquisition on 16th September 1916 for "Fokker No.509 100hp Gnome, presently at National Economy Exhibition". A memo of 27th February 1918 recorded that the museum had finally taken delivery of the E.III but it was "missing engines [sic], propeller, instruments etc which were present when it was handed over." The latter is presumed to relate to an inspection made when the War Office agreed to the deal in September 1916 but its touring with the National Economy Exhibition had clearly taken its toll. The Fokker was displayed until 1923 and put into store. In late 1923 a large amount of material from the Imperial War Museum's exhibition at the Crystal Palace was transferred, among which was the 'missing' Oberüsel! During the Fokker's time on tour and its first airing on show in South Kensington a lot of the fabric had been purloined by the public and so it was a *skeletal* version, but now *with* engine it was put back on display in 1935.

Gloster E28/39 W4041/G
1941 | Single-seat experimental jet | One 860lb st Power Jets Whittle W.1

The pioneering work of Frank Whittle and his Power Jets Ltd in developing his concept for a turbojet came to fruition on 12th April 1937 when the temperamental first unit ran. The Air Ministry issued a contract to Gloster on 3rd February 1940 for two prototypes that could be further developed into a fighter. Under the guidance of designer George Carter the Gloster E28/39 was built at Hucclecote, near Gloucester, before moving to the former premises of Regent Motors in Cheltenham in the spring of 1941. (Carter went on to create the Meteor – see Chapter 5.) Taxying trials, with a non-flight rated W.1X turbojet, started on 7th April 1941 and the following day, with chief test pilot Philip Edward George 'Gerry' Sayer at the helm, W4041/G made a series of 'hops'. (The suffix /G on a serial number denoted that the aircraft was to be permanently under guard when not flying.) The jet was roaded to Cranwell where the combination of a large, all-grass, aerodrome and reasonable seclusion provided a good site for testing. With a flight-rated W.1, at 19:48 hours on 15th May 1941 Gerry Sayer put the throttle forward and now used to the characteristic lull as the turbojet kicked in, the little jet took to the air for a 17-minute test flight. Frank Whittle, a former Cranwell cadet, was there to witness the moment of history and congratulate Sayer upon his return. After several more tests from Cranwell, W4041/G returned to Hucclecote for a 1,160lb static thrust (st) W.1A to be fitted and it first flew in this guise from Edge Hill, Warwickshire, on 16th February 1942. On 27th September 1942, the inaugural test of a new W.1A, Gerry suffered a reduction in thrust as he climbed out of Edge Hill, he got W4041/G around the circuit and down with damage to the tail and a wing tip. The E28/39 was back in the air in November, with Michael Daunt in command. (Tragically, Britain's first jet pilot had been killed in Hawker Typhoon Ib R7867 of 1 Squadron in a sortie out of Acklington on 21st October 1942 while on a courtesy visit to boost morale as the Typhoon was suffering structural problems. Ironically, Gerry Sayer almost certainly died in a mid-air collision and was not a victim of the Typhoon's troubles.)

The E28/39 made its first sortie at the Royal Aircraft Establishment (RAE), Farnborough, on 20th December 1942 to begin investigating the extremes of the flight envelope, including establishing its service ceiling. During this time, Wg Cdr H J Wilson – later to clinch the world air speed record at 606mph in a Meteor IV on 7th November 1945 – declared that the E28/39 was disturbing to fly as the fuel gauge could be seen moving downwards from the moment the engine started! There was room for only 81 gallons of fuel, even with modest demands of the throttle endurance was still less than an hour. On 1st March 1943 W4041/G was joined by W4046/G, but it had a short life. While it was with RAE Sqn Ldr Douglas B S Davie baled out at 37,000ft when the ailerons jammed on 30th July 1943. More and more powerful and refined Whittle powerplants were installed in W4041/G; a W2/500 of 1,700lb st in May 1943 and the first of two W2/700s in August 1944. Retired to Gloster's Bentham facility in March 1945, W4041/G had completed a total of 51 hours, 30 minutes flying time. At Bentham it was readied for public display at the 'Britain's Aircraft' exhibition, held on the bombed-out John Lewis site in Oxford Street, London, June to September 1945. It was back at Bentham by March 1946 and took place inside the Imperial Institute in South Kensington on 28th April 1946. Today, close to where the E28/39 'flies' in the 'Flight' gallery, is the Whittle W.1 that propelled Britain's first jet that evening on 15th May 1941.

Frank Whittle congratulating 'Gerry' Sayer after the first flight of the E28/39 at Cranwell, 15th May 1941. *KEC*

Gloster E28/39 W4041/G under test at Farnborough, 1940. *Peter Green Collection*

Hawker Hurricane I L1592
1938 | Single-seat fighter | One 1,030hp Rolls-Royce Merlin II

It took some pondering before choosing which Hurricanes to profile. Because the Hawker fighter evolved little in shape, construction technique or engine, only two feature in depth, whereas the Spitfire gets more expansive treatment. Shuttleworth's Sea Hurricane (Chapter 3) was an easy choice, but which other? Picking the South Kensington example may raise a few eyebrows, but L1592 is a *very* unsung survivor. Yet, as the 47th off the production line, it is the oldest survivor and *probably* the only one extant with fabric-covered wings. It is a Battle of Britain veteran, having given and taken punishment in that pivotal campaign.

Built at Brooklands, L1592 was issued to 56 Squadron at North Weald on 3rd June 1938 as the unit completed conversion from Gloster Gladiator biplanes. In June 1939 neighbouring 17 Squadron gave up the last of its Gloster Gauntlet II biplanes and on 27th July L1592 was transferred to fill the unit's Hurricane compliment. Germany invaded Poland on 1st September 1939 and the following day 17 Squadron deployed to Croydon for a week of 'sabre-rattling' before settling on Debden. It *seems* that L1592 was destined for 87 Squadron and France as part of the Advanced Air Striking Force on 10th October 1939, but four days later it was on charge with 43 Squadron at Tangmere, so the cross-Channel deployment very likely remained only a paperwork transfer. A month later, it was back 'on the books' of 17 at Debden.

The Hurricane caught up with 43 Squadron again, from 16th February 1940 by which time the 'Fighting Cocks' were at Acklington, but moved to Wick in Scotland on the 26th. With the retreat from France via Dunkirk starting on 27th May, the Hurricanes were called back from the far north, 43 Squadron returning to Tangmere on the 31st. The following day Plt Off Tony 'Wombat' Woods-Scawen was over Dunkirk in L1592 and engaged Messerschmitt Bf 109s. He claimed one, but in the melée this remained unconfirmed as he took hits in his cooling system and returned to Tangmere for a gear-up landing. It was to be late July before L1592 was back in the thick of it, joining 615 (County of Surrey) Squadron at Kenley on the 23rd, taking on the code letters 'KW-Z'. On 18th August the 'Surreys' took a pasting; Plt Off David Looker force-landing at Croydon after engaging Bf 109s over Sevenoaks. Plt Off P H Hugo was killed in combat that day and two other members of 615 were wounded and their aircraft written off. Back at Kenley, three Hurricanes were destroyed during a Luftwaffe bombing raid at lunch time. Repaired again and with a Merlin III fitted, L1592 joined the Special Duty Flight at Christchurch on 10th October 1940. Much of the SDF's duties was co-operation with the Telecommunications Research Establishment at Worth Matravers in Dorset. SDF also manned a battle flight and several times L1592 was launched into action and on 10th November fired on a Dornier, but to no observed effect. Thus ended L1592's frontline career.

Newly refurbished, Hurricane I L1592 at Dunsfold, early 1961. *Hawker Siddeley*

It was withdrawn into storage at 15 Maintenance Unit (MU) at Wroughton – the airfield destined to become ScM's large objects store in 1980. From there L1592 was transferred to what its 'movement card' calls 9 Air Observer School probably in April 1942. Since 1st November 1939 the unit had been known as 9 Bombing and Gunnery School, based at Penrhos, Wales. Either way, this was brief and was followed by stints at 5 (Pilots) Advance Flying Unit at Tern Hill from 21st April and 9 (P)AFU at Errol in Scotland from February 1943. It was retired to 22 MU at Silloth on 8th October 1943. From there on this decidedly war-weary Hurricane should have faced scrapping, but it lingered. By 1945 it was with 47 MU at Sealand near Chester and tagged for museum use. In between storage at various sites, it was used as an exhibition airframe, for example being displayed at Horse Guards Parade in London in circa 1946 and again in 1950 by which time it was wearing spurious 257 Squadron markings as 'DT-A'. In 1952 it was a static 'extra' during the filming of *Angels One Five*. On 16th December 1954 the Hurricane was taken on by ScM and put into its Sydenham, South London, store. It moved to Dunsfold on 22nd August 1960 where Hawker employees restored it for display, painting it in 615 Squadron colours as 'KW-Z'. It was installed in the new gallery at South Kensington in May 1961.

Craning L1592 into the aviation gallery on the top floor of the Science Museum, May 1961. *Science Museum*

For a master-class on how to compile and write an aircraft 'biography' seek out a copy of *Air-Britain Digest* for Winter 2002, within is *The Story of a Hurricane* by Lawrence Hayward which gives chapter and verse on L1592.

Hawker P.1127 XP831
1960 | Single-seat V/STOL fighter prototype | One 12,000lb st Bristol Siddeley Pegasus 2 | On loan from the RAF Museum

Within the South Kensington building, visitors can find all three types that contributed to the UK's predominance in short/vertical take-off and landing (V/STOL) combat aircraft; leading to the incredible Harrier which is still a world-beater even if the RAF and Fleet Air Arm have been robbed of its unique abilities! The Rolls-Royce 'Flying Bedstead' (see below) and the Short SC.1 (Chapter 9) took the path of dedicated lift engines; what became the Harrier adopted the higher-risk, but ultimately more practical vectored thrust.

The first of six prototype P.1127s, XP831, was laid down in May 1959 and rolled out at Dunsfold in July 1960. The first BS53 was run in September 1959. A special gridded area was readied at Dunsfold for a careful, step-by-step, series of ground runs and tethered hovers from late 1960. Things had to be taken in a cautious manner, between them Hawker and BSE were testing a new method of flight and the first-ever vectored thrust engine all at once. (It was 11th March 1963 before test-bed Vickers Valiant B.1 WP199 flew with a Pegasus 3 in its belly.) With Bill Bedford at the controls, XP831 made the first tethered hover on 21st October 1960 and on 19th November a free hover, all from the special pad at Dunsfold. The P.1127 was roaded to the Royal Aircraft Establishment (RAE) at Thurleigh and on 13th March 1961 Bill carried out the type's inaugural sortie as a conventional jet. Back at Dunsfold as the hovers increased in complexity and piloting experience grew, on 12th September 1961 in four sorties Bill Bedford and then Hugh Merewether – Hugh shadowing his boss, both learning from 'raw' – took XP831 from a vertical take-off to a conventional landing and then from a 'normal' take-off to a vertical landing. As Hugh climbed out, the pair had completed XP831's 99th flight – the P.1127 was proven! The Pegasus 2 that XP831 first flew with was changed for a 13,500lb 'Peggie' 3 in 1962 and on 8th February the future was graphically illustrated when it was flown on and off the aircraft carrier HMS *Ark Royal*. Bill Bedford took XP831 to Le Bourget, Paris, in June 1963 to demonstrate the P.1127 at the Salon Aéronautique trade show. On the 16th the flight ended in a cloud of dust with a very public accident; XP831 was badly damaged, Bill was relatively unhurt. The prototype was rebuilt and on 2nd February 1965 was delivered to the Aero Flight at RAE Thurleigh for a long career of research and development. It was retired in late 1972 and issued to the RAF Museum; its last flight being in November 1972 to RAF Northolt from where it was roaded to Hendon on 13th November. With the creation of the 'Flight' gallery at South Kensington, it was agreed to lend XP831 to ScM and it was installed in 'hovering' mode on 31st May 1992. The later story of the Harrier and Sea Harrier can be followed with reference to Chapters 4 and 6.

Test pilot Bill Bedford performed the first vertical landing by a fixed-wing aircraft on a warship on 8th February 1963. Piloting P.1127 XP831, he carried out trials on HMS *Ark Royal*.
Bristol Siddeley

Hill Pterodactyl I J8067
1925 | Single-seat tail-less experimental | One 32hp Bristol Cherub III

Captain (later Professor) Geoffrey Terence Rowland Hill served as a test pilot with the Royal Aircraft Factory at Farnborough, Hampshire, during World War One and with Handley Page from November 1918. Soon he was involved in design, helping to create the leading edge slots that became a cash-cow for HP as they were licenced around the world. (See narrative on the Gugnunc, above.) Like Cierva (see the C.30A above) Hill became fascinated in creating an aircraft that could not stall. He came up with a tail-less configuration with rotating 'controllers' at the wing tips that acted as elevators and ailerons. Small rudders mid-set underneath the wings provided additional directional control. Hill built a glider to prove his point and on the last day of 1924 he flew it at the wonderfully-named Devil's Rest Bottom on the Sussex Downs. This got the Royal Aircraft Establishment (RAE) at Farnborough interested and eventually, the Air Ministry. Along with his wife, Hill built a powered version, the Pterodactyl I which he flew the first time, for five minutes, at Farnborough on 2nd November 1925. Hill used the name Pterodactyl – a winged dinosaur – as the generic term for all of his tail-less designs.

Trials at RAE showed that the concept had prospects and the Mk.I was given the serial number J8067. With official interest increasing, Hill joined the staff of Westland Aircraft at Yeovil in 1926, taking charge of a department established to exploit the concept. With Flt Lt J S Chick piloting, J8067 led the flypast of new types at the RAF Air Pageant at Hendon on 3rd July 1926. After public 'stardom', the Pterodactyl moved to Yeovil and was modified with reduced span 'controllers'. During a taxi trial with test pilot Laurence Openshaw in command, J8067 bounced into the air and was badly damaged upon its return to earth. It was later back at the RAE and was last flown there on 20th February 1928; returning to Yeovil. Four months later the brand-new and radically different-looking two-seater Pterodactyl IA J9251 took to the air and it went through a series of modifications. This machine was due to fly at the June 1930 Hendon display, but its Armstrong Siddeley Genet engine was playing up and J8067 was substituted at short notice. It flew in formation with the HP Gugnunc slot test-bed (held in store at Wroughton – see the narrative above) and a Cierva C.19 autogiro – three 'unstallable' types. The Pterodactyl II and III remained on the drawing board but the Mk.IV two-seat pusher first flew in March 1931 leading to the tractor-configured Mk.V two-seat fighter in May 1934. This could have forward-firing machine guns and had a rear gun position offering an exceptional field of fire. By 1937, interest had waned in the tail-less concept, despite Hill having schemed flying-boat and airliner versions. Professor Hill was not done with 'controller'-like wings; in 1950 he moved to Belfast to create the SB.1 and Sherpa – see Chapter 9. The original Pterodactyl had languished at Yeovil, although it was on show at Farnborough in 1948 and at back at Hendon in 1951 statically exhibited at the *Daily Express* 'Fifty Years of Flying' celebration. Professor Hill donated J8067 to the museum that year and it is displayed with the starboard wing stripped of fabric.

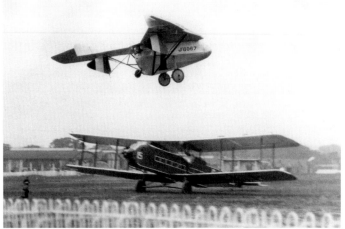

With a huge '1' painted on its 'fuselage', Flt Lt Chick brings Pterodactyl J8067 into land at the 1926 Hendon show. All 'new types' received a number at the Air Pageant, '15', being the prototype Armstrong Whitworth Argosy I, G-EBLF. *KEC*

Messerschmitt Me 163B-1a Komet 191316
1944 | Single-seat rocket-powered interceptor | One 3,750lb st Walter HWK 509A-2

Conceived as a fast-climbing point defence fighter with a heavy armament of two 30mm cannon, the Komet seemed invincible when the Allies gained knowledge of the rocket-powered fighter. Requiring complex infrastructure to look after its potentially lethal rocket fuel, the Me 163 was very difficult to fly and even more so to land. Its huge speed – close to 600mph – meant that it easily overtook its bomber prey, but with little manoeuvrability, or endurance, to return for a second pass. If the little tail-less, swept-wing fighter did achieve a firing solution, the pilot had only milliseconds to react. Blasted to height by its temperamental rocket motor, the Komet had to glide back to its base, landing on the built-in skid; this often resulting in a wrecked aircraft and at times a spinally-injured pilot. Jagdgeschwader 400 deployed the fighter for the first time on 28th July 1944 against USAAF Boeing B-17G Flying Fortresses. Eight months later the production lines closed with around 400 having been created, including a large number used in the tortuously long development process. Nine Me 163s survive, three in the USA, two each in Germany and the UK, one in Australia and one in Canada.

The *second* Me 163B to be displayed at South Kensington – see the narrative above – this example was on charge with JG 400 as *Yellow 6* and captured intact at Husum, close to the Danish border. It was shipped to the Royal Aircraft Establishment at Farnborough and allocated the Air Ministry reference number 210. It moved to 6 Maintenance Unit (MU) at Brize Norton on 21st July 1945 and then to 47 MU at Sealand, near Chester, on 17th June 1946. By 1949 it was at 3 MU, Stanmore Park, Middlesex, as part of what was known as the German Air Force Equipment Centre. Its exact whereabouts beyond this is unconfirmed, but it was issued to the museum in 1958. It moved to Halton, Bucks, in 1961 for refurbishing by apprentices from 1 School of Technical Training prior to going on show at South Kensington with the opening of the aviation gallery in 1963.

Roe 1909 Triplane
1909 | Single-seat triplane | One 9hp JAP

Manchester-born Alliott Verdon Roe had been building model gliders since 1901 and in April 1907 at Alexandra Palace won the considerable sum of £75 for a rubber-powered Wright-like biplane. This cash must have helped with the construction of a full-size machine, powered by 6hp JAP twin-cylinder which was tested at Brooklands, Surrey, in September 1907 but was not successful. With a 24hp French Antoinette installed it managed a few 'hops' in June 1908 before the 30-year old Roe was asked to leave Brooklands and the Antoinette returned to its homeland. In 1909 Roe turned his thoughts to a triplane format and started construction of a one for George Friswell, but this was not completed. The next one, retrospectively referred to as the Roe Triplane Type I, was started at Putney with assembly being completed in a railway arch at Lea Marshes in Essex. Roe's brother, Humphrey, was by then financing the enterprise. It was powered by a vee-format two-cylinder of a hoped-for 10hp, but gave only 9hp, built to order by John Alfred Prestwich – hence the JAP – at his Tottenham works. Roe and JAP had previously been in partnership, but this had been dissolved by the time the engine was delivered in May 1909. (In 1930 Mr Prestwich donated the JAP-Harding Monoplane to ScM – see the narrative above.) The first hops from land close to his workshop were achieved on the 5th June. On the 13th July he made a more sustained flight and ten days later he achieved a distance of 900ft at an altitude of a giddy 10ft. Nevertheless these were the first sustained flights by an Englishman in a British designed and built flying machine with a likewise indigenous engine. In the dawn of 25th July Louis Blériot flew the English Channel and any chance of Roe dominating and headlines vanished.

Like many pioneer aircraft, the Triplane I had a brief flying career, it was last flown at the Blackpool Flying Carnival, held over 18th-24th October 1909. The Triplane was exhibited at the Manchester Industrial Exhibition in 1910 and early in 1914 within the hall at Belle Vue Gardens, Manchester. Beyond this it was put into store, almost certainly at the giant Newton Heath plant at Manchester that was a direct consequence of Alliott's success at Lea Marsh. Other products of the dynasty that he founded can be found throughout this book. But how did this fundamental aircraft gravitate to South Kensington?

At this point, we'll divert into the Roe's correspondence file held in the bowels of ScM; they make fascinating reading. Following approaches from museum staff regarding the status of the Triplane a letter was received on 22nd April 1925 from the Avro HQ at Newton Heath, noting that the directors had "unanimously agreed to offer Mr A V Roe's 9hp aeroplane for exhibition." A one-year loan document was drawn up, dated 27th April 1925 for "one Triplane", inventory number 1925-443. Staff were disappointed that the machine lacked its engine and there was a note that Avro was "hunting". This was fruitful as a (the?) JAP two-cylinder was noted as received on 11th March 1926, inventory number 1926-208. Clearly the museum was looking for more than a 'rolling' one-year loan from Avro but a memo dated 21st October 1927 noted that the company didn't want to increase its commitment as the intention was to fly the Triplane on the occasion of its centenary! Then came two letters that got the author wobbling; being a born-and-bred Avro fan. One signed by Roy Chadwick, the great designer, the other by Roy Dobson, the man who made the company tick; both outline intentions to renovate the Triplane for continued display. A letter on incredibly stylish Saunders-Roe notepaper dated 24th September 1931 was signed on behalf of Sir Alliott Verdon Roe. (Roe sold his interest in Avro to Sir John Siddeley in 1928 and bought into Sam Saunders's boat-building company at Cowes, renaming it Saunders-Roe.) This reads: "I notice that my early Triplane, which is exhibited at the Science Museum is described as being lent by Messrs A V Roe & Co Ltd, actually this machine is my property. I remember the Board Meeting and it did not occur to me at the time to say 'Gentlemen, why should the Board unanimously agree to lend my machine?' However, if you write to Messrs A V Roe & Co Ltd I am sure they will not question the ownership, if so, perhaps you would kindly state it is lent by Sir Alliott

Verdon Roe." A reply from Avro dated 3rd October 1931 can be paraphrased as follows: "It's ours!" After the war, the museum embarked upon a campaign of permanency relating to the Triplane and this was rewarded by 'AV' himself signing a donor document on 20th June 1950. Attribution is always a potential problem for any museum; here's proof that even large corporations and famous individuals may not get it right!

Left: A charismatic image of 'AV' with the 1910 Triplane, the Type III. *British Aerospace*

Below: Roe aloft in his Triplane at Lea Marshes, very likely September 1909. *British Aerospace*

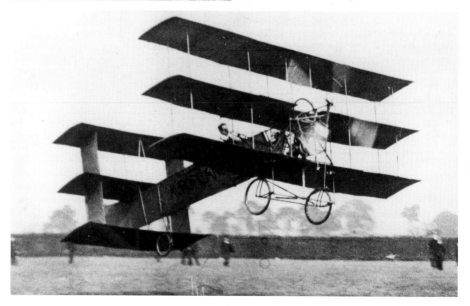

Rolls-Royce Thrust Measuring Rig XJ314
1953 | Single-seat vertical jet-lift test-bed | Two 4,900lb st Rolls-Royce Nene 101-IV

Separated by an impressive 'stack' of motorcars and a German V-2 rocket within the 'Making of the Modern World' gallery at South Kensington are the two earliest UK non-rotor vertical take-off pioneers; the unlikely-looking 'Flying Bedstead' and the Short SC.1. On the top floor, in the 'Flight' gallery is the prototype Hawker P.1127 which is profiled above. Although the vertically-mounted powerplant format was eclipsed by the P.1127's vectored thrust, both the 'Bedstead' and the SC.1 contributed considerably to the global success story of the Harrier through 'puffer' control jets and automatic stabilisation systems.

Co-operation between Rolls-Royce and the Royal Aircraft Establishment (RAE) starting in 1952 led to a jet-powered test-bed to produce data for a dedicated lift engine and a control and stabilisation system for hovering flight. RAE provided the control systems while Rolls-Royce created what was known as the Thrust Measuring Rig (TMR) but which the press readily called the 'Flying Bedstead'. Two horizontally-mounted Nene turbojets were coupled together via T-shaped ducting that provided downward thrust. A small amount of thrust was bled away into four 'puffer' jets to provide stability, projecting starboard and port and fore and aft. The latter two could swivel to provide a limited amount of directional control; it could fly sideways, or in circles. The TMR was rolled out at Hucknall on 3rd July 1953 and was mounted within a complex gantry arrangement that provided a degree of tethered flight, limited by cables on pullies. With Wg Cdr J H Heyworth sitting atop the pair of turbojets in an open cockpit protected by a crash-cage, the first successful tethered hop took place three days after the roll-out. Ronnie T Shepherd piloted the first free excursion on 3rd August 1954. Tests at Hucknall were completed on 15th December 1954 by which time it had clocked up 224 tethered and 16 free flights, the latter amounting to 105 minutes airborne. The TMR was transferred to the RAE at Farnborough on 13th January 1955, moving to RAE Bedford at Thurleigh on 21st June 1956. On 16th September 1957 the TMR crashed following a partial failure of the control system, Sqn Ldr S J Hubbard survived. This was a severe blow for the project made all the more so when the second TMR (XK426, first flown 12th November 1956), crashed fatally at Hucknall just 57 days after the original example. The first TMR was rebuilt, using elements of the second one, and transferred to the museum, reportedly for £600, on 9th January 1961. During the 1980s, the TMR was displayed on loan at three venues: Strathallan Aircraft Collection, Scotland, from June 1982, the Museum of Flight East Fortune (Chapter 10) from June 1987 and the Fleet Air Arm Museum (Chapter 4) from February 1989. It was installed within the 'Making of the Modern World' exhibition at South Kensington in late 1999.

The incredible Rolls-Royce
Thrust Measuring Rig,
understandably called the
'Flying Bedstead' by the press.
Rolls-Royce via Peter Green

Here is a good place to fill in brief details on the TMR's neighbour, Short SC.1 XG900. The background to the type can be found in Chapter 9 where the second SC.1, XG905, is profiled. Tom Brooke-Smith first flew XG900 in conventional mode at Sydenham on 17th December 1956. Following the fatal crash of XG905, its brother was grounded from early October 1963 until June 1967 and from March 1969 it was relegated to ground-running only. On 22nd June 1971 XG900 was transferred to ScM.

Royal Aircraft Factory SE.5a G-EBIB
1918 | Single-seat fighter | One 200hp Wolseley Viper

South Kensington's SE.5a was produced in 1918, almost certainly as F938, by Wolseley Motors of Adderley Park, Birmingham. Its service life, if any, is unconfirmed, but its life beyond that more than makes up for the uncertainty! It was civilian registered as G-EBIB to Major John Clifford Savage at 'The London Aerodrome', Hendon on 26th September 1923. 'Jack' Savage knew Hendon well; he had been a mechanic with Grahame-White and manager of British Aerial Transport. On 16th July 1921 Hendon had reverberated to the sound of half a dozen of the demobbed fighters in a form of combat. Under the aegis of the Royal Aero Club, and with Savage acting as promoter, Oxford and Cambridge Universities competed in an air race, using six SE.5as on loan from the Croydon-based Air Disposal Company. Cambridge won; Oxford having retired. Jack formed the Savage Skywriting Co Ltd at Hendon the following month and, using Vickers-built G-EATE as a test-bed, developed a patented smoke system that utilised the original twin exhausts of the SE.5a, extending them down the fuselage to meet in a Y-junction at the rudder post. This provided white smoke that could be seen in perfect conditions from 50 miles away, and lasted a long time in still air. Chief pilot Cyril Turner gave the first public demonstration of the art of skywriting at Hendon on 30th May 1922. Savage Skywriting put an incredible 33 SE.5As on the British civil register and the company picked up many highly lucrative contracts. Performing extensively in the UK, aircraft travelled to Australia and the USA as well as to Europe. All three of the genuine SE.5as in UK museums came from the Savage fleet. The fortunes of the skywriting trade mirrored that of the world economy and by the early 1930s, the operation was but a shadow of its former self. The last Savage SE.5a flying was G-EBVB which earned its keep performing aerobatics at air displays and other events until it was retired in 1934. The Savage offices at Hendon closed the following year, but several SE.5as lingered in the hangars.

SE.5a G-EBIB in hastily-applied camouflage and roundels, plus short exhausts, at the Hendon Pageant in 1937, note the paddock number '6' on the fin. *KEC*

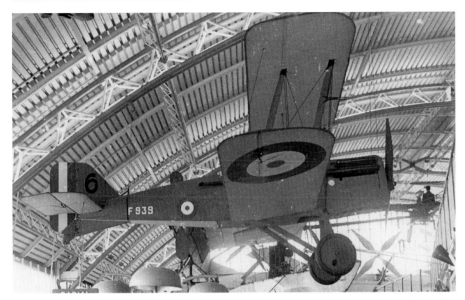

South Kensington's SE.5a after its 1961 re-work, marked as 'F939' and carrying the 1937 paddock number in black on the fin.
Peter Green

In 1936 Flt Lt Buckle and team staged a World War One 'act' at Hendon's Air Pageant. For the 1937 event, they planned a mock combat ending with the destruction of a barrage balloon; Buckle had a knack for finding 'ancients' and reviving them for airshow purposes. Staged on 26th June 1937 and the forlorn 'blimp' was defended by LVG C.VI 7198/18 (now with the RAF Museum, see Chapter 6) and attacked by SE.5A G-EBIB, with the paddock number '6' in period camouflage piloted by Flt Lt R C Jonas, Sopwith Triplane N5912 (paddock number '5' and now at the RAF Museum at Hendon, Chapter 5) flown by Buckle and a Bristol F.2b Fighter, the latter specially on charge with the resident 24 Squadron for the event. The balloon perished amid thunderous applause... After this performance, the SE.5a was put back into store at Hendon. On 1st June 1939 Jack Savage, possibly faced with demands for hangar fees, wrote to ScM explained that he had "discovered" one of his SE.5as at Hendon and wanted to donate it. The paperwork was drawn up on 24th July with Savage agreeing "to lend [it] for a period of eternity" – no ambiguity there, then! In 1961 the SE.5a was refurbished and during research into its provenance decided that its serial number was F939 and this was painted upon the fuselage and on the fin, an accurate rendition of the paddock number worn at Hendon in 1937 ('6') but painted in black, not white. With the major restructuring of the aviation gallery at South Kensington resulting in the excellent 'Flight' gallery in October 1992, it was decided to properly restore the SE.5a. John Bagley (see the narrative above) seized this opportunity to bring it back to a *known* period of its life, using the good offices of Tim Moore's Skysport and John Pothercary's Air South. With two SE.5as in national museums in wartime markings, John chose to revert it to G-EBIB, in overall 'silver' and the long, joined exhaust stacks to honour the Savage Skywriters.

Supermarine S.6B S1595
1931 | Single-seat racing seaplane | One 2,350hp Rolls-Royce 'R'

On 13th September 1931 Flt Lt John Boothman of the RAF High Speed Flight put the throttle forward to 3,200rpm as all 2,350hp kicked in, he worked hard to correct the swing then suddenly boat turned into aircraft and he climbed for height. Blasting past the pier at Ryde on the Isle of Wight, he turned left abeam Bembridge Harbour and headed north east for West Wittering on the Hampshire coast. On reaching the shoreline he hauled hard on the stick and rudder for the longest leg of the course, sharp left due west passing Hayling

Island, Portsmouth and Gilkicker Point at Gosport on the right before turning around a marker-boat off East Cowes, for another gruelling jack-knife left turn to sizzle past Ryde again at the end of the first, 31-miles lap. Another six to go... When all the observers and judges had finished their deliberations, it was announced that he had averaged 340.05mph and had won the Schneider Trophy in perpetuity for Great Britain.

French-born armaments magnate Jacques Schneider had offered the stunning trophy as a way of encouraging greater performance in seaplanes. The competition would be closed when one country was the fastest three times in a row. First staged at Monaco in 1913, the Schneider Trophy was a hard-fought battle of national pride involving France, Italy, Switzerland, UK and USA. Only the British team entered for the 1931 event. Uncontested or not, Boothman, the RAF, Supermarine and Rolls-Royce had achieved a sparkling victory. To emphasize this, 17 days later Flt Lt G H Stainforth put S1595 through its paces and became the first man to travel at over 400mph – setting a new world air speed record of 407.5mph.

The 'S' series of floatplanes had been conceived by Supermarine's gifted design staff, headed by the exceptional Reginald Joseph Mitchell. The S.6B represented the pinnacle of all of their experience and S1595 and sister-ship S1596 were created at a pace almost as hectic as the race itself. Built at the Woolston works, S1595 was taken on charge by the RAF High Speed Flight on 27th July 1931 and first flown two days later by the CO, Sqn Ldr A H Orlebar. Then it was based at Calshot and worked up ready for what became the 12th and final Schneider. Supermarine and Mitchell were 'old hands' at the competition, Henri Biard clinched the 1922 Schneider at Naples in a Sea Lion II at 145.7mph. Biard was at the helm of the first 'S' series, the S.4 at Baltimore, USA, in 1925, but the machine came to grief. Italy won the 1926 event in the USA, so hosted the following year at Venice. Flt Lt S N Webster in S.5 N220 took the honours, bringing the next event, 1929, to Calshot where Fg Off H R D Waghorn won in S.6 N247 at 328.63mph. And so to Calshot in 1931...

After the victory, S1595 was moved to Brooklands, Surrey, for an exhibition staged by Vickers – the owners of Supermarine – in October 1931. From the beginning of June 1932 it was loaned to ScM for temporary display before again going into the care of Vickers on the 18th for a trip to Canada for flag-waving exercise. On 18th April 1934 S1595 was gifted to the museum and eventually joined by the magnificent trophy. Only a matter of 20 miles away from the Schneider race course, at Solent Sky in Southampton, is Supermarine S.6A N248 built at the Woolston works on the opposite bank of the River Itchen for the 1929 contest. It is nestled under the wing of Short Sandringham VH-BRC, another marine aircraft well versed with the waters of the Solent.

Line-up of the High Speed Flight alongside Calshot Castle, 1931. Left to right: S.6B S1596, S.6 N249 and S.6B S1595. *Rolls-Royce*

Above: Flt Lt G H Stainforth, who became the first man to fly at over 400mph in S.6B S1595 on 29th September 1931. *Peter Green Collection*

Left: Supermarine S.6B S1595 and the superb Schneider Trophy. *Ken Ellis*

Vickers Vimy IV
1919 | Two-crew modified bomber | Two 360hp Rolls-Royce Eagle VIII

"'Vickers-Vimy Rolls-Royce Aeroplane' presented by Messrs Vickers Ltd, London." to quote the heading in ScM's *Aeronautics* handbook published in 1929 regarding artefact inventory number 1919-476. This matter-of-fact attribution was followed by: "This aeroplane, which was built at Brooklands, is the original machine on which the first direct trans-Atlantic flight was made by Capt Sir John Alcock KBE DSC and Lt Sir Arthur Whitten Brown KBE on 14th-15th June 1919, flying over a distance of 1,890 miles in 15 hours 57 minutes at an average speed of 118.5mph. The crossing was made from St John's, Newfoundland, to Clifden, County Galway, Ireland." On 15th December 1919 the Vimy was handed over to ScM during the inauguration of the new South Kensington buildings and Vickers company director Douglas Vickers MP declared that: "all would agree that this aeroplane constituted an historical landmark" yet "it was not in any way specially made for the flight, but was to have been a Berlin bomber."

The prototype Vimy bomber first flew on 30th November 1917 but the type saw no operational service during the Great War and huge orders were dramatically cut back, just over 200 being built by 1921. In 1919 the *Daily Mail* offered £10,000 for the first aircraft to make a direct crossing of the Atlantic. (This would equate to about £550,000 in present-day spending values.) Vickers realised that the Vimy was ideal to have a crack at this and set aside the 13th example off the line at Brooklands for modification with extra fuel tanks; this aircraft test flew on 18th April 1919. It was crated and shipped to Newfoundland, Canada, arriving on 26th May. Assembled by a company team at Quidi Vidi, north of St John's, and test flown on 9th June, it settled on Lester's Field, the point of departure for Alcock and Brown's epic venture.

In late 1919, brothers Ross and Keith Smith flew Vimy IV G-EAOU to Darwin, becoming the first to fly from the UK to Australia. This machine is preserved at Adelaide Airport. Vimys entered service with the RAF in October 1918 and the last in the bomber role was retired in the summer of 1928. Training and trials versions flew on until 1933.

Science Museum aircraft

Type	Identity	Built	Origin	With ScM since	Notes
Antoinette Monoplane	–	1910	France	1926	–
Avro 504K*	D7560	1918	UK	22 Jan 1920	see profile
Balloon Factory Airship No.17	–	1910	UK	c1917	gondola, *Beta II*
Blériot XI	–	1909	France	1920	cockpit – see narrative
Cierva C.30A	AP507	1934	UK	24 May 1946	see profile
Cody Military Biplane*	304	1912	UK	26 Nov 1913	see profile
De Havilland Moth*	G-AAAH	1928	UK	21 Jan 1931	see profile
Douglas Dakota IV	KN448	1944	USA	1976	cockpit – see narrative
Fokker E.III	210/16	1916	Germany	27 Feb 1918	see profile
Frost Ornithopter	–	1902	UK	1925	wing, flapping mechanism, engine
Gloster E28/39*	W4041/G	1941	UK	28 Apr 1946	see profile
Hawker Hurricane I*	L1592	1938	UK	16 Dec 1954	see profile
Hawker P.1127*	XP831	1960	UK	31 May 1992	see profile
Hawker Siddeley HS.125-1/522*	G-ASSM	1964	UK	16 Mar 1989	–
Hill Pterodactyl I	J8067	1925	UK	1951	see profile
JAP-Harding Monoplane	–	1910	France	1930	–
Lilienthal glider replica	–	1976	Germany	1976	–
Lockheed 10A Electra*	NC5171N	1935	USA	21 Jun 1982	–
Messerschmitt Me 163B-1a	191316	1944	Germany	1958	see profile
Pitts S-1S Special	G-AZPH	1970	USA	Oct 1991	–
Roe Triplane*	–	1909	UK	1925	see profile
Rolls-Royce 'Flying Bedstead'	XJ314	1953	UK	9 Jan 1961	see profile
Royal Aircraft Factory SE.5a*	G-EBIB	1918	UK	24 Jul 1939	see profile
Saro Skeeter AOP.12	XN344	1960	UK	1975	–
Schempp-Hirth Cirrus glider	DFY	c1975	Germany	1992	–
Short Brothers Gas Balloon	–	1910	UK	c1912	basket only
Short SC.1	XG900	1956	UK	22 Jun 1971	–
Supermarine S.6B	S1595	1931	UK	18 Apr 1932	see profile
Supermarine Spitfire Ia	P9444	1940	UK	16 Dec 1954	–
Vickers Vimy IV*	–	1918	UK	15 Dec 1919	see profile
Wright Flyer replica	–	1948	USA	1948	–

Note: * – illustrated in the colour section

Science Museum aircraft on loan

Type	Identity	Built	Origin	With ScM since	Location
BAC/Sud Concorde 002	G-BSST	1969	UK/France	4 Mar 1976	Fleet Air Arm Museum – Chapter 4
Cierva C.24 autogiro	G-ABLM	1932	UK	Sep 1935	De Havilland Aircraft Heritage Centre, London Colney, Herts
Clarke Chanute glider	–	1910	UK	1914	RAF Museum, Hendon – Chapter 5
De Havilland Sea Vampire F.1	LZ551/G	1945	UK	Oct 1949	Fleet Air Arm Museum – Chapter 4
Mignet HM.14 'Flying Flea'	G-AEHM	1936	France	Sep 1938	M-Shed, Bristol, Glos
Short Sandringham 4	VH-BRC		UK	Nov 1981	Solent Sky, Southampton, Hampshire
Yokosuka MXY-7 Ohka 11	–	1945	Japan	1946 (?)	Fleet Air Arm Museum – Chapter 4

Alcock and Brown departing Lester's Field, Newfoundland, at the start of their epic transatlantic flight 14th June 1919. *Rolls-Royce*

CHAPTER 2

Transforming a Century
Imperial War Museum
South Lambeth, London
www.iwm.org.uk

Just before the end of 2012 the last airframe at South Lambeth was brought down from its 'perch', suspended within the Imperial War Museum's Large Exhibits Gallery, where it has been for the last two decades or so. This was P-51D Mustang *Big Beautiful Doll*, in the colours of the Duxford-based 78th Fighter Group, USAAF. Like the rest of the aircraft that had been at Lambeth, all but one were destined for Duxford. Some will be stored temporarily, or – in the case of the P-51 – bound for the 'Conservation in Action' bay at the front of the 'Superhangar'. With the careful removal and dismantling of the *Doll*, the Imperial War Museum (IWM) closed its doors to the public, ready to re-open partially in July 2013.

The gas mask boxes, the 'tin hat' and the uniforms give away the date of this view of a gallery at South Lambeth. The museum closed its doors to the public in September 1940. RE.8 F3556, carrying the legend 'A Paddy Bird from Ceylon' on the forward fuselage was originally displayed at Crystal Palace in 1920. *IWM*

South Lambeth is embarking on a massive transformation and the first fruits of this will appear in 2014 – the centenary of the start of World War One. Six years after that the IWM itself celebrates its own centenary. Staff at Lambeth face a busy and momentous time! I quote from the museum's web-site for what is to come: "Using the latest historical research and our exceptional collections we will open new world-class World War One Galleries which will offer new stories, new perspectives and new ways of looking at the 'Great War'. Our redesigned atrium will stretch over six floors. We will display the most iconic and unusual of our objects in this dramatic space to explore aspects of war from 1914 through to the present day." As this book closed for press IWM was keeping close to its corporate chest just what aircraft will go back. New will be Harrier GR.9A ZD461 and the former Pacific-salvaged Mitsubishi A6M3. (See the table on page 57 for the latest on transfers.)

With the horrific conflict of World War One still raging, the War Cabinet approved a proposal by Sir Alfred Mond MP on 5th March 1917 to collect and ultimately display material to tell the story of what was then hoped would be the 'War to end all Wars'. The intention was to record all experiences – civilian and military – and commemorate the sacrifices of all sections of society. At first this was referred to as the National War Museum, but with the support of the Dominions, the title was changed to the Imperial War Museum. An Act of Parliament established the IWM in 1920 and on 9th June that year King George V opened the IWM's incredible Great Victory Exhibition within the Crystal Palace, near Sydenham in South London. As will be seen from the table 'Imperial War Museum display at the Crystal Palace 1920-1923' and the illustrations, there were some amazing types that are no longer extant. Most of the airframes on show are assumed to have been scrapped as soon as the event was over; identifying and charting these has been an impossibility. The 10th June 1920 issue of the weekly *Flight* magazine covered some aspects of the event, but the narrative limply noted: "To give a full description of the exhibits would be an interminable task, and we do not propose to attempt it." Diddums! The issue the week before *did* enter into some detail of items that might today seem ghoulish, parts from the aircraft in which the following met their fate: Captain Albert Ball's SE.5a (17th May 1917), Major James McCudden's SE.5a (9th July 1918), Lt Werner Voss's Fokker Dr.I (23rd September 1917) and the engine and rudder of Rittmeister Manfred von Richthofen's Fokker Dr.I 425/17 (21st April 1918).

The Crystal Palace exhibition ran until late 1923. It is worth emphasizing that this was seen as *temporary* to mark the end of the war and to provide the public with an insight into the munitions and machinery used by both sides. Many of the items were destined for the scrapheap and not museum inventory. The Nieuport Nighthawk, Parnall Panther and *possibly* the Sopwith Salamander were billed as the 'Latest types of British aircraft' and *may* well have gone back to the RAF, though they would have 'missed the boat' by 1923. Nine (or possibly eleven) airframes were put into storage in the basement of the Science Museum. By 1936 all are believed to have moved to Cardington, some to face the axe. The Bristol F.2b Fighter, LVG C.VI, Royal Aircraft Factory BE.2 and RE.8, Short 184, Sopwith Camel and Triplane are thankfully still with us. Smaller items from the Crystal Palace were put on show in galleries, close to the Imperial Institute and the Science Museum, while a permanent home was found.

Souvenir postcard of the 1920-1923 Crystal Palace exhibition, showing 'A Corner of the Aerial Section'. NT.2b N2269 is floating in its own pond, behind and to the right is the RE.8 and Bristol F.2b.
Peter Green Collection

Amid the grandeur of the Crystal Palace, the Parnall Panther (with the starboard floatation bag deployed) and Nieuport Nighthawk J2417 illustrate the 'Latest Types of British Aircraft'. *Peter Green Collection*

Imperial War Museum display at the Crystal Palace 1920-1923

Aircraft	Location / Fate
Armstrong Whitworth R29 airship car and engine pod	–?–
Bristol F.2b Fighter E2581 #	IWM Duxford
Friedrichshafen G.III	–?–
'Gotha'	–?–
Junkers J.I remains	–?–
LFG D.VI D7515 #	–?–
LVG C.VI 7198/18 #	RAF Museum
Nieuport Nighthawk J2417	–?–
Norman-Thompson NT.2b N2269	–?–
Parnall Panther	–?–
Roland D.VII D7515	–?–
Royal Aircraft Factory BE.2c 2699 #	IWM
Royal Aircraft Factory RE.8 F3556 #	IWM Duxford
Short 184 8359 #	Fleet Air Arm Museum
Sopwith 2F1 Camel N6812 #	IWM
Sopwith Salamander	–?–
Sopwith Triplane N5912 #	RAF Museum Hendon
Submarine Scout Type Zero airship SS.Z.70 #	–?–

Notes: Aircraft marked # were all stored in dismantled state in the basement of the Science Museum buildings in South Kensington from 1923. *At least* the Camel and the F.2b received Science Museum inventory numbers: 1923-683 and 1923-685, respectively. All are believed to have been moved to No.1 Airship Shed at Cardington, Bedfordshire, for further storage, by 1936. In the case of the LFG and SS.Z.70 (and a Bristol F.2b Fighter fuselage and a Fokker D.VII, both of which are less well characterised and *may well* not have been on show at the Crystal Palace) were scrapped by 1936.

Longevity was achieved on 7th July 1936 when King George VI opened the IWM at its current South Lambeth Home. The building had been the Bethlem Royal Hospital, also known as 'Bedlam'. It was completed in 1815 and served as a hospital until 1930 when it re-located to Kent, allowing for the new 'tenant'. The IWM closed its doors to the public in September 1940. On 31st January 1941 the museum received a direct hit from a Luftwaffe bomb, causing considerable damage. The Sopwith Camel (profiled below) received some damage, but it was the Naval Gallery that took the brunt; the magnificent Short 184 torpedo-bomber floatplane was very badly damaged. (See Chapter 4 for more on this machine.) The building was on the receiving end of more than 40 incendiary hits during the war. With the advent of World War Two the museum's terms of reference were extended to include both conflicts and in 1953 it was decided to portray all military operations involving British and Commonwealth forces from 1914 onwards.

The IWM re-opened in November 1946; remaining much as it had been in 1936 until a small extension to the galleries in the early 1960s. As with the Science Museum (see Chapter 1) space for large objects was a problem. To illustrate this, in the mid-1950s a complete Imperial Japanese Navy Mitsubishi A6M5 Model 52 *Zeke* fighter was offered, but space restrictions meant that it had to be reduced to a cockpit section. Much of the remainder could be found in a scrapyard in Warrington in 1956. As well as the 'Zero' (the A6M5 was known as the Navy Fighter Type 0, hence its nickname) the IWM received three former Luftwaffe aircraft during the 1960s. Among these was a Focke-Wulf Fw 190A-8/R6 on loan from the Royal Air Force Museum. This migrated to Duxford 1986 to 1989 while the Lambeth atrium was remodelled. With the closure in December 2012 it was decided to return the Fw 190 to the care of the RAF Museum – see Chapter 6.

Fw 190A-8 733682 with Mosquito T.3 TV959 'flying' above it, South Lambeth, late 1970s. The Mosquito had its starboard wing removed to fit in. It left Lambeth in 1988 and the Fw 190 was returned to the RAF Museum in late 2012. *IWM*

From the 1970s onwards IWM underwent tremendous changes and expansion, the fruits of which continue with the Great War project. Much of the impetus for the 'rebirth' of the museum was at the hands of a Bomber Command navigator who was awarded the DFC in 1944 – Dr Noble Frankland. From 1948 he worked for the Air Historical Branch (more on the AHB in Chapter 5) and he went on to write the four-volume *Strategic Air Offensive Against Germany*, among many other titles. He became Director of IWM in 1960, a classic example of a round peg in a round hole, and was the man who presided over the acquisition of Duxford – a former Fighter Command airfield, but you can't have everything! In 1982 he was succeeded by Dr Alan Borg who was responsible for the modernisation of the museum in image, appeal and outlook; in-house this was referred to as the 'New' IWM. Physical changes under Dr Borg included in 1978 taking on the 1938-built cruiser HMS *Belfast* and it was anchored close to Tower Bridge to become a unique 'out-station'. This was followed in April 1989 by the Cabinet War Rooms in King Charles Street, the underground nerve centre for

Churchill's War Cabinet and Chiefs of Staff. (Plus the phenomenal evolution of Duxford, as outlined in Chapter 8.) As mentioned above, from 1988 South Lambeth was transformed and the atrium became the very impressive Large Exhibits Gallery, allowing aircraft to be 'flown' within the space and for items like a V-2 rocket and Polaris submarine-launched ballistic missile to be displayed upright. One press report called it "the biggest boys' bedroom in London!" This is the area receiving still further attention in the present transformation. The new IWM was re-opened to great public acclaim on 4th November 1989.

Dr Borg left the IWM in 1995 to take command of the Victoria and Albert Museum and in his place came an IWM 'lifer', Robert Crawford (Sir Robert from 2007) who joined as a research assistant in the late 1960s and worked his way to the top post. On 5th July 2002 another member of the IWM family opened for business: IWM North at Trafford Park, Manchester. Designed by world-renowned architect Daniel Libeskind, the building is clad in aluminium and symbolises a fragmented globe re-assembled in three interlocking shards representing conflict on land, water and in the air. Within the building is former US Marine Corps Hawker Siddeley AV-8A Harrier 159233. Sir Robert Crawford retired in 2008 and was succeeded by Diane Lees who is heading the significant changes to 'HQ' described at the beginning of the chapter. To reflect this multi-location image IWM 'went plural' in October 2011, rebranded as Imperial War Museums with a new logo incorporating the initials.

For most readers of this book, there is one IWM location that dominates all of this and that of course is the off-spring that far outgrew its parent. Turn to Chapter 8 for the venue that became a brand in its own right – Duxford.

Former Imperial War Museum, South Lambeth, aircraft

Type	Identity	Built	With IWM since	Notes, *current status or fate*
De Havilland Mosquito T.3	TV959	1945	1965	To storage in Hounslow, 1988 and then Duxford. To The Fighter Collection, Duxford, 1992. *To the Flying Heritage Collection, Seattle, USA, 2003*
Fairey Swordfish III	NF370	1944	30 Jun 1952	Re-located 1988 to *Duxford, Cambs*
Focke-Wulf Fw 190A-8/R6	733682	1944	1965	On loan from RAF Museum, *returned to RAF Museum Dec 2012 – see Chapter 6*
Hawker Typhoon I	–	1944	1965	Cockpit, Re-located 1984 to *Duxford, Cambs*
HS Harrier GR.3	XZ133	1976	26 Feb 1992	Falklands exhibition Feb 1992 to Jun 1993. Re-located 1993 to *Duxford, Cambs*
Gloster Meteor F.8	WK991	1953	10 Dec 1963	Re-located 1976 to *Duxford, Cambs*
Messerschmitt Me 163A-1a	191660	1945	1961	Relocated 1976 to Duxford, Cambs. *To Flying Heritage Collection, Seattle, USA, May 2005*
Mikoyan-Gurevich MiG-15*bis*	1120	1955	May 1989	Polish-built Lim-2, on loan from RAF Museum, 1988, returned 26 Feb 1992. *National Cold War Exhibition, RAF Museum Cosford*
Royal Aircraft Factory RE.8	F3556	1918	1920	Re-located 1974 to *Duxford, Cambs*

Heinkel He 162A-1 120235
1945 | Single-seat fighter | One 1764lb st BMW 109-003A-1

With the ability to be produced rapidly in dispersed locations and packing the punch of a pair of 20mm MG151/20 cannon the hastily-conceived Heinkel He 162 offered the potential to flood beleaguered German airspace with a 522mph interceptor. Its 'game-changing' image and the intention to find pilots from within the Hitler Youth gave rise to the nickname 'Volksjäger' – Peoples' Fighter. The prototype first flew on 6th December 1944, a staggering achievement as approval to proceed had only been gained in mid-September. In early February 1945 I Gruppe of Jagdgeschwader 1, the first of three intended Gruppen, set about working up the new type at Parchim in northern Germany as manufacture of hundreds of He 162s was initiated. In April I/JG1 moved to Leck, close to the Danish border, with as many as 50 He 162s massed on the airfield. The unit was declared operational on 4th May but four days later British troops over-ran the defences and the promise of 'Volksjäger' was shattered. An encounter at low level with a USAAF P-51 in April showed the stop-gap fighter to be manoeuvrable, but the Mustang appeared to have better speed and acceleration. By then approaching 300 He 162s had been completed and the Allies found evidence of another 800 in the production phase. The Allies were keen to evaluate the type and, because of this, seven survive today; in Canada, France, Germany and two each in the UK and the USA. (The other UK example is in the RAF Museum Hendon, Chapter 5.)

The IWM 'Volksjäger' was one of the JG1 examples captured at Leck and is almost certainly 120235. It was allocated to the Royal Aircraft Establishment at Farnborough and the Air Ministry identification number 68 (AM.68) on 10th August 1945, but was routed on to 6 Maintenance Unit at Brize Norton for storage. By 1947 it was at Cranwell and held there until 1960 when it was transferred to the IWM. During the refurbishment at South Lambeth, it was at Duxford from 1986 to June 1989 when it was placed in Lambeth's atrium suspended in 'flying' pose. The 'Volksjäger' is to remain at Duxford.

North American P-51D Mustang '472218'
1945 | Single-seat fighter | One 1,695hp Packard Merlin V-1650

When former Royal Canadian Air Force (RCAF) Mustang IV 9246 was presented to the IWM, the temptation to paint it in the colours of a Duxford-based example was compelling. Texan Lt Col John David Landers was the commanding officer of the 78th Fighter Group from February to July 1945 and during that time he flew 44-72218 *Big Beautiful Doll*, carrying the codes 'WZ-I' of the constituent 84th Fighter Squadron. The 78th arrived at Duxford in April 1943, initially flying Republic P-47D Thunderbolts, staying until in October 1945. Landers ended the war with 8½ 'kills', 3½ of which were achieved with the 78th.

Lambeth's P-51D was built for the USAAF as 44-73979 at Inglewood, California, and was issued for service on 26th April 1945. It remained Stateside and was transferred to the RCAF on 6th December 1950 as 9246. An accident cut short its flying career and it was struck off charge on 16th May 1951. It became an instructional airframe and on 10th May 1955 officially disposed of, becoming instructional airframe A612 at the College Militaire Royale at St Jean, Quebec, and by 1960 was on display at the gate of the nearby RCAF station. It was presented to the IWM and arrived at Duxford in June 1972. Painted as the *Doll*, it was moved to South Lambeth in June 1989. As related above, it was brought down from its lofty perch within the Large Exhibits Gallery in December 2012 and moved to Duxford where it will stay.

Mustang '612' in a pale green and grey camouflage at St Jean, Quebec, in the mid-1960s. The numbers relate to its Canadian instructional airframe identity, A612. *KEC*

Royal Aircraft Factory BE.2c 2699
1916 | Two-crew, general purpose | One 90hp Royal Aircraft Factory 1A

In Chapter 1 the career of the Cody biplane is detailed. Even then out-moded, this ponderous machine won the Military Aeroplane Trials of 1912 while the Royal Aircraft Factory's exceptional BE.2 designed by Geoffrey de Havilland, was ineligible for judging. Despite the Cody's victory it was BE.2 that was ordered in increasingly large numbers, setting the format for warplanes for much of the conflict. Initially used for reconnaissance, the BE.2 was adopted for home defence but mostly served in the training role. BE.2c 2699 was part of a batch of 100 built in Lincoln by Ruston, Proctor & Co Ltd. It was first issued to 50 Squadron at Dover, Kent, in the home defence role. By April 1918 it was with 190 (Night) Training Squadron at Newmarket, transferring to 192 (N)TS at Cottenham, near Cambridge, in October 1918. Its last use was with apparently with 51 Squadron at Marham. By then then the unit was flying Royal Aircraft Factory FE.2bs, so 2699 is thought to have been a 'hack' for training and communications. A forced landing in May 1918 put paid to the biplane's career and in 1920 it was passed on to the IWM and exhibited at the Crystal Palace. It was displayed at Lambeth until 1979 when it was moved to Duxford for restoration, returning to London in 1989 for another spell of 'duty' until October 2012 when it again travelled to Duxford where it will stay.

Sopwith 2F1 Camel N6812
1918 | Single-seat naval fighter | One 150hp Bentley BR.1

"08:58 hours. Flew from Lighter to attack Zeppelin from 300ft below. Fired seven rounds from No.1 gun which jammed and a double charge from No.2. Zeppelin burst into flames and destroyed." It had been a momentous morning, on 11th August 1918 when Canadian Lt Stuart Douglas Culley had taken off from Thorneycroft Seaplane Lighter H5 being towed by HMS *Redoubt* in the southern sector of the North Sea. His objective was Zeppelin LZ100, tactical number L53, which had first flown a year previously and was a veteran of 19 patrols and four bombing raids against England. As it turned out, this was the last Zeppelin to be shot down during the Great War. As the giant airship fell to Culley's guns there was no time for elation; the very nature of such Royal Naval Air Service (RNAS) operations was that the pilot had to find the ship that

A Camel on the deck of Seaplane Lighter H3 under tow behind a warship. It was from such a short deck that Culley was launched against Zeppelin L53 on 11th August 1918. *KEC*

Camel 'F3043' outside 58 Maintenance Unit's hangar at Honington, 1953. *KEC*

despatched him, ditch alongside in the cold and unforgiving waters (even in summer), be plucked from the water and savour a tot of rum. This was no mean feat, but Culley achieved it and he and Camel N6812 were brought on board. As well as the drink, Culley received a DSO.

With a detachable rear fuselage to permit easier stowage on a ship, a single Vickers gun in the cowling and twin Lewis guns on the top wing the 2F1 version of Sopwith's famous Camel was designed as an airship killer and was known in the RNAS as the 'Ship's Camel' or 'Split Camel'. It was built by William Beardmore & Co Ltd at Dalmuir on the banks of the River Clyde. The destruction of L53 very likely assured the Camel's survival and from 1920 it was shown off at the Crystal Palace. With the closure of the exhibition, the Camel was stored in the basement at the Science Museum, and was given the inventory number 1923-683, until the mid-1930s when it was moved to the airship sheds at Cardington, near Bedford. It was put on show at South Lambeth in 1935 but was damaged when the building took a direct hit on 31st January 1941. The biplane did not re-appear until 1953 when it was at 58 Maintenance Unit, at Honington. Here it was readied for an appearance at the Royal Tournament in Earls Court and painted with the serial number 'F3043' – originally allocated to a Vickers Vimy that was cancelled prior to construction. Beyond this, it returned to Lambeth, leaving in 1988 for refinishing, care of Skysport Engineering, in accurate colours and re-gaining twin Lewis guns on the top wing. The Camel had moved to Duxford by October 2012.

Imperial War Museum, South Lambeth aircraft*

Type	Identity	Built	Origin	With IWM since	Notes
Avro Lancaster I	DV372	1943	UK	1960	cockpit#
Handley Page Halifax A.VII	PN323	1945	UK	1979	cockpit
Heinkel He 162A-1 Salamander	120235	1945	Germany	1960	see profile
Mitsubishi A6M5 *Zeke*	–	1944	Japan	1955	cockpit
North American P-51D Mustang*	'472218'	1945	USA	Dec 1971	see profile
Royal Aircraft Factory BE.2c*	2699	1916	UK	1920	see profile
Sopwith Camel 2F1*	N6812	1918	UK	1920	see profile#
Supermarine Spitfire I	R6915	1940	UK	26 Aug 1946	–#

Notes: Airframes on show at Lambeth in the year up to the closure for re-development in December 2012 – refer to main narrative. * – illustrated in the colour section #Expected to return to Lambeth.

CHAPTER 3

Passion for Flying
Shuttleworth Collection
Old Warden Aerodrome, Biggleswade, Beds

www.shuttleworth.org

In the accepted meaning of the term, Shuttleworth is not a 'national' museum or collection. Yet it is regarded and recognised as a pioneering institution of considerable character and influence. To omit it from the pantheon of the 'biggies' would be wrong. Indeed, the size of this chapter reflects its longevity, the scope of activity and the barrage of important types that have traversed the turf at Old Warden. With its central policy of *flying* its exhibits Shuttleworth is unique in the UK, sitting astride the role of 'national archive' and that of 'warbirds' and airshows. Its steadfast championing of civil aviation has, to date, inspired far too few of the national and regional museums to do likewise.

As a privately-run organisation it need not have a collecting policy as such; whereas the nationals have strict 'rules of engagement' regarding what can, or cannot, be acquired and exhibited. There have been times throughout the post-1963 era, when Old Warden opened its doors on a regular basis to visitors, when collecting 'policies' came and went, including a 'Nothing beyond 1945' rubric, a 'training' theme through to 'sub-sets' such as de Havilland types. During 2013 Shuttleworth celebrates its half-century of public opening and with so many years under its belt, the 'brand' is so well established that audiences know they will witness a rich mix of types and eras, enhanced by aircraft on loan, the bulk of which can be flown.

Above: Shuttleworth's Blackburn Monoplane, the oldest airworthy British aeroplane in the world has now reached its 100th birthday. *Phil Whalley*

Richard Shuttleworth, in Alfa-Romeo '26' delighting in a moment of glory at the Nice Grand Prix 1935. He'd just over-taken legend Tazio Nuvolari in Alfa '2'; this situation did not last long! *Shuttleworth Collection*

The Shuttleworth family made its fortune in manufacturing; Clayton and Shuttleworth in Lincoln built heavy machinery and farm implements from the mid-1800s. During World War One aircraft were also produced, including Handley Page O/400s and Sopwith Camels. The family settled on the wonderful estate at Old Warden in Bedfordshire and there on 16th July 1909 Richard Ormonde Shuttleworth (ROS) was born to Colonel Frank and Dorothy Clotilda Shuttleworth. Frank died in January 1913, aged 68, when his son was four. On his 21st birthday, 1932, ROS inherited £2 million – in present-day purchasing power, around £110 million. Two years previously he had bought a 1900 Panhard motor car and his love for speed and racing was cemented. He built up an impressive and important collection of cars and vehicular transport of all sorts. An accident in South Africa in January 1936 put paid to his racing and nearly cost him his life.

ROS was a regular competitor at the Brooklands motor racing circuit in Surrey and there his passion strayed to aeroplanes. "One second-hand Cirrus II aircraft G-EBWD, as seen, tried, approved and agreed. £300 plus one guinea for re-registration." So read the bill dated 21st January 1932 on Brooklands School of Flying notepaper. ROS paid in crisp 'tenners' for his first aeroplane. Two days later that guinea's worth of re-registration kicked in and the paperwork was complete. (And for those who wonder what a guinea was, it was a pound and a shilling; and there will also be others who need to know what a shilling was... that's 5p these days!)

The first flight Richard ever made was in a Moth, flown by George Stead in 1927 who said of this experience: "From then on, it was the air for him." Richard took lessons at the Scottish Flying Club at Renfrew, Glasgow, on 9th December 1930;

Richard Shuttleworth in RAF uniform, 1940. *Shuttleworth Collection*

later transferring to the Hampshire Aero Club based at Kings Worthy, north of Winchester. ROS went solo in G-EBWD on 14th February 1932 – 25 days after he purchased it. On 3rd March he was issued with Royal Aero Club aviator's certificate 10385. On 6th May 1932 ROS and Jimmy Edmunds took off from Croydon bound for Villacoublay, near Paris. They stayed the night and the following day headed south, but the weather deteriorated and a precautionary landing was the order of the day. The aircraft stalled over trees and a heavy landing ensued. Both occupants were fine, but the Moth was in need of repair. ROS and Jimmy boarded an Imperial Airways Handley Page HP.42 at Le Bourget and returned to Croydon. Having located the spares he needed at Heston, ROS enquired if there was a mechanic available to help with the field repair. Here he met a willing Leonard A Jackson, soon to become Old Warden's resident engineer.

It is important not to see Moth G-EBWD as we do now. It was only four years old and unlike most of his growing fleet of cars was not what we might call today a 'heritage' item; it was his runabout. The first recorded occasion on which the Moth touched down on the Shuttleworth estate was 13th November 1932, with Richard and Jimmy sharing the piloting. At that stage, ROS was using another part of the 'manor' and it was some time before the aerodrome as we know it began to take shape. What is today No.1 hangar – the workshop and offices – was the first real structure. In the 1930s, Old Warden aerodrome was a true flying field, with take-offs and approaches possible in the direction deemed best by the pilot; the longest available run being about 1,700ft.

Whisky-Delta was originally fitted with a 65hp Cirrus II, but in 1933 ROS re-engined it with a 105hp Cirrus Hermes II. The Moth was put into store at Old Warden during the war and the registration was officially cancelled on 1st December 1946. It was restored in the name of Richard's mother, Dorothy Clotilda Shuttleworth, on 28th June 1951 and to Allen Wheeler, on behalf of the trustees on 24th October 1968. Moth G-EBWD has been based continuously at one aerodrome for longer than any other aeroplane in aviation history.

(On 29th August 1925 Alan Cobham delivered the eighth production DH.60 from Stag Lane to its new owners, the Lancashire Aero Club at Barton, west of Manchester as the Air Ministry-sponsored clubs began to take their allocations of Moths. This machine was G-EBLV which today flies from Old Warden on loan from BAE Systems.)

Acquired by Richard Shuttleworth in January 1932, Moth G-EBWD is the collection's flagship. *Alf Jenks*

Today's No.1 hangar in the mid-1930s when it was Old Warden's only hangar. *KEC*

ROS established three companies: Warden Aviation Co and Aeronautical Advertising Co at Heston in Middlesex and Warden Engineering Co at Old Warden. These were intended as profit-making enterprises, helping to finance a collection of historic aircraft. The Heston ventures were wound up in October 1935 and everything was centred on the family estate under the aegis of the Warden Aviation and Engineering Co. Richard was also a director of Comper Aircraft and Pobjoy Airmotor at Hooton Park on the Wirral and he owned three Comper Swifts, G-ABWE, G-ABWW and G-ACBY. Other types acquired for business were: DH Dragon G-ACGG; Desoutters G-AAPS, G-AAPZ and G-AAZI and Spartan Arrow G-ABWP. Desoutter *Papa-Zulu* lingered and is now airworthy with the collection; the Spartan was bought new in 1936, became part of the Trust but was sold off in 1952 and today is airworthy in Surrey. (See the table on former Shuttleworth Collection aircraft.)

A mid-1930s line up at Old Warden. Left to right: Desoutter, Moth, ANEC G-EBJO. *Peter Green Collection*

Chief engineer L A 'Jacko' Jackson was a great practical joker; here grinning at a radical 'modification' to a Desoutter (believed to be G-AAZI) circa 1936. Behind is today's survivor, G-AAPZ. *Peter Green Collection*

Richard's first 'historics' were a Vickers bomber acquired in 1932 and a Blackburn Velos the following year. Then came: the Blériot and Deperdussin (1935); the Sopwith Dove (Pup) and the Avro 504K (both December 1936); Hanriot HD-1 G-AFDX (October 1937); the Blackburn and parts from the Frost steam-powered ornithopter of circa 1900 (October 1938). All except the Vickers, the Velos and the ornithopter are still with us. (Frost's second ornithopter is mentioned in Chapter 1, the Science Museum and he was custodian of the Pilcher Hawk for a while – see Chapter 10.) The Pup and the Avro are profiled in due course and the others are mentioned in the narrative that follows.

ROS was not alone in this 'craze' of acquiring old aircraft, at Brooklands radio and electronics entrepreneur Richard 'Dick' Grainger Jeune Nash was busy doing likewise, setting up the International Horseless Carriage Corporation as the operating arm of his passion. The pair developed a friendly rivalry, keeping one another informed of what they were up to. Nash's collection went on to be a founding mother lode for the RAF Museum – see Chapters 5 and 6.

On 9th May 1937 at the Royal Aeronautical Society's Garden Party at the Great West Aerodrome (now swallowed in Heathrow Airport), Fairey test pilot Flt Lt Chris Staniland put the brand new P27/32 K4303 – the prototype Battle bomber – through its paces. ROS was also on 'the bill', flying the Blériot. Among the crowds many must have thought that what was Richard was doing in his 'old crock' was charming but probably dangerous; the 1920s and 1930s were all about seeking modernity after all. It is a great irony that it was not racing an Alpha Romeo, or flying a Desoutter to the south of France, or straining to get some height in the Deperdussin that Richard lost his life; it was in a plodding Fairey Battle. ROS joined up and in November 1939 started his RAF career at the Central Flying School, Upavon, and then 10 Flying Training School at Tern Hill. While on a solo night exercise with 12 Operational Training Unit at Benson on 2nd August 1940, the 31-year old perished when L4971 crashed near the airfield boundary. The devastating loss suffered by his family and friends apart, the world of aviation heritage had lost a pioneer of the greatest potential.

The Old Warden estate was extensively used during the war and from June 1941 Shrager Brothers Ltd worked in the hangar on contracts for the Civilian Repair Organisation, including overhauling a variety of communications types and modifying Percival Proctors and North American Harvards.

The Trust endowed in her son's name by Mrs Dorothy Shuttleworth OBE on 26th April 1944 gave rise to the magic that is today Old Warden – the aerodrome and aircraft, the motor vehicles, the Swiss Garden, the agricultural college and its grounds. During 2013 the Shuttleworth Collection is celebrating the 50th anniversary of opening its doors to the public on a regular basis. We'll return to the evolution of the collection later, but now is the time to stray a little...

Biplanes... the big and the Belgian

In December 1932 ROS travelled the short distance to the Home Aircraft Depot at RAF Henlow, Beds. He had successfully tendered £3 for a recently-withdrawn and engineless Vickers biplane bomber and, with a crew of friends, set about dismantling it to take it back to Old Warden. (Let's put that £3 into context. An agricultural worker in 1933 would have an average weekly wage of £1/10/6 – one pound, ten shillings and five pence, or present day £1.55.) This was not an attempt to restore the monster to flying condition; ROS had acquired it for its wood, turnbuckles and other useful fittings. Richard referred to it as a Vimy – see Chapter 1 for the famous transatlantic aircraft. Henlow had been home to the Vimys of the Parachute Training Flight but had largely changed over to the Virginia by the time of Richard's visit. Vimy F9147 is known to have still been at Henlow in April 1932, but others could have been candidates. An engineering officer at the station, Flt Lt Allen Wheeler (of whom much more anon), met ROS for the first time on this occasion. Wheeler recorded that it was a pendulous Virginia and not a Vimy. More so, he is quoted in *Richard Shuttleworth – An Illustrated Biography* by Kevin Desmond (Jane's 1982) that: "Unfortunately the two engines – Napier Lion units – had been [a] separate tender and these had gone for £8 previously." That clinches it for me; Vimys had Rolls-Royce Eagles, Virginias were pulled through the sky by Lions. There are several options for Virginias that could have been the one bought by ROS, once the all-metal Mk.Xs and earlier ones brought up to that standard are dismissed. But this is all semantics as the big bomber was never intended for preservation. It does bring up an intriguing notion that its wood can be found today in some of the collection's aircraft, the Blériot or the Blackburn – who knows?

Talking of Napier Lions, 450hp Mk.IIBs powered six Blackburn Velos biplanes that chugged in and out of Brough on the banks of the Humber from 1929 until the last gave up the ghost in 1934. A training version of the Dart torpedo-bomber, Blackburn produced a batch of Velos from 1925 for the Greek Navy and others were licence-built in that country. The half-dozen served Blackburn's own North Sea Aerial and General Transport Co. One of these redundant machines appealed to Ian R Parker and he bought G-AAAW for £15, ferrying it to Hooton Park on 28th April 1933. It is alleged that Mr Parker did not have a flying licence, but this does not seem to have deterred him. On 19th May 1933 he set off on a foray into the deepest south arriving at Heston that day, going on to Brooklands on the 20th and shortly afterwards over to Northolt, where it was 'parked'. The escapade from Hooton is said to have consumed *63 gallons* of petrol. Allen Wheeler was visiting Northolt on 25th November 1933 and was sorely tempted when he heard of the big Blackburn; even more so when he realised there was fuel in the tanks! He fired it up and flew it; another one for the logbook. He contacted Parker and struck a deal, one guinea (that's one pound, one shilling, or £1.05) brought him all 3,945lbs of unladen Velos! He then contacted ROS and it is not clear if it became a Shuttleworth aeroplane, or one of Allen's not inconsiderable 'fleet'. Either way, it was flown by Allen to Old Warden on 30th December 1933. It is not known if it ever flew again; by 1935 it had been dismantled and used as 'stock' for the other 'historics' that were gathering.

In May 1939 ROS was again exercising his chequebook locally by tendering for five Avro Rota autogyros – licence-built Cierva C.30As. These were held at 26 Maintenance Unit, Cardington. Three were intact (K4232, K4233 and K4235) two were stripped-out fuselages (K4230 and K4238); all had been struck off charge on 6th May. The trio cost a guinea each (see above for reminder of what they were!) and in short order the two fuselages had been scrapped. With the outbreak of war, K4232, K4233 and K4235 were re-acquired by the Air Ministry and ROS was duly compensated. All three survived their war service and K4232 is now with the RAF Museum at Hendon (Chapter 4) while K4233 was sold in Belgium in 1948. By an incredible turn of fate, K4235 was registered as G-AHMJ in May 1946 and was donated to the Shuttleworth Collection in 1954 thereby making a *return* to Old Warden. (It was disposed of in 1998, being sold to the USA.)

A classic illustration of how ROS collected things – see it, buy it – is exemplified by the fruits of a holiday in Belgium in 1937. Fresh off the production line in Paris, Hanriot HD-1 single-seat fighter biplane No.75 was handed over to 1e Escadrille de Chasse of the Belgian Air Force in 1918 and put into action from Les Moores. Belgium's

Blackburn Velos G-AAAW, possibly at Hooton Park. *KEC*

entry for the World Aerobatic Competition at Nice in France in March 1922 was 'ace' Willy Coppens and he was the winner, flying HD-1 No.75. The fighter was withdrawn from service by 1934 and acquired by the brothers Drossaert and put on the Belgian civil register as OO-APJ. (Their first names being: André, Paul and Jules – hence the registration.) By 1937 it was with former SPAD pilot Jacques Ledure and ROS saw it outside a cinema being used as an attraction for the film then showing – *Wings*. (This was 'Wild Bill' Wellman's winner of the first-ever best picture Oscar. It was silent, black and white and released in 1927; did it *really* take that long to get to Belgium?)

ROS offered £15 and he flew the Hanriot to Old Warden, arriving there on 24th November 1937. It was UK registered as G-AFDX on 4th May 1938 to Warden Aviation and appeared at special events. On 18th June 1939 ROS departed Brooklands in the Hanriot, not knowing that a wheel had come off on take-off. He was unhurt in the untidy 'arrival' at home, but No.75 was in a bad way. The wings were sent to Chelsea Aeronautical College for rebuild as a student project – and did not survive the war. In 1962 the remainder crossed the Atlantic for the first of four times. It was sold without engine to Marvin Kingman Hand of San Francisco, California. (The 110hp Le Rhône had been used in Shuttleworth's Avro 504.) A superb restoration followed and it was flown again on 27th April 1968 having been conveniently registered in the USA as N75. The Hanriot came eastbound inside a World Airways Boeing 747 in May 1973 and was shown off, statically, at the Paris Salon airshow at Le Bourget; returning back to the US west coast. In December 1978 Mr Hand presented No.75 to the RAF Museum and it was graciously accepted. (Though No.75 and the type were bereft of any direct RAF connection – see Chapter 5.) Transatlantic flight No.4 was in the belly of a RAF Lockheed Hercules taking the Hanriot from San Francisco to Lyneham in January 1979. Restored at Cardington, the Hanriot was taken to Hendon on 10th December 1979 and, as this book went to press, was due for export to New Zealand.

Shuttleworth's first benefactor

A pamphlet published in 1957 by the Shuttleworth Collection was entitled *Memories of Early Flying Days*. It was written by A E Grimmer and sub-titled 'The Shuttleworth Collection's First Benefactor'. The chance meeting of A E Grimmer and ROS brought two early aircraft into the collection. The chance meeting of A E Grimmer and ROS brought two early aircraft into the collection. They met in 1935 at a gathering held to debate an airport to serve Bedford. Albert Edward Grimmer (AEG) ran a garage at nearby Ampthill and in 1912 acquired the first of a pair of monoplanes which he flew beyond the outbreak of war. Clearly two kindred spirits, ROS and Mr Grimmer struck up a rapport, ending with AEG offering his machines for no fee, but the 300-plus empty oil drums that occupied the same building would have to be disposed of. In late 1912 AEG picked up the 1910 Blériot XI from Blackfriars, London. It had been damaged and put into store there. Having repaired it, AEG flew it briefly on Easter Sunday 1912. More flights followed and he even built a hangar to keep it in at Cow Bridge, near Bedford. In 1914, AEG purchased the 1910 Deperdussin, which had been impounded against hangarage debts at Hendon. It seems that the 'Dep' replaced the Blériot with the latter going into store. AEG flew the Deperdussin beyond the declaration of war. All this ended with a nose dive and a very heavy landing, breaking both wings. True to his word, as well as picking up his two prizes, ROS removed all the oil drums which were dispersed in woodland on the Old Warden estate. Under the guidance of Leonard A 'Jacko' Jackson, ROS's engineer and later Curator of the collection, the Blériot and Deperdussin were rebuilt and reflown, in 1936 and 1937 respectively. I wonder if the oil drums are still in the trees?

Magnificent Man

Throughout the history of the Shuttleworth Collection there have been people who have been vital to its progress. It is never easy to single one out, but Richard Shuttleworth continually praised him and regarded him as a close friend; so the choice has been made: Air Cdre Allen Henry Wheeler CBE OBE. AHW completed a degree in engineering in 1924 and decided to join the RAF. He was commissioned on 17th January 1925 and soloed in an Avro 504K at 2 Flying Training School at Digby. In 1926 he was at Old Sarum in Wiltshire at the School of Army Co-operation, moving to 111 Squadron on Armstrong Whitworth Siskin IIIs at Duxford as a Flying Officer. By this time he owned Royal Aircraft Factory SE.5a G-EBQM, but only for a short time. His degree determined more and more of his progress and in October 1927 he embarked on an engineering course at the Home Aircraft Depot (HAD) at Henlow; going back to 'Triple-One' in 1929. AHW was posted oversees the following year, going to Hinaidi, Iraq, in charge of the engine shops as a Flight Lieutenant. There he designed and built a single-seat mid-wing monoplane powered by a Blackburne Tomtit, which he called the Slymph. It didn't fly and he brought it with him to Henlow. Registered G-ABOI in July 1931, he still tinkered with it, fitting an ABC Scorpion; but it never flew. It was stored at Old Warden from about 1934 until it was loaned to the Midland Aircraft Preservation Society (later the Midland Air Museum) in the late 1960s and its remains are stored in Coventry.

After Hinaidi, AHW returned to HAD Henlow and, when a Vickers Virginia was put up for tender, he met and befriended Richard Shuttleworth – see above. AHW became general assistant, test pilot and 'purchasing agent'. Allen had the sorrowful task of identifying the body of his friend in the morgue at Benson in August 1940. That same month, Mrs Shuttleworth asked Allen to look after the collection of aeroplanes and vehicles and this led to him becoming a trustee and later director of the collection.

After two years at Henlow, AHW joined 41 Squadron at Northolt during the change-over from Bristol Bulldogs to Hawker Demons. In November 1933 he bought Westland Widgeon G-EBRN, keeping it at Northolt and later at Andover. He was overseas from late 1935 in Aden; returning for a series of 'desk' appointments within 6 Group. From the middle of 1936 AHW based the latest of his own aircraft, Desoutter G-AATK, at Old Warden. In 1941 the Commanding Officer of the Aeroplane & Armament Experimental Establishment at Boscombe Down asked for AHW, who was by then a Wing Commander. The man doing the asking was Air Cdre Ralph S Sorley – the man who had played a vital role in making sure that Hurricanes and Spitfires carried eight machine-guns – and he wanted AHW to head the Performance Testing Squadron. In this capacity Allen became the first RAF officer, outside of de Havilland, to fly the Mosquito.

The head-hunting hadn't stopped. The Director of the Royal Aircraft Establishment (RAE) at Farnborough, W S Farren, asked in 1942 for AHW to be OC of Experimental Flying, with the rank of Group Captain. With RAE he flew a bewildering numbers of types, ranging from the Gloster E28/39 (Chapter 1) to a captured Focke-Wulf Fw 190. RAE also had a policy of 'operational attachments', giving pilots a taste of the 'sharp end'; AHW flew with Bomber Command, on fighter sweeps over France and with Benson's Photographic Reconnaissance Unit. In early 1944 he was appointed as Officer Commanding RAF Fairford setting up the station and readying it for airborne forces use at D-Day. He ferried a Spitfire XI out to India in 1945 by way of getting him to his assignment as Senior Air Staff Officer, South East Asia. Back in the UK in April 1946, he became Deputy Director, Auxiliary and Reserve Air Forces before moving to Beaulieu in the New Forest as officer commanding the airfield that was home to the Airborne Forces Experimental Establishment. In January 1949 he returned to the RAE, as CO Experimental Flying before going overseas again as Air Officer Commanding Cyprus with the rank of Air Commodore. This service career was crowned by a return to Boscombe Down in August 1952, becoming Commandant A&AEE; a post he held until April 1955.

As mentioned earlier, Allen had owned and flown an SE.5a pre-war, arguably Britain's best fighter of World War One. In similar fashion on 25th October 1946 he had registered in his name, not one but *two* Spitfires: Mk.Ia AR213 (G-AIST) and Mk.V AB910 (G-AISU). The Mk.I was stored at Old Warden until it was put into flying trim for use in the film *Battle of Britain*, 1967-1968. Afterwards, AHW flew *Sierra-Tango* from Booker, near High Wycombe, until it was sold to Patrick Lindsay in May 1974. Painted blue with white trim,

Allen Wheeler, with his wife in the cockpit, alongside his SE.5a G-EBQM, circa 1926. *Peter Green Collection*

the Mk.V was flown until May 1955 when it was passed on to Vickers-Armstrong and presented to the Battle of Britain Memorial Flight a decade later.

Before *Battle of Britain*, Allen had been heavily involved with another film, the fantastic *Those Magnificent Men in Their Flying Machines or How I Flew from London to Paris in 25 Hours, 11 Minutes* released in 1965 by 20th Century Fox. AHW was the technical adviser and also did some of the flying. Working closely with the producer, Stan Margulies, Allen joined the team in October 1963 with shooting set to start on 1st May 1964. In between, he had to commission the construction and flight testing of five different replicas (Antoinette, Avro Triplane, Bristol Boxkite, Eardley Billing and Santos-Dumont Demoiselle) as well as a bunch of non-flying 'funnies'. The Shuttleworth collection was involved in the film, lending the Blackburn and Deperdussin and the workshop created a taxiable replica of the Picat Dubreuil monoplane. This took part in the hilarious scene played out by actor Jeremy Lloyd as a naval officer pilot who threw an anchor out to stop his machine, with the expected abrupt result! In 1965 AHW wrote up his experiences in *Building Aeroplanes for 'Those Magnificent Men'*. The Avro Triplane and Bristol Boxkite in today's collection had previously 'starred' in the film. Other movie work followed, AHW was air supervisor for *The Blue Max* (1966), chief aeronautical adviser for *Mosquito Squadron* (1969) and technical adviser on *Aces High* (1976). An incredibly gifted pilot and engineer, Allen Henry Wheeler OBE DFC died on New Year's Day 1984, aged 80. (AHW penned the excellent books *That Nothing Failed Them: Testing Aeroplanes in War* about his times with A&AEE and RAE and *Flying Between the Wars*, both now much sought after.)

The Boxkite flying at Filton in 1966 just prior to presentation to Shuttleworth. *Rolls-Royce*

To fly, or not to fly?

On 1st July 2012 a stunned silence fell over Old Warden. An aeroplane fell to earth and took with it the life of 52-year old Trevor Roche. That afternoon's airshow was cancelled in consideration for a well-respected and much-loved collection pilot. Trevor had come to grief in the one-of-a-kind ABC Scorpion II-powered de Havilland Humming Bird ultra-light G-EBHX of 1923. His career was typical of many Shuttleworth pilots. During an engineering degree at Oxford he learned to fly with the University Air Squadron after which he joined the RAF and was selected for fast-jets. He piloted swing-wing Panavia Tornado strike fighters; Trevor and his navigator, David Bellamy, flew 27 operational sorties during the first Gulf War – no crew did a greater number. Early strikes included night-time low-level assaults on Iraqi airfields; high-risk missions that required a special sort of aircrew. In 1994, then a Squadron Leader, he was selected for the Empire Test Pilots' School at Boscombe Down, passing out top of the course. He served with the Experimental Flying Squadron at Boscombe until leaving the RAF in 1998 to fly Boeing 757s and 767s for British Airways. The year before he settled into the cockpit of a big Boeing, he started flying as a pilot for the collection. He became Chief Pilot in 2009 and qualified on every type other than the Avro XIX and DH Comet.

　　DH.53 G-EBHX was the first of a pair built for the *Daily Mail*-sponsored Light Aircraft Trials at Lympne, Kent, in October 1923 and it had its inaugural flight on the 2nd of that month. (See the profile on the English Electric Wren below for more on the trials.) It was flown to and from Belgium in December 1923 by Alan Cobham. In classic Shuttleworth style, *Hotel-X-Ray* was 'discovered' in storage in 1955 by Sqn Ldr L A Jackson and was substantially rebuilt, returning to the air at Hatfield on 4th August 1960. Fifteen DH.53s were constructed, including eight for the Air Ministry. Two of the latter gained fame by flying off and back to the airship R-33 in 1925, using a trapeze device above the cockpit to hook-up with the airborne leviathan. No decision has been taken on the future of G-EBHX, but its crash revived the perennial debate about the merits and perils flying rare, or unique, aircraft.

The DH.53 during its post-restoration test flight at Hatfield on 4th August 1960. Two aircraft from the DH Engines test fleet are on the ramp; Avro Ashton (the forward section of one is preserved at the Newark Air Museum) and a Canberra. *De Havilland*

This was not the first major accident suffered by Shuttleworth, but it was the first fatality. In front of a large audience at the Society of British Aircraft Constructors airshow at Farnborough on 13th September 1964, the engine of Bristol Bulldog IIA G-ABBB cut during aerobatics. The biplane impacted severely on the airfield – its pilot, thankfully, suffering only minor injuries. A special trials and development aircraft, the Bulldog had been presented to the Science Museum (Chapter 1) in 1938. It was restored to airworthiness by Bristol at Filton in 1961 and presented to Shuttleworth. When *Bravo-Bravo* crashed it had a total of 16 hours, 10 minutes of flying time since its return to flight – averaging about four hours annually. The remains were salvaged for the Air Accident Investigation Branch and it was considered a write-off. There was a Mk.IV in a museum in Finland, so the breed was not extinct. Thanks to the endeavours of the RAF Museum the remains of G-ABBB were gathered and rebuilt and it is today on display at Hendon – see Chapter 5.

It could be said that the Science Museum was deficient in letting the Bulldog go and that it might today be gracing the 'Flight' gallery at South Kensington. Yet the argument that the best way to preserve a piece of equipment is to keep it 'live' – in the case of an aeroplane that means *flying* it – is a powerful one. Let's go off on a tangent for a moment, to the Lombardy region of Italy in the town of Cremona is the Stradivari Museum dedicated to the violins created by Antonio Stradivari. There is an incredibly fortunate gentleman in Cremona who gets to play the precious instruments regularly, on the basis that the best way to preserve them is to let them make wonderful music.

Curators declare that it is vitally important to interpret an exhibit vividly and *in its context* – Shuttleworth certainly does that. There are other plus points, such as conserving skills – piloting and maintenance for airframes, engines and systems. On the minus side, modern certification requirements may not allow original materials as they are no longer approved or that more practical constructional solutions are employed – see the comments in the profile on the DH Comet *Grosvenor House* below. There are more basic considerations; take a look at the audience at any airshow and they will go through a gamut of feelings – appreciation, empathy, exhilaration, joy, awe. It's hard – but by no means impossible – to get that lot walking around a museum gallery...

With aircraft like the DH.53, the need to be flown only in the most benign of conditions means that flying hours are necessarily sparse and pilot experience on type is therefore minimal. At other end of the scale, a gas-guzzling warbird has huge operating costs which also preclude frequent use. With warbirds this need for 'currency' can be mitigated by building hours on similar types, say a Harvard for World War Two fighters, or a Tiger Moth for inter-war biplanes. For one-offs with no closely similar types and/or powered by rare engines for which operating experience is thin on the ground, currency can be difficult to achieve. It is hard to imagine a suitable 'introductory' type for the DH.53 Humming Bird, or the DH.88 Comet for that matter. This is where pilots with a wide experience of types and circumstances come in.

Where there are examples of types already within static museums, the 'to fly, or not to fly?' debate is less acute. So should sole-survivors be flown at all? If one is written off, isn't this robbing generations to come of the opportunity to see and even *touch* a rarity? Illustrations and movie clips are no substitute. Human endeavour being as it is, there is no guarantee that popping a precious prototype into a museum's clutches secures it for eternity. On 17th May 1990 at Dugny on the far side of Le Bourget airfield near Paris a fire raged through a hangar. It was the main storage and restoration site for the Musée de l'Air – France's national aeronautical collection. That blaze took out *forty-four* airframes, including one-offs of vital significance to France. In December 1997 a fire gutted the Museo Aeronáutico in Montevideo, Uruguay, destroying all of the airframes within. That said, these two cataclysmic events brought about a wave of fire suppression installations in museums worldwide and there have been no losses in that manner since.

And the risk of injury or worse to pilots – is that worth it? Trevor Roche would have emphatically said so; that's why he flew for Shuttleworth. He also knew that potentially the most dangerous thing he did on 1st July 2012 was the drive to Old Warden.

Ringing the changes

For any collection some change to the artefacts held is bound to occur. As can be seen in this and other chapters, acquisition policies do change for one reason or another. All collections are guilty at times of saying 'yes' to something when they really should be saying 'no'. *Some* donations are very difficult to turn down, eg government-to-government or from a prominent organisation/business. Besides, 'ringing the changes' is an important factor in the constant need to encourage visitors to return. The table 'Former Shuttleworth

Collection Aircraft' outlines machines that have moved on, some hardly attracting any comment, others fomenting considerable disquiet. Two in the latter category demand further examination.

In 1950 Spitfire PR.XI PL983 was ferried to Old Warden with the 'B Condition' ('trade plate') marks G-15-109 as a gift from Vickers. It was displayed statically for nearly 25 years. It's difficult to condense its provenance, but it flew operations with 4 and 2 Squadrons from February 1945 with the 2nd Tactical Air Force. Retired in January 1946, it was acquired by Vickers-Armstrongs in July 1947 for a special purpose. On 27th January 1948 with the US civil registration N74138 the Spitfire was handed over to the US Air Attaché, Livingstone Satterthwaite, for use by the US Embassy Flight. (See Chapter 1 for Satterthwaite and the Wright Flyer in October that year.) On 28th August 1948 N74138, piloted by Lettice Curtis, came fifth at the Lympne International Air Race. During that contest, Lettice broke the national 100km closed circuit record at 313mph. Satterthwaite dearly wanted to take the Spitfire back to the US when his term of office expired, but it was on loan and instead it was presented to Shuttleworth, becoming the collection's *first* Spitfire.

The second example was Mk.V AR501 which arrived at Old Warden from Loughborough in 1961. At Duxford on 27th June 1975 a volunteer team celebrated as AR501 took to the air after a two-year restoration. Sixty-five days later a lorry pulled up at Duxford with PL983 on board, ready for the crew to start again. By late 1982 Shuttleworth faced a cash crisis and the unfinished PL983 was auctioned on 14th April 1983. The £110,000 (that's £440,000 in present-day values) was a vital cash injection to keep the collection functioning, but for the team who had been working on it, to have it whisked away was a bitter blow. But Old Warden's already had a flying Spitfire and ready sale of the Mk.XI was a certainty.

Frenchman Roland Fraissinet had bought PL983 and it moved to the workshops of Trent Aero, was registered as G-PRXI and first flew at East Midlands Airport on 18th July 1984. Later acquired by Warbirds of Great Britain *X-Ray-India* went to Justin Fleming and Martin Sergeant in December 1999. While performing at a display in France on 4th June 2001, PL983 encountered engine troubles and it crashed on approach, tragically killing Martin.

In November 1935, 'Kiwi' Jean Gardner Batten, in brand-new Percival Gull G-ADPR, also called *Jean*, set a record for flying from the UK to Brazil: 2 days, 13 hours, 15 minutes. She and the Gull set a new record for flying to Darwin, Australia, of 5 days, 21 hours, 3 minutes during October 1936. Not content with this she flew on to Sydney and from there to Auckland. On the way she broke the record for crossing the Tasman Sea and became the first-ever person to fly solo to New Zealand, in a time of 11 days, 1 hour, 25 minutes. The following year she broke the record for Darwin to the UK, at 5 days, 18 hours, 15 minutes.

In 1940 G-ADPR was impressed for war service as AX866. 'Demobbed' in April 1945 *Papa-Romeo* was acquired by Percival Aircraft and from 1959 stored at Luton. It was gifted to Shuttleworth and delivered to Old Warden on 25th April 1961. Its certificate of airworthiness lapsed in 1969 but thanks to Shuttleworth's workshop, other

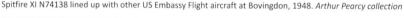
Spitfire XI N74138 lined up with other US Embassy Flight aircraft at Bovingdon, 1948. *Arthur Pearcy collection*

contractors and with input from Hunting Engineering (as the descendants of Percival), the Gull was restored to flying condition in the 1980s. On 1st August 1990 G-ADPR flew to New Zealand again, but this time at much greater speed – in the hold of a Boeing 747! Celebrations over, it returned and made its flying debut at Old Warden in 1991. On 23rd February 1995 this exercise was repeated with G-ADPR again travelling by 747 to New Zealand.

During a re-assessment of assets, the Trust had declared *Papa-Romeo* surplus to requirements and sold it. It would leave a significant 'hole' in the collection, but generate much-needed income. Even as the Gull was in transit, an attempt was made in the UK to have the export stopped, but ultimately this failed. In New Zealand, the Gull flew briefly as ZK-DPR, before going on permanent display at Auckland Airport. Jean Batten was a New Zealander and her record flight was as much a 'Kiwi' heritage as it was British, so Auckland is just as deserving a place as Old Warden, but G-ADPR's departure was still a sad loss for the UK. The argument remains, if its export could have been rescinded, what institution in the UK would have bought it? The Science Museum has the most obvious remit. The RAF Museum was more and more appreciating some civilians to help interpret the wider history of aviation (and G-ADPR had worn camouflage for a while), but otherwise there were no other obvious hosts. Acquisition by a 'national' and then presentation on loan to Old Warden was a possibility; but then the issue of keeping it flying would crop up.

Of the airframes listed in the table 'Former Shuttleworth Collection Aircraft' it is important to remember that some generated cash to help look after the others or the purchase of new exhibits. It is of note that nine airframes listed are airworthy today with individuals or other collections and 14 are preserved in static condition in museums or similar collections.

Above: Crowds gather around Jean Batten and Gull G-ADPR at Seletar, Singapore, on the way to Australia and New Zealand, October 1936. *Paddy Porter Collection*

Left: Spartan Arrow G-ABWP was owned by Richard Shuttleworth from new in 1936 and later joined the collection. It is airworthy with an owner in Surrey. *KEC*

Former Shuttleworth Collection Aircraft

Type	Identity	Built	Arrived	Notes, current status or fate
Auster AOP.9	G-AXRR	1962	Jan 1970	ex XR241. To British Aerial Museum, Duxford. *Airworthy with Essex owner*
Avro Triplane replica	–	c1953	1965	To Northern Aircraft Pres Soc (became The Aeroplane Collection – TAC) 24 Oct 1969. *Displayed at Museum of Science and Industry, Manchester, on loan from TAC*
Avro Anson C.19 Phase 2	TX183	1947	6 Mar 1968	Moved to Duxford for restoration. *Auctioned at Duxford 14 Aug 1983, becoming G-BSMF. To Dubai May 2001 for the Gulf Air Museum*
BAT FK.23 Bantam	G-EACN	1919	1950s	Remains only. *Sold to the Aviodome, Netherlands, Jan 1990*
Blake Bluetit	–	1930	1968	Reg'd as G-BXIY Jun 1997 and some restoration undertaken. Sold off in Feb 2000. *Believed stored in Herefordshire*
Bristol F.2b Fighter	–	1917	1960s	fuselage frame. Acquired by Aero Vintage for restoration as G-AANM. Returned on loan as 'D7889' Mar 2001. *To Canada Dec 2006*
Bristol Bulldog IIA	'K2227'	1931	Jul 1961	G-ABBB. Crashed at Farnborough 13-9-64. *Restored to static and display at RAF Museum Hendon – see Chapter 5*
Cierva C.30A	G-AHMJ	1934	1954	Avro-built Rota I K4235 – see narrative. *Sold to Kermit Weeks, Fantasy of Flight, Florida, USA Nov 1998*
De Havilland DH.60G Moth	G-ABAG	1930	13 Oct 1977	Sold Jan 2004, but remained based, on loan
De Havilland Tiger Moth T.2	XL716	1941	late 1960s	spares use. *To London Colney, Herts, by Jul 1975, no further details*
De Havilland Queen Bee	LF858	1944	1960s	Sold 1983. *Airworthy as G-BLUZ, based at Henlow*
De Havilland Hornet Moth	G-ADND	1936	Sep 1971	Loaned to Hawker Siddeley Fg Club, finally based at Old Warden from 1979. *Sold Dec 2005, airworthy, Bristol-based owners*
De Havilland Hornet Moth	G-ADOT	1935	c1962	*To Hatfield for restoration, but transferred to Mosquito Aircraft Museum, London Colney, 1977 – still on display*
DHC Chipmunk T.10	G-AOTD	1950	Aug 1977	Restored at Kingston, first flown 1983. Sold by Sep 1994. *Airworthy at Old Sarum*
DFS Grunau Baby IIb	VN148	c1940	1960s	Presented to Russavia Clln, 1975, as BGA.2400 'DUW'. *Believed stored in Wales*
DFS Grunau Baby IIb	–	c1940	1960s	Presented to Russavia Clln, 1975, as BGA.2362 'DTF'. *Last reported in Buckinghamshire, 1976*
Elliotts of Newbury Primary	–	c1950	1960s	Loaned to Torbay Aircraft Museum, Higher Blagdon from Jun 1971. *No further details*
Fieseler Fi 103 V-1 replica	–	1965	c1970	Loaned to IWM Duxford 1985 to 1987 then to *Kent Battle of Britain Museum, Hawkinge*
Gloster Gladiator II	N5903	1939	c1970	Spares for G-AMRK. To Fleet Air Arm Museum, Yeovilton for restoration 1978. Sold to The Fighter Collection 30 Nov 1994. *Airworthy as G-GLAD at Duxford*
Hafner R.II	–	1932	1966	Loaned to the Torbay Aircraft Museum Aug 1972. *Displayed at The Helicopter Museum, Weston-super-Mare*
Halton Jupiter MPA	–	1972	29 Nov 1978	*Disposed of in the 1980s, last reported stored in Sussex*

Type	Identity	Built	Arrived	Notes, *current status or fate*
Hanriot HD-1	G-AFDX	1918	May 1938	See narrative. Sold in USA as N75 1963; acquired by the RAF Museum 1978; exported to New Zealand 2013 – *see Chapter 5*
Hunting Jet Provost 1	G-AOBU	1955	Apr 1961	Loaned to Loughborough College as instructional airframe. Finally arrived at Old Warden Jan 1991. Sold Sep 1991. *Airworthy with Kennet Av at North Weald, Essex, as 'XD693'*
LVG C.VI	7198/18	1918	late 1959	See narrative. *Under restoration at MBCC, RAF Museum Cosford – see Chapter 6*
Miles Magister	G-AIUA	1940	1960s	Spares use. To Vintage Aircraft Team, Cranfield 1981. *With Wings World War Two Remembrance Museum, Balcombe*
Miles Magister	G-ANWO	1938	1960s	Spares use. To Vintage Aircraft Team, Cranfield 1981. *Believed with Bury, Lancs, owner, stored*
Pedal Aeronauts Toucan MPA	–	1972	Oct 1978	ex Radlett. Forward section only retained; *to Mosquito Aircraft Museum, London Colney, Nov 1985. Gone from there by 1995, no further details*
Percival Gull IV	G-ADPR	1932	25 Apr 1961	See narrative. *To New Zealand as ZK-DPR 23 Feb 1995, displayed at Auckland Airport*
Percival Prentice T.1	G-AOKL	1949	1999	Restoration suspended stored. *Sold to private owner, Scotland, Mar 2013.*
Percival Provost T.1	WV605	1954	c1968	Loaned to Torbay Aircraft Museum, Higher Blagdon, from 1971. *To Norfolk & Suffolk Av Museum, Flixton, 1978*
Percival Provost T.1	G-AWRY	1955	18 Apr 1969	Auctioned at Duxford 14 Aug 1983. *Damaged 28 Jul 1987, stored at Thatcham, Berks*
Saunders-Roe Skeeter AOP.12	XN351	1960	c1968	Loaned to Torbay Aircraft Museum, Higher Blagdon from May 1971 then to Wales Aircraft Museum, Cardiff, from 1980. *Privately owned, reg'd as G-BKSC, believed stored in Ipswich area.*
Southampton Univ MPA	–	1961	c1966	'SUMPAC'. *To Hall of Aviation, Southampton (now Solent Sky – Chapter) 1984*
Spartan Arrow	G-ABWP	1936	1936	owned from new by R O Shuttleworth; stored at Old Warden from 1939; sold in 1952 and flown out. *Airworthy with private owner in Surrey*
Supermarine Spitfire PR.XI	PL983	1944	1950	To Duxford for restoration Aug 1975. *Auctioned at Duxford 14 Aug 1983 to Roland Fraissinet, becoming G-PRXI. Fatal crash France 4 Jun 2001. Under restoration*
Volmer Swingwing	–	1977	8 May 1981	powered hang-glider, made last flight at Old Warden and presented to collection. *Left 29 Sep 1983 and displayed at Museum of Science and Industry, Manchester*
Westland Wallace replica	–	1991	2004	Fuselage frame, on loan. Removed in early 2013

Note: MPA – man-powered aircraft. * – Illustrated in the colour section.

Our friends in the north... and at home

As with most museums, Shuttleworth relies on the support of volunteers. A unique asset is located not in Bedfordshire, but Yorkshire – Northern Aeroplane Workshops (NAW). This was the brainchild of John Langham and it came into being in March 1973. NAW started off with a workshop in Harrogate, but these days it is located at Batley, both in Yorkshire. The intention was to perpetuate traditional skills involved in the creation of aircraft made of "wood, wire and linen" and providing the collection with fine flyable replicas of extinct types, or ones that it could not expect to be able to own. Two firm requirements are needed before a project can start: *original* drawings must be available and an appropriate engine; the latter coming from Shuttleworth's stock. The first machine was a Sopwith Triplane, constructor's number NAW-1. The RAF Museum at Hendon (Chapter 5) holds an original and there is another in Moscow. With a 130hp Clerget 9B and financing coming from the collection, a volunteer team led by Eric Barraclough set to. The result was G-BOCK, bedecked in the colours of 'N6290' *Dixie* of 'Naval 8' – 8 Squadron Royal Naval Air Service. *Charlie-Kilo* was delivered to Old Warden in June 1990 and was flight tested on 10th April 1992. Shuttleworth's website proudly declares: "Sir Tom Sopwith, the founder of the original aircraft company, who supported the project throughout his later life, honoured [Shuttleworth] when he decreed that Northern Aeroplane Workshop's Triplane should be considered as a late production example. This is reflected in manufacturer's plate in the cockpit: No.153."

With the completion of the Triplane, NAW moved seamlessly to the creation of a 110hp Le Rhône rotary-powered Bristol M.1C monoplane fighter. Only one M.1 survives, in Australia. NAW-2, G-BWJM, was delivered to Old Warden on 28th October 1997 and first flew on 25th September 2000. It is painted in the colours of 'C4918' of 'C' Flight, 72 Squadron in 1917. As this hits the keyboard, NAW-3, Sopwith Camel G-BZSC, which will be fitted with a 130hp Clerget rotary, is due to arrive at Old Warden before the end of 2013. Thanks to work by the DH.2 Research Group, it is *likely* that the next project will be an Airco DH.2.

Working steadfastly to support the collection in many ways is the Shuttleworth Veteran Aeroplane Society (SVAS), founded in the early 1960s as Old Warden opened its doors to the public on a regular basis. SVAS volunteers carry out work on both aircraft and vehicles, ranging from major overhauls and restorations to making sub-assemblies and components. Attend any flying day at Old Warden and you will see SVAS members on the flight line, positioning aircraft, walking the wingtips, driving vintage cars, stewarding arriving cars, and all the many other tasks needed at an airshow. Members are kept in touch via the excellent house journal *Prop-Swing*. Fund-raising is a vital SVAS task and in its time many hundreds of thousands of pounds have been donated to the collection. Much of this being used to fund aircraft and to date the tally is: Chipmunk, Jungmann, Lysander, Provost and Super Cub. The Cub, used to tow aloft the collection's gliders, arrived on 13th October 2008 and was registered as G-SVAS in honour of the Society.

Glider-tug Super Cub G-SVAS, honouring Old Warden's support organisation. *Ken Ellis*

With a large font of aircraft acquired from the passions of Richard Shuttleworth and continued under the guidance of Allen Wheeler, Leonard 'Jacko' Jackson and General Managers and Trustees ever since, the collection has always had an operating caucus of aircraft. Since the late 1960s, the loan of suitably 'period' aircraft has been encouraged. Listing all of these is beyond the scope of the book, but visitors to Old Warden have been able to bask in additional airworthy types thanks to this policy. From the late 1970s, the extensive de Havilland collection gathered by Anthony Haig-Thomas (later to be a Trustee) was resident and there was a dedicated 'De Havilland' hangar for a while. These included: Puss Moth G-AEOA (built 1931), Fox Moth G-ACEJ (1933), Dragonfly G-AEDU (1937) and Moth Minor G-AFNG (1939). A pair of aircraft acting as a tribute to long-distance flyer and test pilot Alex Henshaw were loaned by Desmond Penrose from 1982. These were Arrow Active II G-ABVE of 1932 (Alex owned the other Active, G-ABIX) and Percival Mew Gull G-AEXF. In 2002, Shuttleworth was given first refusal on acquiring them outright but, tempting though the offer was, it was declined and they are now at Breighton in Yorkshire. A look at the table 'Shuttleworth Collection Aircraft' includes machines presently on loan, including Philip Meeson's Dragon Rapide G-AGSH and Peter Holloway's Fieseler Storch G-STCH and Miles duo, Falcon Major G-AEEG and Magister G-AKPF. Detailed in the profile section are two machines on loan from BAE Systems: Avro XIX and DH Moth.

On 28th September 1972 Allen Wheeler was at the helm for a very significant maiden flight at Old Warden; he was flying Luft Verkehrs Gessellschaft LVG C.VI 7198/17. Built in 1918, the battlefield reconnaissance biplane became the world's only genuine airworthy World War One German two-seater after an exceptionally demanding restoration. It is one of three of the type extant, the other two being in Brussels and at the Musée de l'Air at Le Bourget, Paris. The LVG was presented to the Imperial War Museum (Chapter 2) in August 1919 and displayed at Crystal Palace but was returned to the Air Ministry in 1932. It was flown at the 1936 and 1937 Air Pageants at Hendon before entering a long and migratory period of storage interspersed with attempts to have it scrapped! In late 1959 the LVG was presented by the Air Council to Shuttleworth on "indefinite loan". It was civil registered as G-AANJ on 9th October 1981 as part of the Civil Aviation Authority's clean-up of the collection's otherwise anonymous aircraft. In 1994, the loan status was reconfirmed, under the aegis of the RAF Museum, and it was given the Ministry of Defence instructional airframe number 9239M. Following negotiations with Hendon, it was decided to retire the LVG and it had its last official flight on 20th September 2003, travelling by road to the Michael Beetham Conservation Centre at the RAF Museum Cosford on 12th November 2003 where it is under restoration.

A Robinson helicopter's eye view of Old Warden, looking along Runway 03 to the north-east, 2006. *Ken Ellis*

An evolving collection

As explained at the beginning of this chapter, 2013 is the 50th anniversary of the Shuttleworth Collection opening its doors on a full-time basis to the public. The airfield as established by Richard Shuttleworth in the mid-1930s is essentially the same, but more hangars have been constructed and other buildings have changed their role. The impressive 'run' of hangars that extends southwards from what is today the visitor centre continued its expansion in 1978. The first major structure on the aerodrome, No.1 hangar, became the workshop in 1986 with the public allowed access to monitor the progress of restoration projects. With expansion of the loans policy and the welcome revenue stream that hangarage was bringing to the collection, Hangar No.9 was completed in late 2008 in the wooded area to the east of the runways and in the same site No.10 was inaugurated in the spring of

2012. (This area is not available for public inspection.) Hangar 2 was completely remodelled in 2006, becoming the impressive visitor centre. In 1999 there was a major change in the 'shape' of the aerodrome with the doubling of the length of Runway 21/03. The extension runs south of College Road providing about another 2,000ft for collection aircraft, it is not available to visitors. In the spring of 2012 a small building was refurbished on the eastern side of the aerodrome, acting as a reminder of the 'roots' of the collection. This garage-like construction was erected in 1932 to house Richard Shuttleworth's DH Moth G-EBWD and that very machine was on hand to roll into the restored structure on 19th April 2012. From that first biplane came a bustling aerodrome now with ten hangars and the home of a world-renowned aircraft and vehicle collection.

Avro XIX Series 2 G-AHKX
1946 | Eleven-seat general purpose | Two 420hp Armstrong Siddeley Cheetah 17

Like the 504 and the trainer dynasty it founded, the Anson became a mother lode for Avro. It evolved so much that to choose the Mk.I at Duxford alone would be misleading; a later variant is also needed. A former RAF Mk.19 would serve the purpose, but the BAE Systems 'heritage flight' civilian version provides great contrast.

Avro test pilot Ken Cook was at the controls when G-AHKX first took to the air from Woodford in November 1946. It had been registered to its customer, Smiths Aircraft Instruments Ltd, the previous May and served the company faithfully on development work and communications, from Staverton. *Kilo-X-ray* joined Meridian Air Maps at Shoreham from March 1961 on photo-survey work. From May 1965 it became Treffield Aviation Ltd's second aircraft; the first being Anson C.19 G-AGWE. Based at Sywell, the 'Annies' were used for charters until they were sold off in January 1967. Both G-AGWE and G-AHKX moved in January 1967 to Thruxton, joining Kemps Aerial Surveys. By late 1973 they were parked up at Thruxton and six of the fleet, including *Whisky-Echo* and *Kilo-X-Ray* were acquired by Sir William Roberts, destined for his Strathallan Aircraft Collection in Scotland. G-AGWE and G-AHKX flew north on 16th and 22nd January 1973, respectively. To allay ever-increasing costs, G-AHKX was among 23 aircraft sold by auction at Strathallan on 14th June 1981. *Kilo-X-ray* went under the hammer for £600 (around £2,400 in present-day values) and was acquired British Aerospace plc. It was returned to its birthplace at Woodford and an exacting restoration was started. On 8th March 2001 the venerable Avro was taken on its second flight test at Woodford, 56 years after its first. Wearing a striking two-tone blue with white trim colour scheme, it was ferried to Old Warden on 29th June 2002. It is on loan from BAE Systems (Operations) Ltd along with DH Moth G-EBLV and the Blackburn B-2.

Alan Crossthwaite (left) and Harry Wheeler working on G-AHKX's port Cheetah at Woodford, mid-1992.
British Aerospace

Blackburn Monoplane No.9 G-AANI
1912 | Single-seat monoplane | One 50hp Gnome

The collection's Blériot and Deperdussin have already gone through the centenary milestone and by the time this book goes to the printers, Old Warden's Blackburn will have definitively done the same. Since its restoration, completed in 1949, the 'Mono' has been the oldest *airworthy* British aeroplane in the world.

As might be imagined of a device of such antiquity, there are a few uncertainties about its provenance. It is believed to have been a one-off; but *very probably* there were two. There is a line of thought that December 1912 was *not* its birthday and that event came in February 1913.

Robert 'Bob' Blackburn studied engineering at Leeds University and he watched the Wright brothers demonstrating their biplane in France in 1908. The following year, aged 24, he set about creating an aircraft. The dynasty ended with the awesome Buccaneer strike fighter of the late 1950s. Bob's first aeroplane lifted off from the sands at Filey on the Yorkshire coast in 1910 and several Mercury monoplanes followed. The Blackburn Flying School at Filey taught the new-found skills of aviation but in September 1912 it was moved to Hendon, northwest of London. Managing this outfit was Gloucestershire-born Harold 'Harry' Blackburn, who was no relation to the Leeds family. By June 1913 at the latest, the London venture was over and Harold was in Yorkshire acting as test pilot for young Bob's designs until mid-1914.

Cyril E Foggin took flying lessons in France, gaining his Royal Aero Club (RAeC) aviator's certificate on 29th October 1912 at the Eastbourne Aviation Company on a Blériot. That same month he ordered a single-seat monoplane from Robert Blackburn. This was most likely tested by Harry that December and used as a demonstrator in early 1913 and this is Shuttleworth's centenarian.

By January Cyril was at Hendon and first flew in a Blackburn two-seater – probably with Harry in command – on the 17th. By the end of the month another student of Harry's, Lincolnshire-born Montague Francis Glew, qualified for his RAeC 'ticket' on a Blackburn at Hendon. Cyril and Francis became friends and Francis eventually married Cyril's sister, Rene. Blackburn company archives give 17th February 1913 as the day Cyril was charged for the new machine, which was called a 'Type D'. Harry flew the 'Mono' to Lofthouse Park, Leeds, on 17th March and it was shown off to the public. Three days later Cyril took his first trip in it, for 20 minutes.

Harry was busy with the 'Mono' at Stamford, Lincs, on 2nd-3rd April when he dropped leaflets and on the 22nd he took it from Wakefield to Harrogate, landing in front of the 'Queen's Hotel'. Either that day or the next, Harry suffered a take-off accident that badly damaged the aircraft; it went back to the workshop.

Around this time, Cyril seems to have lost interest in the 'Mono'. On 3rd June 1913 company archives refer to it as the property of Francis at his farm at Wittering, near Stamford, Lincs. Francis is believed to have paid £325 for it – about £35,750 in present-day purchasing power. If this seems steep, a Blackburn sales brochure for 1910 was offering Mercury-type monoplanes from new at £550. It is important to remember that this was not an 'old crock', Cyril and Francis had embarked upon the purchase and operation of a state-of-the-art flying machine – the equivalent of buying a high-end sports car. With this in mind, Francis and his elder brother, Aubrey, were determined to make the Blackburn an 'earner' and, with their friend Jack Burkitt, set about organising public appearances. Displays at Market Rasen and Horncastle were advertised for July 1913.

There is a photo of a stoic-looking Francis standing in front of the wreck of his Type D at Market Rasen, dated 4th July, 1913. Undaunted, he promised it would be up and running the following week. And so it was, but on the 11th it suffered another mishap. Such 'prangs' were all part of the 'learn as you go' nature of early aviation. Over the weekend of 23-24 July Francis was flying at Crooks Field, Horncastle. Again, the exhibition ended in a crunch.

During 23-25 July Harry Blackburn was piloting a 'Mono' from Leeds to the York Agricultural Show carrying copies of the *Yorkshire Evening Post* in a brilliant publicity stunt. At 70 miles, Horncastle to York was not an easy commute in 1913, by air or otherwise. Harry's newspaper-delivering machine *has* to be different – proof of a second example?

By 1914 Francis had the 'Mono' at Park Farm, Wittering, and he was working on it, removing around 18in of structure from behind the engine, apparently with plans to install a more potent powerplant. This may have been the result of yet another argument with gravity that year, or just to give it more 'poke'. With the outbreak of war, the dismantled Blackburn was secreted away. In December 1916, just a stone's throw away from the farm, the RFC began operating from what was then called Stamford airfield but destined to become the famous RAF Wittering in May 1924.

A stoic-looking Francis Glew with his smashed Monoplane at Market Rasen, 4th July 1913. *Peter Green Collection*

Richard Shuttleworth (ROS), tracked down rumours of a 'monoplane' at Wittering and met up with Francis Glew in 1937. It is said that the 'Mono' was hidden under a haystack and the Gnome engine was in pieces, 'pickled' in a barrel in the granary. ROS had to purchase the haystack as well in order to obtain the aeroplane! ROS took this incredible survivor back to Old Warden and restoration started. After the war, Richard's chief engineer, Sqn Ldr L A 'Jacko' Jackson completed the work in 1949, fitting a different 50hp Gnome rotary. The first flight was at RAF Henlow, to the north of Old Warden, on 17th September 1949 in the hands of Air Cdre Allen H Wheeler. Nine days later, it made its post-1914 public debut at the Royal Aircraft Establishment's display at Farnborough. (Not to be confused with the Society of British Aircraft Constructors airshow, which had been staged at Farnborough over 6th to 11 September.) In 1981 the Civil Aviation Authority realised that several Shuttleworth machines had no official identity, including the Blackburn. On 29th October 1982 it was given the vacant G-AANI, which should have been allocated in 1929 or 1930.

De Havilland DH.88 Comet G-ACSS
1934 | Two-seat long-distance racer | Two 210hp De Havilland Gipsy Six Series II

Sir MacPherson Robertson offered a glittering prize of £10,000 for the winner of an air race from England to Melbourne, Australia, to mark the centenary of the establishment of the State of Victoria. The flag would go down at 06:30 hours on 20th October, 1934 at Mildenhall in Suffolk. The contest attracted a lot of interest, not the least at Hatfield where Arthur Hagg and team decided they could design and build a twin-engined long distance racer specifically for the event, which was just *nine months* ahead. This became the DH.88 Comet and three orders were received, conditional on them being ready on time. Hubert Broad piloted G-ACSP on its maiden flight on 8th September at Hatfield, just six weeks prior to the start.

The three Comets for the race were: G-ACSP *Black Magic* owned and flown by Jim and Amy (née Johnson) Mollison; the unnamed G-ACSR owned by Bernard Rubin and flown by Owen Cathcart-Jones and Ken Waller; G-ACSS *Grosvenor House*, owned by Arthur Edwards of the Grosvenor House Hotel and flown by C W A Scott and Tom Campbell Black. Two other DH.88s were later commissioned: F-ANPZ, a mailplane for the French Government and G-ADEF *Boomerang* for Cyril Nicholson. (*Black Magic* is the subject of an ambitious restoration project by the Comet Racer Project Group at Derby.)

It was *Grosvenor House* that clinched the race. Scott and Campbell Black crossed the finishing line at 05:34 on 23rd October after a gruelling 70 hours 54 minutes 18 seconds, travelling 11,333 miles and averaging 158.9mph. This was a new point-to-point record, and the crew clocked up other records for Mildenhall-Darwin, Mildenhall-Singapore, Mildenhall to Allahabad and Allahabad to Singapore. After static display in Melbourne, G-ACSS came back to the UK by ship as deck cargo, coming back to Hatfield in January 1935.

The Air Ministry acquired G-ACSS for £7,000 from Arthur Edwards. It was to be used for performance evaluation by the Aeroplane & Armament Experimental Establishment (AA&EE) at Martlesham Heath and for assessment of its wooden structure at the Royal Aircraft Establishment (RAE), Farnborough. In overall silver dope and the serial K5084 it was put on charge at RAE on 15th May 1935. While with A&AEE the undercarriage jammed on 30th August 1935 and it was belly landed at Martlesham. De Havilland carried out repairs and it was back on the RAE's books on 20th July 1936. Just 31 days later, again with A&AEE, K5084 crashed at Butley in Suffolk having been carrying out gross weight landing trials. It was declared beyond repair and struck off charge in November.

The hulk was acquired by Frederick Tasker of Essex Aero, based at Gravesend and G-ACSS was registered to him on 7th June 1937. The huge task of restoring the DH.88 began; Gipsy Six Series IIs replaced the original Gipsy Six Rs of 230hp. The red and white scheme was forsaken for pale blue and with the new name *The Orphan*. Entered into the Damascus air race, 20-21 August 1937, G-ACSS was flown from Marseilles to Damascus and then to Le Bourget, Paris. Fg Off Arthur Clouston and Flt Lt George Nelson came fourth in at an average of 196mph. Ken Waller than competed in the King's Cup, centred upon Hatfield, that September, coming 5th overall in *The Orphan*.

The out-and-back record to and from Cape Town, South Africa, was the aim of Arthur Clouston and Betty Kirby-Green during November 1937. Sponsorship from the famous clothing brand Burberry included bespoke flying gear for the crew and G-ACSS became *The Burberry*. The flight took 57 hours, 23 minutes, traversing 14,690 miles and knocking a staggering 88 hours of the previous record. There was still more to be had from G-ACSS and it was renamed *Australian Anniversary*. After an abortive attempt in February, on 15th March G-ACSS departed Gravesend bound for Blenheim in New Zealand. Arthur Clouston and Victor Ricketts set an outbound record of 4 days, 8 hours, 7 minutes and finished the return leg at Croydon on the 26th having been away 10 days, 21 hours and travelled 26,500 miles. It was the first direct to and from to New Zealand and another four point-to-point records were notched up.

After all this fame, G-ACSS should really have been acquired for the nation and put in a museum, but that was not the case. There was not the machinery for that sort of thing then, but I'm not altogether sure that it could be achieved in similar circumstances today. On 5th November 1938 it flew for the last time and at Gravesend, the engines were stripped off *Australian Anniversary* and it was unceremoniously put into store outside with just a tarpaulin to stave off the elements. In 1944 de Havilland's publicity manager, Martin Sharp, discovered the mouldering hulk, recognised it for what it was and the importance of his next actions. He secured G-ACSS for £150 and had it moved to his company's apprentice training centre at Salisbury Hall, near Hatfield. (Today the home of the de Havilland Aircraft Heritage Centre.) For the Festival of Britain staged in London in 1951, the Comet was earmarked for display and this involved suspending it in 'flying' attitude, using wires. Holes were drilled in the airframe to achieve this and a whole-hearted lightening exercise was carried; large amounts of metal fittings were removed – never to be seen again. After this, the Comet taken to the de Havilland Engines facility at Leavesden and mounted vertically on a hangar wall.

At a ceremony at Hatfield on 30th October 1965, G-ACSS was donated to Shuttleworth by Hawker Siddeley Aviation (HSA). In February 1974 the collection announced that the Comet was to be restored to airworthy condition under the guidance of general manager David Ogilvy and workshop manager John Briggs. A grant from the Transport Trust has been secured along with some financial support from HSA, both amounting to £8,000 and at the time the whole project was estimated to cost £25,000. The registration G-ACSS was restored on 8th July 1975. From the beginning the restoration to fly project was full of controversy – see the narrative above. The venture was vast, complicated and swallowing money. Work stopped in November 1982 when it was declared that another £100,000 was needed.

In April 1983, the project moved to the RAE at Farnborough where technicians at apprentice school, with lots of input from the wider aerospace industry, were to oversee its completion. In February 1984 *Grosvenor House* was flown to Melbourne inside a Lufthansa Boeing 747 to take part in the 50th anniversary celebrations of the Robertson race – a date that had always been a target for the restoration's first flight. On its return to the UK, G-ACSS was shown off to the public outside its workshop at the September 1984 Farnborough airshow. After Farnborough, the Comet returned to its birthplace, where British Aerospace and many other agencies combined to make sure that the project came to fruition. Bearing in mind that after the Festival of Britain, G-ACSS was little more than a wooden shell, the restoration needed radical solutions to make it a safe and practical flying machine. The nose cone was originally made of magnesium alloy; this was replaced by a glass-fibre reinforced plastic version and the pilot's seats were also created from GRP. The undercarriage was a triumph of 'reverse engineering' with the addition of electronic actuation, with manual over-ride, being installed. Power for this came from an electric motor originally used to open and close the canopy on a Buccaneer and a modified flap-shaft mechanism from a BAe 146 jetliner was employed. The fuel tank in the rear fuselage was removed and the remaining tankage was reduced. We shall probably never know the total man-hours and cash lavished on the Comet project.

On 17th May 1987 George Ellis eased the throttles forward at Hatfield and DH.88 G-ACSS entered its second flying phase. That month, *Grosvenor House* appeared at the Mildenhall Air Fete, going back to its point of departure for the great adventure to Australia 54 years before. With Old Warden's runway too short to allow safe operation of *Sierra-Sierra*, the Comet was based at Hatfield. When touching down on runway 06 on 4th July 1987 G-ACSS ground-looped to starboard and the port main undercarriage collapsed; the aircraft coming to a halt facing in the way it had come. Repairs were immediately put in train.

A press release from Old Warden on 29th March 1994 brought about a not unexpected statement about the Comet's future. General manager Peter Symes declared: "The sensitive handling of this historical aeroplane make it impossible to operate from... Old Warden. It has been flown successfully from the London Business Aviation facility at the British Aerospace airfield at Hatfield... Six years' experience of operating in this way, whilst confirming the attraction of the Comet in the air have exposed limitations associated with lack of access on the ground. With the closure of the airfield at Hatfield in the immediate future, alternative operating arrangements have been carefully explored, none of which, unfortunately, meet our requirements satisfactorily. Being fully aware of the collection's responsibility to ensure the preservation of this aircraft... we have resolved that we should cease to continue to fly the aircraft but rather to transport it to Old Warden and put it on display to the public in a taxiable condition."

Right: Race No.34, DH.88 G-ACSS at Mildenhall in October 1934, prior to the start of the MacRobertson race. As is evident, construction of the 'C' type hangars at the RAF station was underway. *Peter Green collection*

Comet K5084 after its first mishap at Martlesham Heath, 30th August 1935. The forward fuel tank has been removed from the nose. *Peter Green Collection*

Grosvenor House arrived by road at Shuttleworth on 22nd May 1994 and its permit to fly lapsed on 2nd June that year with a declared total flying time of 549 hours, which will have included all of its 1930s globe-trotting. With the extension of the main runway at Old Warden in 1999 the tantalising prospect of flying G-ACSS from the Bedfordshire turf has arisen from time to time. An air test on 28th October 2002 for renewal of its permit to fly ended with the starboard main gear collapsing after the aircraft bounced four times on landing. It came to rest 150-degrees from its landing heading. Thankfully the pilot was unharmed. The collection is committed to flying the Comet again, perhaps as early as 2013.

English Electric Wren II No.4 G-EBNV
1923 | Single-seat ultra-light | One 3hp ABC

Inspired by the new sport of gliding, English Electric's (EE) designer W O Manning set his mind to creating an ultra-light that could fly on the least power possible. The outcome was a very clean, glider-like, aircraft with robust undercarriage and foldable wings. Designated S.1 Monoplane, the design came together in late 1922 and an ABC flat-twin motorcycle engine was chosen. The Air Ministry was approached about the concept and it accepted the offer to build a prototype, which was embodied in Specification 4/23 as a 'training machine' capable of 30-minutes endurance. Construction started at Preston on 5th February 1923 and a price of £600 was agreed upon; it was allocated the serial number J6973 and given the name Wren. With Sqn Ldr Maurice Wright at the controls, J6973 made its first sustained flight on 8th April 1923 from the sands at Lytham St Annes. It appeared at the RAF Pageant at Hendon on 30th June and was taken on charge by the Aeroplane Experimental Establishment at Martlesham Heath in July, but its flying career lasted only until November. (At that point it was AEE, the wording 'and Armament' – as in A&AEE – being added from March 1924.)

Manning hoped that the Wren could become a cheap to operate light aircraft and two more, referred to as Mk.IIs, were built. They were entered into the *Daily Mail*-sponsored Light Aircraft Trials at Lympne, in October 1923. The two were identical apart from the competition numbers, '3' and '4', worn on the rudders. During the trials '3' was flown by Sqn Ldr Wright and '4' by Flt Lt W Longton. During the competition A H James, flying ANEC I G-EBIL flew 87.5 miles on a gallon of petrol and Longton then matched this incredible performance. The pair shared the newspaper's £1,000 and £500 awarded by the Duke of Sutherland.

(The collection has another Lympne trials competitor, ANEC II G-EBJO, which was entered in the 1924 competition. An optimistic two-seater, it was powered by a 30hp Anzani twin-cylinder; which proved troublesome, preventing it from taking part. Registered as G-EBJO on 17th July 1924, the little monoplane passed through a series of owners and was passed on to Richard Shuttleworth in January 1937. Fitted with an ABC Scorpion it flew again on 9th March 2004.)

Wrens '3' and '4' returned to Lancashire, with the former stored at Lytham and the other at Strand Road, Preston. When EE vacated Lytham in 1926, '3' was acquired by Alan Smith of Roundhay, Leeds, and it was registered to him as G-EBNV on 9th April. By 1929 it was in store in Bradford and in the mid-1930s was with collector R H Grant in Dumfries. Meanwhile '4' 'flew' over the EE stand at the British Empire Exhibition at Wembley, April to October 1924. Beyond this, '4' was presented on loan to the Science Museum (inventory number 1924-603) and displayed at South Kensington, London.

On 4th February 1946 Wren '4' was taken to Preston for planned restoration by EE, but was put back into store as the company started a huge expansion programme. Shuttleworth approached EE in late 1954 and with the co-operation of test pilot and light aircraft enthusiast Peter Hillwood, '4' moved to the EE airfield at Warton. Engineer Bill Eaves was in charge and W O Manning on hand for advice. At this point, both Wrens were re-united for the first time since 1923 as Bob Grant's G-EBNV had been tracked down and secured. Inspection revealed that G-EBNV was too far 'gone' to really help the project, although its little ABC engine was in far better trim than that of '4'.

Peter Hillwood conducted the first 'hop' along Warton's generous runway in July 1955, but it was 25th September the following year before real sustained flight was achieved. Famed EE test pilot Roland Beamont also sampled the Wren. At the Royal Aeronautical Society's Garden Party at Wisley, Surrey, on 15th September 1957, the Wren was officially handed over to the collection. In attendance was W O Manning and Dorothy Clotilda Shuttleworth, mother of Richard. It was flown for a long time merely as '4' but in 1981 the Civil Aviation Authority requested that Shuttleworth register its aircraft that had slipped through the 'system'. On 29th October '4' adopted the registration of '3', the long decayed and gone sister-ship G-EBNV. Trials with bungee launching started in April 1968 and this method is often used to help the 3hp flat twin propel the Wren into the air.

Both Mk.II Wrens in the same photo, or probably not, proudly wearing Lympne competition numbers '3' and '4' on their rudders. No.3 has been crudely re-touched to show the top of the wing and the curve of the nose. Close inspection of No.4 shows the propeller to be motionless and precious little evidence of a pilot. It is likely the 'flying' aircraft has been super-imposed to take advantage of No.3's pilot apparently watching it land! *KEC*

Hawker Hind (Afghan) G-AENP
1935 | Two-seat light bomber | One 640hp Rolls-Royce Kestrel

During the mid-1930s there was a joke that the RAF was to be renamed as the 'Hawker Air Force'. This was based upon the incredible success of the family of two-seat military biplanes devised by Sydney Camm with no less than *seven* variants entering RAF service. The RAF ordered 2,549 units and the series was extensively exported, using a variety of powerplants. The wider British aircraft industry gained from this apparently monopolistic situation with extensive sub-contracts. As well as this airworthy Hind, the RAF Museum's Hart Trainer is profiled in Chapter 5.

Shuttleworth's Hind flies in the colours of 'K5414' with 15 Squadron. It has also flown in two other guises, one potentially accurate, the other certainly so. The potential one was 'K5457', a former 211 Squadron machine which was transferred to the Afghan Air Force in July 1939 as part of a batch of 20 surplus to RAF needs. The other scheme was an Afghan one. (Afghanistan had taken eight new off the production line in 1937.)

In the late 1960s, someone passing through Kabul noted a hangar open with some biplanes in it. Questions were asked and it was discovered that they were Hinds! Depending on the source, the Afghans operated the type until 1954 or 1956. One joined the RAF Museum, two went to Canada in 1975 and one was donated to Shuttleworth. Old Warden's example was collected with the help of the Ford Motor Company in 1970; the epic land journey of 6,000 miles took four weeks. First flown after restoration on 17th August 1981, it initially wore Afghan national markings. The Hind was civil registered as G-AENP on 29th October 1981; this identity had not been allocated in September 1936 and was a very suitable 'period' allocation. *November-Papa* is thought to come

While not claiming that this is the Shuttleworth machine, a rare view of an Afghan Hind in its element. *KECa* from the surplus RAF stock. If it had been from the new batch, it very likely would have seen action against insurgents in 1938 in Katawatz province. Aerial warfare in Afghanistan is not a just a 21st century activity.

Hawker Sea Hurricane Ib Z7015
1941 | Single-seat carrier-borne fighter | One Rolls-Royce Merlin III

Shuttleworth's example is the *only* airworthy and 'hooked' Sea Hurricane in the world. Built by Canadian Car and Foundry at Montreal, Canada, for the RAF as Mk.Ib Z7015, it was received in the UK at 13 Maintenance Unit, Henlow, on 18th March 1941. It was moved to General Aircraft Ltd at Hanworth, specialising in Sea Hurricane conversions, on 27th June 1941. Its operational debut came on 29th July when Z7015 joined 880 Squadron at St Merryn and it is these colours that the Sea Hurricane wears today. By February 1942 the Hurricane had moved to Tain in Scotland, flying with 801 Squadron. An accident in April that year had the aircraft at Barton, Manchester, for attention by Civilian Repair Organisation David Rosenfield Ltd. With this complete, Z7015 joined its last unit, 759 Squadron at Yeovilton on 8th December 1942 where it carried the codes 'Y1L'.

Retired in August 1943, in November Z7015 became an instructional airframe at Loughborough College's Department of Aeronautical Engineering. In March 1946 the college took delivery of a Spitfire V AR501 – which of course rubs shoulders again with Z7015 at Old Warden. On 21st February 1961 the Hurricane was acquired by Shuttleworth and moved to Old Warden, where it was given a basic RAF camouflage scheme by 1966. It had a brief spell of 'stardom', taxying in the film *Battle of Britain* at Henlow in 1967-1968. Restoration to flying condition started on 26th April 1975 when the fuselage was delivered to Staverton, where a team from Dowty set to. The wings migrated to Heathrow Airport, for attention by BEA Engineering. In July 1981 the Sea Hurricane restoration became a combined Imperial War Museum/Shuttleworth operation and the entire airframe settled in at Duxford. Registered as G-BKTH on 24th May 1983, *Tango-Hotel* first flew at Duxford on 16th September 1995. In 1996 ownership was transferred solely to Shuttleworth and it returned full-time to Old Warden. Although other Sea Hurricanes survive, Z7015 is the only one of its type that is once again 'hooked'.

Inside the Loughborough college hangar immediately post-war. Left to right: Grumman Martlet AL246 (now at the Fleet Air Arm Museum – Chapter 4), Spitfire V AR501 and Sea Hurricane Z7015. *KEC*

Mignet HM.14 'Flying Flea' G-AEBB
1936 | Single-seat ultra-light | One 16hp Scott A2S 'Flying Squirrel'

Frenchman Henri Mignet was undeterred by his inability to learn to fly in a conventional manner. Through a line of this own designs he got airborne. With his HM.14 Pou du Ciel (literally Sky Louse, but universally called the Flying Flea in Britain) of 1933 he created a practical ultra-light that he claimed could be built by anyone who could make a packing case. The 'Flea' had a tandem-wing layout, was of all-wood construction and could use a wide variety of engines, mostly converted motorcycle units. Mignet published an engagingly-written book, *Le Sport de l'Air*, which became a best-seller in France and when translated and published by the Air League as *The Flying Flea: How to Build It*, it appealed to a huge number of would-be aviators. Hundreds were started, many never to take to the air, many more not completed. Others flew often and well. The Flea brought about the Authorisation to Fly (A to F) method of certification, effectively the forerunner of today's Permit to Fly. After a series of fatalities, in December 1936 the Air Registration Board brought in what has frequently been misinterpreted as a 'ban' on the little machine. In essence it was only prohibiting those without what Mignet called the 'conjugated wing', a modification that prevented the forward wing from masking the rear wing from the airflow. Several British Fleas received an A to F after the 'ban'.

As will be seen below, a healthy number of Fleas can be found in UK museums. Some took advantage of reprints of the Air League book and were built from the 1960s onwards. As the HM.14 is a homebuild, there is no reason why an example built decades after the mid-1930s should not be considered original, although none were constructed with the intention of flying. Shuttleworth's G-AEBB has been chosen because it is an original pre-war example *and* it flew. Also Old Warden is a most appropriate location as the entire aerodrome is a shrine to civil aviation endeavour.

Kenneth William Owen built G-AEBB in Southampton. Powered by a converted 1300cc Henderson motorcycle engine it flew successfully, although from exactly where is unknown. Its A to F was issued on 24th January 1936, expiring on 1st March 1937. After that it is reported to have been stored in a fish and chip shop in the city. In 1941 G-AEBB was donated to 424 Squadron Air Training Corps in Southampton and kept in good trim by generations of cadets. The Flea was presented to Shuttleworth in 1968, initially on loan. It was rebuilt by Tony Dowson and fitted with a Cherub and later with a Scott A.2S and was taxied at events for a while. These days, it 'flies' along with replicas from previous eras from the rafters of the main hangars.

Sopwith Pup '9917'
1920 | Single-seat fighter biplane | One 80hp Le Rhône

The Pup hit the headlines when the RNAS experimented with its suitability to operate from ships. Sqn Cdr E H Dunning achieved the first landing on a vessel underway on aircraft carrier HMS *Furious* on 2nd August 1917. Pups became the backbone of early RNAS shipboard fighter operations; Shuttleworth's machine is painted in the colours of '9917' that served from HMS *Manxman*. During 1919-1920 Sopwith developed a two-seat dual-control 'sporting' version, the Dove. It had a longer fuselage, to accommodate a second seat and to keep the centre of gravity within bounds; the wings were slightly swept back. At least nine were completed for private owners; the last being handed over in mid-1920.

Shuttleworth's Pup started off as a Dove and its early history was revealed by Harald Penrose in *British Aviation – The Adventuring Years*, the third of his exceptional five-volume history of British aviation from 1903 to 1939. After serving with the RFC and the RNAS, D L Hollis Williams was working in Hawker Aircraft's design department at Kingston-on-Thames. The company had secured a contract to recondition a batch of de Havilland DH.9As in 1922-1923 and Hollis Williams (HW) was helping to clear space in the factory for this to be carried out. During this he: "found six partly-finished uncovered airframes intended as conversions from Pups to Doves for a joy-riding company that failed to find the money." Thomas Octave Murdoch Sopwith's huge aero engineering enterprise centred on Kingston had gone into liquidation in September 1920; only to re-emerge phoenix-like on 15th November as H G Hawker Engineering. It was so named in honour of his gifted test pilot-come-designer, Australian Harry Hawker. The well-known scrap merchant R J Coley was going to take these airframes away. (Coley was still going strong at Hounslow in the early 1970s, handling scrap from the demise of the TSR-2 from Brooklands and Handley Page at Radlett, among others.) HW turned to his friend C H Lowe-Wylde, a Hawker draughtsman, and suggested the two combine and restore one of the Doves. They turned to works manager Fred Sigrist and he offered the pair: "Anything you can put on a lorry is £5 to you." (HW was earning £5 a week in those days.) They sorted out the best-looking airframe, but this had no tail, but they found a fin and rudder from a Sopwith Snipe and this explains why the finished aircraft was distinctive in having a horn-balanced fin-rudder. The bundle was hauled off to a lock-up garage in Kingston and Coley supplied a Le Rhône rotary for another 'fiver'.

The project was registered as a Dove to HW as G-EBKY on 27th March 1925. By this time Hollis Williams had moved to the design department of Fairey Aviation (he was to become chief designer) and Lowe-Wylde withdrew to develop his interests in gliding, but maintained his interest in the Dove. Hollis Williams, assisted by H H Robinson, also at Fairey, ploughed on when time allowed. The Air Registration Board did not like the work on the wings and, for a fee, Fred Sigrist was happy for Kingston to improve on the job. The Dove gained its Certificate of Airworthiness (C of A) on 12th April 1927 but it did not fly much as it was expensive. HW could not afford any form of insurance and: "the engine burned almost as much Castrol [oil] as petrol". A force-landing after take-off from a strip near Bournemouth left the machine, as far as HW was concerned, a write-off. The imposing Richard Fairey, mogul behind the company that carried his name, heard of the 'prang' and told the disconsolate HW that he had instructed the Hayes factory to rebuild it.

The Dove was kept at West Malling in Kent, where Lowe-Wylde had established the British Aircraft Company, and its C of A lapsed on 23rd September 1932. Lowe-Wylde was killed while flying a BAC Planette motor-glider at West Malling on 13th May 1933. HW left Fairey in 1934 to join General Aircraft at Hanworth and with the death of Lowe-Wylde and pressures of the new post led to the disposal of the Dove. (HW later re-joined Fairey and in 1951 became chief engineer for Westland.)

We next turn to Geoff A Chamberlain flying G-EBKY wholly unofficially from a strip at Kempston, Bedfordshire. Mr Chamberlain had acquired the Dove from collector C P B Ogilvie of Watford, Hertfordshire, in 1935, for £45. (The following year Ogilvie acquired Bristol F.2b Fighter D8096, which joined the Shuttleworth Collection in February 1952.) In the summer of 1936, ROS had learned of Geoff A Chamberlain and went to visit. As described in another Penrose's volume *British Aviation – Ominous Skies*, Mr Chamberlain was less interested in money, more in another flying machine. He was offered Avro 504K G-ABSN – the *first* Shuttleworth 504. Built in 1918 by Brush Electrical Engineering at Loughborough as H2965 it served 9 Squadron as a 'hack' during 1924-1926 before being civilianised as three-seater G-ABSN in July 1932. It was last registered to Plt Off Francis Blowfield Chapman on 10th December 1934 and based at Gosport. The RAF officer moved it on and it seems that ROS was its next custodian. A deal was secured, Richard got the Dove and Mr Chamberlain the 504. (ROS has snapped up another 504 for the collection by the end of 1936.)

The Dove was registered to ROS 12th July 1937 and work started to convert it to Pup status, complete with 0.303in Vickers machine-gun. Allen Wheeler carried out the air test at Old Warden on 26th February 1938 and the following day ROS took it up. The paperwork lapsed during the war and G-EBKY was restored to the register on 11th July 1947 to Warden Aviation and Engineering Co. The marks were cancelled as 'transferred to military marks' on 24th September 1956, but were renewed in October 1981. Post-war the Pup flew with the serial 'N5184' and later 'N5180' (the Pup prototype) before taking on its present RNAS colours.

The Pup, complete with civilian registration but carrying a machine-gun, during air testing in 1948. *KEC*

Shuttleworth Collection Aircraft

Type	Identity	Built	Origin	Arrived	Notes
Abbott-Baynes Scud II	BGA.231	1937	UK	Dec 2009	glider
ANEC II	G-EBJO	1924	UK	Jan 1937	Lympne 1924 No.7
Avro Triplane Type IV replica	G-ARSG	1964	UK	1966	–
Avro 504K*	G-ADEV	1918	UK	Dec 1936	–
Avro Tutor I	G-AHSA	1933	UK	1959	–
Avro XIX Series 2	G-AHKX	1946	UK	29 Jun 2002	see profile
Blackburn Monoplane*	G-AANI	1912	UK	1937	see profile
Blackburn B-2 Series 1	G-AEBJ	1936	UK	Mar 2008	–
Blériot XI*	G-AANG	1909	France	1935	see narrative
Bristol Boxkite replica	G-ASPP	1964	UK	1966	–
Bristol M.1C replica	G-BWJM	1997	UK	28 Oct 1997	built by NAW – see narrative
Bristol Scout replica #	'A1742'	1962	UK	17 May 2009	static, on loan
Bristol F.2b Fighter	G-AEPH	1918	UK	Feb 1952	D8096
Bücker Bü 131 Jungmann	'4477'	1967	Germany	23 Oct 2003	G-RETA, Spanish-built, by CASA. Accident 3 Jul 2011. Stored
Chilton DW.1	G-AESZ	1937	UK	Jun 2011	on loan
Chilton DW.1 replica	G-CDXU	2009	UK	2010	on loan
Comper Swift*	G-ACTF	1932	UK	16 Aug 1996	–
De Havilland DH.51	G-EBIR	1924	UK	Jul 1965	see profile
De Havilland Humming Bird #	G-EBHX	1923	UK	4 Aug 1960	see narrative
De Havilland Moth	G-EBLV	1925	UK	1993	on loan
De Havilland Moth*	G-EBWD	1928	UK	21 Jan 1932	see narrative
De Havilland Moth	G-ABAG	1930	UK	Jan 2004	formerly Shuttleworth owned, on loan
De Havilland Tiger Moth II	G-ANKT	1942	UK	Sep 1972	'K2585'
De Havilland Comet*	G-ACSS	1934	UK	30 Oct 1965	see profile
De Havilland Dragon Rapide 6	G-AGSH	1945	UK	27 Feb 2009	on loan
DH Canada Chipmunk 22	G-BNZC	1952	Canada	Mar 2000	'671'
Deperdussin Monoplane	G-AANH	1910	France	1935	G-AANH – see narrative
Desoutter I	G-AAPZ	1931	Netherlands	5 Jan 1935	–
Dixon Ornithopter #	–	1964	UK	1960s	–
EE Wren II	G-EBNV	1923	UK	15 Sep 1957	see profile
EoN Primary	AQQ	1947	UK	late 1960s	glider
Fieseler Fi 156A-1 Storch	G-STCH	1944	Germany	5 Dec 2006	on loan
Gloster Gladiator I	G-AMRK	1938	UK	Nov 1980	'K7985'
Granger Archaeopteryx #	G-ABXL	1930	UK	28 Apr 1967	on loan, stored
Grumman FM-2 Wildcat #	N49JC	1944	USA	23 Feb 2012	under restoration
Hawker Cygnet replica	G-EBJI	1977	UK	Apr 2010	on loan
Hawker Cygnet replica	G-CAMM	1992	UK	1995	–
Hawker Tomtit	G-AFTA	1929	UK	May 1960	–
Hawker Hind	G-AENP	1935	UK	1970	see profile
Hawker Demon I	G-BTVE	1937	UK	23 Jul 2009	K8203, on loan
Hawker Sea Hurricane Ib*	G-BKTH	1941	UK	21 Feb 1961	see profile
Lilienthal glider replica #	–	1984	Germany	Apr 2007	–
Mignet HM.14 'Flying Flea'	G-AEBB	1936	France	1968	see profile
Miles Falcon Major	G-AEEG	1936	UK	2002	on loan
Miles Magister I	G-AKPF	1941	UK	Sep 2001	on loan, N3788
Miles Magister I	G-AJRS	1942	UK	3 Apr 1970	P6382

Type	Identity	Built	Origin	Arrived	Notes
Parnall Elf	G-AAIN	1932	UK	Jul 1951	–
Percival Provost T.1	G-KAPW	1955	UK	2 Nov 2001	XF603
Pilcher Bat Mk.3 replica #	–	2000	UK	Nov 2008	–
Pilcher Triplane replica #	–	2003	UK	2006	–
Piper Super Cub 150	G-SVAS	1961	USA	13 Oct 2008	glider tug
Polikarpov Po-2 *Mule*	G-BSSY	1944	USSR	31 Jul 2003	'28'
Royal A/c Factory SE.5a	G-EBIA	1918	UK	Aug 1959	F904
Ryan ST3-KR	G-BYPY	1941	USA	2008	on loan, '001'
Slingsby Grasshopper TX.1 #	XA241	1953	UK	Dec 1995	stored
Sopwith Triplane replica*	G-BOCK	1980	UK	2004	built by NAW – see narrative
Sopwith Pup	G-EBKY	1920	UK	1937	see profile
Sopwith F.1 Camel replica	G-BZSC	–	UK	off site	being built by NAW – see narrative
Southern Martlet	G-AAYX	1930	UK	1955	–
Supermarine Spitfire Vc*	G-AWII	1942	UK	1961	under restoration, AR501
Westland Lysander III	G-AZWT	1942	UK	1997	'V9367'

Notes: All are airworthy except for those marked #. * – Illustrated in the colour section. Additionally, the Trust owns the static Blériot XI replica on loan to the Midland Air Museum at Coventry Airport, Warwickshire. The fuselage of this was built at Old Warden for Blériot collector Cdr L D Goldsmith in 1959 and used in *Those Magnificent Men...* See Chapter 10 for an important restoration undertaken by Leonard Jackson and the Old Warden workshops in 1961 for the Royal Scottish Museum.

The essence of a Shuttleworth event, traction engine and the Avro XIX. *Ken Ellis*

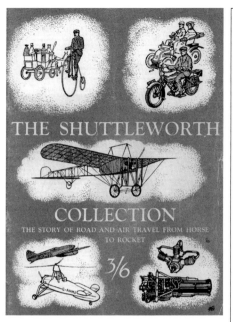

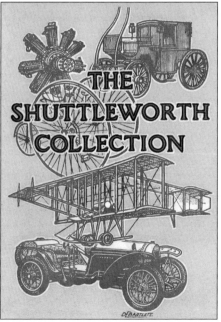

A selection of 1970s and 1980s Shuttleworth literature.

CHAPTER 4

First and Foremost
Fleet Air Arm Museum
Yeovilton, Somerset

www.fleetairarm.com

Before the M5 motorway allowed traffic to hurtle into the West Country, the A303 was a way by which holidaymakers made the trek to the beaches. After having glanced at Stonehenge as they drove through Wiltshire, the number of places where a break could be taken was few and far between. Coming over the crest of Sparkford Hill, aviation-minded travellers could not fail to notice the huge Royal Naval Air Station (RNAS) at Yeovilton. As they got closer, it was clear that the A303 skirted the northern boundary of the airfield. In the early 1960s, de Havilland Sea Vixens thundered in and out and there was also the hope that a glimpse could be had of the venerable Fairey Swordfish biplane flown as a memorial. The grass verges alongside the fence became a welcome place to stop, brew up and watch the flying. By 1963 a layby had been built and a couple of historic aircraft held on the base were parked up to add further interest.

From the A303 we turn to the Angel Parkway alongside Naval Air Station Pensacola, Florida. In 1961 the US Navy had opened up a hangar and was busy filling it with exhibits to tell the story of American naval flying. The collection was open to the public and very popular; what went on to become the National Museum of Naval Aviation was in business. Favourable comments were passed on by visiting Royal Navy personnel; the public relations value of a similar set-up in the UK was too good to pass up. Besides, there had long been schemes for a museum devoted to the Royal Air Force and it was only right that the 'Senior Service' be first and foremost! Plans were forwarded to the Admiralty Board and these were approved in September 1963. Cdr Robin Foster

Lt Cdr 'Winkle' Brown flying alongside HMS *Ocean* in December 1945 in the third prototype Vampire LZ551/G. *KEC*

Above: View of part of Hangar 11 in the early days of the FAAM. From the rear: the cockpit of Sea Vampire T.22 XA127, Seafire F.17 SX137, Vampire LZ551/G, Sea Fury FB.11 WJ231. *HMS Heron*

Right: Models and photos from the mid-1960s framed by the Sea Fury. The cabinets came from the Imperial War Museum and the Science Museum. *HMS Heron*

Below right: Swordfish II HS618 has worn a variety of colour schemes in its time. In the mid-1970s it 'flew' as 'V6105'. *KEC*

was tasked with creating the Fleet Air Arm Museum (FAAM) and a date was given for the opening – just nine months away! On 28th May 1964 RNAS Yeovilton was to host a Royal Review on the occasion of two anniversaries, the 25th of British naval aviation under Admiralty control and the 50th of the founding of the Royal Naval Air Service. HRH Prince Philip was to attend and he could open the FAAM at the same time. No pressure then!

The year 2014 will witness another 50th anniversary, that of FAAM itself and it is hoped that all involve push the boat out – pun intended! In the hectic time running up to the grand opening in May 1964, even the keenest advocate of the heritage of the Fleet Air Arm could not have envisaged the scope, size and status that the museum went on to achieve in the next half-century.

No.11 Hangar, a T2 Bellman closest to the A303, was made available and the finding of artefacts and airframes was initiated. Favours were pulled and both the Imperial War Museum and Science Museum passed on showcases and other display materials. So, with Corsair KD431, Seafire SX137, Sea Fury WJ231 and Swordfish HS618 among the 'founder members', FAAM was opened on schedule on 28th May 1964. The UK had its first 'service' aviation museum – and a brand new visitor attraction for the South West was born. That year FAAM attracted 29,000 visitors and 33,000 in 1965 – an excellent start. From these small beginnings, Yeovilton went on to become the third-largest aviation collection in UK and Europe's largest naval aviation museum.

During 1966 the Science Museum delivered de Havilland Vampire LZ551/G – which made the world's first landing by a jet on an aircraft carrier in December 1945. This was forging a relationship that was to see another Science Museum jet come to Yeovilton a decade later. Also in 1966, FAAM was established as a Charitable Trust. Lt Cdr L A 'Harpy' Cox became the first curator and by the early 1970s, there were nearly 40 airframes, most of which were outside.

In 1976 Cdr Dennis White was appointed as Development Director, to capitalise on the museum's popularity and to steer it on the course of expansion. Dennis was a larger than life character with a warm, booming, laugh and the ability to galvanise others to support the cause. He joined the Navy as a Sub-Lieutenant in the Volunteer Reserve and got his 'wings' at Pensacola in 1941. Piloting a Grumman Wildcat from the escort carrier *Fencer* on 2nd April 1944 he shadowed Fairey Barracudas attacking the German warship *Tirpitz* moored in a Norwegian fjord. Post-war he took a permanent commission, becoming a qualified flying instructor and a deck landing control officer. He was Naval Attaché to Ethiopia and his final duties were with NATO in West Germany.

The Board of Trustees was expanded to include civilians for the first time, notably Sir Donald Gosling, Bill Regan and Cdr Sam MacDonald Hall. Under their direction, Dennis set about planning the expansion of the museum and finding the finance for the new buildings essential to the long term preservation of the aircraft collection. Naturally flamboyant, typically he was out on the runway when Concorde touched down and 'batted' the jetliner in! Dennis retired in 1987, having seen the museum dramatically expand into a world-renowned collection. Cdr Dennis White OBE died on 2nd November 2007, aged 84. His Fleet Air Arm (FAA) career had been exceptional, but his influence on the development and maturity of the aircraft preservation movement shines out not just at Yeovilton but in the countless people within the sector he inspired. The author is proud to be among the latter.

The museum bought Sopwith Pup replica N6452 at the auction of the former Whitehall Theatre of War in June 1985 for £19,000. In this publicity shot showing the Pup leaving for the journey to Yeovilton, FAAM Director Cdr Dennis White is holding the propeller, while Curator (now Director) Graham Mottram has his hand on the wheel and apprentice Dave Morris (now Curator of Aircraft) is holding the fin. *FAAM*

Frontline HMS Heron

From the car park and the Airfield Viewing Area within the museum, visitors can see the comings and goings of the very active FAA airfield. Yeovilton's fascinating history started in July 1939 when the Admiralty acquired large tracts of land east of Ilchester and set about construction of a typically Navy format of four runways. Intended as a training station, the Naval Observer School (NOS) was the founder occupant in early 1940. The airfield was officially commissioned as a Royal Naval Air Station, HMS *Heron*, on 18th June 1940. Fighters and strike aircraft became the dominant theme; the first frontline unit was 827 Squadron with Fairey Albacores, from March 1941. Five miles to the south was the Westland factory at Yeovil which was suffering from capacity problems while churning out Supermarine Spitfires and Seafires. From 1942 the company established a final assembly and flight test facility at Yeovilton; the RNAS and Westland having maintained a close co-operation ever since. Wildcats, Sea Hurricanes, Seafires and Fireflies became the stock-in-trade of HMS *Heron* through the war years.

In the early post-war years Sea Furies and 'second generation' Fireflies were the major types. Yeovilton increasingly took on a headquarters role, it became the home of the Flag Officer Flying Training in 1953 and, from November 1970, Flag Officer Naval Air Command. De Havilland Sea Venoms heralded the all-weather jet era in November 1953. The advent of the big, capable, de Havilland Sea Vixen required a major rework of the airfield's infrastructure and in November 1958 the 'Vixen trials unit, 700Y Squadron became operational. By the mid-1960s the McDonnell Phantom FG.1 was to be the next focus and again a major rebuilding programme was instituted to prepare for the new machine. The roar of reheated Speys filled the Somerset skies from August 1967 with the establishment of 700P Squadron. The Phantoms moved north to Leuchars in Scotland during 1972 to amalgamate operations with the RAF's fleet. The scrapping of the last of the large carriers, HMS *Eagle* and *Ark Royal*, co-incided with the influx of more and more helicopter units to Yeovilton. The age of the carrier was not over with the so-called 'through-deck' carriers and the first frontline Sea Harrier unit, 800 Squadron, became operational in April 1980. Sea Harriers bowed out in March 2006, Navy V/STOL pilots moving to Cottesmore where Joint Force Harrier had been established. Today, HMS *Heron* remains a major base, with 702 and 815 Squadrons flying anti-submarine Westland Lynx HAS.3s. Four units supply airlift capability for the Royal Marines and the Army as part of Joint Helicopter Command, 845, 846 and 848 Squadrons with Westland Sea King HC.4s and 847 Squadron with Lynx AH.9As. No.727 Squadron with Grob Tutors provides primary fixed-wing training.

HMS Heron, RNAS Yeovilton, ready for an Air Day in the 1980s and looking north, towards both the old and new A303.
HMS Heron

Also resident is the Royal Navy Historic Flight (RNHF) which can trace its origins to 1961 when Westland donated Fairey Swordfish LS326 to the Royal Navy as a flying memorial, initially operated by RNAS Yeovilton's Heron Flight. In 1971 Hawker Siddeley gave Hawker Sea Fury FB.11 TF956 to Heron Flight and the following year FAAM passed on Firefly AS.5 WB271 to the Navy and RNHF was born. Although initially manned by Service personnel, successive rounds of defence cuts led to the Flight being civilianised in the early 1990s and the Swordfish Heritage Trust was formed to raise funds. The Flight remains a Royal Naval Squadron, initially run by a civilian general manager, but since 2009 by a serving officer. RNHF pilots are all serving or Reserve Officers who fly as volunteers during their spare time. RNHF is not open to the public at Yeovilton, but its aircraft are regular performers at airshows all over the UK.

Long-term sentinel

On 21st November 2001 a well-known Yeovilton landmark was trundled out of the main gate and off to the warmth and protection of Cobham Hall. This was the third prototype Blackburn Buccaneer and it had 'guarded' the museum's entrance faithfully for 34 years. FAAM's operational Buccaneer S.1 XN957, nestled on the flight deck of the Carrier exhibition, is profiled below but the opportunity to tell the story of this long-serving stalwart *must* be taken. No less than *nine* prototypes of the highly advanced Blackburn NA.39 (later to be named the Buccaneer) were ordered in 1955. The third to fly was XK488 which was completed at Brough on the Humber and then roaded to Holme-on-Spalding Moor for flight trials. It had its maiden flight on the last day of October 1958 and was destined for a life of engine trials. By January 1959 it was with the Royal Aircraft Establishment (RAE) at Thurleigh, and three months later at Hatfield, Hertfordshire, for trials with de Havilland Engines (DHE), makers of its Gyron Junior turbojets. The NA.39 flitted between RAE and DHE until July 1960 when it was at the Aeroplane & Armament Experimental Establishment, Boscombe Down, for an entire 72-hours! It was back at Hatfield from 28th July and flew at the 1960 Farnborough Airshow.

Strapped into XK488 on 24th July 1961 was test pilot David Lockspeiser and flight test observer R A 'Tony' Buxton. David had flown for Hawker at Dunsfold, with the legendary Neville Duke. He'd worked on a wide range of Hunters and also on the Sea Fury target-tug. He then joined the Buccaneer development programme, helping to perfect the auto-pilot and the navigation-attack system. He was seconded to DH for Gyron Junior performance, surge investigation and specific fuel consumption calibration. The Buccaneer had a revolutionary boundary layer control (BLC) system that blew air at very high pressure through perforations

Blackburn NA.39 XK488 where it finished up after failing to take-off at Hatfield on 24th July 1961. *KEC*

NA.39 XK488 as many will remember it, the faithful sentinel of the FAAM entrance. *Peter Green*

in the wing skin to dramatically increase lift. For the 24th July sortie, David was to make an 'unblown' take-off; not engaging the BLC. Throttles forward, XK488 blasted off down Hatfield's runway but refused to unstick no matter what David did. He abandoned the take-off, knowing that the safety barrier would come into action. The NA.39 hit the net and a combination of 115 knots and a loaded weight of around 42,000lb combined to let XK488 shoot straight through. It careered off the end of the runway, impacting in a set of glasshouses. After the sound of breaking glass finally stopped came the realisation that neither of the crew were hurt, nor was anyone on the ground.

Buccaneers are made of stern stuff and XK488 was repaired and was with Bristol Siddeley Engines (having taken over responsibility for the Gyron Junior) at Filton, Bristol from July 1962. Its work done, XK488 was retired at Filton on 16th February 1966. The following year it was trucked to Yeovilton and started its long stint 'on duty' outside the museum.

Concorde at the Leading Edge

By the mid-1970s, the A303 just outside the northern perimeter of HMS *Heron* had morphed into the B3151 as the main road was swung northwards to bypass Ilchester. Something was needed to help attract more visitors off that dual carriageway. As related in Chapter 1, the Science Museum had been honoured with custodianship of the British prototype BAC/Sud Concorde and needed to find a venue with a suitable runway *and* the ability to show off such an icon. FAAM's Sir Donald Gosling was a major factor in convincing the Government that the museum was a credible home for 002; keeping it in the south west, close to its Filton birthplace. So, Yeovilton ticked all the boxes *and* the supersonic airliner offered a way of extending the appeal of the FAAM beyond the core of Naval aviation. Concorde 002 touched down on 4th March 1976 – see the profile below for its full pedigree.

From the earliest moments of the Concorde project, the teams at Yeovilton and South Kensington wanted to generate a visitor attraction that was not just about one particular aircraft. As an interim arrangement, *Sierra-Tango* was placed on a purpose-built 'apron' alongside the main FAAM hangar and was opened to the public on 26th July 1976. Cleverly, as part of an evolutionary expansion, this apron was to become part of the floor within the large display hall that would take G-BSST and almost quadruple the indoor floor area. The Concorde Hall was opened in July 1980, offering visitors close views of the airliner from different aspects and an incredible degree of access to the interior. Two development airframes, the Handley Page HP.115 and BAC 221 were also exhibited, extending the story of the incredible technological achievement. Yeovilton's Concorde continues to offer the best way by far to appreciate this iconic jetliner.

Cdr Dennis White 'batting' Concorde 002 on to the 'flight deck' of RNAS Yeovilton, 4th March 1976. *FAAM*

Captain Jim Flindell followed Dennis White and with Graham Mottram, who became Curator in 1983, further developed the potential of Concorde Hall, expanding it with funds from retiring Trustee Bill Regan, to include another British design and engineering triumph, the Harrier, in 1990-1991. Later still, after Graham became Director in 1995, the whole area was completely reworked with Heritage Lottery funding to produce the interpretive and 'hands-on' Leading Edge exhibition. British Aerospace at Dunsfold took on a badly damaged Sea Harrier FRS.1 in October 1995 and, by using elements of a Harrier GR.3, created a complete display airframe. This was mounted on the ski-ramp that was previously occupied by a former US Marine Corps AV-8A Harrier. (More details in the profile of Sea Harrier FA.2 XZ499 below.) Alongside was Hawker P.1127 XP980 to illustrate the earliest days of the V/STOL fighter. A skeletal Bristol Scout replica and the unflown Westland Wyvern prototype provided warplane and aerodynamic contrasts to complete Leading Edge. This was the first time that the museum availed itself of lottery funding and its £3.7 million this provided the bulk of the £5.3 million required to create the exhibition and to build Cobham Hall (of which more anon). Leading Edge opened on 10th July 2000 and that year visitors topped 100,000.

Moving Hawker P.1127 XP980 during the re-jigging of the Concorde Hall in readiness for 'Leading Edge'. *FAAM*

On deck with Carrier

Over four decades of writing on aviation heritage matters, the author has seen a large number of innovations, exhibitions and launches. Two stand out in his mind as by far and away the most ground-breaking and exciting. One of these is Carrier, which continues to give a feeling of excitement and fun with every visit. (The other is in Chapter 6!) Deputy Director Graham Mottram headed a complex project involving not just the many talents he had within the FAAM team, but a wide range of external agencies. The concept was born around 1991 with the realisation that by using a standard hangar coupled with special lighting effects, the illusion of being on the flight deck of an aircraft carrier at night could be achieved. This was extended by 'flying' visitors to that 'deck' using two specially-modified, inter-connected, Westland Wessex helicopters. Having watched a Phantom hit the reheat and blast off, visitors could tour other exhibits arranged on deck before touring the carrier's 'island', including going into 'Flyco' where the captain and his team would oversee operations. This was far from the end, with more back-projection and clever effects, the tour would be completed by descending into the 'hangar deck' on an aircraft lift. Thus filled with wonderment, youngsters from 8 to 80 leave to glimpse the museum's workshop and from there back into the rest of the museum. Carrier is sheer magic!

As Carrier evolved, the 'story' of the tight-knit, skilled, community that is at the heart of a warship became central to the presentation. Architects, special effects maestros, outfitters, builders, all needed precise co-ordination. About 18 months were expended in developmental thinking; then came two years of construction. Teams from Yeovilton could be found pulling bits off decommissioned ships that might have a direct application or act as a reference for the creation of a lighter weight replica. Speeches had to be written for the mannequin sailor that takes the role of 'guide' and for the other personnel on board. It was decided that the opening of Carrier would be a great way to celebrate the museum's 30th birthday. The incredible exhibition was opened on schedule on 28th May 1994.

Vampire LZ551 touching down on HMS *Ocean* – the first jet to land on a carrier flight deck, December 1945. *KEC*

World's biggest cupboard

Over the years FAAM has amassed an incredible amount of archive material, artefacts ranging from medals through to missiles and airframes from drones to a supersonic airliner. What most museums put on public display is but the tip of the iceberg in terms of what is held and this is certainly the case with FAAM. From the earliest days, FAAM had use of hangars at the Royal Naval Aircraft Yard (RNAY) at Wroughton, near Swindon, Wiltshire, as a large objects repository. (Wroughton is now the Science Museum's out-station, see Chapter 1 for more details.) While Wroughton was very useful, the journey from there to Yeovilton was 70-plus miles, much of it on narrow roads and aircraft moves were far from easy and only undertaken rarely. The search for an alternative to Wroughton had been underway from the mid-1980s and when the RNAY was scheduled for closure in September 1992, there was an even greater imperative to find or create a new version. Thankfully, with the Science Museum having moved in, the FAAM had some leeway and could slide from one 'landlord' to another... but this incurred significant new expense and was not a long term solution.

The ideal would be a huge storage facility at Yeovilton. This would be capable of taking entire airframes, ideally without the need to dismantle them – by their very nature most naval aircraft are of reasonable dimensions. This would allow the museum to be able to 'ring the changes' for short-term exhibitions by rolling machines out of the store and straight into display, or vice versa. Areas for keeping of archives, images and all of the other material needed to support a museum were also required. All of this need not be on the active airfield, what was needed was essentially a specialised warehouse. Suitable land was found to the north, adjacent to RNAS *Heron* and purchased from the Church Commissioners. Funding was provided by FAAM Trustee Sir Michael Cobham, who had put his support behind the search for a new store for several years and the building was named in his honour.

Cobham Hall was never going to set the blood racing over its looks, it was not intended as an architectural gem; functionality was king. As with any new 'store cupboard', empty it looked vast but as the airframes and equipment started to arrive from Wroughton it was amazing how quickly it filled! Cobham Hall was ready to receive the first airframes in the autumn of 1999 and FAAM left Wroughton completely on 16th December that year – the entire operation dovetailing seamlessly. Regular open days are staged so visitors can have the opportunity to go behind the scenes and take a look at the treasures in store. The regular changing of airframes for special events 'across the road' is a testament to the flexibility that Cobham Hall gives FAAM.

Cobham Hall in late 1999 as the main floor began to take the aircraft previously stored at Wroughton. *Ken Ellis*

Science Museum: Lifting Hawker Siddeley HS.125-1/522 G-ASSM into the Flight gallery 28th June 1992.
Science Museum

Science Museum: The Cody
Military Biplane 304, November
2012. *Ken Ellis*

Science Museum: The Roe
Triplane, April 2007. *Steve
Fletcher-Key Publishing
www.flypast.com*

Science Museum: Left to right, de
Havilland Moth G-AAAH, Cody
Military Biplane 304, Vickers Vimy,
April 2007. *Steve Fletcher-Key
Publishing www.flypast.com*

Science Museum: Avro 504K
D7560 in 'Making of the Modern
World', November 2012. *Ken Ellis*

Science Museum: Royal Aircraft
Factory SE.5a G-EBIB, November
2012. *Ken Ellis*

Below: Science Museum:
Lockheed 10A NC5171N in
'Making of the Modern World',
November 2012. *Ken Ellis*

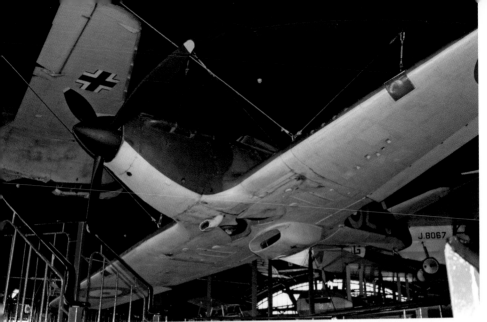

Above: Science Museum: Hawker Hurricane I L1592, November 2012. *Ken Ellis*

Science Museum: Gloster E28/39 W4041/G, November 2012. *Ken Ellis*

Below: Science Museum: Hawker P.1127 XP831, November 2012. *Ken Ellis*

Imperial War Museum South
Lambeth: Royal Aircraft Factory
BE.2c 2699, March 2012. *Ken Ellis*

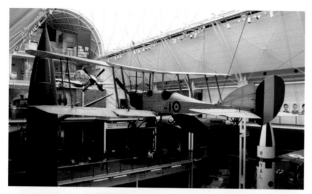

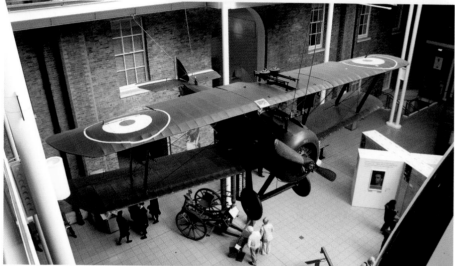

Above: Imperial War Museum
South Lambeth: Sopwith Camel
N6812, March 2012. *Ken Elli*s

Imperial War Museum South
Lambeth: North American P-51D
Mustang 472218, March 2012.
Ken Ellis

Left: Shuttleworth Collection: Blackburn Monoplane G-AANI, October 1982. *Alf Jenks*

Middle: Shuttleworth Collection: Blériot XI G-AANG, August 1998. *Alf Jenks*

Bottom: Shuttleworth Collection: Sopwith Triplane replica N6290, September 2005. *Alf Jenks*

Shuttleworth Collection: Avro 504K H5199, July 2009. *Alf Jenks*

Above: Shuttleworth Collection: De Havilland Moth G-EBWD, July 2009. *Alf Jenks*

Shuttleworth Collection: Comper Swift G-ACTF, September 2012. *Alf Jenks*

Above: Shuttleworth Collection: De Havilland DH.88 Comet G-ACSS, September 1989. *Alf Jenks*

Left: Shuttleworth Collection: Hawker Sea Hurricane I Z7015, May 2011. *Alf Jenks*

Below: Shuttleworth Collection: Supermarine Spitfire V AR501, May 1994. *Alf Jenks*

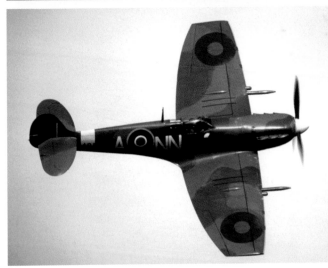

Above: Fleet Air Arm Museum:
The Science Museum's Short 184
8359 in its display case, May 2012.
Terry Dann

Right: Fleet Air Arm Museum:
Fairey Swordfish II 'W5984',
August 1970. *Alf Jenks*

Below: Fleet Air Arm Museum:
Fairey Fulmar II N1854, June 1975.
Alf Jenks

Fleet Air Arm Museum: Grumman Martlet I AL246 inside the conservation workshop, November 2012. *Terry Dann*

Above: Fleet Air Arm Museum: Grumman Avenger ECM.6B XB446, November 2012. *Terry Dann*

Left: Fleet Air Arm Museum: The Science Museum's de Havilland Sea Vampire I LZ551/G, inside 'Carrier', November 2012. *Terry Dann*

Fleet Air Arm Museum: Agusta
A.109A AE-331, November 2012.
Ken Ellis

Fleet Air Arm Museum: Westland
Sea King HAS.6 XZ574, November
2012. *Ken Ellis*

Below: Fleet Air Arm Museum:
Westland Lynx HAS.3GMS XZ720,
November 2012. *Ken Ellis*

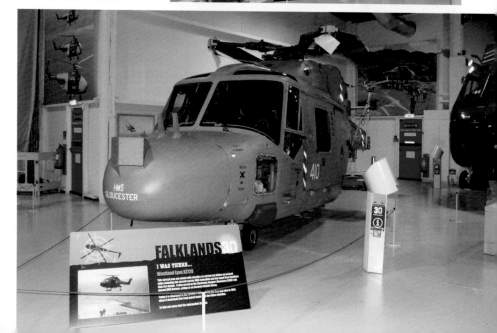

Above: Fleet Air Arm Museum: McDonnell Phantom FG.1 XT596, inside 'Carrier', September 2005. *Fleet Air Arm Museum*

Left: Fleet Air Arm Museum: Hawker Siddeley Sea Harrier FA.2 XZ499, November 2012. *Ken Ellis*

Below: Fleet Air Arm Museum: The Science Museum's BAC/Sud Concorde 002 G-BSST inside 'Leading Edge', June 2008. Bristol Scout D replica N5419, BAC 221 WG774 and Hawker Hunter T.8M XL580 in the foreground. *Alf Jenks*

Royal Air Force Museum Hendon: Sopwith Triplane N5912 inside the Grahame-White Factory, March 2008. *Alf Jenks*

Royal Air Force Museum Hendon: Sopwith Dolphin C3988 inside the Grahame-White Factory, October 2012. *Alf Jenks*

Below: Royal Air Force Museum Hendon: Sopwith Snipe E6655, at Old Warden October 2012. *Terry Dann*

Royal Air Force Museum Hendon: Airco DH.9A F1010, April 2010. *Alf Jenks*

Below: Royal Air Force Museum Hendon: Fokker D.VII 8417/18 inside 'Milestones of Flight', September 2012. *Ken Ellis*

Royal Air Force Museum Hendon: Bristol Bulldog IIA K2227, April 2010. *Alf Jenks*

Above: Royal Air Force Museum Hendon: Supermarine Stranraer 920, April 2010. *Alf Jenks*

Right: Royal Air Force Museum Hendon: Fiat CR-42 Falco MM5701 inside the Battle of Britain Experience, March 2008. *Alf Jenks*

Below: Royal Air Force Museum Hendon: Hawker Hurricane I P3175 inside the Battle of Britain Experience, September 2012. *Ken Ellis*

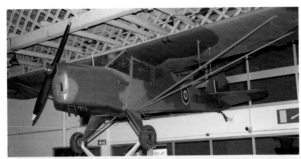

Royal Air Force Museum Hendon:
Auster I LB264, April 2010. *Alf Jenks*

Above: Royal Air Force Museum
Hendon: Boeing B-17G Flying
Fortress 44-83868 inside the
Bomber Command Hall, April
2009. *Alf Jenks*

Royal Air Force Museum Hendon:
North American P-51D Mustang
413317 inside 'Milestones of
Flight', September 2012. *Ken Ellis*

Royal Air Force Museum Hendon:
McDonnell Phantom FGR.2 XV424,
October 2005. *Alf Jenks*

Right: Royal Air Force Museum
Hendon: Panavia Tornado F.3 ZE887,
November 2010. *RAF Museum*

Below: Royal Air Force Museum
Hendon: Eurofighter Typhoon DA2
ZH588 and Lockheed-Martin F-35
full-size model inside 'Milestones
of Flight', November 2010.
RAF Museum

Royal Air Force Museum Hendon:
Bristol Belvedere HC.1 XG474,
October 2005. *Alf Jenks*

Above: Royal Air Force Museum
Hendon: Westland Wessex HCC.4
XV732, April 2010. *Alf Jenks*

Left: Royal Air Force Museum
Hendon: EHI EH-101 PP8 ZJ116,
March 2008. *Alf Jenks*

Above: Royal Air Force Museum Cosford: CASA 352L (Ju 52) G-AFAP, July 2005. *Ken Ellis*

Royal Air Force Museum Cosford: Kawasaki Ki-100-1b 16336, May 2012. *Terry Dann*

Royal Air Force Museum Cosford: Douglas Dakota C.4 KN645 inside the National Cold War Exhibition, June 2011. *Ken Ellis*

Royal Air Force Museum Cosford:
Avro Lincoln B.2/4A RF398,
November 2009. *Alf Jenks*

Above: Royal Air Force Museum
Cosford: Gloster F9/40 Meteor
DG202/G, June 2011. *Ken Ellis*

Royal Air Force Museum Cosford:
De Havilland Comet 1XB G-APAS,
June 2012. *Ken Ellis*

Above: Royal Air Force Museum Cosford: Vickers Valiant BK.1 XD818 inside the National Cold War Exhibition, May 2012. *Terry Dann*

Right: Royal Air Force Museum Cosford: Hunting Jet Provost T.1 XD674, November 2012. *Alf Jenks*

Below: Royal Air Force Museum Cosford: Bristol 188 XF926 and Sikorsky MH-53M 68-8284, May 2009. Note Lockheed SP-2H Neptune 204 in the background. *RAF Museum*

Royal Air Force Museum Cosford:
Hawker Siddeley Dominie T.1
XS709, June 2012. *Ken Ellis*

Above: Royal Air Force Museum
Cosford: Hawker Siddeley Andover
E.3A XS639 and Scottish Aviation
Bulldog T.1 XX654, November 2009.
Alf Jenks

Royal Air Force Museum Cosford:
Short Belfast C.1 XR371 in the
National Cold War Exhibition, May
2012. *Terry Dann*

Above: Imperial War Museum Duxford: General view of 'AirSpace' with English Electric Canberra B.2 WH725 to the fore, July 2011. *Ken Ellis*

Right: Imperial War Museum Duxford: Fairey Gannet ECM.6 XG797, April 1988. *Alf Jenks*

Below: Imperial War Museum Duxford: British Aerospace Harrier GR.9A ZD461 (destined for South Lambeth), July 2012. *Terry Dann*

Imperial War Museum Duxford: Duxford Aviation Society's Airspeed Ambassador 2 G-ALZO, July 2012. *Terry Dann*

Imperial War Museum Duxford: Duxford Aviation Society's Vickers Viscount 701 G-ALWF, April 1988. *Alf Jenks*

Imperial War Museum Duxford: Duxford Aviation Society's Bristol Britannia 312 G-AOVT, April 1988. *Alf Jenks*

Ulster Folk and Transport Museum: Short SC.1 XG905, September 2011. *Ken Ellis*

Above: Ulster Aviation Collection: English Electric Canberra PR.9 XH131 ready to be unveiled, September 2011. *Ken Ellis*

Ulster Aviation Collection: Hawker Siddeley Buccaneer S.2B XV361, September 2011. *Ken Ellis*

National Museum of Flight Scotland: View of the main display hangar, June 2002. Left to right: Piper Comanche G-ATOY, Miles Monarch G-AFJU, the Pilcher Hawk, GAL Cygnet G-AGBN. *Ken Ellis*

National Museum of Flight Scotland: Scottish Aviation Twin Pioneer Series 2 G-BBVF, June 2002. *Ken Ellis*

National Museum of Flight Scotland: De Havilland Comet 4C G-BDIX, October 2006. *Ken Ellis*

National Museum of Flight
Scotland: English Electric Lightning
F.2A XN776, June 2002. *Ken Ellis*

Below: National Museum of Flight
Scotland: Hawker Siddeley Harrier
GR.1 XV277, June 2002. *Ken Ellis*

Bottom: National Museum of
Flight Scotland: BAC/Concorde 102
G-BOAA, October 2006. *Ken Ellis*

Imperial War Museum Duxford: Fairchild A-10A Thunderbolt II 77-0259, Boeing PT-17 Kaydet 27786 and Republic P-47D Thunderbolt 226413 in the American Air Museum, July 2011. *Ken Ellis*

Under the paint

Currently inside the workshop is Grumman Martlet AL246 – see the profile below. It is the second machine to undergo a painstaking and innovative process that the author believes is so far unique to FAAM. Yeovilton's Curator of Aircraft and Chief Engineer is Dave Morris, who joined the museum as an apprentice engineer in 1981. He and his team have developed an exacting technique of peeling back paint to uncover the past. Certain airframes lend themselves to being returned to their original paintwork, presuming it survives beneath the later layers. This is *restoration* in the truest sense of the word.

In November 1999 Corsair IV KD431 was rolled into the workshop. Dave and his crew decided to pioneer a 'whole aircraft' method of paintwork conservation. As will be seen in the profile below, KD431 arrived at Yeovilton in June 1963. It was hastily given a 'top coat' so that it could appear in the static at the Air Day that month, after that it was handed on to the museum. Inch by inch, layer by layer, that hastily-applied paint job was removed. Underneath was as near to original condition from 1944 as it is possible to achieve. Markings, stencilling, even scratches and scuffs were revealed. The Yeovilton team had unpeeled the Corsair's 1944 reality and unveiled it on 9th August 2005. Dave Morris wrote *Corsair KD431: The Time Capsule Fighter* which was published in 2006 by Sutton in association with FAAM. It remains a seminal study of the application of aviation history, the meaning of markings and the wealth of information that can come from even the smallest of details.

Now going through the same intense scrutiny is Grumman Martlet I AL246. Once again a well-meant but inaccurate paint scheme is coming off with the hope of revealing the markings of a very rare survivor – see the profile for AL246's pedigree. As this was being written it is best not to steal the thunder of what the team is discovering, but when the work is complete it should cast considerable light on the marking conventions of the early days of World War Two. The experience gained during the investigation of the Corsair has brought Dave and the team into contact with other bodies that can help, including Bournemouth University's School of Conservation Science.

With heightened awareness that colour schemes are as much in need of conservation as turbine blades, a decision has already been made about the latest FAAM exhibit, Harrier GR.9A ZD433. This joined FAAM on 20th December 2011, having come from Cottesmore, the former home of Joint Force Harrier. The GR.9A was fresh off active service at Kandahar in Afghanistan and wearing the colours of the RAF's 1 Squadron but was also crewed by 800 Squadron FAA. The nose carries detailed mission tallies and other markings from its time in Afghanistan. When given the choice of a GR.9A for the FAAM Dave Morris could have picked a newly-overhauled, spick-and-span example, but his eyes were drawn to the 'war weary' look of ZD433 and its 'scoreboard' on the nose. This Harrier will be conserved 'as is', a 'time capsule' with the museum from Day 1. To emphasize this status, the crew at Yeovilton have nicknamed ZD433 'Dirty Harry'!

Corsair IV KD431 in the museum workshop in 2003 as it began to reveal its wartime colours and codes. *Ken Ellis*

Harrier GR.9A ZD433, otherwise known as 'Dirty Harry'. *FAAM*

BAC 221 WG774
1955 | Single-seat high-speed ogee wing test-bed | One 9,300lb st Rolls-Royce Avon 28

The author's enthusiasm for the exhibition centred *around* Concorde at Yeovilton is vented in the introduction to this chapter. One of the reasons for this is because it tells a much wider picture and includes some of the other aircraft used to pave the way for the supersonic transport. One of these is the BAC 221, standing on stalky undercarriage and boasting a wing shape very close to Concorde. This fascinating machine has a 'dual personality' having started life as the Fairey FD.2, but radically re-engineered in the early 1960s.

Responding to an experimental requirement for a high-speed delta research platform issued in September 1950, Fairey designed the Avon-powered FD.2 and received a contract to build two examples at Hayes. Long before Concorde was ever thought of, a 'droop snoot' tilting the cockpit and nose down by 10-degrees allowed for a better view on approach to land. Test pilot Peter Twiss was at the controls for the first flight of FD.2 WG774 at Boscombe Down on 6th October 1955. Twenty-two days later, the sleek delta went supersonic and hopes were high that this was a potential record-breaker. As related graphically in his superb autobiography, *Faster than the Sun*, the 17th November 1955 was a challenging day. At 30,000ft or so, a good 30 miles out from Boscombe, Peter found that all had gone quiet. Fuel starvation had made the Avon stutter and die. A 'twitchy' aircraft with the power on, Peter was rapidly evaluating its gliding characteristics and trying to 'find' home base through the cloud. Six miles out from Boscombe he discovered that WG774's long nose was pointing directly at the runway. He made a successful landing, without the luxury of the 'droop snoot' or airbrakes and was presented with a Queen's Commendation for his determination. Operating out of Boscombe on 10th March 1956 Peter and WG774 combined to seize the World Absolute Airspeed Record at an astonishing 1,132mph, crushing, by 310mph, the previous record held by an American F-100 Super Sabre. In the month beforehand, Peter had flown WG777, the second FD.2. This was used alongside WG774 by the Royal Aircraft Establishment (RAE) at Thurleigh, for high-speed research. 'Triple-seven' was retired in June 1966 and is now on display at the RAF Museum Cosford.

On 5th September 1959, WG774 was ferried from Bedford to Filton, Bristol, and disappeared into the huge hangar in which the monstrous Bristol Brabazon airliner had been built in 1949. Here the FD.2 was treated to radical surgery so that it could have a new life as the BAC 221, a high-speed test-bed for the ogee

Above: Fairey Delta 2 WG774 in the guise that it wore after achieving the World Air Speed Record, 10th March 1956. *KEC*

Right: Fabulous angle on the unpainted BAC 221 WG774 when it was shown off to the press at Filton early in 1964. *BAC*

wing planned for Concorde. It was given an entirely new wing and long-stroke undercarriage requiring considerable re-engineering. Now, there is no denying this was a vital research project, but the author has never been able to figure why it was that the record-breaking WG774 was chosen and not WG777. There *has* to be a valid engineering reason; let it *not* be a case of nobody with an eye to heritage, or a short memory...

In its radically new configuration, WG774 had its maiden flight from Filton on 1st May 1964 and was used by the British Aircraft Corporation for trials before moving on to the Aero Flight at RAE on 20th May 1966. The 221 was grounded at Thurleigh after 273 sorties on 9th June 1973 and the following year was roaded to East Fortune in Scotland for display at the Museum of Flight. It travelled south in January 1980, coming to the FAAM to complement Concorde 002.

BAC/Sud Concorde 002 G-BSST
1969 | Supersonic airliner prototype | Four 34,730lb st Rolls-Royce/SNECMA Olympus 593-3B | On loan from the Science Museum

With test pilot Brian Trubshaw at the controls, the prototype British-built Concorde G-BSST touched down at Yeovilton for the 438th and final time on 4th March 1976. Fifty-three days earlier, the type's commercial life had begun with a simultaneous inauguration by Air France and British Airways from Charles de Gaulle and Heathrow airports, respectively. (Kicking off the Concorde era for BA was G-BOAA now preserved at East Fortune – see Chapter 10.) In Chapter 1, the Science Museum's role and background is outlined and in the narrative above, there is more on the subject.

The second Concorde prototype, and the first to be assembled in the UK, G-BSST was rolled out at Filton, Bristol, in September 1968 for extensive ground tests. (The specially-granted out-of-sequence civil registration – a rare thing in 1968 – stood for: 'Great Britain's Super Sonic Transport.') Piloted by Trubshaw, it took off on its maiden voyage on 9th April 1969 and landed at Fairford, which had been set aside for flight testing. Mach 2, twice the speed of sound, was reached during the 57th sortie on 12th November 1970. The test fleet notched up 'firsts' and 'greatests' with regularity; 002 achieving the 'highest' on 1st January 1971, reaching 57,700ft. A marketing tour in the summer of 1972 took it on a 12-country excursion, including Singapore, Japan and Australia. South Africa was its next overseas venue in early 1973 for 'hot and high' trials at Johannesburg. Back in the UK, G-BSST switched from the tropical to testing the de-icing system. These were conducted by flying behind tanker-configured English Electric Canberra B2/8 hybrid WV787 of the Aeroplane & Armament Experimental Establishment. (WV787 is today at the Newark Air Museum, one of a number of aircraft directly involved in the development of Concorde. The BAC 221 – profiled above – and HP.115 – below – being other examples.)

The test schedule for 002 was completed on 10th April 1975 when it was put into temporary storage at Fairford while the debate about its final resting place was finalised. Flights 435 and 436 were also spent in close formation with another aircraft, a Hawker Siddeley HS.125, to assess the wake turbulence characteristics of the delta-winged airliner. *Sierra-Tango's* penultimate excursion was in front of the crowds at the Weston-super-Mare airshow on 26th August 1975. This very nearly ended in disaster. Test pilot John Cochrane noted that 'three greens' were not registering; the port undercarriage leg appeared not to have locked in the 'down' position. Cochrane brought 002 gingerly 'over the numbers' at Fairford, letting it down gently and successfully. A stay on the main undercarriage leg had failed when the gear was deployed in a relatively tight turn; 'mods' were introduced across the fleet. So, to the final flight, to Yeovilton, and the completion of 723½ flying hours, 173½ of which had been at beyond the speed of sound.

Blackburn Buccaneer S.1 XN957
1963 | Two-crew carrier-borne strike | Two 7,100lb st de Havilland Gyron Junior 101

Built at Brough on the Humber, Buccaneer S.1 XN957 was roaded to Holme-on-Spalding Moor and test flown on 3rd April 1963. It was issued to 801 Squadron at Lossiemouth, Scotland, on 10th May 1963. 'Lossie' was destined to be XN957's only operational shore base. With 801, regular deployments were made to the carrier HMS *Victorious*. From January 1965, XN957 moved across the ramp to 809 Squadron, regularly embarking upon *Hermes*. This assignment lasted until 27th March when XN957 was put on charge with the Jet Strike Training unit, 736 Squadron. A serious engine problem in March 1966 put the Buccaneer out of commission. It was first taken to the Royal Naval Aircraft Yard at Sydenham, Belfast, then to Lossiemouth's Naval Aircraft Support Unit, until re-joining 736 on 3rd August 1966. It was retired from service on 26th February 1971 and on 19th November 1971 joined the FAAM. See the narrative at the beginning of this chapter for details of the museum's long-serving NA.39 Buccaneer development machine and Chapter 5, the RAF Museum Hendon, for a profile of a Spey-powered S.2.

British Aerospace Sea Harrier FA.2 XZ499
1981 | Single-seat carrier-borne V/STOL fighter | One 21,500lb st Rolls-Royce Pegasus 104

The story of the incredible and much missed Harrier is told via the profiles of several stepping stones in the history of the vertical/short take-off and landing (V/STOL) miracle: The P.1127 prototype at the Science Museum (Chapter 1) and the much-evolved GR.9A at RAF Museum Cosford (Chapter 6). With respect to the air and ground crews of the RAF GR.3s that took part in Operation CORPORATE, the Falklands campaign, it is the image of the Sea Harriers that dominates the air war. Yeovilton has 'pointed nose' FRS.1 XZ493 on show within the Leading Edge exhibition. It has a Falklands era outline and indeed went down to the South Atlantic on HMS *Invincible*, in April 1982, but saw no action. It is a composite, having the forward fuselage of XZ493 and much of GR.3 XV760. FA.2 XZ499, however, has a far better provenance.

Test flown at Dunsfold for the first time on 12th June 1981, FRS.1 XZ499 joined 801 Squadron at Yeovilton on 16th June 1981, transferring to 809 in April 1982. On the 30th it was flown to Banjul in Gambia, en route to Ascension Island, arriving there the following day. The Sea Harrier ('SHAR' in Naval parlance) transferred to the *Atlantic Conveyor* for the cruise to the Falklands Exclusion Zone, before settling on the deck of the CORPORATE command vessel, the carrier HMS *Hermes*, on 18th May. Just 72 hours later, Lt M Hale got an Argentine IAI Dagger fighter in his sights and unleashed an AIM-9L Sidewinder heat-seeking missile, but it blew up prematurely. Next day, Hale attacked a patrol boat, the *Rio Iguazu*. On the 8th June Lt D A Smith was at the helm of XZ499 and succeeded in getting an AIM-9L to lock-on to Douglas A-4B Skyhawk C-204, shooting it out of the sky and killing its pilot. After 38 combat sorties XZ499 returned on the *Hermes* to the UK in July 1982. With 809 Squadron, it joined the carrier *Illustrious* for a cruise to the Falklands and back, August to October 1982, gaining the name *Ethel* on the nose. SHARs moved around units at quite a rate and XZ499 had short stays with all of the Yeovilton-based frontline units, 800, 801 and 899. In March 1996 it was returned to Dunsfold for transformation to FA.2 status. It first flew in the new guise on 28th July 1998, but was placed into store at St Athan on completion. It was issued to 801 Squadron at Yeovilton on 7th November 2000 until it was retired on 20th June 2002. Towed across to Cobham Hall on 13th November 2002, it started its life with FAAM.

Chance Vought Corsair IV KD431
1944 | Single-seat carrier-borne fighter | One 2,250hp Pratt & Whitney R-2800-8 Double Wasp

Corsair IVs were the equivalent of the US Navy's FG-1D and KD431 was first flown by Goodyear test pilot C J Clarke at Akron, Ohio, on 22nd August 1944. Shipped across the Atlantic, KD431 was accepted by Lockheed at Renfrew, Glasgow, for preparation for service. It was June 1945 before this Corsair was issued to an operational unit, 1835 Squadron at Eglinton, Northern Ireland. On the last day of July it was loaded on to the carrier HMS *Patroller* at Sydenham Docks, Belfast, bound for the war with Japan. At 08:15 on 6th August, as *Patroller* continued to provision, accept personnel and prepare to sail, Boeing B-29 *Enola Gay* dropped an atomic bomb on the city of Hiroshima, Japan, and the era of nuclear apocalypse had dawned. Orders had been given that *Patroller* was not to weigh anchor and by the 8th, KD431 had been lifted off its deck and towed back to adjacent Sydenham airfield. Next day, Nagasaki was hit with another atomic weapon and six days later Japan surrendered and World War Two was at an end. The Corsair stayed in Northern Ireland, joining 768 Squadron at Ballyhalbert in September and it was involved in deck-landing practises on HMS *Premier*. No.768 Squadron moved to East Haven in Scotland on 25th October 1945, and KD431 took on the code letters 'E2-M'. By early January 1946, its flying days were over and it was in store at Donibristle.

Acquired by the College of Aeronautics at Cranfield, the fighter moved south by road and by 3rd July 1946 it was assembled, taking its place in the famous 'Library of Flight' as a teaching aid. With the pace accelerating to open the FAAM, Admiralty approval was given to transfer KD431 to Yeovilton and it arrived in June 1963, appearing at the station's Air Day that month. In readiness for this 'stardom', KD431 was given a 'top coat' paint job prior to handing on to the museum. As is detailed at the beginning of this chapter, in November 1999 the Corsair was rolled into the workshop where Curator of Aircraft, Dave Morris, and his team carefully stripped back the layers of paint to reveal the hoped-for 'time capsule' of its finish in 1944. Complete with scuffs and dents, on 9th August 2005 the Corsair IV was unveiled and put back on display. Dave and his team are repeating the process with the Grumman Martlet – see below.

De Havilland Vampire 1 LZ551/G
1944 | Single-seat jet fighter prototype | One 2,700lb st de Havilland Goblin II | On loan from the Science Museum

Geoffrey de Havilland JNR sat inside the small moulded plywood shell that constituted the 'fuselage' of LZ548, the prototype DH.100 and eased it into the air at Hatfield on 29th September 1943. This was the third jet aircraft type to fly in the UK – the others being the Gloster E28/39 (see Chapter 1) and the Gloster Meteor (see Chapter 5). The DH.100 was originally to have been called the Spider Crab, but common sense prevailed with the far more pugnacious choice – Vampire. Intended as the second to fly was LZ551, but this honour was taken by MP838. No matter, LZ551 had another piece of history awaiting it.

With a forward slash and a 'G' at the end of its serial number, denoting it was to be guarded at all times when not flying, DH.100 LZ551/G had its maiden flight on 17th March 1944. Then it was back into the factory where it was 'navalised', principally with increased flap area, lengthened travel in the undercarriage and – most importantly – an arrester hook at the end of an A-frame attached to the centre section. It re-flew in this guise on 23rd August 1945. Fifteen days later the little twin-boom jet was despatched to the Royal Aircraft Establishment (RAE) at Farnborough, for arrester trials. On 26th November, LZ551/G was issued to RNAS *Peregrine*, Ford, Sussex, which had Aerodrome Dummy Deck Landing (ADDLs) training equipment and runway markings.

At Hatfield on 19th May 1945 famed naval test pilot Lt Cdr Eric M 'Winkle' Brown strapped himself into a Vampire at Hatfield for a familiarisation flight. He was well versed with jets, and had even flown the Messerschmitt Me 163 rocket-plane, and was busy evaluating which type would be best for potential use by the Fleet Air Arm (FAA). After sampling de Havilland's little jet, he knew this one was the winner. Next step was to see what it would behave like flown on and off a carrier – something no jet had done at the time. Eric went down to Ford on 2nd December and took up LZ551/G for ADDLs. In his superb book *Wings on My Sleeve*, Eric laconically describes this preparation for an historic event: "...did just one brief ten-minute session of ADDLs, and put my Vampire on ice in the hangar." The following day, Eric and the Vampire were awaited by the Captain and crew of HMS *Ocean*. Commanding the trials carrier was Caspar John – more of him in the profile of Hellcat KE209 below. At 11:28 local on the 3rd the hook of LZ551/G engaged with *Ocean*'s arrester wire No.1, an over-deck wind of 42 knots having reduced the landing speed to a mere 41.4 knots. 'Winkle' and LZ551 made a comfortable arrival, having achieved the world's first landing on an aircraft carrier by a jet. To prove it was no fluke Eric performed another three landings that day and, on the 6th, made it all look so unremarkable with eight more take-offs and landings. The Vampire returned to Farnborough that afternoon for stress tests on the arrester gear. From 19th January 1946 LZ551/G was on charge with the Aeroplane & Armament Experimental Establishment (A&AEE), Boscombe Down, carrying out ADDLs and 24 landings and take-off from HMS *Triumph*.

On 6th June 1946 LZ551/G joined the FAA, going to 778 Squadron at Ford which had the dual brief of Service Trials Unit and Carrier Trials Unit. The Vampire was back with RAE on 10th January 1947 for over-run barrier tests. But its flying life was fast running out and on 13th August it was struck off charge. Thankfully, 34 days later it was bought by a heritage-aware de Havilland and *probably* kept at Hatfield. In October 1949 it was gifted to the Science Museum and was stored at Waddon, Surrey; there being no available space to show it off – see Chapter 1. With the opening of the FAAM, the opportunity to put a round peg in a round hole was realised and LZ551/G moved to Yeovilton in 1966. Today it has pride of place alongside the 'island' on the flight deck of Carrier.

Personnel gather around Vampire LZ551/G after its landing on HMS *Ocean*, 3rd December 1945. *KEC*

De Havilland Sea Venom FAW.22 WW138
1955 | Two-crew all-weather carier-borne fighter | One 5,300lb st de Havilland Ghost 105

Yeovilton's Sea Venom is painted in the yellow and black stripes used as a ready identifier for aircraft involved in Operation MUSKETEER, the Suez campaign of November 1956. Built at Christchurch, Dorset, as an FAW.21 WW138 was issued to 809 Squadron at Yeovilton on 3rd May 1955, then embarking on HMS *Ark Royal* for a cruise to Malta. The unit was shore based at Ta Qali and then Hal Far from 14th November. Its life on Malta was curtailed just 18 days later when a runway accident put WW138 out of commission. It was returned to the UK and in June 1959 was at the Royal Naval Aircraft Yard Sydenham, Belfast, where it was upgraded to Mk.22 configuration by replacing its Ghost 104 turbojet with a higher-rated Series 105. It was returned to service on 11th January 1961 with the electronic warfare specialist 831 Squadron at Culdrose, before moving to Watton in 1962. No.831 disbanded in May 1966 and WW138 transferred a year later to the Airwork-operated Air Direction Training Unit at Yeovilton. Struck off charge on 4th September 1969, WW138 was taken on by the FAAM.

De Havilland Sea Vixen FAW.2 XS590
1966 | Two-crew all-weather carrier-borne interceptor/strike | Two 11,250lb st Rolls-Royce Avon 208

When the test pilot put the throttles forward on FAW.2 XS590 at Hawarden, near Chester, for its first flight on 3rd February 1966, he brought the production history of the Sea Vixen to a close; for this was the last new-build example. Cleared for service by the FAA, XS590 joined 892 Squadron at Yeovilton on 5th March. When not flying from its Somerset headquarters, 892 deployed to HMS *Hermes*. Use with 892 was brief, with XS590 going into store, in turn, at Yeovilton, Belfast and then Brawdy. On 12th March 1969 it was back at Yeovilton and in frontline trim, issued to 899 Squadron, which spent plenty of time on *Eagle*. The Naval Aircraft Support Unit (NASU) at Yeovilton accepted XS590 for long-term storage on 16th April 1970, the Sea Vixen having clocked up 789 flying hours. On 26th November 1970 it was allocated to FAAM, but it was not until the spring of the following year that is was trundled out of NASU and handed over.

Sea Vixen FAW.2 XS589 carrying out 'buddy-buddy' refuelling with fellow 892 Squadron machine XS590 – now with the FAA Museum. *KEC*

Fairey Swordfish II 'P4139'
1943 | Two/three crew torpedo-spotter-reconnaissance biplane | One 750hp Bristol Pegasus XXX

Appearing wholly inadequate in a world increasingly dominated by nimble monoplanes, the Swordfish is the stuff of legend. It outlasted the Albacore, its intended replacement. The combat exploits of Swordfish crews are too many to do justice here; but four iconic incidents head the list of exceptional valour: Battle of Narvik April 1940, Battle of Taranto November 1940, sinking the *Bismarck* May 1941; the 'Channel Dash' February 1942.

Built by Blackburn at Sherburn-in-Elmet, Swordfish II HS618 was accepted by the FAA on 30th April 1943 and it joined 834 Squadron at Donibristle, Scotland, the following month. Its operational career was cut short inside the hangar deck of the escort carrier HMS *Hunter* during the night of 4-5th August 1943 in the heat of an intense gale. Lashed-down Seafires broke loose, smashing against the biplane. In an amazing survival story, HS618 could have been thrown overboard to free up space, but instead it 'surfaces' next in 1960 as instructional airframe A2001 at the Royal Naval Engineering College at Manadon. It was with the FAAM by 1962 and has worn several different colour schemes and identities.

Fairey Fulmar II N1854
1939 | Two-crew carrier-borne fighter | One 1,300hp Rolls-Royce Merlin 30F

The first true Fulmar, N1854, flew at Ringway (now Manchester Airport) on 4th January 1940. It was used for trials, initially with Fairey, then briefly at the Royal Aircraft Establishment, Farnborough, in May 1940 before moving on to the Aeroplane & Armament Experimental Establishment at Boscombe Down, for performance trials. In December 1940 it returned to Fairey and was converted into a Mk.II by fitting a Merlin 30. It was put to good use by the company for trials and communications; the rear compartment being fitted with two seats. It was registered as G-AIBE in July 1946 and continued in use for 'comms', wearing Fairey house colours of blue and silver but was repainted in wartime camouflage in June 1959. Its last flight came on 18th December 1962 when it was donated to the Fleet Air Arm at Lossiemouth. The world's only surviving Fulmar moved to Yeovilton to join the museum on 22nd September 1972.

Fairey Firefly TT.1 Z2033
1944 | Two-crew ship-borne fighter/strike/reconnaissance I One 1,990hp Rolls-Royce Griffon XII

A bright yellow Firefly I entered the circuit at Staverton, near Gloucester, on 5th May 1964, creating quite a stir, because it was an 'international' flight from Gothenburg and it was taking up residence. Swedish civil registered as SE-BRD it was joining the pioneering Skyfame Museum. It was re-registered as G-ASTL on 1st June and quickly given FAA colours and the name *Sir Richard Fairey*. Built at Heaton Chapel in Manchester and test flown from Ringway (now Manchester Airport), it was issued to the FAA as Z2033 in April 1944, joining 731 Squadron at East Haven, Scotland, in March 1945. Reconditioned as a TT.1 target-tug, it was delivered to Svensk Flygtjanst AB for contract work with the Royal Swedish Air Force in March 1949.

Fulmar II G-AIBE at Heston in April 1947, with Fireflies in the background. *KEC*

Firefly TT.1 Z2033 *Evelyn Tentions* arriving at Yeovilton from Duxford, July 2000. *FAAM*

Replacing its Fireflies with Douglas Skyraiders, the Swedish company was happy to respond to the pleas of Skyfame's Peter Thomas and presented SE-BRD to the museum. As related in the companion volume *Lost Aviation Collections of Great Britain*, Skyfame closed its doors in January 1978. A rescue of most of the airframes was staged by the Imperial War Museum and they were moved in an exceptional operation to Duxford. There, Z2033 was refurbished and painted in the colours of DK431 *Evelyn Tentions* of 1771 Squadron serving on HMS *Implacable* in August 1945, while retaining its original serial number. It moved to FAAM at Yeovilton on 25th July 2000, joining TT.4 VH127 which had been with the collection since November 1972.

Fairey Gannet AEW.3 XL503
1961 | Three-crew carrier-borne early warning I One 3,875hp Armstrong Siddeley Double Mamba 102

Developed as an advanced anti-submarine aircraft, the Gannet was also dramatically re-thought to turn it into the airborne radar picket Mk.3. Its first incarnation, the sub-hunter airframe, is dealt with in Chapter 8, the Imperial War Museum Duxford. For many AEW.3s service was hard-working, but from a 'life history' point of view it can be summarized as: issue to the various flights of 849 Squadron with embarkations on carriers. The FAAM example followed much of this pattern, but was also involved in trials early in its life and radar training in its twilight years. Built at Hayes in Middlesex, it was taken by road to White Waltham and had its maiden flight on 13th April 1961. It was retained by Fairey for trials before being released to the Aeroplane & Armament Experimental Establishment (A&AEE) at Boscombe Down, on 8th October 1963 for canopy jettison tests. In October 1963 it was briefly at Culdrose for radar assessment with 849 Squadron. Then came a spell with the Royal Aircraft Establishment at Thurleigh in April 1964, using the airfield's catapult and arrester gear. Very probably XL503's first carrier embarkation occurred in July 1964 with an A&AEE crew performing single-engined 'bolters' on HMS *Eagle*. A 'bolter' is naval parlance for a 'missed approach' or a 'go-around'. While appearing to be a *single*-engined aircraft, the Gannet was powered by a *Double* Mamba turboprop driving counter-rotating propellers – one behind the other using a shared drive-shaft and spinner – via a gearbox. For

Gannet AEW.3 XL503 with 849 Squadron's 'D' Flight while shore-based at Brawdy, or embarked upon HMS *Eagle*, 1969. *MAP*

long-endurance patrols, the Gannet was designed to shut one Mamba down, with the 'live' engine driving one of propeller assemblies. Full release to 849 Squadron, with 'A' Flight at Brawdy, was achieved on 26th May 1966. Life with 849 continued for the next seven years, including time afloat on HMS *Victorious*, *Hermes* and *Eagle*, in turn. From 5th October 1971 XL503 was attached to the Royal Radar Establishment (RRE), headquartered at Pershore, to help train RAF crews for Avro Shackleton AEW.3s which were using AN/APS 20 radars extracted from Gannets – see Chapter 5. It was back with RRE for six months the following year, this time helping with radar recording kit. On 12th July 1972 XL503 was back with 849 Squadron at Lossiemouth, but the wind-down of the type was well in hand; it flew to its new home with FAAM on 26th April 1973.

Grumman Martlet I AL246
1940 | Single-seat fighter | One 1,200hp Wright Cyclone G205A

After having toured the incredible Carrier exhibition, visitors vacate via a lift that takes them past the workshops. A wall of glass, the length of the 'shop, allows great views of the work going on within. As explained at the beginning of this chapter, currently receiving meticulous attention inside is Martlet AL246. This is receiving the now well-established layer-upon-layer 'paint archaeology' treatment. Martlet Is were diverted from a French order for 32 land-based fighters and had fixed wings, four 0.5in machine-guns in the wings and were powered by a Wright Cyclone. From the Mk.II through to the VI all had folding wings, and Pratt & Whitney R-1830s. This makes the FAAM's example a very distinctive survivor.

Built at Bethpage, New York, the British Purchasing Commission accepted AL246 on 22nd August 1940 and it was received at Scottish Aviation, Prestwick, near Ayr, on 22nd November, after having crossed the Atlantic by ship. It was issued to 802 Squadron on 10th December, transferring to 882 Squadron on 18th July 1941, both units being based at Donibristle. No.882 moved to Machrihanish, near Campbelltown, on 17th March 1942 in readiness for embarking upon the carrier HMS *Illustrious*. As a non-folder, AL246 was left at 'Mac' to await another purpose. This came briefly when it was noted returning to Machrihanish from the Royal Aircraft Establishment at Farnborough, in June 1942. On 1st March 1943 the training unit 768 Squadron arrived at Machrihanish which was ideally placed for its aircraft to practise deck landings from carriers off the coast. Martlet I AL246 joined this unit in June 1943 after it had recovered from an accident when it swung on take-off the previous September. By early 1945 at the latest, the Martlet was delivered to Loughborough College's Department of Aeronautical Engineering to join its expanding fleet of instructional airframes. (The Shuttleworth Collection Spitfire V and Sea Hurricane also came from Loughborough – see Chapter 3.) In 1963 the FAAM took on AL246 and nearly half a century later, this fascinating fighter is slowly giving up some of its secrets.

Grumman Avenger ECM.6B XB446
1945 | Three-crew electronic countermeasures platform | One 1,750hp Wright Cyclone R-2600-20

Despite its present World War Two camouflage and 'Invasion stripes', FAAM's Avenger was unborn when D-Day happened. It was built by General Motors at Trenton, New Jersey, for the US Navy as TBM-3E 69502. Accepted for service on 22nd February 1945, it served with two units; torpedo squadron VT-87 from Alameda, California, from April 1945 and composite squadron (hunter/killer pairs) VC-11 from January 1950. From 4th May 1953 carrier HMS *Perseus* shipped 69502 and others from Norfolk, Virginia. In July the Avenger was roaded to Scottish Aviation at Prestwick, near Ayr, where it was converted to AS.4 status as XB446. It joined 820 Squadron at Eglinton in Northern Ireland on 4th March 1954, but the following year it was withdrawn and taken to Gosport. Here it was turned into an electronic countermeasures-configured ECM.6, joining 751 Squadron at Watton, Norfolk, on 13th March 1957, moving to Culdrose that September. No.751 was re-numbered as 831 Squadron on 1st May 1958. With converted ECM Gannets coming on strength (including ECM.6 XG797 now at the Imperial War Museum Duxford and profiled in Chapter 8), XB446 was relegated to general duties with the Station Flight at Culdrose on 29th November 1960. It was retired to storage at Abbotsinch in October 1962, before returning to Culdrose in in the spring of 1963. It was delivered to the FAAM on 9th April 1968.

Grumman Hellcat II KE209
1945 | Single-seat carrier-borne fighter | One 2,000hp Pratt & Whitney R-2800-10W Double Wasp

Built as an F6F-5 at Bethpage, New York state, *probably* as US Navy serial 79301, the Yeovilton Hellcat was taken on charge at Roosevelt Field, New York, on 13th June 1945. Shipped across the Atlantic, it was prepared for Fleet Air Arm service by the Receipt and Despatch Unit at Anthorn, before moving in November 1945 to the Aircraft Holding Unit (AHU) at Stretton. On 18th June 1946, KE209 was issued to the Station Flight at Lossiemouth and by 1950 had acquired an overall gleaming 'Midnite' blue colour scheme. It was the personal aircraft of Captain J A Ievers (pronounced 'Ivers') the commanding officer of Royal Naval Aircraft Station *Fulmar* – Lossiemouth – and later it was flown with similar appreciation by Captain Caspar John. (Caspar John gets a mention under Vampire LZ551, above.) This could not last and by July 1954 the Hellcat was in the hands of Lossiemouth's AHU, its worth as a fortunate survivor recognised. In 1970 it made the long road journey south, to join the FAAM.

Handley Page HP.115 XP841
1961 | Single-seat slender delta research test-bed | One 1,900lb st Armstrong Siddeley Viper 9

Specification ER.197D was issued on 21st December 1959 for a simple jet-powered low-speed test-bed to explore the characteristics of a slender delta wing. The Handley Page HP.115 had fixed undercarriage, a 'podded' cockpit – complete with ejection seat – and, for those days, the engine innovatively placed above the rear fuselage, with the fin and rudder mounted above it. Built at Radlett, it was moved to its base for its entire flying career, the Royal Aircraft Establishment (RAE) at Thurleigh, and first flew on 17th August 1961, piloted by Jack Henderson.

Handley Page HP.115 XP841 displayed at Farnborough, 1961. *KEC*

Very quickly, the HP.115 moved from theoretical research to practical trials, as it was ideal to investigate the slow speed characteristics of the upcoming Concorde programme. Towards the end of its flying career it flew with Hartmann noise generators mounted either above or below the wing leading edge to assess the noise of the airliner on take-off and approach. With a design life of just 500 hours, RAE decided to retire XP841 early in 1974. Flt Lt John Reid flew it to the RAF station museum at Colerne on 1st February 1974, completing 493 flying hours in just over 1,000 flights. With the closure of Colerne, the jet was trucked to Cosford on 9th October 1975 before moving to Yeovilton on 6th June 1979 to take its place under the wing of Concorde 002.

Hawker Sea Fury FB.11 WJ231
1951 | Single-seat carrier-borne fighter | One 2,480hp Bristol Centaurus 18

The last British piston-engined fighter, in production until November 1952, the Sea Fury has a unique appeal and is today highly prized by 'warbird' owners and air race pilots. The Sea Fury's greatest moment came during the Korean War. On 9th August 1952 when Lt Peter 'Hoagy' Carmichael was flying WJ232 of 802 Squadron off HMS *Ocean* he engaged Mikoyan-Gurevich MiG-15 *Fagots* at low level, downing one with his four 20mm cannon.

In 1958 WJ232 was delivered to the Burmese Air Force. FAAM managed to claim WJ231 after it was offered for disposal in 1962. This was not because its serial was just one behind Carmichael's, but because WJ231 also served with 802 Squadron on *Ocean* in the summer of 1952, although it was not embarked when the MiG 'kill' took place. Accepted into service in November 1951, WJ231 was loaded on to the carrier *Vengeance* in January 1952 and shipped to the Far East. It joined 802 Squadron at Iwakuni in Japan in June 1952 and embarked on *Ocean*. On 5th August it was on shore at Iwakuni again and was on its way home on *Ocean* during November 1952. By March 1954 it was at Ford in Sussex, serving with 810 Squadron, embarking on HMS *Centaur*. A heavy deck landing on 23rd July 1954 put paid to WJ231's frontline days and it was off-loaded to Hal Far on Malta before being shipped back to the UK. Repaired, it joined the Airwork-operated Fleet Requirements Unit at Hurn – now Bournemouth Airport – on 24th March 1960. Its last use was with the Station Flight at Yeovilton from May 1962 but by December it was up for disposal and the scrapmen began to circle. Thankfully, FAAM held sway and the Sea Fury became a 'founder member'.

Sea Fury FB.11 WJ231 at Yeovilton in 1962 during its last flight assignment, with the Station Flight. *KEC*

Hawker Sea Hawk FGA.6 WV856
1954 | Single-seat carrier-borne ground attack fighter | One 5200lb st Rolls-Royce Nene 103

Sea Hawk FGA.4 WV856 test flew on 22nd November 1954 at Bitteswell, where it had been built by Armstrong Whitworth. After a period of storage, it was taken to Hal Far, Malta, in April 1955, joining 806 Squadron on the carrier HMS *Centaur*. By June 1956 it was with 898 Squadron at Brawdy and embarked upon HMS *Ark Royal*. A flying accident on 2nd February 1957 brought the Sea Hawk to the RNAY at Fleetlands and the opportunity was taken to upgrade it to FGA.6 configuration. From April 1958 it was at Lossiemouth with 806 Squadron, or on the deck of HMS *Eagle*, followed by shore-basing at Brawdy with 801 Squadron from May 1960. The fighter's next assignment was far from the norm, with the communications unit 781 Squadron at Lee-on-Solent, on 9th January 1962. It took on a striking green and white Admiral's 'barge' colour scheme – now *there* would be a challenging repaint project! Briefly loaned to the Royal Aircraft Establishment at Farnborough, from September to November 1966, WV856 saw its days out with 781, retiring to Yeovilton and joining the museum on 3rd July 1967.

McDonnell Phantom FG.1 XT596
1966 | Two-crew carrier-borne strike fighter | Two 12,250lb st Rolls-Royce Spey 201

Combine the best from St Louis with Rolls-Royce engines and sub-assemblies by the British Aircraft Corporation and Shorts and many would argue the ultimate Phantom was the outcome. With its nose leg extended for catapult take-off FG.1 XT596 is the centre-piece of the action on the flight deck of the incredible Carrier exhibition at Yeovilton – phabulous! FAAM's example was the second of two FG.1 prototypes and spent all of its life in development and trials work. Designated by McDonnell (which merged with Douglas on 28th April 1967) as YF-4K2, XT596 first flew at St Louis, Missouri, on 30th August 1966. It spent nearly three years in the States, much of the time at St Louis, but also at Edwards Air Force Base, California, and at the Naval Aircraft Test Center at Patuxent River, Maryland. It was flown across the Atlantic, arriving at Holme-on-Spalding Moor on 28th April 1969. Holme had been turned into the flight test and maintenance receipt centre for the UK Phantom programme; later Scampton in Lincolnshire took on the role. With the Speys being the major element of the Anglicized Phantom, XT596 was sent to the Rolls-Royce airfield at Hucknall, near Derby, for the first time on 1st May 1969 for engine upgrade and reheat trials and was based for nearly 13 months. The Royal Aircraft Establishment (RAE) at Thurleigh also provided a home for XT596, the first time in the summer of 1970 and in January 1974 for heavy landing trials – full fuel load and weapons. On 11th October 1974 it was badly damaged when a tyre burst on landing and it ran off the runway. It was at Holme again in January 1975 and trucked to Brough on the Humber for what turned out to be a major repair. The Phantom was back at Holme by late 1982 and was prepared for air test. It was ferried to Scampton on 5th December 1983 and used for trials, although it did not fly often. On 19th January 1988 it was ferried to Yeovilton for FAAM.

Phantom FG.1 XT596 touching down for the last time, Yeovilton 19th January 1988. *FAAM*

Short 184 8359

1915 | Two-crew ship-borne torpedo/bomber floatplane | One 225hp Sunbeam | On loan from the Science Museum

Genuine aircraft from World War One are rare, ones that have *operational* use even more so. Inside a large, glass-fronted display case at Yeovilton is the battered centre section and engine from a true Great War warrior that was secured for preservation as long ago as December 1917. Sadly, nobody told the Luftwaffe of its cherished status and it became a victim of the London Blitz in January 1941.

The Short 184 is wonderfully summed up in Owen Thetford's seminal *British Naval Aircraft since 1912*: "In any history of the development of British naval aviation the Short Type 184 must occupy an honoured place. It was to the First World War what the Swordfish became in the Second World War; both types made history as torpedo-carrying aircraft and earned reputations in every theatre for solid reliability." The 184 (also known as the '225' from the horse power of its engine) emerged in 1915 as a dedicated torpedo-carrier. Over 900 were built and many were still in service at the Armistice in November 1918. On 12th August 1915, Flt Cdr C H K Edmunds pointed his 184 at a target in the Dardanelles, let go the torpedo and moments later became the first person in the world to destroy a warship using an air-launched torpedo. Just to keep his hand in, Edmunds repeated the feat five days later. Flt Lt G B Dacre also scored a torpedo hit from a 184 in this same period. Three drops, three hits and the RNAS never unleashed another 'tin fish' in anger before the end of the war!

Built by Westland – as its fourth aircraft – at Yeovil, 8359 was delivered by rail to the Isle of Grain, Kent, and accepted for service by the Royal Naval Air Service on 4th March 1916. It was first issued to *Engadine* on the 30th and was to operate with the warship mostly out of Dundee. It was one of two 184s embarked upon HMS *Engadine* when it sailed out of Dundee on 31st May 1916. This was the first of two days that came to be called the Battle of Jutland, the only time during all of the Great War that the fleets of the Royal Navy and the Imperial German Navy came to blows. With Flt Cdr F J Rutland as pilot and Assistant Paymaster G S Trewin as observer, 8359 was lowered over the side of *Engadine* and launched on a patrol. The floatplane's crew was able to report some movements of vessels, although this was probably not of help to the battle. Nevertheless, 8359 was at a scene of history and it had flown in a battle zone. (Assistant Paymaster Trewin was a qualified pilot. Many early naval officer pilots came from the permanent service so had 'strange-looking' ranks. FAAM has Trewin's medals within its collection.)

The floatplane was briefly detached to HMS *Furious* in September 1917. Someone with an eye for history allocated 8359 for use with the nascent Imperial War Museum (IWM) in December 1917. It was dismantled and crated at Buncrana, near Donegal in Northern Ireland, and moved to a store to await the opening of the museum. As described in Chapter 2, the Short was displayed at the Crystal Palace 1920 to 1923 and beyond that was shown off inside the IWM at South Lambeth. On the night of 31st January 1941 the Luftwaffe bombed the IWM and the Short was one of the casualties. Stored for a long time, the forward fuselage was

A Short 184 showing how the FAAM's example would have looked had the Luftwaffe not 'modified' it! *KEC*

shown off at Duxford before being handed over to FAAM on 28th January 1976. While it may lack the presence of a fully-fledged Short 184 with a span of 63ft 6in and a height over the floats of 13ft 6in, this is a remarkable and very significant survivor.

Sopwith Baby 'N2078'
1916 | Single-seat naval fighter floatplane | One 110hp Clerget

Derived from the Sopwith Schneider military floatplane, 171 examples of the more powerful Baby were built 1915-1916 and used extensively for anti-Zeppelin patrols from warships and shore stations. Two Babies, 8214 and 8215, built at Kingston-on-Thames, appear not to have flown in the UK and were delivered to the Central Supply Depot at White City, Hammersmith, in April 1916. From there they were transferred to the Italian Government in July, destined to act as patterns for licence production by Macchi. And so the trail goes cold until aircraft and vehicle collector Richard 'Dick' Grainger Jeune Nash acquired 8214 and 8215 and stashed them at Brooklands as part of his International Horseless Carriage Corporation. Nash referred to his Italian prizes as 'Schneiders', but he may have been using a generic phrase, not attempting to 'up' their provenance. By June 1940, Nash had been given notice to quit Brooklands to make way for vital war work. A dispersal plan for the collection was underway, but an air raid on 6th September at the airfield badly damaged at least two Blériots and the Baby floatplanes. A fuselage, various mainplanes and a float from the pair survived and were passed on to the Royal Aeronautical Society and stored post-war at Hendon and later at Heathrow, London Airport. In the late 1960s, FAAM curator Lt Cdr L A 'Harpy' Cox took the Sopwith Baby remains and a major restoration started at the Royal Naval Aircraft Yard at Fleetlands. Sourcing as many original parts as possible, the project was rolled out in May 1970. The Baby was finished as Blackburn-built N2078 *The Jabberwock* in which Flt Sub Lt G F Hyams bombed a U-boat off the coast of Scarborough on 26th March 1918.

Sopwith Baby 'N2078' on roll-out at Fleetlands at the end of its restoration, May 1970. *Peter Green Collection*

Supermarine Walrus I L2301
1938 | Three-crew general purpose ship-borne amphibian | One 775hp Bristol Pegasus VI

Yeovilton's Walrus had a multi-faceted life, starting at Woolston, Southampton, in 1938 when it was built to the order of the RAF as L2301. It is believed to have been taken on charge on 13th December 1938 and been stored, along with L2302 and L2303 at Tern Hill. The trio were destined to fulfil a request from the Irish Air Corps (IAC) to join its Coastal Patrol Squadron to keep an eye on the west coast from Shannon airfield. All three were returned to Supermarine to be readied for service and L2301, '2 and '3 were test flown as N18, N19 and N20 on 24th February, 10th January and 17th January 1939 respectively. These numbers were 'B Condition' (or trade-plate) numbers used by Supermarine for test and trials purposes and were adopted by the IAC as serials, but the 'N' was dropped. On 3rd March 1939 all three amphibians took off from Eastleigh on delivery to the IAC at Baldonnel, near Dublin. Bad weather over the Irish Sea broke up the loose formation. One Walrus turned back, one got as far as Dun Laoghaire on the Dublin coast while Lts M Quinlan and M Higgins in N18 (the former L2301) suffered engine trouble, landed in rough water and successfully managed to get it to Wexford harbour. N18 completed its journey to Baldonnel with its wings and tail section in a lorry, and the fuselage being towed behind on its own landing gear! By 1945 Walrus 18 was the only one of the three surviving and it was sold to the Irish national airline, Aer Lingus, that August. It was registered as EI-ACC but was not used and was put into store at Dublin Airport.

Following up a lead about a 'flying-boat' being available, Wg Cdr R G Kellett of 615 (County of Surrey) Squadron, Royal Auxiliary Air Force, operating Spitfire XIVs from Biggin Hill, travelled to Dublin in November 1946 to inspect the Walrus. Kellett was after something to fly the ground crew around in and to generally have fun with. He snapped up the amphibian for £150 (£4,500 in present-day values) and had it registered as G-AIZG on 20th December. In the following March, Kellett and Flt Lt Freddy B Sowery flew the Walrus from Dublin to Croydon (to clear Customs) and then on to Biggin Hill. *Zulu-Golf* was used for a variety of jaunts, including at least one that involved a water landing. The 'fun' came to an end in 1949 and it was sold to a scrap merchant at Thame, Oxfordshire. Here G-AIZG languished until it was 'discovered' by members of the Historic Aircraft Preservation Society and bought, reportedly for a 'fiver'. In the mid-1960s Freddy Sowery, who crewed the Walrus on its flight to Biggin Hill in 1946, was a Group Captain, and he was instrumental in saving the amphibian for a second time, securing it for FAAM. It was roaded to the Royal Naval Engineering College at Arbroath in Scotland for restoration. It was officially handed over to the museum on 6th December 1966.

The Walrus started life named the Seagull V, and at one time the there was a proposal to call it the Stingray. Early customer, the Royal Australian Air Force, stuck with the Seagull V designation and the RAF Museum at Hendon has a former RAAF Seagull V on display (Chapter 5).

Walrus I G-AIZG with 615 (County of Surrey) Squadron, circa 1948. *KEC*

Supermarine Seafire F.17 SX137
1945 | Single-seat carrier-borne fighter | One 1,850hp Rolls-Royce Griffon VI

The story of the Spitfire and its sea-going brother the Seafire is too vast and involved to insult readers by presenting a hideous précis here. Three versions have been chosen to profile: Hendon's Mk.I (Chapter 5), Duxford's F.24 (Chapters 8) and Yeovilton's Seafire. Mk.17s first entered service with the Fleet Air Arm at Arbroath, Scotland, in September 1945 and were to have a long career, with Royal Navy Volunteer Reserve (RNVR) Units and in the training role. No.764 Squadron disbanded on 23rd November 1954 at Yeovilton and the Seafire F.17 was retired from service. The FAAM's example was with 764 at this time, but its flying days were not quite over. Built by Westland at Yeovil, SX137 was issued to the Receipt and Despatch Unit at Culham, on 25th September 1945. It was not until 18th June 1951 that it started operational flying, with the RNVR unit 1831 Squadron at Stretton. This sojourn was brief, the Seafire moving on to 759 Squadron at Culdrose on 6th November. Finally, SX137 was issued to 764 Squadron on 9th July 1954. The Yeovilton-based unit mainly operated as a pilot pool keeping aircrew current on type until a frontline posting could be found. As related above, SX137 was with 764 when it disbanded and it was written off charge in May 1955, but the decision had been made to keep it going. It was restored to full flight condition from 1957 and on 16th June 1959 issued to the Station Flight at Yeovilton. It was last flown just over a year later, on 16th July 1960, but it stayed at Yeovilton as part of the 'attractions' displayed to motorists in need of a break on the A303. In June 1962 it was loaned to the RAF and was painted up as a Spitfire, given the serial 'W9132' and the name *Suzy* for an appearance at Earl's Court, London. It was returned to Yeovilton in April 1963, thankfully returned to its Seafire self and became a 'founder member' of FAAM.

Seafire F.17 SX137 at an unknown moment in its career. *KEC*

Supermarine Attacker F.1 WA473
1951 | Single-seat carrier-borne fighter | One 5,100lb st Rolls-Royce Nene 3

The Fleet Air Arm's first frontline jet fighter, the Attacker was a bridge between the piston era and the jet age. Its wing was essentially the same as the Spiteful, the final iteration of the Spitfire; its laminar flow aerodynamics having confined the iconic elliptical planform to history. The Attacker could not hide its ancestry as it was a 'taildragger' and gained a reputation for damaging runways and flightdecks with its jet efflux. The world's sole surviving Attacker, WA473, was ready for service at South Marston on 25th July 1951. It joined 800 Squadron at Ford on 17th August 1951. It then transferred to 702 Squadron at Culdrose on 20th April 1952, the unit converting piston pilots to jets. No.702 was re-numbered as 736 Squadron on 26th August 1952 and WA473 served on until August 1954 when it was taken to Gatwick for reconditioning by Airwork General Trading. It was moved to the Aircraft Holding Unit at Abbotsinch on 12th December 1956 and by 1959 was displayed on a pole as the station 'gate guardian'. It joined FAAM in 1964.

Attacker F.1 WZ473 with 800 Squadron, when based at Ford, 1951. *MAP*

Supermarine Scimitar F.1 XD317
1959 | Single-seat carrier-borne strike fighter | Two 11,250lb st Rolls-Royce Avon 202

Supermarine's last throw of the dice, the exceptional Scimitar, deserves a greater image. Side-lined by the Sea Vixen, it was the Scimitar that prepared the way for the Buccaneer and Phantom era far more than its twin-boom cousin. The Scimitar gave the Fleet Air Arm (FAA) a range of 'firsts': nuclear-capable strike fighter, supersonic in a shallow dive, swept-wing single-seater, area-ruled fuselage aerodynamics, powered-flying control systems and blown flaps greatly reducing approach speed. All of this took the FAA from the delightful, but simplistic, Sea Hawk to the realms of a 'heavy-hitter'. Production ended in September 1960 and, out of 76 production examples, only two others survive intact. Solent Sky at Southampton has XD332 in deep store. Across the Atlantic is XD220, on loan from FAAM to the Empire State Aerosciences Museum at Glenville, New York.

Scimitar XD317 had its maiden flight, from South Marston on 6th October 1959. It joined 807 Squadron at Lossiemouth on 23rd February 1960 and was then shipped to Singapore, where it was embarked on the carrier HMS *Centaur*, for a cruise westwards. Across the Indian Ocean, up the Red Sea and via Suez into the Mediterranean, *Centaur* steamed to Malta. On 18th April 1962 an incident occurred which thankfully caused no human damage other than embarrassment but was to become a classic quirk of fate. During a formation flypast at Malta, XD317's port outer drop-tank touched the wing of another Scimitar; both machines landed safely. On the receiving end of XD317's attentions was none other than 21st century survivor XD332! On 29th November 1962 XD317 joined 800 Squadron at Lossiemouth and was embarked upon HMS *Ark Royal*. Repairs and upgrades at the Royal Naval Aircraft Yard at Fleetlands took XD317 out of the sky from late 1963 to the autumn of 1965. Next came a spell with the Royal Aircraft Establishment (RAE) starting off at Thurleigh in January 1966 with arrester gear trials, followed in March with weapons experimentation at Farnborough. Its final spell of flying came with the Fleet Requirements Unit at Hurn from 2nd November 1966. On 4th August 1969, the Scimitar was issued back to RAE Farnborough, but during that month it was trucked out to its new life with FAAM at Yeovilton.

Westland Wyvern TF.1 VR137
1949 | Single-seat carrier-borne fighter/torpedo attack fighter | One 2,690hp Rolls-Royce Eagle 22

The only turboprop fighter to enter operational service with British armed forces, the Wyvern had an exceptionally long and much-altered development. When Wyvern S.4 WP345 took off from Yeovil in May 1956, it was the last Westland fixed-wing design to be built. One of a batch of 20 pre-production TF.1s, VR137 got as far as having its 24-cylinder Eagle fitted at Yeovil in 1949, but it never flew. The ebbs and flows of the Wyvern programme had put paid to the piston version. Unpainted, it was sold by the Ministry of Supply to the College of Aeronautics at Cranfield, arriving there by lorry on 30th November 1950. Here, among the varied fleet of instructional airframes, it joined Corsair IV KD431, also destined to join the FAAM. In May 1963 VR137 was acquired by Biggin Hill-based Historic Aircraft Preservation Society, but resolutely remained at Cranfield. Its worth to FAAM was beyond dispute and the museum took it on in 1965 and it was moved to Yeovilton in February 1966. During the winter of 1970/1971 it was painted in representative FAA colours. In 1998, the Wyvern was moved into the workshop where it was returned to its Spartan 'colours' from its days at Cranfield and it took its place inside the Leading Edge exhibition in July 2000. This was a brave move risking some visitors deciding it was an incomplete exhibit – which of course is exactly its provenance – but it provides a striking contrast with the other exhibits and is true to itself. Gleaming, Eagle-engined VR137 is fabulous, but if I may be permitted a moment of random 'what iffing', oh for it to have been a turbine-propelled S.4, ideally one that had fought in the skies over Suez!

Very likely the first Eagle-engined Wyvern prototype, TS371. *Westland*

Westland Wessex HAS.3 XP142
1962 | Four-crew anti-submarine and anti-surface vessel helicopter | One 1,600shp Napier Gazelle 165

During an intense four days in April 1982 a 20-year old helicopter called *Humphrey* became a major news item during the first 'shooting' days of the Falklands conflict. In the twilight of its Fleet Air Arm service, *Humphrey* had turned itself into a very desirable museum piece. Westland built the Sikorsky S-58 under licence, in increments re-engineering and greatly developing it. Built as a HAS.1, XP142 first flew at Yeovil on 18th June 1962 and joined 845 Squadron in the troop transport role 13 days later. With 845, XP142 was called *Jinks*, and was based at Culdrose and embarked on the carrier HMS *Albion*. In September 1965

Dramatic image showing the 'white-out' conditions on South Georgia on 22nd April 1982. Wessex HU.5 XT464 is lying on its side, while troops from XT473 look on. Wessex XP142 *Humphrey* was to rescue all of the personnel from *both* HU.5s that day. *KEC*

Humphrey's mission tallies, record the attack on the submarine *Santa Fe* and the rescue operations. *Ken Ellis*

the Wessex was converted to its originally intended role – anti-submarine warfare, entering service with 706 Squadron, also at Culdrose, in October 1966. By July 1967 it was back at Yeovil, having its Gazelle turboshaft upgraded from a Series 161 to a 165, thus becoming an HAS.3. From September 1969 it joined 814 Squadron at Culdrose when not stationed on the carrier HMS *Hermes*.

In November 1970 XP142 returned to 706 and spent time detached to HMS *Hampshire* and then HMS *Fife*. On 6th February 1981 the Wessex moved to Portland, going on strength with 737 Squadron.

It was with 737 that XP142 was issued to County Class destroyer HMS *Antrim* and was given the name *Humphrey*. In April 1982 *Antrim*, with *Humphrey* in its hangar at the stern, set sail for the South Atlantic as part of Operation CORPORATE. Antrim was not bound for the Falklands themselves, but tasked with securing South Georgia, a set of tiny islands further eastwards in the unforgiving Atlantic. Three Wessex, *Humphrey* and HU.5s XT464 and XT473 ferried Special Forces personnel to the Fortuna Glacier on South Georgia, on 21st April before returning to the confines of the *Antrim*. It was apparent early the following morning that the weather was horrific and that the men needed to be taken off. The three 'choppers' deployed through appalling blizzard conditions to the glacier and uplifted the frozen troops. Visibility was minimal and the pilots of XT464 became disorientated and the helicopter fell on to its side; there were no serious injuries. The crew and soldiers scrambled aboard the remaining two Wessex and the sortie got underway again. While climbing away, XT473 hit a snow bank and, like XT464, collapsed on its side, amid flailing rotors. *Humphrey* set off for Antrim, dropped its passengers and returned to the glacier, picking up everyone from XT473. The crew of four, led by Lt Cdr I Stanley, had shown exceptional determination and flying skills in the harshest imaginable weather conditions.

This was just the beginning of the adventures of *Humphrey*. The following day, the 23rd, the same crew took it to rescue four Special Forces personnel from their inflatable motor boat in a South Georgian cove. Two days later Lt Cdr Stanley and his team encountered the surfaced Argentine submarine *Santa Fe* at Grytviken and unleashed four depth charges which were seen to impact on the boat's port side. The day was going to go from bad to worse for *Santa Fe* – see the profile on Wasp XS527 below. On May 21, 1982 *Antrim* was attacked by Argentine IAI Dagger jets that caused considerable damage. *Humphrey* received many shrapnel hits and these can be seen to this day at Yeovilton. *Antrim* arrived back at Portsmouth on 17th July 1982 and *Humphrey* was handed over to FAAM ten days later. The hard-working Wessex had earned its place in history.

Westland Wasp HAS.1 XS527
1963 | Two-crew ship-borne anti-submarine and anti-surface vessel helicopter | One 710shp Bristol Siddeley Nimbus 103

From the Saunders-Roe P.531 light helicopter two production versions arose, the Scout Army general purpose type and the Wasp. Chapter 7 on the Museum of Army Flying details the former. Built at Hayes, Wasp XS527 was the first from the initial production batch and made its inaugural flight at White Waltham, Berkshire, on 23rd March 1963. For the next five years it spent most of its time on development flying with Westland, either at White Waltham or Yeovil and with the Aeroplane & Armament Experimental Establishment at Boscombe Down. Brought up to full HAS.1 status, it was first issued to the Fleet Air Arm at the Naval Aircraft Support Unit at Culdrose, on 10th January 1968. It was embarked on the warship HMS *Rothesay* from June 1968 and then to HMS *Rhyl* from October 1971. While flying from the *Rhyl* on 3rd December 1972 the Wasp encountered a problem and was ditched alongside, its flotation bags allowing the crew to escape and keeping XS527 buoyant. The helicopter was salvaged by a Dutch naval vessel and it was repaired, reconditioned and then modified by the Royal Naval Aircraft Yard at Fleetlands. The 'mods' allowed XS527 to be stationed with the Ice Patrol Ship HMS *Endurance*, from 3rd September 1976. Briefly with 703 Squadron at Portland, Dorset, from March 1980, XS527 was back on *Endurance* on 15th May 1980 and heading for the South Atlantic. As related in the profile of Wessex XP142 *Humphrey* above, the Argentine submarine *Santa Fe* was caught on the surface off South Georgia on 25th April 1982. *Endurance* was one of the ships that directed attacks on the boat and XS527, crewed by Lt Cdr J A Ellerbeck and Lt D A H Wells, launched three AS.12 wire-guided missiles, damaging the 'sail' (conning tower). By the end of the day, the submarine was run aground close to Grytviken; its war over and the following day, Argentine forces on South Georgia threw the towel in. Back in the UK, XS527 was issued to 829 Squadron at Portland on 14th September 1984, with deployments on the Royal Fleet Auxiliary *Olwen* and the anti-submarine frigate HMS *Lowestoft*. The Wasp was delivered to FAAM on 31st July 1986.

Westland Sea King HAS.6 XZ574
1976 | Four-crew ship-borne anti-submarine and rescue helicopter | Two 1,535 shp Rolls-Royce Gnome 122/123

Based on the Sikorsky S-61B, the Westland-produced Sea King represents a considerable development over its American forebear. Both Fleet Air Arm (FAA) and RAF (search and rescue HAR.3s) Sea Kings are now in the twilight of their years, having given exceptional service. Only three 'dark blue' Sea Kings have so far been preserved and it is not clear if others will be made available, although it is believed that the RAF's 'yellow' search and rescue examples will be widely offered. The FAAM was beaten to the post by the Yorkshire Helicopter Preservation Group, who were the first to secure one, HAS.6 XV677, on 25th July 2006 and it is displayed at the South Yorkshire Aircraft Museum at Doncaster.

Yeovilton was biding its time hoping to achieve HAS.6 XZ574. Like XV677, it was a veteran of Operation CORPORATE, the Falklands conflict, but it had the additional cachet of having a Royal pilot! Built as a HAS.2, XZ574 had its maiden flight at Yeovil on 2nd September 1976 and was issued to 826 Squadron at Culdrose on 19th January 1977. With 826, the Sea King was embarked upon the cruiser HMS *Tiger* and on 30th March 1978, while exercising in the Arabian Sea, XZ574 had a gearbox problem and carried out a precautionary water landing close to the ship. The helicopter capsized, but the four crew and four passengers were rescued. That would have been game over for most military operators, but not the FAA. Plucked from the water, the Sea King was off-loaded in Valetta Harbour, Malta, to start a long journey home and back to health.

It next re-joined 826 Squadron, then shore-based at Culdrose and deployed on the carrier HMS *Invincible*. On 5th April 1982 *Invincible* left for the South Atlantic and one of the helicopter's pilots was Sub Lt HRH Prince Andrew. The Prince flew XZ574 during the rescue of 846 Squadron Sea King HC.4 ZA311 which had crashed into the sea at night on 23rd April; one of its pilots was saved, sadly the other died, becoming the first British casualty of the Falklands conflict. An Argentine Euromissile Roland surface-to-air-missile hit 801 Squadron Sea Harrier FRS.1 XZ456, off *Invincible*, near Port Stanley on 1st June. RAF Flt Lt I Mortimer 'banged out' and landed in the water very close to the coast. Eight hours later, the sound of XZ574 approaching was comforting and he was whisked from the water back to the carrier. The battles over, XZ574 returned to the UK on board HMS *Illustrious* and it was back at Culdrose on 18th September 1982. In

December it joined 706 Squadron briefly before going to 810 in January 1983. During 1991 XZ574 was upgraded to HAS.6 status at the Royal Naval Aircraft Yard at Fleetlands. It returned to service with 819 Squadron in September 1992 and this was followed by 820 (from June 1996), 810 (October 2000) and finally 771 Squadron (July 2001), all shore-based at Culdrose. With a total flying time of 9,168 hours, XZ574 was retired and became an instructional airframe at HMS *Sultan*, Gosport. By 2008, patient lobbying by FAAM paid off and the helicopter was prepared for the museum with help from AgustaWestland and Vector Aerospace and issued to Yeovilton on 11th June 2008.

Westland Lynx HAS.3GMS XZ720
1980 | Two-crew ship-borne anti-submarine and general duties helicopter | Two 1,120shp Rolls-Royce Gem 204

First flown on 21st March 1971, the Westland Lynx utility/battlefield and anti-submarine helicopter family has been in continuous production at Yeovil, Somerset, ever since. From July 2000 the company has been known as AgustaWestland and the latest iteration of the Lynx is the AW159 Wildcat. The Museum of Army Flying at Middle Wallop has 'mud-mover' versions, including a record-breaker – see Chapter 7. First flown at Yeovil on 30th April 1980 in HAS.2 guise, XZ720 joined 815 Squadron at Yeovilton, on 6th November 1981. Like the Westland Wasp before them, most Lynx were destined to be detached to a warship when not being flown by the 'parent' unit – 815 Squadron. Carrying the name *Phoenix* on its nose, XZ720 joined HMS *Alacrity* and was on board when the Type 21 frigate set sail for the South Atlantic in April 1982 as part of the task force to re-take the Falklands Islands, Operation CORPORATE. The Lynx came home from the conflict on the carrier HMS *Hermes* in July. In 1983 the helicopter was fitted out to carry BAC Sea Skua anti-ship missiles and during that summer was embarked upon HMS *Hermione* and was named *Lobo*. From 24th November 1986, XZ720 was shore-based at Portland, Dorset, with 829 Squadron's headquarters flight. Conversion to HAS.3 status, replacing its Gem 100s for Series 204s, took place in mid-1987. That September, now named *Asterix*, XZ720 was resident on HMS *Battleaxe*, followed by sojourns on HMS *Brazen* (inevitably taking the name *The Harlot*) and HMS *Coventry* before joining the Type 42 destroyer, HMS *Gloucester* in July 1990. By January the following year *Gloucester* was in the Arabian Gulf ready to take part in what became the First Iraqi War. Sea Skuas fired from XZ720 proved their worth, sinking *three* Iraqi vessels in different engagements on 30th January. Back with 815 at Portland by March 1992, XZ720 was detached to a string of Royal Navy warships: HMS *Edinburgh* (named *The TARDIS II*), HMS *Liverpool*, HMS *Edinburgh* again, HMS *Manchester* and HMS *York* (named *Jorvik*). From January 2008, XZ720 was back with 815 and from there was despatched to HMS *Iron Duke* and re-acquainted itself with the landing pad on the back of *Manchester*. By late 2010 the helicopter had been placed in storage at Fleetlands, Hampshire, but covetous eyes at Yeovilton were gazing upon it. This interest bore fruit on 26th April 2012 when the veteran of two conflicts was handed over to FAAM.

Yokosuka MXY-7 Ohka Model 11
1945 | Single-pilot piloted attack weapon | Three 1,764lb (combined) Type 4 Mk.1 Model 20 solid-propellant rockets | On loan from the Science Museum

A selection representing Japanese warplanes of World War Two has to include the macabre Ohka (Cherry Blossom) piloted flying-bomb. In a world terrorised by the spectre of hijacked jetliner flying-bombs and explosive waistcoats the Kamikaze serves as a reminder that determination can manifest itself in many ways. Ensign Mitsuo Ohta, a pilot of the 405th Kotukai, came up with the idea of a simple to mass-produce, largely wooden construction, easy to fly, piloted bomb as an anti-invasion device but instead it was used against capital ships. Launched from a Mitsubishi G4M *Betty* twin-engined bomber the Ohka – with a 1,200lb warhead – would glide towards its target, the pilot igniting the rockets at close range. Glider trials proved the concept in October 1944 and on 12th April 1945 the first sinking was achieved. The Allies quickly developed countermeasures, with a massive barrage of firepower of all calibres proving decisive in the last moments. Most effective was early warning of the approach of the vulnerable 'mother-ships' and their interception. Post-war analysis of shipping losses revealed that the shock effect of the Ohka far outweighed its efficiency as a weapon, but more sophisticated developments were under test in the run up to VJ-Day.

Fleet Air Arm Museum aircraft on loan at other locations and Former Fleet Air Arm Museum aircraft

Type	Identity	Built	Arrived	Notes, *current status or fate*
Albatros D.Va replica	'D5397'	1978	1985	*Sold in the UK late 2013; exported to the USA as N428UT.*
DH Sea Venom FAW.22	XG737	1958	7 Mar 1969	To Wales A/c Museum, Cardiff, 1977. *East Midlands Airport Aeropark, Leics*
Fairey Firefly AS.5	WB271	1949	19 Jul 1967	*Transferred to RN Historic Flt, Yeovilton, and first flown 27 Sep 1972. Fatal crash Duxford 12 Jul 2003*
Fairey Gannet T.2	XA508	1955	11 Sep 1975	To Midland Air Museum, Coventry, 26 Sep 1982, *on loan*
Fairey Gannet T.5	XG883	1957	3 Jun 1970	To Wales A/c Museum, Cardiff, 12 Apr 1983. *Museum of Berkshire Aviation, Woodley*, *on loan*
FMA Pucará	A-522	c1980	7 Dec 1982	ex Argentine Air Force. *To North East A/c Museum, Sunderland 22 Jul 1994 on loan*
Gloster Gladiator II	N5903	1939	1978	ex Shuttleworth Clln (Chapter 3), On loan. *To The Fighter Collection, Duxford, 30 Nov 1994. Airworthy as G-GLAD*
HS AV-8A Harrier	159233	1974	6 Jun 1987	*Transferred to Imperial War Museum North, Manchester, 21 Nov 2001 – Chapter 3*
Macchi MB.339AA	0761	1981	14 Jun 1983	ex Argentine Navy. Composite, nose of 0761, remainder 0767. To Filton 1992 for Rolls-Royce, mock-up of US JPATS T-Bird II contender. *Rolls-Royce Heritage Trust, Derby, on loan*
McDonnell F-4S Phantom II	155848	1968	6 Nov 1986	*To Museum of Flight, East Fortune, Scotland, 11 May 2001 – Chapter 10*
Percival Sea Prince C.1	WF137	1950	6 Dec 1968	To Second World War A/c Pres Soc, Lasham Apr 1979. *Stored dismantled, Booker, Bucks*
Percival Sea Prince C.2	WJ350	1953	27 Jun 1972	*To Guernsey Airport fire service, Channel Islands, 21 May 1979. Perished by Sep 1992*
SPAD XIII replica	'S3398'	1977	18 Sep 1986	*To the Imperial War Museum Duxford 17 Sep 1996 – in American Air Museum – Chapter 8*
Supermarine Scimitar F.1	XD220	1957	22 Jul 1970	Shipped to USA 7 Jun 1986 in exchange for F-4S 155848. *Displayed on board USS Intrepid, now at the Empire State Aerosciences Museum, New York, USA, on loan*
Westland Whirlwind HAR.3	XJ402	1955	13 Feb 1976	Stripped for spares 1988. *To fire dump at Yeovilton by Jul 1989, gone by 1991*
Westland Wessex HAS.1	XS881	1966	18 Jan 1980	*To instructional use Yeovilton 1993. To RN Fire School Predannack Sep 1997, hulk scrapped 2001*

Fleet Air Arm Museum aircraft

Type	Identity	Built	Origin	Arrived	Notes
Agusta A.109A*	AE-331	1980	Italy	Oct 2010	ZE411
BAC 221*	WG774	1955	UK	Jan 1980	see profile
BAC/Sud Concorde 002*	G-BSST	1969	UK/France	4 Mar 1976	see profile
Bristol Scout D replica*	N5419	1990	UK	30 Nov 1998	on loan
BAe Sea Harrier FA.2	XZ499	1981	UK	13 Nov 2002	see profile
Blackburn Skua II	L2940	1940	UK	1974	–
Blackburn Buccaneer S.1	XN957	1963	UK	1974	see profile
Blackburn Buccaneer S.2B	XV333	1966	UK	23 Mar 1994	–
Chance Vought Corsair IV	KD431	1944	USA	1964	see profile
De Havilland Vampire 1*	LZ551/G	1944	UK	1966	see profile
De Havilland Sea Vampire T.22	XA127	1954	UK	1968	fuselage
De Havilland Sea Vixen FAW.2	XS590	1966	UK	26 Nov 1970	see profile
Fairey Flycatcher replica	'S1287'	1979	UK	5 Jun 1996	G-BEYB
Fairey Swordfish II*	'P4139'	1943	UK	1962	see profile
Fairey Albacore I	N4172	1943	UK	1983	composite reconstruction
Fairey Fulmar II*	N1854	1940	UK	1962	see profile
Fairey Firefly TT.1	Z2033	1944	UK	25 Jul 2000	see profile
Fairey Barracuda II	DP872	1943	UK	1968	forward fuselage, remainder stored
Fairey Gannet AEW.3	XL503	1961	UK	26 Apr 1973	see profile
Grumman Martlet I*	AL246	1940	USA	1963	see profile
Grumman Avenger ECM.6B*	XB446	1945	USA	9 Apr 1968	see profile
Grumman Hellcat II	KE209	1945	USA	1970	see profile
Handley Page HP.115	XP841	1961	UK	6 Jun 1979	see profile
Hawker Sea Fury FB.11	WJ231	1951	UK	1965	see profile
Hawker Sea Hawk FGA.6	WV856	1954	UK	Jul 1967	see profile
Hawker Hunter T.8M*	XL580	1958	UK	21 Nov 1994	–
Hawker P.1127	XP980	1963	UK	6 Mar 1989	–
HS Sea Harrier FRS.1	XZ493	1980	UK	1 Mar 1995	–
Mikoyan-Gurevich MiG-15bis	01420	1964	USSR	14 May 1987	Polish-built Lim-2, G-BMZF
McDonnell Phantom FG.1*	XT596	1966	USA	19 Jan 1988	see profile
North American Harvard IIA	EX976	1941	USA	1981	–
Short S.27 replica	–	1979	UK	1980	–
Short 184*	8359	1915	UK	28th Jan 1976	see profile
Sopwith Baby floatplane	'N2078'	1916	UK	May 1970	see profile
Sopwith Triplane replica	'N5459'	1976	UK	25 Mar 1987	–
Sopwith Pup replica	'N6452'	1983	UK	10 Jun 1985	G-BIAU
Supermarine Walrus I	L2301	1939	UK	6 Dec 1966	see profile
Supermarine Seafire F.17	SX137	1945	UK	1964	see profile
Supermarine Attacker F.1	WA473	1951	UK	1964	see profile
Supermarine Scimitar F.1	XD317	1959	UK	18 Sep 1969	see profile
Westland Dragonfly HR.5	WN493	1953	USA	19 Oct 1966	–
Westland Wessex HAS.3	XP142	1962	USA	26 Jul 1982	see profile
Westland Wessex HU.5	XT482	1966	USA	24 Feb 1994	–
Westland Wessex HU.5	XT765	1966	USA	Mar 2011	–
Westland Wessex HU.5	XT769	1967	USA	7 Sep 1993	–
Westland Sea King HAS.6*	XZ574	1976	USA	9 Jun 2008	see profile
Westland Lynx HAS.3GMS*	XZ720	1980	UK	26 Apr 2012	see profile
Yokosuka Ohka 11	15-1585	1945	Japan	1977	see profile

Notes: * – illustrated in the colour section

Fleet Air Arm Museum aircraft held at Cobham Hall

Type	Identity	Built	Origin	Arrived#	Notes
BAe Harrier GR.9A	ZD433	1989	UK/USA	20 Dec 2011	–
Beech T-34C-1 Turbo-Mentor	0729	1978	USA	7 Jul 1983	–
Bell Sioux AH.1	XT176	1965	USA	6 Jun 1994	–
Bell UH-1H Iroquois	AE-422	1974	USA	6 Jun 1989	–
Bensen B.8M	G-AZAZ	1971	USA	2 Dec 1999	–
Blackburn NA.39	XK488	1958	UK	22 Jul 1967	–
De Havilland Tiger Moth	'G-ABUL'	1940	UK	1972	XL717
De Havilland Sea Vampire T.22	XA129	1954	UK	14 Jul 1970	–
De Havilland Sea Venom FAW.22	WW138	1955	UK	Sep 1969	see profile
De Havilland Sea Vixen FAW.1	XJ481	1958	UK	7 Mar 1974	–
Douglas Skyraider AEW.1	WT121	1951	USA	1962	–
Douglas Skyraider AEW.1	WV106	1950	USA	1964	–
Eclipse Super Eagle hang-glider	G-BGWZ	1979	USA	1981	–
Fairey Firefly TT.4	VH127	1947	UK	29 Nov 1972	–
Fairey Gannet COD.4	XA466	1957	UK	12 Dec 1978	–
Focke-Achgelis FA 330A-1	100545	1944	Germany	25 Aug 1993	–
Fokker Dr.I scale replica	'102/17'	1968	Germany	1975	–
Gloster Sea Gladiator II	'N5579'	1939	UK	17 Jul 2002	–
Gloster Meteor T.7	WS103	1952	UK	8 Jan 1971	–
Gloster Meteor TT20	WM292	1953	UK	4 Jun 1969	–
Hawker P.1052	VX272	1948	UK	Feb 1990	–
Hawker Sea Hawk FGA.6	XE340	1955	UK	21 Oct 1970	–
Hiller HT.1	XB480	1953	USA	5 Oct 1971	–
Hunting Jet Provost T.3A	XN462	1960	UK	25 Mar 1998	–
Percival Sea Prince T.1	WP313	1953	UK	Jan 1987	–
Saunders-Roe P.531	XN332	1958	UK	1980	G-APNV
Saunders-Roe P.531	XN334	1958	UK	1978	–
Sopwith Camel replica	'B6401'	1969	UK	1985	N1917H
Sud Gazelle HT.2	XW864	1973	France	21 Oct 2002	–
Supermarine 510	VV106	1948	UK	Feb 1990	–
Westland Wyvern TF.1	VR137	1949	UK	Feb 1966	see profile
Westland Dragonfly HR.5	VX595	1949	USA	23 Nov 1998	–
Westland Whirlwind HAR.1	XA864	1953	USA	10 Mar 1970	–
Westland Whirlwind HAR.3	XG574	1955	USA	12 Mar 1975	–
Westland Whirlwind HAS.7	XG594	1957	USA	23 Mar 1970	–
Westland Whirlwind HAS.7	XL853	1958	USA	7 Dec 1998	–
Westland Wessex HU.5	XS508	1964	USA	28 Jun 1993	–
Westland Wasp HAS.1	XS527	1963	UK	31 Jul 1986	see profile
Westland Wasp HAS.1	XT427	1965	UK	28 Mar 1984	–
Westland Wasp HAS.1	XT778	1966	UK	15 Feb 1999	–
Westland Lynx HAS.3	XZ699	1980	UK	Nov 2006	–

Notes: # First taken on by FAAM.

A variety of Fleet Air Arm brochures.

CHAPTER 5

Milestones to Hendon
Royal Air Force Museum
Hendon, London

www.rafmuseum.org

Over ten million visitors have made the pilgrimage to the Royal Air Force Museum at Hendon. In November 2012 forty years of being open to the public were celebrated. In that time the nature and extent of the site has changed beyond the wildest dreams of those who achieved the transformation of the 'Belfast truss' hangars (more correctly Double General Service Sheds) from forgotten architectural heritage to national institution. Always evolving, Hendon is gearing up for the centenary of the Great War and, on 1st April 2018, the 100th anniversary of the Royal Air Force itself. Beyond that are still more challenges, not the least of which is the ambitious Battle of Britain Beacon, announced in May 2010 and in currently the early phases of fund-raising. Taller than St Paul's Cathedral, this striking 350ft tower will re-interpret the story of the decisive struggle of 1940. The original Battle of Britain Hall, the Bomber Command Hall, the Grahame-White Factory and Watch Tower, Milestones of Flight and now the Beacon attest to just how much the museum has progressed with its gigantic task of telling the story of the RAF and the history of aviation. In 1972 when Hendon opened up, comment at the time was that it would rapidly assume the role of a sleepy hollow; this has been proven wildly inaccurate!

Above: Hart, Meteor and Fokker D.VII, part of the chronology of aviation vividly presented within Milestones of Flight at Hendon. *RAF Museum*

And then there's Cosford… The Shropshire site has long been recognised as an equal and not a subsidiary, so it gets its own treatment, from the days as the Aerospace Museum, and for ease of reference it follows, in Chapter 6.

Secreting treasures away

It was in the 1930s that the notion of collating and presenting the heritage of the RAF was first discussed. Some far-seeing chiefs appreciated that, although the RAF had only been created in 1918, too many artefacts, large and small, had already slipped the net, probably never to be regained. But the 1930s were not good years to establish a museum, swinging from a chronic lack of funding to massive expansion to meet the threat of Fascism. Plans for a formal collection were shelved, but a small department established in 1920 was already carrying out a vital task, and would assume greater responsibility – the Air Historical Branch (AHB). Tasked with advising the Air Staff on historical matters, with collating Air Ministry/RAF records of all sorts and producing official histories, AHB has essentially the same role today. To the praise of all involved, during World War Two AHB was recognised as the best body to itemise, locate and reserve artefacts important to RAF heritage. A look through the exhibit profiles below and in Chapter 6 will show how often the AHB intervened to save a gem. With limited resources and without a clear view of 'outcome', the personnel at AHB, and some gifted COs realising what history was slipping through their hands, managed to secure for future generations some incredible aircraft. A full study of the AHB is beyond the remit of this book – it is not a 'museum' body as such – and an examination of the treasures that were asked for and secured, and which were lost would make fascinating reading.

By 1945, the work of the AHB was such that several generic phrases were in use: "an AHB aircraft" and "the AHB collection", even "the AHB museum". During the late 1940s a series of RAF stations looked after AHB aircraft; many of which were dismantled and in packing cases and destined to move around the country as airfields closed down or changed priority. In September 1946 what became widely known as the Cranwell 'museum' was established on the North Airfield and it can be regarded as the prototype 'station museum'. It was 1989 when the last of these containing a major collection of airframes, St Athan in Wales, closed. This is not to say that RAF stations no longer cherish their heritage, several bases have 'history rooms' or similar: for example the Trenchard Museum at Halton, Bucks; the RAF Signals Museum at Henlow; and the Historical Museum at Scampton, Lincs.

At Cranwell enterprising, volunteer, personnel set out these treasures, each with a display board and associated artefacts – there was no budget and 'scrounging' was the predominant skill. The doors would open and the lights go on mostly for visiting 'brass' or the occasional party of enthusiasts. RAF stations holding AHB airframes would occasionally be tasked with providing static items for Standard presentations, disbandment ceremonies, Royal visits etc. Major 'AHB' storage sites through to the early 1960s were as follows:

Location	Unit (if any)	From	To
Pengam Moors, Cardiff	52 Maintenance Unit	1943	Oct 1945
Cranwell, Lincs	–	Sep 1946	1961
Sealand, Flintshire	47 Maintenance Unit	1945	late 1947
Stanmore Park, Middlesex	GAFEC*	1945	Nov 1949
Wroughton, Wiltshire	15 Maintenance Unit	1945	late 1950s
Fulbeck, Lincs	Cranwell satellite	1960	mid-1960s
Biggin Hill, Kent	–	1960	mid-1960s

* German Air Force Equipment Centre

As the RAF Museum neared reality, Biggin Hill was wound down and four major 'station museums' had emerged: Colerne, Wiltshire; Cosford, Shropshire; Finningley, Yorkshire; and St Athan, Wales. The story of all but Cosford is told in the companion volume, *Lost Aviation Collections of Britain*, and will not be repeated here; Cosford is dealt with in Chapter 6. By 1962, Henlow, Bedfordshire, had become the major repository for what were still being referred to as 'AHB airframes', along with workshop facilities. Before long, this store had a purpose other than holding a holding unit for a conceptual museum; Henlow had a target, it was the 'funnel' through which the RAF Museum would be 'fed'.

Wellington T.10 MF628 on a rare 'outing' from the storage hangar at Biggin Hill in the early 1960s. *KEC*

No building, no site, no money

In November 1958 the imposing Air Ministry, now the Ministry of Defence (MoD), building was fully open for business in Whitehall, London. Designed by Vincent Harris, this enormous creation called with great imagination 'Main Building', had been started in 1938 and struggled its way through the war and budget considerations to completion. Consideration was given to opening up a room, or two, to the public at weekends – when the mandarins had vacated. Material on view was to include uniforms, medals, photographs and documentation. For a variety of reasons, this was turned down. But the idea of 'opening up' stuck and in 1961 the Air Council set up the Historical Advisory Committee, chaired by Sir Dermot Boyle with the brief of identifying *what* and *how* to display the RAF's heritage.

In 1953 John Benedict Ian Tanner (Dr Tanner from 1960) became librarian of the RAF College at Cranwell, home to the first station museum. As well as organising enthusiast parties to tour the 'museum' hangar on Cranwell North, John Tanner developed a memorabilia room within the fantastic college building, and this was open to cadets, teaching staff, visiting 'brass' and small parties of the public by prior arrangement. In many ways this was a taste of what *nearly* happened at Whitehall and he wrote to Sir Dermot Boyle in 1962 outlining what would make *an* RAF Museum. In 1963 John Tanner was given a job co-ordinating the inaugural steps in forming the Royal Air Force Museum (RAFM from now on). A board of trustees, with Sir Dermot chairing, was up and running and John Tanner was appointed as its founding Director.

It is around this time that John Tanner's oft-quoted and almost certainly apocryphal 'job definition' was delivered. It was not about what he *had*, it was about what the post *lacked*: "There is no collection, there is no building, there is no site, there is no money". MoD would facilitate the site, staff and running costs; Dr Tanner would have to find around £2 million to achieve the building. That's a cool £40 million in present-day values and this massive hurdle was achieved. An assessment of *where* was initiated and a location in Carlton House Terrace, off The Mall near St James Park was quickly discounted – an airfield was the answer. Among those short-listed were: Biggin Hill in Kent, Upavon in Wiltshire and Hendon in Middlesex. In 1967 Hendon was announced as RAFM's home.

An early staff appointment was inspirational, Jack M Bruce who later became Keeper of Aircraft

Jack Bruce joined RAFM in 1966. He is illustrated with the SE.5A upon his retirement in 1983. *RAF Museum*

and Research Studies. Genial, learned, patient, Jack had time for everyone including, in the middle of 1977, the author who was then deep in his 'sprog' years. An unflagging enthusiast, Jack was happy to share his knowledge and there are many, many people who can thank him for taking the time to put them on the right path. Jack's over-riding love was World War One aviation and his seminal 'Putnam' *The Aeroplanes of the Royal Flying Corps* must be a trusted companion on many a bookshelf.

Cradle of Aviation

Flat land off the Edgware Road, where Colindale Avenue ground to a halt near Hendon looked ideal. In 1908 H P Martin and George Handasyde built a monoplane in the ballroom at the back of Hendon's 'Old Welsh Harp' public house and tested it in a nearby field; it was not a success but the pair went on to form the Martinsyde Aeroplane Company. A year later instrument maker E J Everett created a monoplane to his own design and housed it in a specially-built shed, but this machine was only ever destined to be the 'Grass Hopper' that the locals nicknamed it. In the first days of 1910 Everett leased his shed to Claude Grahame-White who began testing a Blériot on 20th January. The brand-new pilot was taken with the possibilities of the location and during 1911 the Grahame-White Aviation Company (GWAC) acquired a ten-year lease on 207 acres of land – London Aerodrome was born. Sheds were built and several operators, including the Blériot School and the Blackburn School took up residence. On 12th May 1911 the Parliamentary Aerial Defence Committee witnessed a display of flying machines, including Samuel Cody dropping flour bombs on a mock-up of a battleship. More and more individuals and organisations came to fly from Hendon with a string of 'firsts' and record flights achieved; for example Gustav Hamel flew the first aerial post, flying between Hendon and Windsor on 9th September 1911. George Holt Thomas established the Aircraft Manufacturing Company – Airco – in 1912 and along with GWAC started to build aeroplanes at Hendon. Grahame-White was determined that Hendon would be a place the public would throng to and on 8th June 1912 he staged the first Aerial Derby and a crowd of 45,000 turned up.

Hendon was commandeered under the Defence of the Realm Act on 4th August 1914 and it became a Royal Naval Air Station. Airco, GWAC and the British Caudron Company received orders for aircraft for the Royal Flying Corps and Royal Naval Air Service. In June 1914 Geoffrey de Havilland joined Airco, having previously designed for the Royal Aircraft Factory. His DH.1 first flew from Hendon in 1915 – the start of a huge wartime production run. Hendon became a large flying school, churning out pilots for both RFC and RNAS. With the formation of the RAF on 1st April 1918 Hendon ceased to be a Navy station, but was not known as RAF Hendon, keeping the title 2 Aircraft Acceptance Park. By the time of the Armistice, the factories had peaked with over 15,000 employees and nearly 8,000 aircraft produced, but the wind-down was dramatic with mass lay-offs and terminated contracts.

In December 1918 the negotiations at Versailles that were to bring World War One to a formal end brought into being 1 (Communications) Squadron with DH.4As and Handley Page O/400 shuttling between Paris and Hendon with diplomats and administrators. Air Travel and Transport Ltd formed at Hendon and on 1st May 1919 set off on the first commercial post-war flight, in a DH.9. The Aerial Derby returned, on 21st June 1919. The following year it was all change, the RAF staging a spectacular tournament on 30th July; this was the precursor of the famous annual Air Pageants. The aerodrome was bought by the RAF in 1926, becoming the preserve of 600 (City of London) and 601 (County of London) and later 604 (County of Middlesex) Squadrons Auxiliary Air Force. Hendon's closeness to London meant that it was also home to communications units, the most significant was the King's Flight which formed there on 20th July 1936.

During World War Two it was 'comms' units that held sway at the airfield, with the varied fleet of 24 Squadron being the most prominent. The Metropolitan Communications Squadron (MCS) was established in April 1944, being re-designated as 31 Squadron in July 1948 until in March 1955 it reverted to MCS. Post-war 601 and 604 re-formed, soldiering on with Spitfire 16s until the advent of jets forced a move to North Weald, Essex, in 1949. US Army and Navy units were also based, flying Douglas R4D Skytrains and types such as DHC L-20 Beavers during the early 1950s. In 1957 the airfield closed to regular flying and it fell to the MCS to perform a farewell flypast on 4th November, comprising a DH Devon C.2, DHC Chipmunk T.10 WZ875 and Avro Anson C.19 TX214. Devon VP952 was present on that day, and *may* have been the one taking part in the flypast; it is preserved at Cosford. The last aircraft to depart was TX214 on the 7th – this is also now at Cosford – see Chapter 6. Hendon remained a functioning RAF station with a variety of ground-based units;

SKYWRITING

Avro 504Ns of 2 Flying Training School, Digby, performing the ever-popular 'crazy flying' routine at the 1930 Hendon Air Pageant. The pilots were Fg Off Campbell and Plt Off Whittle – the latter soon to become the father of the jet engine. Behind are the Savage Skywriting hangars – see Chapter One. *Peter Green Collection*

the silent wings of 617 Gliding School (1959 to 1968) and the occasional helicopter provided flying content. From mid-1968 Barnet Council began building houses on the airfield site, the RAF presence being reduced to the ten-acres destined to become RAFM, and the East and West Camps. RAF Hendon closed on 1st April 1987, but the site continued to house the Joint Service Air Trooping Centre (JSATC) and the Supply Control Centre (SSC) as an enclave. East Camp finally closed in February 1988, the Grahame-White Factory and the Watch Tower being within its confines. Both listed buildings, it was to be some time before their future could be defined. West Camp closed in August 1988, but the RAF Ensign is still to be seen flying from the refurbished and repositioned RAF Hendon Station Headquarters flagstaff, courtesy of RAFM.

Wrapping 1915 in modernity

Dr John Tanner's list of the things he didn't have – a collection, a building, a site, money – was thinning down. When he was appointed as the founding Director he had the most extensive of collections, thanks to the efforts of the AHB and thousands of RAF personnel who had recognised the value of this artefact or that aircraft. At Henlow, rapidly called the 'Pickle Factory', airframes were gathering from RAF stations and from the results of an extensive search from the 'shopping list'. A significant addition was the Nash Collection, previously in the custody of the Royal Aeronautical Society: two Avro 504s, Blériot XI and XXVII, Caudron G.3, Fokker D.VII, Royal Aircraft Factory SE.5a, Farman F.41 and Sopwith Camel. Latterly held at London Heathrow Airport, courtesy of the British European Airways Engineering centre, the whole collection was placed on loan to the nascent RAFM in March 1963 and the trek to Henlow began. During 1968 there was to be another gathering at the Bedfordshire airfield, as it took on the role of 'headquarters' for the filming of Guy Hamilton's *Battle of Britain*; as will be seen in the profiles below, several RAFM airframes were used – some *abused* – during the production. While there were workshop facilities at Henlow, the farming out of airframes for restoration to other RAF stations began.

Former Nash Collection Blériot XXVII inside the Grahame-White Watch Tower building at Hendon, September 2012. *Ken Ellis*

The collection was healthy and expanding; and the 'site' was in hand. The money the all-deciding factor and the determinant of the *when*. All of the airframe sleuthing, restoration and research meant nothing if in the end there was no cash to translate all of these efforts into a building suitable for a national collection and to showcase the RAF in its true glory. A large publicity and advertising campaign was launched to solicit donations from the public, but more vitally to attract corporate sponsors, signing large cheques or offering facilities and services. A Founders' Roll of Honour was created, allowing John Smith to rub shoulders with Rolls-Royce within its pages. Mention must be made of the determination and innovation of Gp Capt Bill Randle who came up with the idea of 'flown covers' – special commemorative stamped envelopes which were a major source of revenue from around 1968 well into the 1980s. Gp Capt Randall's fund-raising was crucial to the existence of RAFM, the Battle of Britain Museum and the Bomber Command Museum.

Hendon had been chosen as the venue, but just *which* bit of the RAF station was open to appraisal. The 'Belfast truss' hangars built in 1915 on the eastern perimeter of the airfield, alongside the railway line, became the focus of attention. There had been six of these, but two were destroyed, along with 14 aircraft, most from 24 Squadron, during a raid by the Luftwaffe on 7th September 1940. The space created by the raiders today forms the car park to the south of the Historic Hangars and the area on which the Milestones hall is sited. Dr John P Milford Reid, a former RAF officer, came up with the concept of linking the four hangars and 'wrapping'

An extensive advertising campaign was launched to raise funds for the Hendon project.

Construction underway around the 'Belfast truss' hangars at Hendon, with Beverley XH124 looking on, 1970. *KEC*

them in a modern facade providing entrance hall, shop, restaurant, theatre/conference facilities etc. Architect Geoffrey Bodker turned this into an impressive and remarkably cost-effective building. The edifice was 650ft long, 170ft wide and encompassing over 175,000 square feet of display space. With the 'space' defined, under the guidance of Ray Lee and John Tanner, the job of deciding on exhibits and how to arrange them was embarked on, using the time-honoured method of models within a scale mock-up of the building.

Outside, the runways at Hendon occasionally had an unplanned arrival – including a Luftwaffe Nord Noratlas on 25th January 1967 convinced it was on finals to Northolt. During 1968 an *intended* arrival; the last RAF fixed wing, powered, machine to use the airfield was greeted by a large crowd. As soon as the 50th anniversary celebrations at Abingdon, Oxfordshire, were complete, Blackburn Beverley C.1 XH124 was prepared for its last-ever sortie on 19th June 1968. With air traffic long since gone, a green flare was fired to let the crew of the giant airlifter know that the runway was clear; XH124 required less than half the length and taxied to a stop on the hard standing 'created' by the Luftwaffe 28 years previously. The Beverley, having completed 4,478 flying hours, was technically the 'gate guardian' for RAF Hendon; but it was there to await the opening of RAFM and provided a reminder to construction crews that the project was all about aviation.

As everything started to come together 1972 was declared as the target and on 15th November HM Queen Elizabeth II opened the Royal Air Force Museum at Hendon. The 'open' presentation of the airframes, with 'kerbs' providing a subtle, but very effective, barrier to any adventurous visitors was praised. So were the lighting levels and the very 'airy' feel, plus the elevated galleries providing views from a variety of angles and aspects. Special events and exhibitions were planned to 'ring the changes', for example the incredible 'Wings of the Eagle' event staged 1975-1976 and these have been a hallmark of the museum ever since. Hard on the heels of the main museum opening was the inauguration of the Dermot Boyle Wing – in honour of the guiding light from 1961 and the Historical Advisory Committee – to house special displays.

Battle of Britain and Bomber Command

A vast amount of time had been spent agonising over which aircraft to display at Hendon. The original building had been designed to provide ease of access so that even large airframes could be replaced. But this would allow for a one-in, one-out treatment, whereas Hendon was showing off less than a third of the airframes to hand. Growth was on the cards from the earliest days. The Hendon site could accommodate more buildings without the need to expand its boundaries. Two themes were obvious – the Battle of Britain and Bomber Command – and once again the two-pronged process of developing exhibits alongside the lifeblood of funding were put into action. First on Dr John Tanner's list was the Battle of Britain and while RAFM would have no trouble in filling it with aircraft and artefacts directly from the conflict, there was no on-site building to incorporate and thereby ameliorate some of the costings. Land was chosen on the south-western boundary, close to Grahame Park Way and the Battle of Britain Hall was opened in November 1978. A multi-layer design was adopted, allowing once again for the well-regarded viewing from different vantage points.

Genuine Hurricane and Spitfire Battle of Britain veterans were arranged in a mock-up of an 'E-pen' that also acted as a venue for small exhibits. A line-up of other 1940-era types along the southern wall was a very potent sight, especially the Luftwaffe types. The opportunity was taken to accommodate the Short Sunderland flying-boat that had been on external display since 1971. A large restaurant was built alongside, allowing for more space within the main building.

In 1989 the 'rebranded' 'Battle of Britain Experience' was launched to great acclaim. Visitors travel through exceptionally well-staged scenes with mannequins 'explaining' events; the bombed-out street scene being particularly effective. Entering into the main hall, visitors have the option of ascending into a set of theatre seats above and behind the 'E-pen' from which a totally engaging series of projections tell the story of the Battle while lighting effects highlight individual aircraft. The building underwent another transformation in 2010 with the east wall becoming all-glass.

Left: The Battle of Britain Hall, shortly after opening in 1978. In the foreground is a Bofors gun, the Gladiator, Defiant and Bolingbroke. *RAF Museum*

Below: Sunderland MR.5 ML824 inside the Battle of Britain hall with the gantry that allows public access inside. 'Moored' alongside is Seaplane Tender 206, part of the marine craft collection. *Ken Elis*

Brochure launching the appeal for the Bomber Command Hall, with a Terrence Cuneo painting of Halifax *S-for-Sugar* on the cover.

IS PAST HISTORY PAST CARING FOR ?

The Bomber Command Hall, opened in 1983, required huge scale to meet the ambition of containing the Lake Hocklingen Halifax, Lancaster *S-for-Sugar*, Valiant and Vulcan V-Bombers and, as part of a tribute to the United States Army Air Corps, a Boeing B-17 Flying Fortress and North American B-25 Mitchell, among others. Where to put this structure? Land behind the original building, with the railway line, the M1 motorway and the Barnet By-pass beyond, was chosen for the two linked halls. This was clever use of land but also allowed for a radical change within the main building. The new hall not to be separate, but would 'break into' the 1972 structure. The eastern wall would have a large access door, the area in front of which could act as a 'receipt and dispatch' for large artefacts moving and in and out of *both* the main and the new building. Use of space was kept to the absolute minimum – take a look at the distance from the end of the Vulcan's in-flight refuelling probe to the north-east corner of the hall to see how precisely managed every square inch was! An example of this practicality can be seen under the mainwheels of Lancaster *S-for-Sugar* – purpose-built skates. This allows the bomber to be moved with ease, to facilitate the 'chess game' needed to reshuffle airframes. These skates were invented by Sqn Ldr Bruce James and have gone on to help museums all over the world. Sqn Ldr James ran the Michael Beetham Conservation Centre for many years and his skills are to be found all over RAFM.

Hostage to fortune

Where is the Shackleton? Is a question often put to RAFM staff, particularly inside the National Cold War Exhibition hall, where an example of the venerable sub-hunter would seem most appropriate. As will be seen in the profiles below, RAFM's Shackleton is to be found in Manchester. A look through the table 'Former Royal Air Force Museum Aircraft' reveals that RAFM had three other Shackletons, all no longer with the collection. How this came about is a good case study of the dilemma RAFM found itself in until 1998 and, in some ways still, does. Tasked with being custodian of the heritage of the Royal Air Force, the museum had no direct control over its exhibits, actual or potential; that was the domain of the MoD. (And in terms of *potential* airframes, still is.)

Two of the 'other' Shackletons were the final version, the tricycle undercarriage and Viper 203 turbojet-assisted MR.3/3 introduced in the early 1960s. At 64,300lb empty and with a wingspan of 119ft 10in, the massive Mk.3 is not to be sniffed at when it comes to re-locating by road. The year 1971 looms large in the preservation history of Shackletons. No.201 Squadron at Kinloss had started working up on the mighty HS Nimrod in 1970 and the days of the Shackleton MR.3 were numbered. (When 204 Squadron disbanded at Honington on 28th April 1972 the final MR.3s were retired.) On 23rd September 1971, former 42 Squadron XF703 touched down at Henlow, for RAFM. That November, MR.3 WR977 was allocated for fire practise at Thorney Island, but this was rescinded and instead the former 203 Squadron machine flew to Finningley on the 9th to join the station museum. At the Shackleton's birthplace, Woodford, on the last day of September 1971 a new breed of the venerable patroller took to the air for the first time – this was WL745, the prototype AEW.2. Fitted with the AN/APS 20 radars previously in the Fleet Air Arm's Gannet AEW.3s (see Chapter 4) the Shackletons were intended as 'stop-gaps' until the Nimrod AEW.3 programme became operational. To recap, during 1971 RAFM had a 'primary' Mk.3 at Henlow, plus a 'reserve' at Finningley and the prospect – some time during the mid-1980s – of a choice of the dozen AEW.2 conversions.

Things changed rapidly... Space pressures at Henlow meant that XF703 was scrapped by MoD in September 1975. No matter, WR977 was secure at Finningley. Plans to hold the Royal Review of the RAF, as part of the Queen's Silver Jubilee celebrations, at Finningley in July 1977 brought an abrupt end to the station's collection. Newark Air Museum stepped up to the breach and moved WR977, piece by piece, to Winthorpe in April. On 7th July 1979 MR.2 WL801, fresh from acting as a crew trainer for 8 Squadron, flew into Cosford

Newark Air Museum's Shackleton MR.3/3 WR977 was brought piece by piece from the closing station museum at Finningley in April 1977. *Ken Ellis*

for the museum. And there was always Plan B – at 2 School of Technical Training at Cosford, MR.3s WR971, WR974, WR982 and WR985 had been in use for instructional purposes since arriving in 1970. And then there was still the AEW.2s by then plying their trade from Lossiemouth. In 1982, the first tranche of AEW.2s were retired and included in these was *Dougal*, WR960, which touched down at Cosford on 22nd October for the Aerospace Museum. Soon plans for the Manchester Air and Space Museum were being formulated, and RAFM played a major part in getting this up and running. Dismantled, WR960 made the journey to Manchester in January 1983. During June 1984 MR.2 WL801 was offered for tender and the following year it was scrapped.

All four instructional MR.3/3s were put up for disposal by the MoD in September 1988, much to the surprise of many pundits who would have expected one to stay with the Aerospace Museum. (WR974 and WR982 are with the Gatwick Aviation Museum, the fuselage of WR971 is with the Fenland and West Norfolk Aviation Museum and WR985 languishes at Long Marston.) In terms of a 'global' view at the end of 1988, the Imperial War Museum at Duxford had been looking after MR.3/3 XF708 since it touched down on 23rd August 1972, so a Mk.3 was comfortably with a 'national'. Since then, XF708 seems to have slipped in IWM's priorities and indeed there was a time when the AirSpace hall was being schemed that it was to be dismantled and turned into a 'walk-through' exhibit. (While its wings, 'tail feathers' etc were to be kept, should it ever need to become whole again.) Today, XF708 remains effectively stored in the conservation area of AirSpace. The nation's 'reference' Shackleton MR.3 is the Newark Air Museum's example, lovingly looked after, albeit in the open.

In the summer of 1991 the final AEW.2s were retired from service with the Boeing Sentry AEW.1 fully up and running at Waddington. (The Nimrod AEW.3 programme having been laid to rest in December 1986.) So it is that *Dougal* is RAFM's Shackleton, displayed in what is now the Museum of Science and Industry in Manchester, close to its birthplace. Returning it to Cosford, or Hendon would be an expensive and complex exercise and would also involve MOSI (now a Science Museum franchise) planning well in advance what to do with the not inconsiderable 'hole' it would create. Besides, moving WR960 would only make sense if it were to slip straight into covered accommodation and a building of the same scale and potential as the National Cold War Exhibition is a long way off.

Gate guardian collateral

While being the custodian of airframes not 'owned' by the museum can be a considerable drawback, there are also advantages. Most of its airframes, vehicles, items of equipment etc come from MoD; and, of course, myriad items being donated by companies, societies and most important of all, the public. Donations do not have to be aircraft, or medals; from its earliest days, RAFM has relied upon cash gifts, bequests and the results of trading enterprises. So, how does an organisation that is not cash-rich acquire high-profile items to extend its collection and shorten its 'shopping list'? Thankfully, MoD has had a progressive view of the collateral power of its historic airframes. A couple of examples will serve to illustrate this flexibility. In exchange for Hawker Typhoon MN235, the Smithsonian Institute in the USA took Hurricane II LF686 in 1968. As a mark of thanks for help during the acquisition of Bolingbroke IVT 10001 in Canada in 1969, Beaufighter TT.10 RD867 was sent to the national collection at Rockcliffe. Supermarine Seagull V VH-ALB was secured in Australia by trading Spitfire XVI TE384 in 1973. This system has worked the other way around; in 1997 RAFM gained a CASA-built Bücker Jungmann from Spain by way of a 'thank you' for the loan of Cierva Rota I K4232 which was used as a 'template' to help in the construction of an airworthy replica.

From 1988, RAFM's 'war chest' was swollen considerably thanks to a proposal from AHB or RAFM or a combination of both and Tim Routsis of Cambridge-based Historic Flying Ltd (HFL) who responded with a workable scheme. This was simple, the time had come to remove Hurricanes and Spitfires from 'gate guardian' duties at RAF stations; they were far too precious to be exposed to the elements year after year. In exchange for some Spitfires that his company could restore to flying condition and sell onwards, HFL would supply the MoD with high-quality full-scale replica Hurricanes and Spitfires to take over duty on the gates. This was 'win-win' and MoD readily drew up the necessary paperwork. This released Spitfires that Hendon could use in exchanges and, as will be seen from the table, the museum still has a working stock at its long-term store at Stafford. Currently nearing completion by Precision Aerospace at Wangaratta, Victoria, Australia, is Douglas A-20G Havoc 43-9436 *Big Nig*; and for this complex restoration, Precision will receive two Stafford Spitfires. In Lincolnshire, Vintage Skunk Works is under commission to supply RAFM with an Ilyushin Il-2M2 'Sturmovik' for eventual display within Milestones in exchange for another Spitfire.

Hendon is 'guarded' by Hurricane and Spitfire full-scale replicas created by Historic Flying Ltd. *Ken Ellis*

Spitfire V EP120 'on guard' at Wattisham in 1988. Wattisham was the fourth RAF station it had been displayed at, and it moved to Church Fenton before being released for 'trade' by RAFM. Today it flies with The Fighter Collection at Duxford. *KEC*

Royal Air Force Museum 'gate guardian exchange' Spitfires

Variant	Identity	Previously 'guarded'	Notes
Mk.V	BM597	Church Fenton	Restored as G-MKVB, airworthy with the Historic Aircraft Collection at Duxford
Mk.V	EP120	Boulmer	Exchanged ex store at St Athan with The Fighter Collection for Sabre XB812 during Jan 1993. Restored to flight as G-LFVB, airworthy at Duxford
Mk.XVI	RW382	Uxbridge	Restored as G-XVIA, later N382RW. Restoration project, Isle of Wight, registered G-BPIX
Mk.XVI	RW386	Halton	Restored as G-BXVI. Airworthy in Sweden as SE-BIR
Mk.XVI	RW393	Turnhouse	Stored at Stafford
Mk.XVI	SL542	Coltishall	Exchanged ex store at St Athan for Hampden P1344 1992. Shipped to the USA, becoming N2289J
Mk.XVI	SL574	Bentley Priory	Displayed at San Diego, California, USA
Mk.XVI	SL674	Biggin Hill	Stored at Stafford
Mk.XVI	SM411	71 MU Bicester	Exchanged for DH.9A F1010, displayed in Krakow, Poland
Mk.XVI	TB252	Bentley Priory	Became G-XVIE, under restoration in New Zealand
Mk.XVI	TD248	Sealand	Restored as G-OXVI, airworthy at Humberside Airport
Mk.XVI	TE356	Leeming	Restored as G-SXVI, airworthy as N356TE, Oregon, USA
Mk.XVI	TE392	Credenhill	Restored as N97RW, airworthy in Texas, USA
Mk.XVI	TE476	Northolt	Restored as G-XVIB, airworthy as N476TE in Florida, USA
F.21	LA198	Leuchars	To East Fortune, Scotland, ex-Cardington for restoration 4 Mar 1998 for Kelvingrove Art Gallery and Museum, Glasgow. See narrative
F.21	LA226	Biggin Hill	Stored at Stafford
F.22	PK664	Binbrook	Stored at Stafford
F.24	PK624	Abingdon	Exchanged ex store at St Athan with The Fighter Collection, 1994. Stored at Duxford

Spitfire power

A potential addition to the exchange 'fleet' was Spitfire F.21 LA198, but while it is now on show in a museum, it did not contribute to bringing a new type to Hendon or Cosford. Its story helps to underline the notion that RAFM did not 'own' most of its airframes and illustrates the life of a typical gate guardian. Built at South Marston in October 1944, LA198 joined 1 Squadron at Coltishall, the following May. Within a year the unit exchanged its Spitfires for Gloster Meteor F.3 jets and LA198 was put into store. Its flying career was not over, Mk.21s were ideal for the newly-revived Auxiliary Air Force (with a 'Royal' prefix from 16th December 1947) and LA198 was enlisted with 602 (City of Glasgow) Squadron at Abbotsinch on 12th May 1947. The Spitfire flew from what is today Glasgow Airport until it was retired to storage in July 1950, as Spitfire F.22s became the bulk of 602's fleet. A further spell of activity started on 19th September 1951 at Exeter with 3 Civilian Anti-Aircraft Co-operation Unit, where it flew as a willing target for Army gunners.

Its propeller blades finally stopped turning in late 1951 when it was retired and presented the following year to 187 Squadron Air Training Corps at Worcester and displayed outside its headquarters at Portiswell. It was whisked off to Henlow in Bedfordshire in 1967 for use as a non-flying 'extra' in the film Battle of Britain. From mid-1969 it was erected on a plinth outside RAF Locking, near Weston-super-Mare. This lasted until 25th March 1986 when LA198 returned to Scotland. Resplendent in 602 markings again, LA198 was mounted at the main entrance to Leuchars, the station then flying magnificent Rolls-Royce Spey-powered McDonnell Phantoms. This 'stardom' did not last long, LA198 becoming part of the gate guardian replacement programme. The Mk.21 was kept initially at St Athan before moving to Cardington, for potential exchange for other exhibits.

From LA198's arrival at Leuchars, former 602 Squadron members and others intensified their lobbying about the Spitfire's particular relevance to Glasgow. Michael Bruce Forsyth, Member of Parliament for Stirling since 1983 and, from 1995, Secretary of State for Scotland, took up the cudgel to 'repatriate' LA198. (He was also heavily involved in bringing the Stone of Scone home. It was installed in Edinburgh Castle in November 1996, six centuries after it had been appropriated by Edward I and moved to Westminster.) Eyes turned to railway enthusiast Michael Denzil Xavier Portillo MP, Secretary of State for Defence in John Major's Conservative government and the decision was made to gift LA198 to the City of Glasgow. For many bemused onlookers, including the author, it became known as 'Portillo's Spitfire'.

On 4th March 1998, LA198 arrived at the Museum of Flight, East Fortune (Chapter 10). In a joint project between Glasgow Museums and the National Museum of Scotland a workshop was created, with viewing facilities so that the public could monitor progress, with restoration funded by the Scottish Executive. The small, full-time, team worked miracles and the completed restoration was put on temporary display at East Fortune from August 2002. It was moved west unveiled at Glasgow's Museum of Transport on 17th September 2003, then transferred to the newly-refurbished Kelvingrove Museum for a further inauguration on 17th October 2005. As a postscript, Michael Forsyth's efforts in returning Scottish heritage seem not to have been appreciated by the people of Stirling; in the General Election of 1997, the Labour candidate more than reversed his 40-percent majority achieved in 1992.

Three sites, tough choices

For Sgt Desmond Fopp the odds were far from good and Messerschmitt Bf 110s got the better of him. The Australian-born pilot parted company with his Hurricane; he was badly burnt and rushed to hospital. It was 3rd September 1940, and he had been flying Hurricane I P3673 of 17 Squadron. Desmond recovered and resumed a career in the RAF that included flying Royal Auxiliary Air Force Gloster Meteors. Seven years after taking to the silk, Desmond became the father of Michael Fopp.

Bearing in mind that he's written the Foreword, the author has to be careful with his words henceforth! Now Dr Michael Fopp, he says that with a Battle of Britain background: "a love of aviation was inescapable". Michael was elected as the first volunteer Secretary of the Society of Friends of the Museum in 1974. In September 1979 he left the Police, having been injured in riots the previous April, and joined RAFM's full-time staff and within a year became, highly appropriately, Keeper of the Battle of Britain Museum. He left in 1985, taking the post of Director of the London Transport Museum. The gravitational pull of Hendon was far too strong, in 1988 John Tanner retried as Director and Michael slipped seamlessly into the hot seat.

Construction of the Bomber Command Hall had put RAFM into debt – close on £2 million. Michael needed to get things firmly on to a business footing. He'd already got a track record, when the Battle of Britain Hall was being readied, Michael proposed that it should be run separately – with an admission fee – and it worked. Under Michael's direction, RAFM charged admission across the site and more income streams were sought, including the arrival of simulators for the public to sample. Without a firm financial base, development was impossible. By 1988 the Director RAFM was responsible for three sites, Hendon, Cosford and the restoration centre at Cardington, Bedfordshire. Much of Michael's time was devoted to upping both the status and capabilities of Cosford. This and the story of the stores and workshops beyond Henlow are related in Chapter 6.

Among tough decisions there was a very obvious one in early 1990 as a scrap merchant tore into Hendon's 'gate guardian' of 21 years, Blackburn Beverley C.1 XH124. As related earlier, with the Battle of Britain hall, the Sunderland could be wheeled into the snug and the dry, but at 38ft 9in tall, a wingspan of 162ft and an empty weight of 79,000lb, the Beverley was a very different proposition. When it flew in to Hendon, there was no 'vision' for it two decades hence. Inspections inside XH124 showed that it was steadily decaying; a restoration programme was possible but would be horrifically expensive and draining on resources and pointless without a plan to put a roof over its head. In November 1989 the bullet was bitten and it was offered for tender and in January the giant was felled. Logic similar to that related in the 'case study' on the Shackletons above was that there was another example, XB259, with the Museum of Army Transport, appropriately at Beverley in East Yorkshire. (This machine faced an uncertain future when the Museum of Army Transport closed. Miraculously, XB259 was dismantled and moved by road to the Fort Paull Armouries in May 2004 – the *second* time this monster had been taken apart and trucked to a new home.) In some ways, the scrapping of the Beverley gave rise to the notion that was to take substantial form in the Cold War hall at Cosford.

January 1990 and the Hendon Beverley falls to the scrapman's axe. *Alan Curry*

Already mentioned, the former Nash collection had been placed on long-term loan to RAFM from the Royal Aeronautical Society (RAeS). In the early 1990s, RAeS wished to dispose of the collection to RAFM permanently and required a settlement. This would be to the advantage of both parties as technically any work RAFM craftsmen carried out on former Nash airframes could be negated as they were sold on. Grants, lottery funding etc would not be available as the museum did not own its exhibits. Eventually, a solution was found which included the disposal of DH Mosquito T.3 TW117 and MoD acquiring the Nash machines on behalf of RAFM until September 2004 when MoD gifted them to RAFM.

Ambitious plans to develop Cosford and the emerging Milestones of Flight project meant that the nettle of being custodian to exhibits technically owned by another body had to be grasped. As recounted above under the headings 'Hostage to Fortune' and 'Spitfire Power' above, RAFM could find itself at the whim of politicians wishing to bear gifts, or changes in MoD attitudes to particular airframes. The point-prover that settled things was 'Portillo's Spitfire' (F.21 LA198) in 1998. RAFM Trustees agreed that the time for change had come and the Treasury and MoD responded positively. Director Michael Fopp undertook not to seek the return of an RAFM aircraft on loan unless they came off public display at a prime site. Examples of this being the LVG C.VI on loan to the Shuttleworth Collection. When Old Warden announced the intention to stop flying it, RAFM elected to bring back into the fold, its last official flight taking place on 20th September 2003 and it is now being prepared for the centenary of the Great War anniversary. For a long time on show by the Imperial War Museum (IWM) at South Lambeth, London, Focke-Wulf Fw 190A-8 733682 was brought down from its lofty perch in the atrium in December 2012 in preparation for that museum's 1914-1918 exhibition. IWM had decided that it no longer had a place in its plans, so it was taken back by RAFM. To overcome RAFM's 'hostage to fortune' quandary, Parliamentary approval had to be acquired for what was a transfer of assets. In an unprecedented arrangement, on 3rd August 1998 the MoD assigned ownership of 121 airframes to the museum. At a stroke, RAFM was master of its own destiny in terms of applying for lottery funding and other forms of finance. Doors were opening and plans were crystalizing.

Keeping 'em flying

Releasing former gate guardians into the world of 'warbirds' is just one way in which RAFM has contributed to keeping historic aircraft in the air. The research and archival facilities at Hendon are very much a 'back room' operation that seldom gets the praise they deserves; yet a huge list of owner/operators/restorers will stand up and praise the help they have received. Manuals, drawings, part lists, specifications, photographs, the loan of components allowing copies to be made and the exchange of surplus items is part and parcel of how RAFM functions. As might be imagined, the Battle of Britain Memorial Flight has received invaluable assistance from RAFM.

A look through the exhibit profiles below will reveal several examples of this largely unsung aid to 'warbirds'. Sqn Ldr Howell Davies, owner of the Old Warden-based Hawker Demon K8203 (G-BTVE) donated undercarriage legs for the museum's Bristol Bulldog. In return, from RAFM stores, his project received a Demon rear fuselage.

Peter Vacher's superb Hurricane I R4118 flew thanks to the loan of an RAFM Merlin III. *Ken Ellis*

The Shuttleworth Collection's Gloster Gladiator has also benefitted from spares from RAFM. The narrative below on Hendon's B-17G Flying Fortress mentions the unprecedented exchange that took place after the final flight at Stansted, Essex, in November 1983. The Wright Cyclones on Hendon's example were lower-houred than those on B-17 Preservation's famous *Sally B* and it made no sense to let them hang forever more on a museum piece when they could be keeping the 'flyer' operational. The same rationale saw the two bombers exchanging ailerons.

At Cambridge Airport on 23rd December 2004, Hawker Hurricane I R4118 (G-HUPW), piloted by Pete Kynsey, took to the air for the first time since 1943. Owned by Peter Vacher, the discovery of former Battle of Britain veteran R4118 mouldering in a college yard in India, its repatriation to the UK and its restoration to flying condition is a story of epic patience, tenacity and skill. Initial euphoria about the state of R4118's extremely rare Rolls-Royce Merlin III was shattered on strip-down; wasps had made a home within the bores, the rust was beyond redemption and the aluminium around the valve seats was corroded. Peter wrote of the life and times of his project in 2005 in the superb book *Hurricane R4118*. Faced with nowhere to go with his Merlin, he hoped he had an option: "During my various visits to study the Mk.I Hurricane in the RAF Museum at Hendon, I had noticed two Merlin III engines on display. I tentatively approached the Director, Dr Michael Fopp, to ask if there might by any possibility of securing one of these. The trustees deliberated and most kindly proposed that an engine could be let for a period of seven years, which wold get R4118 off the ground whilst another engine could be sourced. I accepted with alacrity this most positive offer of help."

Important milestones

Within the confines of RAF Hendon's East Camp were two listed buildings, both from the days of Claude Grahame-White's transformation of Hendon. Built in 1915 the Watch Office gave views over the comings and goings of the aerodrome and was the nerve centre of the organisation and was last used as a control tower in 1957. The imposing Factory, with offices over-looking the shop floor, was completed in 1917 as the UK's first purpose-built aircraft manufacturing plant, but came too late for production to take place. As related above, the East Camp did not close until February 1988 and disposal to developers and plans for the site took time to emerge. Part of the deal that brought about today's Beaufort Park was the re-location of the Watch Office and the Factory to the southern-most edge of the RAFM site. This was no trivial undertaking, requiring detailed liaison between local authorities, developers, the many specialist contractors and RAFM. During the creation of the original museum building, the 'Belfast truss' hangars stayed rock solid while everything grew up around them. For the Grahame-White projects the structures need relocating, using the maximum amount of original materials while meeting modern regulations and visitor requirements. Skills in building relocation and restoration were well established, with centres like Blists Hill Victorian Town at Ironbridge in Shropshire, the Beamish North of England Open Air Museum near Durham and the Ulster Folk and Transport Museum (Chapter 9) east of Belfast. Despite this, the two-phase project was an enormous undertaking for RAFM.

The Vickers Vimy replica inside the Grahame-White Factory building. *Ken Ellis*

The Factory was the first element to be re-sited and aircraft were rolled into it in February 2003 and it opened to the public later in the year. Attention to detail is superb, including the replica Thomas Crapper & Co cisterns and plumbing in the loos! While the Watch Office was smaller, in terms of challenges it was a far bigger project than the Factory. The building was adapted and extended so that it linked to the Factory with the space in between telling the story of Grahame-White, Hendon, aircraft manufacture in the area and the history of RAFM itself. 'G-W's' personal office is breath-taking, the fireplace containing off-cuts of aircraft grade wood in a typical example of Edwardian waste not, want not! Site developers St George completed the migration of the Watch Office in 2010 and it was formally opened by the Duke of Gloucester on 17th March 2011.

From 2001, government policy decreed that national museums should open to the public at no charge. While this increased the footfall at Hendon overnight, it decreased income for day-to-day running and future schemes. With the site becoming more complex, in 2003 referring to the 'main building' or the 'original building' was becoming misleading and the title Historic Hangars was adopted. On 17th December 2003 the world celebrated the centenary of powered flight – the Wright brothers at Kitty Hawk as noted in Chapter 1. For this Michael Fopp and his team had set their sights on a long-held wish, to portray the history of flight itself. While many UK museums, with a greater or lesser aviation flavour deal with the subject, none specifically did so. The history of the RAF reflects the development of aviation and so both stories need telling; the RAFM's collections already had artefacts and airframes required to do the job. During November 2000 the museum announced that it had secured £4.7 million from the Heritage Lottery Fund towards the £7.4 million needed for the Milestones of Flight hall to celebrate the centenary and to be opened on the day of the anniversary. Like the Grahame-White projects, the Milestones building belies the work involved by museum staff. Research into the chronology running along the length of the hall was extensive, taking in political and social change as well as aeronautical. The 'Navigator' online collection was launched in the same timeframe and was another major leap in facilities. Located to the south of the Historic Hangars, Milestones changed the 'shape' of the museum, becoming the entrance hall from which visitors could fan out as they wished. Milestones serves to provide a 'primer' for the rest of the site, setting the heritage of the RAF in the context of aeronautical achievement. Emphasis was placed on the 'ringing the changes' concept that has always been central to RAFM philosophy and Milestones has the ability to move aircraft in and out with ease and already there have been changes in the line-up. The Duke of Edinburgh opened Milestones of Flight and the Grahame-White Factory on the 17th December as the world paid tribute to the Wright brothers.

Grahame-White's office in the Watch Tower. *Ken Ellis*

The Grahame-White Watch Tower in its new location, amid the modern development of the East Camp, now known as Beaufort Park. *Ken Ellis*

Dr Michael Fopp retired as Director in 2010 with a string of major projects successfully delivered, at Hendon, Cosford and Stafford (see Chapter 6 for the last two). The present Director General, AVM Peter Dye, took the helm on 9th June 2010; the first former RAF officer to take command of the museum. Peter hit the floor running, with the centenary of World War One looming and the all-important 100th anniversary of the RAF four years after that. As noted at the beginning of the chapter, incredible plans for a new presentation of the Battle of Britain will maintain Hendon's status of as the beacon of aeronautical heritage.

Before the exhibit profiles start, it is time to 'fess up and explain that if you 'go' the Royal Air Force Museum website and select 'Research', you will be propelled to the 'Collections' section where there are brief details of all of the aircraft on show at Hendon and Cosford. Should you hanker for more, there is an option to download the official museum history of each exhibit. These have been carefully researched and updated by Andrew Simpson and these words serve to praise him and RAFM for the information treasure they have created. I am grateful to the museum for being able to plunder Andrew's painstaking work over many, many years. I've said it before and I'm saying it again, *every* UK museum should have such a practical method of research and its own Andrew Simpson!

Impression of the Battle of Britain Beacon – another challenge for Hendon. *RAF Museum*

Airspeed Oxford I MP425
1943 | Two-three seat multi-engined trainer/crew trainer: Two 375hp Armstrong Siddeley Cheetah X

Built by the Standard Motor Car Company at Coventry – almost certainly without a gun turret – MP425 was issued to 1536 Beam Approach Training Flight at Spitalgate, near Grantham, on 12th March 1943 and today it wears again those markings. 'BAT' flights taught the 'dark arts' of instrument landings. To warn aircraft in the non-radio traffic patterns that the crew were very likely 'eyes down' and not aware of their surroundings, yellow triangles were painted on the nose, rear fuselage and wing tips. From Spitalgate, MP425 moved on to more general twin-engined training with 18 (Pilots) Advanced Flying Unit at Church Lawford from February 1945 and 2 Service Flying Training School at Westwood, Peterborough, from May 1945. It was retired to 12 Maintenance Unit at Kirkbride in January 1946.

In May 1947 MP425 was acquired, along with Percival-built ED290, by Air Service Training, becoming G-AITB and G-AITF respectively. AST, based at Hamble on the Solent, used the two for contract training of airline pilots, eventually getting another two, G-ALTP and 'R, to expand its operation. In 1960 *Tango-Bravo* and *Tango-Fox* were ferried to Perth in Scotland to become instructional airframes with AST's engineering school. Both were snapped up by RAFM in March 1969 and moved to Henlow. As will be seen in the table 'Former Royal Air Force Museum Aircraft', G-AITF was used in trade with the South African Air Force Museum in February 1984 for the Lockheed Ventura stored at Cosford. Restored to 1536 BAT Flight colours at Cardington, MP425 was displayed at the Newark Air Museum during 1991 to 1994 before travelling to Hendon in October that year.

Cardington in November 1988, in the foreground is the newly-completed Oxford MP425, behind is Hart Trainer K4972. *Peter Green*

Auster I LB264
1942 | Two/three seat air observation post | One 90hp Cirrus Minor

Managing Director of textile machinery manufacturers Crowther Ltd at the Britannia Works, Thurmaston, Leicester, A L Wykes, was also an avid member of the County Flying Club not far away at Rearsby. He combined both experiences and formed Taylorcraft Aeroplanes (England) Ltd in 1938 with factory facilities at Syston and assembly and flight test at Rearsby. Lance Wykes had a licence to build the US-designed Taylorcraft high-wing two-seater, known as the Plus C. The type's ability to become an air observation post (AOP) for the Army led to a small batch of Cirrus Minor-powered versions, Plus Ds, being eagerly accepted for the role in 1939. Originally to have been called the British Taylorcraft Icarus, the name Auster – a warm and gentle Mediterranean wind – was adopted instead. By the end of the war 'Auster' had become a generic name for a military light aircraft and hundreds had been built. In March 1946 the company was renamed Auster Aircraft Ltd to take advantage of this association and because it had developed the type far beyond the original American version. Post-war Auster developed a series of civilian and military versions and in 1960 was absorbed into the Beagle organisation. Such was the diversity of Austers that it is impossible to choose one to profile; so the tactic is to go for 'book ends', the earliest military survivor and in Chapter 7 the last of the breed, the AOP.9.

Lance Wykes piloted LB264 on its miaden from Rearsby on 22nd May 1942 and three days later took it to the Aeroplane & Armament Experimental Establishment at Boscombe Down. By September 653 Squadron was using LB264 to get used to the type at Penshurst in Kent. On 25th May 1943 it joined 1 Elementary Flying Training School (EFTS) at Panshanger, moving on to 22 EFTS at the end of the year. Based at Caxton Gibbet, west of Cambridge, 22 EFTS converted pilots to AOP types. Retired in August 1944, LB264 was sold to the Cotswold Aero Club on 24th May 1946, with just 328 flying hours 'on the clock'. Registered as G-AIXA in January 1947 it flew with a variety of owners until the late 1980s. Peterborough-based Geoff Brown acquired it on 28th March 2000 and he set to restoring it to Auster Mk.I status at a workshop in Loughborough, Leics. Geoff entered into negotiations with RAFM and he piloted it on its last flight, from Spanhoe, Northants, to Cosford on 23rd October 2002. It moved to Hendon on 27th August 2003.

Lance Wykes, the founder of Auster, was the man who carried out the first flight of LB264, at Rearsby on 24th May 1942. *KEC*

Avro Lancaster I R5868
1942 | Seven-eight crew heavy bomber | Four 1,640hp Rolls-Royce Merlin 20

Cheek-by-jowl at Hendon are two World War Two heavy bombers: Halifax and Lancaster. By co-incidence both carry the individual code letter 'S', so were known as *S-for-Sugar*. There are several aircraft within this book that prove that 'exhibit profiles' will never do justice to the subject matter. This is the case with the chosen Lancaster. The reader is directed to the RAF Museum's exceptional website and the 'Research' section, thereby to download the *32-pages* of official history of Lancaster I R5868... Also, try to find a copy of *A Very Special Lancaster*, by F E Dymond and published by Pitkin Pictorials in association with RAFM during 1976. Go into the Bomber Hall at Hendon and look up to the nose of *S-for-Sugar* and you will find a quote from Reichmarshall Hermann Goering: "No enemy aircraft will fly over the Reich territory". Also painted there are 139 bomb tallies, amounting to a tonnage of about 466, taking up about 795 hours of 'ops'. This was only surpassed – by one 'op' – by Lancaster III ED888 'PM-M[2]' of 103 Squadron. All of this makes R5868 very special indeed; but its importance pales against those of the crews who flew and fought in *S-for-Sugar* from July 1942 to April 1945.

So how to pay tribute? Unimaginatively, the first and last 'op', plus a *very* close shave in November 1943 have been chosen and those undertaken by 'Aussie' Plt Off John 'Jack' William McManus, who is illustrated here. Lancaster I R5868 was intended to be a Manchester, the twin Rolls-Royce Vulture-powered bomber from which the Lancaster was descended. Built by Metropolitan-Vickers in Manchester, it was assembled and flight tested at Woodford in June 1942. Taken on charge by 83 Squadron at Scampton on 29th June 1942 it was given the code letters 'OL-Q' – *Q-for-Queenie*. Sqn Ldr Ray Hilton DFC, commander of 'B' Flight eased R5868 off the runway at just gone midnight, 9th July 1942 with 1,260 four-pounder incendiaries in the bomb bay, bound for Wilhelmshaven; returning without incident 4 hours, 13 minutes later. Sixty-seven sorties later, on 15th August 1943, *Q-for-Queenie* completed its last 'run' with 83 Squadron.

In September R5868 arrived at Bottesford, joining 467 Squadron Royal Australian Air Force – the code letters 'PO-S' – *S-for-Sugar* – were painted either side of the fuselage roundel. The stay at Bottesford was not long and on 11th November R5868 was ferried to Waddington, 467's new base. Sortie No.82 was to 'The Big City' – Berlin – with Fg Off Jack Colpus at the helm on 26th November 1943. Just after bomb release, *Sugar* was coned by searchlights, Colpus corkscrewed and dived to throw the enemy off the scent. At 20,000ft or so, the rear gunner reported that they had collided with another aircraft. (This turned out to be Lancaster I DV311 *P-for-Peter* of Skellingthorpe-based 61Squadron – its crew also lived to tell the tale.) After much agonising, and not knowing the full extent of the damage, Jack put *Sugar* down at Linton-on-Ouse with 5ft missing from the wing tip. *Sugar* was sent back into 'the system' for repair-in-works. It was not ready until February 1944 and the crew of Australian Plt Off 'Jack' McManus took it on, with the following results:

Lancaster I R5868 'PO-S' 467 Squadron, 'ops' with Plt Off Jack McManus, 1944

Op	Date	Target	Sortie Time	Comments
83	15/16 Feb	Berlin	6 hrs 48 mins	Lost engine over the target
84	19/20 Feb	Leipzig	7 hrs 24 mins	Some crew sick through "bad oxygen"
–	20/21 Feb	Stuttgart	1 hr 47 mins	Port outer cut at 13,000ft. Bomb load jettisoned and returned – R5868's first abort
85	24/25 Feb	Schweinfurt	7 hrs 32 mins	–
86	25/26 Feb	Augsburg	7 hrs 45 mins	Against the Messerschmitt works
87	1/2 Mar	Stuttgart	8 hrs 8 mins	–
88	18/19 Mar	Frankfurt	5 hrs 58 mins	467 Sqn record – 22 aircraft put up, 118 tons dropped
89	22/23 Mar	Frankfurt	5 hrs 12 mins	Tail wheel tyre deflated on landing
90	24/25 Mar	Berlin	3 hrs 19 mins	Port outer failed, port inner showing oil leaks. Bombs jettisoned. Shadowed by night-fighter for 15 mins, but lost in cloud

Sugar's 139th and last 'op' took place on 23rd April 1945 when Fg Off Laurie Baker took it to Flensburg, but he did not drop his eight thousand-pounders and half-dozen 500-pounders because of the 10/10ths cloud cover over the harbour. Six days later Italian partisans killed Mussolini and 48 hours after that Hitler shot himself; the war in Europe was over bar the formalities. From late April 1945 to 28th May 1945 the crews of 467 Squadron

Plt Off Plt Off 'Jack' McManus in the cockpit of Lancaster *S-for-Sugar. KEC*

– and others of Bomber Command – were involved in Operation EXODUS, the repatriation of prisoners of war. *Sugar*, for example, collected 24 personnel from Jouvincourt, France, on 6th May. By this stage, unit records and Bomber Command's publicity machine were having problems attributing exactly how many 'ops' *Sugar* had been on. It took a lot of archival work two decades later to iron this out.

No.467 moved to its fourth and last base on 16th June 1945, taking the brief 'hop' from Waddington to Metheringham and disbanded there on the last day of September 1945. It would seem that *Sugar* was left at Waddington. The Air Historical Branch (AHB – more on it in the introduction to this chapter) were informed of R5868's availability on 14th July 1945 and six days later came a reply that *Sugar* be retained. The venerable Lancaster was issued to 15 Maintenance Unit (MU) at Wroughton on 23rd August 1945. Part of the working party of seven men that dismantled *Sugar* was Yorkshireman Cpl H Smith. The team took the opportunity for a 'group shot' alongside the cockpit section, next to the famous bomb tallies and quote from an infamous German who at that point was two months away from taking his own life at Nuremburg. Still in dismantled state, R5868 was moved in 1958 to Fulbeck where other AHB airframes were gathered.

The following year, *Sugar* was transferred to its first operational base, Scampton, for display purposes and in 1960 it was put 'on the gate'. In July 1970 a team from RAFM, led by Deputy Keeper Jack Bruce, surveyed the 'Lanc' and a team from 71 MU – the specialist 'crash and smash' unit, tasked with dismantling and moving flightless airframes by road – dismantled it. No.71 MU's base was Bicester and that's where *Sugar* was taken for restoration. This was completed in March 1972 and R5868 travelled to Hendon and it was repainted in 467 Squadron colours. As a postscript, Scampton was not long without a 'guardian'. Lancaster VII NX611, previously languishing at Blackpool Airport, was officially unveiled close to Scampton's guardroom, overlooking the busy A15 on 10th April 1974. This machine is now *Just Jane* and regularly taxied at the Lincolnshire Aviation Heritage Centre at East Kirkby. The team are well into plans to return it to flight status.

Avro Shackleton AEW.2 WR960
1954 | Ten-crew airborne early warning radar picket | Four 2,450hp Rolls-Royce Griffon 57A | On loan to the Museum of Science and Industry Manchester

The story of the Shackleton and RAFM is covered in detail in the introductory narrative of this chapter. Built as an MR.2, WR960 first flew at Woodford, south of Manchester, on 5th February 1954, entering service with 228 Squadron, at St Eval on 22nd July. The Shackleton being a complex anti-submarine platform, service life was interspersed with 'special fit' sessions when systems were updated or replaced. Airframes were also subjected to more comprehensive programmes, including life-extension modifications and armament upgrades. No.228 Squadron disbanded on 1st April 1959 and WR960 transferred to 42 Squadron, also at St Eval, but only for six months as it was destined for Avro facility at Langar, and Phase 1 upgrade. Work done, it joined 210 Squadron at Ballykelly in Northern Ireland on 19th December 1960. In March 1962 it was back at Langar for Phase 2 mods and was rolled straight into the Phase 3 programme; thus being designated MR.2/3. It was not until 2nd February 1968 that it was back in the frontline, this time with 205 Squadron at Changi in Singapore. WR960 was retired to 5 Maintenance Unit at Kemble in November 1970 to await its fate.

On 27th May 1971 WR960 was sent to Bitteswell to become the fourth AEW.2 airborne radar picket conversion. It was delivered to 8 Squadron at Kinloss in Scotland on 7th June 1982. All of 8's AEWs were named after characters in the children's (of all ages!) TV series *The Magic Roundabout* and WR960 became *Dougal*. No.8 moved eastwards along the Moray Firth from Kinloss to Lossiemouth on 17th August 1973. Defence cuts in 1981 halved the AEW.2 fleet and *Dougal* was ferried to Cosford for the Aerospace Museum on 22nd October 1982, completing 9,712 flying hours. It was destined to become the centre-piece of the Manchester Air and Space Museum and it moved to its new home on 27th January 1983.

Blackburn Buccaneer S.2B XW547
1972 | Two-crew low-level strike/reconnaissance | Two 11,200lb st Rolls-Royce Spey 101

Turn to Chapter 4 for a Gyron Junior-engined S.1 survivor. The RAF came late to the Buccaneer, taking the sophisticated strike jet on in the wake of the cancellations of the 1960s: the BAC TSR-2 and the still-born General Dynamics F-111K. Hendon's S.2B was ordered directly for the RAF and was built at Brough, near Hull, and roaded to Holme-on-Spalding Moor for flight test. It was issued to 15 Squadron at Laarbruch, West Germany, on 8th November 1972. A series of units, all based at Honington, followed: 12 Squadron, (1974-

Nimrod AEW.3 XZ285, intended as the first production example, banking away from Shackleton AEW.2 WR960, in 1982. *BAe*

1976); 237 Operational Conversion Unit (OCU – 1976-1978) and 216 Squadron 1979-1980. On 28th April 1981 XW547 was issued again to 12 Squadron, by then at Lossiemouth in Scotland. During 1983, XW547 was involved in two very interesting 'ops'. On 3rd March three Buccaneers, XV353, XV868 and XW547, touched down at Wideawake airfield, Ascension Islands, after a ten-hour transit from the UK. Hendon's XW547 acted as an airborne spare for a sortie 48-hours later and it was back at 'Lossie' on the 7th. Just what this deployment was for, in the year following the Falklands conflict, has never been clarified. Staying at Lossiemouth, XW547 moved across the ramp to 208 Squadron from 1st July. On 9th September 1983 six S.2Bs of 12 and 208 (including XV168, XV865 and XW547) deployed to Akrotiri on Cyprus as part of Operation PULSATOR. Along with Boeing Chinooks, also Cyprus-based, and shipboard Fleet Air Arm Westland Lynx and Sea Kings, the aircraft were acting in support of the British element of the peace-keeping Multi-National Force during another flare-up of the Lebanese civil war, 1983-1984. BRITFORLEB – British Forces in Lebanon – was a small Army contingent based in the Beirut suburb of Hadath. On the 11th, Buccaneers from Akrotiri, including XW547, flew at *very* low level to achieve a 'heads down' to relieve BRITFORLEB during a tense moment. (Carrier-based Dassault Etendards of the French Aéronavale were also involved in similar tactics that day.) A similar show of force was staged by the 'Buccs' on the 13th. The PULSATOR deployment lasted on Akrotiri until 26th March 1984. From 17th December 1985 XW547 was on charge with 237 OCU at Lossiemouth, re-joining 12 Squadron there on 18th April 1986.

In late January 1991 XW547's appearance was radically altered, it was painted in overall desert sand (universally called 'pink') for use by the RAF Gulf Detachment, acquiring nose-art and the names: *Pauline, Guinness Girl* and *The Macallan*. It and eleven others deployed from Lossiemouth to Muharraq, Bahrein, for Operation GRANBY (British military actions within Operation DESERT STORM) to liberate Kuwait from Iraqi aggression on 27th January. Between 2nd and 25th February XW547 flew eleven 'ops', mostly against bridges or airfields. The first involved dropping laser-guided bombs (LGBs) on a high-level road bridge at Samawah, the other ten were designator flights on behalf of LGB-toting Panavia Tornados. The Gulf War came at the twilight of the Buccaneer's service life; XW547 was back at Lossiemouth on 17th March but ferried to Shawbury in July 1991 in readiness for its removal to Cosford for the Aerospace Museum on 20th January 1993. All 29,980lb empty weight of XW547 moved by road to Hendon on 9th February 2003.

Boeing B-17G Flying Fortress 44-83868
1945 | Eight-crew heavy bomber | Four 1,200hp Wright Cyclone GR-1820-97

After abortive operational use of Fortress Is by 90 Squadron in 1941, the RAF found the B-17 a reliable maritime patroller, the last ones leaving service in early 1946. The B-17G on display inside Hendon's Bomber Hall is partially there to 'stand in' for an RAF Fortress, but primarily to honour the men and machines of the USAAF Eighth Air Force during World War Two. Built by Douglas at its Long Beach, California, plant as B-17G-95-DL 44-83868, it was flight tested on 4th July 1945. Its time with the USAAF was fleeting, on the 14th it was transferred to the US Navy for use in Project CADILLAC II – to create a fleet of land-based airborne early warning (AEW) pickets – taking on the Navy Bureau of Aeronautics serial 77233 and designation PB-1W. This and others, straight off the Long Beach line, were ferried to Navy Air Station (NAS) Johnsville, Pennsylvania, where the main modification was the installation of an AN/APS 20 radar under the centre section, in place of the bomb bay, plus operator stations within the fuselage. (This radar was effectively the same as installed in Shackleton WR960 26 years later – see above.) BuAer 77233 was issued to NAS Quonset Point, Rhode Island, in the spring of 1947 for use with experimental trials squadron VX-4. This was in readiness for the US Navy's first operational AEW unit, VPW-1 based at San Ysidro and detached to Miramar, California, from April 1948 (later renamed VW-1). By May 1955 PB-1W 77233 was parked out at the Naval Air Facility at Litchfield Park, Arizona, and struck off charge on 10th July 1956.

On 2nd December 1957 the PB-1W was sold to the American Pressed Steel Corporation and civil registered as N5237V in March 1958 and ferried to Love Field, Dallas, Texas. The Fortress passed through a couple of owners until on 27th September 1961 it was sold to Aero Union and flown to its base at Anderson, California. Aero Union was well-known for its conversions of former military aircraft, particularly to what the Americans call 'air tanker' status but what is best known in Britain as 'fire-bombers'. Thus converted, from December 1961 Butler Aircraft of Redmond, Oregon, operated N5237V as call-sign *Tanker Echo-15*. By the summer of 1962 the B-17 had acquired spray bars along the trailing edges of the wings to allow it to undertake agricultural application work when not involved in the fire season. By 1979 it was being operated by TBM Inc of Sequoia, California, with the call-sign *Tanker-65*. The fire-bomber was retired in 1982 and TBM began a special commission on behalf of the USAF Museum to return it to B-17G status, complete with replica turrets, and it was painted in the colours of the Bury St Edmunds-based 94th Bomb Group's 332nd Bomb Squadron. *Three-Seven-Victor* was to be presented to RAFM in appreciation for a trio of Vulcan B.2s delivered by the RAF during 1981 to USAF museums: XM573 to the Strategic Air Command Museum, Offutt, Nebraska, 16th June; XM605 to the Castle Air Museum, Atwater, California, 8th September; and XM606 to the Eighth Air Force Museum, Barksdale, Louisiana. RAFM elected to have the B-17 restored to flying condition, at its cost, and have it delivered by air across the Atlantic. On 28th September 1983, N5237V was flight tested at Sequoia Field and six days later, piloted by Air Cdre Ron Dick and TBM's Ken Stubbs as P2 with the call-sign *Rafair B17*, the eastwards migration began. The B-17G arrived at Brize Norton, Oxfordshire, on 13th October and on the 25th a sortie was made to overfly its future home, Hendon. Two days later came a memorable formation sortie over former 'Mighty Eighth' bases with the Duxford-based B-17G *Sally B*, operated by Elly Sallingboe's B-17 Preservation Ltd. Its last-ever flight came on 7th November 1983 from Duxford to Stansted, completing a grand total of 5,724 hours. At Stansted, *Sally B's* engines were exchanged for the lower-houred examples on N5237V and both bombers also exchanged ailerons. Early in December the B-17G arrived by road at Hendon and on 17th April 1984 an official hand-over was staged. At this Gen William P Acker, C-in-C of the US Third Air Force presented the B-17 to MRAF Sir Michael Beetham on behalf of RAFM. As well as the B-17, Sir Michael accepted a cheque from Boeing for £35,000 to pay for the restoration costs – a perfect day!

Boulton Paul Defiant I N1671
1940 | Two-crew turret-armed fighter | One 1,030hp Rolls-Royce Merlin III

During 4th December 2012 a low-loader made its way west from Rochester in Kent bound for Hendon. Its cargo was 30,000 man hours of highly skilled endeavour spread over three years; the latest painstaking restoration by the Medway Aircraft Preservation Society for RAFM. MAPS has a unique relationship with Hendon, consistently achieving miracles within its small workshop at Rochester aerodrome. The only intact survivor of the breed, N1671 was built by Boulton Paul at its Pendeford, Wolverhampton, plant and on 17th

September 1940 it was on charge at Kirton-in-Lindsey with the Polish 307 Squadron. The concept of the turret fighter at first held considerable promise by virtue of the firepower that could be brought to bear on bomber streams from unexpected angles, but the Defiant proved to be a disappointment as a day fighter as the Luftwaffe learned to recognise its weak points. Because of this, 307 Squadron was moved to Jurby on the Isle of Man on 7th November 1940 for convoy patrol duties. No.307 moved to Squires Gate on 13th March 1941 but 14 days later had upped sticks to Colerne. From the new base, the Defiants were to be flown in a new regime, as night-fighters and N1671 was flown on its first nocturnal sortie on 8th April. Eight days later Sgt Wisthal caught sight of another aircraft about 300ft above him. This opened fire on N1671, whose gunner did not get the opportunity to bring his four 0.303in Browning machine-guns to bear. It next joined 153 Squadron at Ballyhalbert in Northern Ireland, before relegated to second-line duties with 285 Squadron at Wrexham in June 1942, moving to Honiley, Warks, in October. No.285 specialised in providing targets for anti-aircraft gunners to train on – using blanks! The Defiant was retired to 10 MU at Hullavington on 16th May 1943. In April 1944 N1671 was retained by the Air Historical Branch as a Battle of Britain era aircraft and it was ferried to 52 MU at Pengam Moors, near Cardiff, for packing. By December 1944, it had moved – still in its substantial crate – to 82 MU Lichfield, Staffs, and then to 76 MU Wroughton. Storage at several sites was interspersed with an occasional static appearance at a special event and the greatest of these was at Abingdon in June 1968 for the Royal Review of the RAF, celebrating its 50th anniversary. After that it joined the station museum at Finningley until it moved to Hendon on 1st April 1971.

Bristol Bulldog IIA 'K2227'
1930 | Single-seat fighter | One 490hp Bristol Jupiter VIIIFP

This machine is mentioned in three chapters, reflecting the changing fortunes and priorities of its custodians. It was presented to the Science Museum (Chapter 1) by the manufacturer but returned to airworthiness in 1961. Bristol then handed the fighter to the Shuttleworth Collection (Chapter 3) and it was flown until crashing at the Farnborough Airshow in 1964. Parts of the badly smashed Bulldog were put into store at Old Warden and other elements were secreted away by RAFM. In 1994, Hendon decided to commission a reconstruction, the result today stopping visitors in their tracks as they move around the Historic Hangars.

The Bulldog was built at Filton as a company demonstrator and trials aircraft and civilian registered as G-ABBB in June 1930. It was fitted with a Gnome-Rhône 9ASB radial, the French version of the Jupiter, and late that year it was exhibited inside the Paris Salon Aero Exhibition. The Gnome-Rhône and the appearance in Paris were part of a 'push' for an order from the Armée de l'Air and in the spring of 1931 'Three-Bees' was demonstrated to the French at Villacoublay. By September 1935 G-ABBB had undergone major surgery and been fitted with a tightly-cowled Bristol Aquila radial for a 100-hour endurance trial. For this, the Bulldog flew with the lettering 'R11' under the cockpit. This was what the Air Ministry called an 'under B conditions' identity, but perhaps is better termed as a 'trade-plate' for test and ferry purposes. By 1936 the Aquila trial was complete and R11 was put into store at Filton. Bristol offered the fighter to the Science Museum and in February 1939 it was exhibited at South Kensington but swiftly was put into store. During the summer of 1955 the Bulldog was given the spurious serial 'K2496' for use as an 'extra' in Lewis Gilbert's film *Reach for the Sky*, based on Paul Brickhill's book on Douglas Bader, with Kenneth More playing the legless fighter pilot. (Also appearing was Shuttleworth's Avro 504 and Tutor and Hurricane I P2617, on show at Hendon.)

Following approaches from Bristol, the Bulldog was returned to Filton for restoration to flying condition. On 23rd June 1961 Godfrey Auty took G-ABBB up for a test flight. The biplane provided considerable contrast from his 'day job' which was preparing the first Bristol 188, XF923, for its first flight after roll-out on 26th April; the second example of this Mach 2 experimental is preserved at Cosford. The Bulldog was painted as 'K2227' in the glorious red and white chequers of 56 Squadron's 'A' Flight. On 12th September 1961 Bristol handed the Bulldog to the Shuttleworth Collection, but it continued to be operated by the manufacturer and kept at Filton. The Bulldog made its first public appearance at Old Warden on 14th June 1964 with Bristol deputy test pilot Ian 'Willie' Williamson at the helm. Williamson was flying the fighter again on 13th September in front of a huge crowd at the Society of British Aircraft Companies airshow at Farnborough. At the top of a loop the Jupiter cut and the Bulldog plummeted to earth; miraculously Williamson suffered only minor injuries. This was G-ABBB's third display during the week-long event; it had 'clocked' a total of 16 hours 10 minutes flying time since restoration. At that point the Finnish Air Force Museum's much-modified Mk.IVA BU-59 became the sole survivor of type.

Bulldog G-ABBB in its original configuration, circa 1930, with the radio hatch removed. Visible on the original, just above the top of the undercarriage strut, is an AA badge. *KEC*

After the Air Accident Investigation Unit had picked through the wreckage and written its report, much of the Bulldog was left in the famous yard outside the organisation's hangar at Farnborough. The Jupiter, engine bearers, firewall, rudder plus other elements went to Old Warden, while a large cache of bits was squirreled away at Henlow and later Cardington. In the 1980s, as Shuttleworth reviewed its stores, more of the Bulldog was transferred to RAFM care. By 1992 it was clear that there was the basis of a restoration and in 1994 Tim Moore's Skysport Engineering successfully tendered for the work. Back from oblivion, Bulldog 'K2227' was formally unveiled at Hendon on the last day of March 1999 and Finland's BU-59 was no longer the last-of-breed.

Bristol Bolingbroke IVT 'L8756'
1942 | Four-crew navigation/gunnery trainer | Two 920hp Bristol Mercury XX

In Finland, Blenheim IV BL-200, built under licence in 1944 and flown by the Finnish Air Force until June 1957 is the sole intact surviving Blenheim. Across the planet other 'Blenheims' are preserved, but all are Canadian-built Bolingbroke IVs. The Royal Canadian Air Force (RCAF) wanted large numbers of Blenheims and Fairchild Aircraft of Longueuil, Quebec, was contracted to build Bolingbroke IVs under licence from 1939. A crew trainer, the Mk.IVT, followed the patrol bomber version and the last was struck off charge in 1947; it is from these stocks that so many survived to the present day. Hendon's Mk.IV, RCAF serial 10001, was taken on charge on 20th October 1942 and is known to have served with 3 Bombing and Gunnery School at McDonald, Manitoba, and *probably* with 5 BG&S at Dafoe, Saskatchewan. Struck off charge on 15th May 1946 it amassed 905 flying hours.

Aviation heritage owes a huge debt to Canadian farmers, rural contractors and homesteaders. From 1946 into the early 1950s the RCAF offered equipment at very reasonable rates to locals in an attempt to overcome chronic shortages of aluminium, rubber and other useful commodities. All over Canada, individuals were buying up war surplus airframes and towing them on their undercarriage to farmsteads where they could be robbed of parts to help repair a tractor, a roof, or provide a cart with new wheels. Farmers the world over are genetically programmed never to throw anything away and this meant that in the 1960s and beyond, there were rich pickings to be found in the undergrowth. Perhaps the most famous example of this is the two Bolingbroke IVT airframes that produced the two airworthy Blenheims that delighted crowds at UK airshows in 1987 and 1993-2003. One such farmer was Mr Yuill of Portage La Prairie, Manitoba, who dragged away Bolingbroke IVT 10001 from McDonald, having parted with $200 for the privilege. Bless him, that's all he wanted all those years later when RAFM offered to buy the hulk on 25th April 1966. The RCAF provided facilities during its removal, storage and shipping and for this Beaufighter TT.10 RD867 was despatched to Canada from Henlow. The 'Boly' arrived at Henlow in crates in 1969 and in February 1972 it moved to the Aeroplane & Armament Experimental Establishment at Boscombe Down for restoration by volunteers. It was painted as Rootes-built L8756 of 139 Squadron; that unit took part in the RAF's first operational sortie of World War Two, on September 4, 1939. Restoration completed, 'L8756' was delivered to Hendon on 17th July 1978.

Bristol Beaufighter TF.10 RD253
1944 | Two-crew maritime strike/torpedo-bomber | Two 1,670hp Bristol Hercules XVII

As the plans to create the RAF Museum gathered pace, the world was scoured for types that were on the 'shopping list'. In February 1963 a major 'tick' was achieved when Beaufighter TT.10 RD867 was salvaged from Ta Qali, Malta, and brought to the UK. Last serving with the Communications and Target Towing Squadron at Ta Qali, RD867 had been struck off charge in December 1958 and consigned to rescue training duties. Engineless and in poor condition, RAFM assessed it as far from ideal. Where else to get a Beaufighter?

TF.X RD253 was built at Old Mixon, Weston-super-Mare, and issued to 19 Maintenance Unit (MU) at St Athan on 2nd November 1944. It went to Pershore, the home of 1 Ferry Unit, on 7th March 1945 as one of a batch of 16 destined for the Aviação Naval (Portuguese Naval Air Arm) to replace Blenheim IVs. All had arrived at Portela, near Lisbon, by the 22nd, RD253 taking on the Portuguese serial BF-13. The Beaufighters were withdrawn from service in 1949 and by the following year BF-10 and BF-13 were instructional airframes with the Lisbon Technical Institute. (BF-10 is now at the National Museum of Flight Scotland, see Chapter 10.) In 1965 BF-13 was presented to RAFM and it was received at 71 MU at Bicester, near Oxford, during the summer. The team at 71 MU used elements of BF-13 in the rebuild of RD867 until in 1967 all of the Beaufighter 'kit of parts' was transferred to 4 School of Technical Training at St Athan. Assessing the available material, it was decided that RD253 would become the RAFM airframe and that engineless RD867 would be shipped to the Canadian National Aeronautical Collection at Rockcliffe, Ontario, as a 'thank you' for the facilities granted during the acquisition of Bolingbroke IVF 10001 – see above. Restoration of RD253 was completed in 1968 and it was trucked to Hendon on 15th March 1971.

Bristol Belvedere HC.1 XG474
1962 | Two-crew transport helicopter | Two 1,650shp Napier Gazelle 2

The first twin-rotor *and* turboshaft-powered RAF helicopter, 26 HC.1s entered service after a long and protracted development programme. This stemmed from the Type 173 which first flew on 24th August 1952 and this machine, XF785, is on RAFM charge and on loan to the Bristol Aero Collection. Built at Old Mixon, Weston-super-Mare, XG474 was awaiting collection on 14th March 1962 and the following month was en route to Singapore as deck cargo with five others. It was issued to 66 Squadron on 8th June, based at Seletar. On 18th December a trio of Belvederes, including XG474, deployed to Brunei – northern Borneo. Ten days previously, encouraged by Indonesia, the 4,000 or so men of the TNKU (North Kalimantan National Army) staged a revolt and began attacks on strategic installations in the Sultan of Brunei's territory. As well as the rebellion, there was the worry that this would escalate as part of long-held Indonesian desire to dominate the entire archipelago. This quick-reaction was called Operation ALE, but in a predominantly teetotal region, this was changed to Operation BORNEO TERRITORIES. Along with other aviation assets, 66's Belvederes worked in co-operation with Gurkhas, Royal Marines and the Special Air Service. The Belvederes re-located from the airport at Brunei Town to the island of Labuan, off the west coast of North Borneo. By August, XG474 was operating from Kuching, in Sarawak. It was during this confrontation that the twin-rotor helicopters were nicknamed 'Flying Longhouses' by the local tribes.

Hitching a 'lift' on the carrier HMS *Albion*, XG474 returned to Seletar on 18th December 1963 and on 14th May 1964 it was positioned on to the deck of HMS *Centaur* for the voyage to Aden and the helicopter's next 'hot spot'. Nine days later XG474 was flown off the carrier to Khormaksar, joining 26 Squadron and immediately deploying in support of anti-insurgent forces in the Radfan area. On 23rd November 1965 XG474 was back on *Albion*, heading *back* to Singapore and 66 Squadron and onwards to Kuching. On 11th August 1966 a peace treaty was signed and British forces began a pull-out. That said, British personnel, supported by 7 Flight Army Air Corps with Bell 212s were *still* stationed in Brunei in 2013. By February 1967 XG474 was at Seletar, with occasional detachments to Butterworth in Malaya. No.66 disbanded at Seletar on 20th March 1969, the last RAF operational Belvedere squadron, and XG474 and five others flew to mark the occasion. Almost immediately scrapping started but thanks to 66's CO, Sqn Ldr P L Gray, RAFM accepted XG474 if it could be returned without charge. The services of HMS *Albion* were again called up; it docked in Portsmouth on 1st August 1969 and six days later XG474 arrived by road at Henlow. On 25th March 1971 it was installed at Hendon.

Consolidated Liberator VI KN751
1944 | Eight-crew heavy bomber | Four 1,200hp Pratt & Whitney R-1830-65 Twin Wasp

Liberators found two major applications in RAF service, making the most of the type's long endurance: with Coastal Command operating from the UK and as a bomber in the Middle East and particularly in India-Ceylon. Built by Ford Motors at Willow Run, Detroit, Michigan, as USAAF 44-50206, it was completed as a B-24L-20-FO in December 1944. Diverted to the RAF, as Liberator VI KN751, it set out on a long ferry flight to India from Dorval, Canada, on 4th June 1945. Today, the Liberator carries the lettering 'SNAKE' alongside its serial number. This was used to denote an aircraft destined for Air Command South East Asia and not to be diverted to other taskings or theatres during its long ferry flight. The lettering worked, the bomber routing via the Azores, Morocco, Libya, Palestine, across Iraq and onwards to Dhubalia, Bengal, India, and accepted by ACSEA 19 days after leaving Canada. No time was wasted, 72-hours later KN751 was issued to 99 Squadron which was in the process of moving to the Cocos (or Keeling) Islands, in the Indian Ocean to the west of the coast of Sumatra. It was a remote, but ideal, location to stage long-range sorties against Japanese forces from the single runway carved into the peninsula of the islands' South Lagoon. KN751's first 'op' occurred on 26th July and on 1st August, with Wg Cdr Webster at the helm, it attacked shipping off the coast of Java. The Japanese surrendered on 14th August, but the area remained hostile with dislocated Japanese forces at large and guerrilla forces vying for regional control. On the 21st US President Harry S Truman revoked the Lend-Lease Bill of March 1941 and instructions went out to ACSEA forces that belligerent operations were to cease; in 99 Squadron's case this meant the removal of guns from the turrets and no more dropping supplies to 'friendly' insurgent groups. No.99 disbanded on 15th November and the Liberators were flown north-west to India.

   By 1948 KN751 was at Bangalore being converted to maritime patrol status for the Indian Air Force by Hindustan Aircraft Ltd (HAL). On 2nd March 1949 KN751 was officially taken on by India, with the serial HE807. By 1951 it was serving from Poona, on the west coast near Bombay, with 6 Squadron, 'The Flying Dragons'. The Liberators of 6 were set for a long career and during the Indo-Pakistan War of August-September 1965 were on the order of battle and flew what were technically operational sorties – the B-24's last war. No.6 staged its final Liberator flight on the last day of 1968, having replaced the type with another venerable four-prop, Lockheed Super Constellations. The surviving Liberators were parked out at Poona and many were scrapped, but in February 1970, HE807 was offered to RAFM. Officially accepted by the museum at HAL's Bangalore facility on 1st July 1974 HE807 touched down at Lyneham on the 7th and on the 11th completed its last flight when it arrived at Colerne for the station museum. This stay turned out to be short-lived as Colerne was soon slated for closure and the Liberator was moved by road to Cosford in January 1976 and migrated to Hendon in September 2005.

Liberator VI KN751 shortly after arrival at Cosford from Colerne, 1977. *KEC*

De Havilland DH.9A F1010
1918 | Two-crew light bomber/general duties | One 400hp Liberty 12

In Chapters 1 and 4 are details of Westland-built Short 184 8359 that served operationally in World War One and was badly damaged when the Science Museum was bombed by the Luftwaffe in 1941. In a quirk of fate, Hendon's DH.9A was also made by Westland and saw action in World War One. In 1943 it may well have been damaged by Bomber Command in a raid on Berlin and certainly became a refugee, suffering more harm in the process. Built at Yeovil, DH.9A F1010 was delivered to 110 Squadron at Kenley in August 1918. Like the other 'Ninaks' (a contraction of 'Nine' and 'A-for-Ack' phonetics) it carried stencilling on the engine cowling to acknowledge the generosity of the man who had funded all 18 of the unit's biplanes: 'Presented by His Highness the Nizam of Hyderabad: Hyderabad No.12A'. In F1010's case, '13' was not considered a suitable number, but '12A' probably didn't fool anyone! Deploying to Bettoncourt in France, 110 went into action on 14th September. On the 25th, with Liverpudlian Capt Andrew Glover at the controls and South African 2nd Lt W G L Badley as observer/gunner, F1010 was part of a raid on Frankfurt. On the way to the target, the DH.9As were engaged by German fighters and six of the bombers were lost. One of the attackers, a Fokker D.VII, fell to a burst of fire from 2nd Lt Badley's Lewis gun. On October 5 F1010's crew were Inglis and Badley and they found themselves were in the firing line; F1010 failed to return from an 'op' against targets around Cologne. Forced down, Inglis made a good crash-landing and he and Badley were taken prisoner.

The story fast-forwards to 1936 and the more or less intact 'Ninack' was part of the truly amazing Berlin Air Museum. On the night of 23rd/24th November 1943 the museum was hit by Bomber Command during the first phase of the 'Battle of Berlin'. Over half of the precious contents were wiped out, including the massive Dornier Do X flying-boat, von Richthofen's Fokker Dr.I 528/17, the Heinkel He 176V-1 rocket-plane and a German-built Wright biplane. At some point, it may have even been *before* the raid, many lorry-loads evacuated exhibits to Czarnikau in eastern Germany. By March 1945 Soviet and Polish forces had liberated the area and it was destined to become Polish national territory. Moving on again, by 1963 the Museum of Aviation and Aeronautics at Krakow was basking in many of the former Berlin exhibits. In late 1967 the wingless and worse-for-wear F1010 was 'discovered' in a dark recess by an Australian enthusiast and negotiations began with the Soviet Bloc regime to bring the sole-surviving DH.9A to Hendon. An exchange was arranged with Spitfire XVI SM411 – even the 'Cold War' could thaw occasionally to bring a veteran home. Vehicles set out from Krakow on 15th June 1977 bringing F1010 to Cardington eight days later. With Bill Sayer co-ordinating, work set to create replacement wings and put right many other omissions and damage. The DH.9A was delivered to Hendon in the spring of 1983.

De Havilland Tiger Moth II T6296
1941 | Primary trainer | One 130hp de Havilland Gipsy Major

This is RAFM's second Tiger Moth, the first was NL985 which was part of the Finningley station museum. Moved to Hendon in 1971 it was burnt out in a fire on 23rd May before it could go on display. Thanks to the Fleet Air Arm (FAA), a replacement was to hand. On 13th December 1969 Tiger Moth T6296 made what turned out to be its last-ever flight while on charge with the FAA general duties unit 781 Squadron at Lee-on-Solent. In need of a major overhaul, it was moved to the nearby Royal Navy Aircraft Yard (RNAY) at Fleetlands for attention, but was assessed as not worth the effort. When RAFM started a search for a replacement Tiger, T6296 was an obvious choice and it was transferred to Henlow on 15th March 1972 before moving to Hendon 56 days later.

Like NL985, T6296 was built by Morris Motors at Cowley, Oxfordshire, but four years earlier, being issued to 1 Elementary Flying Training School (EFTS) at Hatfield on 13th June 1941. It joined 7 EFTS at Desford in February 1942 before retiring to 5 Maintenance Unit at Kemble, in September 1946. Already with a reasonable service career behind it, another one was looming. Transferred to the FAA on 11th December it was sent to the RNAY at Donibristle for a major service. Life in the Navy was varied with a lot of unit changes, giving cadets air experience flying, glider-towing, general communications work and simply providing pilots with a very pleasant change from their normal 'office'. Simplified, T6296's 'CV' was as follows: Gosport Station Flight (1951), Royal Naval Engineering College, Roborough and Manadon, Devon (1952), RNAS Bramcote, Warks (1955 and 1958), Station Flight / *Heron* Flight, Yeovilton (1959, 1961 and 1966), Naval Flying Grading School / Britannia Royal Naval College, Dartmouth, Devon, then to 781 Squadron at Lee-on-Solent from 29th November 1966, as described above.

De Havilland Mosquito TT.35 TJ138
1944 | Two-crew target-tug | Two 1,690hp Rolls-Royce Merlin 113/114

As noted in the Introduction, frequently the choice of which particular aircraft to profile is difficult. As this book deals with the 'nationals', the 'daddy' of all 'Mossies', prototype W4050 at the de Havilland Aircraft Heritage Centre at London Colney, Herts, cannot be included. RAFM has two of the breed and as TJ138 served with a frontline unit, it comes to the fore. Built as a B.35 bomber at Hatfield, Herts, it was issued to 27 Maintenance Unit (MU) at Shawbury on 28th August 1945 for what became long-term store. It was allocated to 98 Squadron at Celle in West Germany on the last day of October 1950; the unit re-locating to Fassberg the following day. During February 1951, the squadron started conversion to DH Vampire FB.5s and TJ138's brief sojourn with an operational unit came to a close; it was sent to 38 MU at Llandow. It touched down on the hallowed turf of Sywell in July 1953 for major surgery by Brooklands Aviation to turn it into a TT.35 target-tug. In a silver overall scheme and distinctive yellow with black diagonal stripes on the undersides, it joined 5 Civilian Anti-Aircraft Co-operation Unit at Llanbedr on 8th March 1954. As can be gathered from the title, CAACUs were operated by civil contractors – in this case Short Brothers and Harland. They provided gunnery targets for the Army, Navy and RAF Regiment by towing sleeves, or acting as actual targets in which case there would be blanks in the breech! Additionally, CAACU aircraft 'worked' RAF and Navy radar facilities, providing tracking experience for plotters. On the first day of 1958, 5 CAACU moved to Woodvale, near Southport, and Mosquito TT.35s TJ138 and Airspeed-built VR806 made the transit. At Woodvale TJ138 seems to have been used more by the resident THUM Flight, also run by Shorts. The acronym THUM was derived from 'Temperature and Humidity', the Flight operated daily climbs to 30,000ft recording weather statistics on the way for use by the Meteorological Office and the military. On 18th April 1959 TJ138 carried out the last THUM Mosquito sortie and 14 days later the unit disbanded, the role taken over by balloons equipped with radio-sondes.

By May 1960 TJ138 was stored at Thorney Island under the aegis of the Air Historical Branch and soon gained camouflage and 98 Squadron codes 'VO-L'. It was at Colerne by late 1966 and, with the base's closure, transferred to the collection at Finningley on 17th October 1975. With Finningley selected as the venue for the Royal Silver Jubilee Review of the RAF in the summer of 1977, TJ138 moved yet again, this time to Swinderby, Lincs, in February, serving as a backdrop for passing out parades before going again to St Athan by late 1986. Finally, on 6th February 1992 it settled on Hendon; changing venue slightly in June 2003 by going into the Milestones of Flight hall.

De Havilland Canada Chipmunk T.10 WP962
1952 | Primary trainer | One 145hp de Havilland Gipsy Major 8

Like the Mosquito above, RAFM has two Chipmunks – so which to go for? At Cosford, WP912 was the aircraft in which HRH Prince Philip went solo five days before Christmas Day 1952. With respect to the Duke of Edinburgh, the Hendon example got to do what a lot of RAF frontline aircraft were *intended* to, but thankfully never got the chance – to fly to Moscow. Designed and originally built in Canada, the Chipmunk was produced by the parent company in the UK for use by the RAF, Army and Fleet Air Arm plus military exports and some civilian examples. Built at Hawarden, near Chester, WP962 also had a royal connection; it was first issued to Odiham on 25th April 1953 as part of the huge static display for the Coronation Review of the RAF by HM Queen Elizabeth II. The lives of most Chipmunks were complex and varied, changing units – and sometimes service – frequently and building high flying hours. The 'CV' for WP962 was no different and is summarised as follows: 662 Squadron, Colerne, as a 'hack' for the Army Auster unit (from 1954); 61 Group Communications Flight, Kenley (1957); London University Air Squadron, White Waltham (1957); Army Air Corps Centre, Middle Wallop (1959); 3 Air Experience Flight (AEF), Filton (1962) changing base to Hullavington (1989).

By 1992 WP962 was with 5 AEF at Teversham, and it soldiered on until the unit phased out its Chipmunks on 31st March 1996; in favour of the SAL Bulldog. With the tearing down of the Berlin Wall from November 1989 and the winding up of the USSR on Boxing Day 1991 the opening up of a light aircraft route from Europe across the bulk of the former Soviet Union (FSU) to North America via Alaska was at last a possibility. Operational NORTHERN CIRCLE, a special expeditionary RAF exercise was proposed and Chipmunks WP833 and WP962 were allocated. The team departed the UK on 21st July 1996 getting as far as Moscow before massive forest fires in Siberia looked set to curtail the venture and they turned back. The two Chipmunks were put into store to await another go. On 20th May 1997 the pair left Cranwell, Lincs, arriving at Kinloss, Scotland, on 17th July having circumnavigated the northern hemisphere; across Europe, the FSU, Alaska and Canada, Greenland, Iceland and the Faroe Islands, a journey of 16,259 miles. On 4th February 1998 WP962 had its last flight, from Teversham to Newton, clocking up a total of 13,775 flying hours and 24,813 landings. It was moved to Hendon on 5th May 2000.

English Electric Canberra PR.3 WE139
1953 | Two-crew photo-reconnaissance | Two 6,500lb st Rolls-Royce Avon 101

With such an extensive history and a prolific number of versions, picking which Canberras to feature was not easy. Hendon's London to New Zealand air race-winning PR.3 stands for the B.2 and B.6-based versions and Cosford's PR.9 highlights the incredible evolution of the airframe. Built at Warton, WE139 first flew on 22nd January 1953 and was issued to the Handling Squadron at Manby 13 days later. This organisation prepared Pilot's Notes and other publications regarding the day-to-day operation of RAF types. It was then earmarked for entry into the England to New Zealand air race and it was returned to the manufacturers for the fitment of special equipment. On 10th August 1953 it joined the NZ Air Race Flight, a sub-unit of 540 Squadron at Wyton. For practise, a sortie on 4th September flew out to the Cocos Islands and back to get the crew used to the aircraft, to 'fix' the autopilot and to calibrate fuel consumption. London's Heathrow Airport, with construction work happening across the site, was the starting point, and WE139 arrived there on 3rd October, joining the other participants which included fellow PR.3 WE142 and PR.7 WH773 (the latter is preserved at the Gatwick Air Museum). Piloted by Flt Lt Roland 'Monty' Burton AFC* and Flt Lt Don Gannon DFC as navigator, WE139 was declared the winner of the speed section, flying London to Christchurch, 12,270 miles in 23 hours 50 minutes at an average speed of 494.48mph; thereby clocking a world record at the same time. The Canberra returned to Heathrow on 13th November 1953 and was ferried to the English Electric facility at Samlesbury, Lancs, for the 'once over'. The same crew collected WE139 on 11th December, departing for the USA on the 16th, arriving at Kitty Hawk, North Carolina, the follow day to take part in the 50th anniversary celebrations of the Wright brothers' flight.

Standard RAF life started on 1st October 1954 when WE139 was issued to 69 Squadron at Gütersloh in West Germany. No.69 moved to Luqa, Malta, in 1st April 1958, only to disband there on 1st July. The same day 39 Squadron re-formed, taking on 69's machines, including WE139. From October 1962 the Canberra PR.9 was coming on stream with 39 Squadron and WE139 was transferred to 231 Operational Conversion Unit at Bassingbourn on 19th December. The Canberra was retired on 23rd April 1969 and made its last flight into Henlow for RAFM, transitting to Hendon on 14th January 1971.

Canberra PR.3s WE142 (background) and WE139 at Heathrow for the start of the race to New Zealand, October 1953. *Peter Green Collection*

English Electric Lightning F.6 XS925
1967 | Single-seat interceptor | Two 12,690lb st Rolls-Royce Avon 301

Picking which Lightnings to highlight will inevitably stir the blood. The P.1A prototype at Cosford (Chapter 6) was a temptation, but so was the 'pilot-less' F.1 at IWM Duxford (Chapter 8) and the latter held sway. At the other end of the dynasty, it *had* to be an F.6. Test pilot Roland Prosper Beamont DSC DFC took XS925 on its miaden flight, a 'hop' from Samlesbury to Warton on 26th January 1967. It was delivered to 5 Squadron at Binbrook, on 2nd March; the base on the Lincolnshire Worlds destined to be its only frontline home. Apart from overhauls and a repair (in early 1970) XS925 remained loyal to 5 Squadron until August 1975 when it 'crossed the ramp' to join 11 Squadron for three months. Camouflaged in late 1976, it was put into open store at Binbrook until the summer of 1979 when it was back on strength with 5. It was in store again from February 1980, going on-line in October 1982 for a brief spell with 11 before re-joining 5 the following month. It was put through the wing modification and life-extension programmes during 1984 and 1985, re-entering service at Binbrook in June 1985 with 11, moving to 5 in February 1986 and back to 11 in April. Its last flight was on 21st July 1987, bringing its total flying hours to 4,015. After a spares recovery programme it went by road to Hendon on 26th April 1988.

Eurofighter Typhoon DA2 ZH588
1994 | Prototype single-seat interceptor | Two 13,490lb st Eurojet EJ200-01A

It will be decades before an in-service Typhoon joins RAFM to complement, or supplant ZH588. While there will be little external difference, inside the newer machine will have software that is a quantum leap ahead. It might very well have seen action, the type was 'blooded' in Libya 2011 and who know where-else in the future? British Aerospace Director of Air Operations, Chris Yeo, was in command of ZH588, the first UK-assembled Typhoon to fly, at Warton, Lancashire, on 6th April 1994. (German-completed DA1 had taken to the skies at Manching just eleven days previously.) Both were fitted with Turbo Union RB.199 Mk.104E turbofans in place of the intended Eurojet EJ200s. DA2 was displayed statically at the Paris Salon, Le Bourget, in June 1995 and was displayed at Farnborough in September 1996. Sqn Ldr Simon Dyde became the first RAF pilot to sample the new type, flying ZH588 from Warton on 9th November 1995. In November 1996 DA2 was put through a major inspection, system upgrades and a spin-recovery parachute was mounted on a rig behind the base of the tail. It reached Mach 2 for the first time on 23rd December 1997 and was involved in 'wet' tanking trials with RAF VC-10 K.3 ZA149 in January 1998. DA2 was grounded at Warton later that year for installation of EJ200-01A turbofans. By July 2000 it had gained its all-over black colour scheme adopted when the airframe was covered with 490 pressure sensors. DA2 was back in the limelight at Farnborough in July 2002 before embarking on trials with inert MBDA AMRAAM missiles. Its last tasks included trialling a towed-decoy system and on 29th July 2007 it was retired to Coningsby for spares recovery. Flightless, it was still useful, going by road in October 2007 to Brize Norton, for air portability proving, being loaded in and out of a 99 Squadron McDonnell Douglas Globemaster airlifter. That work completed, it was prepared at Coningsby to 'fly' within the Milestones of Flight hall and was trucked to Hendon on 22nd January 2008.

Fairey Battle I L5343
1939 | Three-crew light day bomber | One 1,030hp Rolls-Royce Merlin II

Shortly after the oil seal broke, the Merlin gave up the ghost and seized, it was lousy weather and the ground below could not have been more unwelcoming. Canadian-born Clayton 'Willy' Wilcox went through his force-landing drills and tried to get his passenger, Lt Col H L Davies of the Royal Engineers, ready by getting him to *stand* behind the pilot's seat. This was not normal procedure, but the alternative did not bear thinking about, although Willy was very pleased it *had* crossed his mind. Inside the cockpit was a spare propeller blade, the tip of which would have been pointing directly at the Royal Engineer's belly – not a desirable situation when an 'emergency stop' was looming. It was September 1940 and of course it just *had* to be Friday the 13th. Willy was at the controls of 98 Squadron Battle I L5343 on a sortie out of Kaldadarnes, Iceland, to allow the Lt Col to inspect construction work at a new airstrip near Akureyi on the north of the island. The glacial area Willy had selected to come down on looked reasonable, but close-in he could see it was strewn with boulders, but he was committed. The Battle was smashed about as it slid to halt. Both occupants were not badly hurt and commenced a walk of over 40 miles to find help.

The recovery party at the boulder-strewn crash site of Battle L5343, Iceland, September 1940. *via Len Woodgate*

Built by Austin Motors at its Longbridge, Warwickshire, plant Battle L5343 was issued to 266 Squadron at Sutton Bridge, as a conversion trainer for what was to become a Spitfire I unit. By July 1940 it was with 98 Squadron at Gatwick, the unit was licking its wounds after being part of the Advanced Air Striking Force in France. No.98 was now destined to the part of the wonderfully-named Operation FRIGIDAIRE, deploying to Iceland for coastal patrols. The Battles, including L5343, were shepherded by a Sunderland flying-boat on the 5 hour, 20 minute over-water sector. Four days after the crash, a RAF team including Wally Forney reached the wreckage of L5343 and set about recovering what equipment they could before firing a flare into the carcase which was impossible to recover. In 1971 Wally approached RAFM with details of the crash and at team from Leeming, led by Flt Lt Erik Mannings with deputy Flt Lt Len Woodgate (who went on to become Keeper of the Aerospace Museum at Cosford in 1983), arrived at Keflavik to attempt a salvage. On 21st November 1972 a 53 Squadron Short Belfast C.1 touched down at Leeming, Yorskhire, and the remains of the Battle were unloaded. In 1977 the project received a boost with the acquisition of fuselage sections from Austin-built L5340 and wing sections from the Strathallan Collection in Scotland – see the companion volume *Lost Aircraft Collections of Britain* for more. In 1983 the Battle moved to St Athan, where Len Woodgate was in charge of the station museum. The restoration was rolled out on 6th March 1990 and moved to Hendon and unveiled on 19th May. The cockpit had not completed at St Athan and corrosion problems in the rear fuselage and wing roots reared their head eventually. So it was decided to move L5343 to the workshops of the Medway Aircraft Preservation Society at Rochester in Kent. Arriving on 19th January 2006, the MAPS team subjected L5343 to an intensive restoration over 25,000-plus man hours. After final work by the team at the Michael Beetham Conservation Centre, Cosford, the immaculate Battle was re-delivered to Hendon on 13th July 2010.

Fokker D.VII 8417/18
1918 | Single-seater fighter | One 160hp Mercedes D.III

Fokker D.VIIs were regarded as so potent that their disposal following the Versailles Treaty of 1919 was vigorously monitored. Hendon's example was built by Ostdeutsche Albatros Werke at Schneidemuhl in eastern Germany and very likely never saw action. Upon the Armistice in November 1918 it was abandoned at Ostend and taken on by Belgium, *probably* joining the Air Force. In 1931 three D.VIIs, including 8417/18, were placed on the Belgian civil register as OO-AMH, 'I and 'Y. In September 1934 OO-AMY was re-registered as OO-UPP; but crashed in France in July 1937. In that year, UK collector Richard Nash found a D.VII stored at Versailles and snapped it up for his growing collection at Brooklands, Surrey. (For more on Nash see the companion volume *Lost Aircraft Collections of Britain*.) It *could* have been OO-UPP, or one of the others, or a composite of OO-AMH and 'I.

Dispersed during the war, the D.VII next surfaced at 39 Maintenance Unit, Colerne, along with other elements of the Nash Collection, circa 1949. In 1953 the Royal Aeronautical Society (RAeS) acquired most of the collection and by 1954 the D.VII had been restored by Vickers at Brooklands, featuring an 'interesting' lozenge camouflage. In 1957 it had gravitated to Hendon, going on to Heathrow Airport by 1959 and to Upavon by 1962. It was loaned to RAFM and by March 1966 was at Henlow and painted in a red and white scheme; going on to Cardington by 1974. With the purchase of the Nash Collection from RAeS in March 1992, RAFM was clear to invest in a serious restoration. With its flying career in Belgium and several, well intentioned, rebuilds during its time in the UK, the D.VII was an amalgam of periods and parts, including a lot of British 'spec' nuts, bolts and bits. At Cardington, years of research were put into just *what* authentic lozenge camouflage was, its colouring and how it was applied to fabric. A workshop in East Germany was tracked down that still had the machinery for printing lozenge camouflage and was commissioned to create another batch; this being used to help similar projects with other museums and collections. In September 1997 the magnificent result of all this work and co-operation was delivered to Hendon.

Gloster Gladiator II K8042
1937 | Single-seat fighter | One 840hp Bristol Mercury VIIIA

There are two examples of the RAF's last biplane fighter at Hendon. As well as the intact K8042 there is the poignant forward fuselage of former 263 Squadron N5628 which was lost during the Norwegian campaign in April 1940. Built at Hucclecote, K8042 was issued straight to 1 Aircraft Storage Unit at Waddington, on 27th August 1937 and it was not until August 1941 that it was despatched for flying duties. Sent to the Aeroplane & Armament Experimental Establishment at Boscombe Down, the biplane was used for trials of a faired-in 0.303in Browning at mid-span under each upper wing with a magazine for 425 rounds per gun; adding to the existing two in the centre section and two under the lower wing. Probably with the additional guns removed, K8042 was in store at 27 Maintenance Unit (MU), Shawbury by April 1942. On May 27th the Gladiator was ferried the short distance to Tern Hill, joining 5 (Pilots) Advanced Flying Unit, which mostly had Miles Masters and Hawker Hurricanes. Staying within the county, it transferred to 61 Operational Training Unit at Rednal on 27th October 1943. The OTU was predominantly a Spitfire unit, but nine Gladiators and at least one Wellington were assigned to 'Q' Flight which was co-operating in the making of a film about the Greek campaign, based on James Aldridge's 1942 book *Signed with their Honour*; although it does not seem to have made it to the 'silver screen'. On 17th October 1944 K8042 was retired to 8 MU at Little Rissington and it was still there when struck off charge in March 1948. This would ordinarily have brought the aircraft's career to an end, but it seems that K8042 was allowed to linger as a historic airframe and by 1954 it was at the Air Historical Branch's store at Stanmore Park, Middlesex. By the early 1960s it was kept at Biggin Hill, Kent, and later with 71 MU at Bicester. It was issued to RAFM at Henlow in November 1965 and painted as the CO's mount of 87 Squadron of 1938. The Gladiator was installed at Hendon on 30th November 1971.

Gloster F9/40 Meteor DG202/G
1942 | Single-seat prototype fighter | Two 1,200lb st Rolls-Royce W.2B/23

As with several other major types in this book, the very first Meteor is to be featured while in Chapter 10 one of the last versions, an NF.14, is outlined. After the success of the E28/39, powered by Frank Whittle's pioneering jet – see Chapter 1 – it made sense to let Gloster and its designer W G Carter create a twin-jet fighter. A contract for prototype/development airframes to Specification F9/40 was placed in February 1941. As the programme evolved, the availability of engines became the pacing element. Production of Whittle W.2s had been passed to Rover but in November 1942 this was terminated and Rolls-Royce at Barnoldswick, Lancashire, took over; this work leading to the Welland and Derwent turbojets. As insurance, it was decided to fit two of the F9/40s with centrifugal de Havilland Halford H.1s – the progenitor of the Goblin turbojet – and another with axial-flow Metropolitan-Vickers F.2s. The honour of the first F9/40 to fly fell to the fifth example, DG206/G with H.1s, on 5th March 1943 at Cranwell, with Michael Daunt at the controls. Next away was the W.2B/23-equipped DG205/G on 12th June, but its performance was disappointing. (The suffix /G on a serial number denoted that the aircraft was to be permanently under guard when not flying.)

Although it was the first airframe completed, DG202/G was the third to take to the skies. It undertook ground runs, fitted with Rover-built W.2B/23s at the Gloster site at Bentham, to the west of Brockworth, from 29th June 1942. It was taken by road to Newmarket Heath on 2nd July and Flt Lt P E G 'Gerry' Sayer started taxi trials, but the low power available prevented anything more than the occasional 'hop'. (It was Gerry Sayer that took the Gloster E28/39 on its maiden flight on 15th May 1941.) In August the engines were removed from DG202 and it was put under wraps to await a more suitable powerplant. It was moved to Barford St John, Oxfordshire, on 22nd May 1943 and fitted with a pair of Rolls-Royce W.2B/23s. In this form, Michael Daunt took it up for a 7-minute sortie on 24th July. On 5th November Daunt ferried DG202 to Hucknall, the main Rolls-Royce test airfield and Church Broughton in Derbyshire, for increasingly intensive engine trials. The port engine exploded on take-off on 13th December 1944, causing considerable damage and a skilful forced landing. The Meteor was taken to Gloster's test airfield at Moreton Valence for repair, the work taking five months. On 11th August 1945 test pilot Sqn Ldr Eric Greenwood flew DG202 to Abbotsinch, Glasgow, where it was taken by road to the River Clyde, loaded onto a lighter and floated over to the carrier HMS *Pretoria Castle*. Craned on board, DG202 taxied around to test its suitability for operation from a 'flat top'. (As detailed in Chapter 4, the Navy did things differently, five months after DG202 was *taxied* on the *Pretoria Castle*, Capt Eric Brown *landed* Vampire LZ551/G on HMS *Ocean*.)

Wearing the instructional airframe number 5758M, Meteor DG202 at Yatesbury, circa 1962. *KEC*

The excursion to and from Scotland was DG202's last flight and it was issued to 5 School of Technical Training at Locking, near Weston-super-Mare, in April 1946. In January 1951 it moved to 2 Radio School at Yatesbury, Wiltshire, for further use as an instructional airframe. It was restored in June 1958 and a pair of Wellands were fitted. In 1965 it was trucked to Cosford for storage, later becoming a founder-member of the Aerospace Museum. On 26th September 2011 it made the journey to Hendon to take its place in the Milestones gallery. Inside the Historic Hangars, Meteor F.8 WH301 is also on show.

Handley Page Halifax II W1048
1942 | Seven-crew heavy bomber | Four 1,390hp Rolls-Royce Merlin XX

Half past eight, the evening of 27th April 1942 at Kinloss, Scotland, 35 Squadron Halifax II W1048 *S-for-Sugar* took off en route for Foettenfjord, near Trondheim, Norway. Target: the 42,000 ton Bismarck-class battleship *Tirpitz*. Crew: Plt Off Don P MacIntyre (pilot); Sgt Vic C Stevens (flight eng); Plt Off Ian Hewitt (nav)/bomb aimer); Sgt Dave L Perry (wireless op/air gunner); Sgt Pierre G Blanchett RCAF (mid-upper gunner); Sgt Ron H D Wilson (tail gunner). Part of a force of 31 Halifaxes and 12 Lancasters despatched from Lossiemouth and Kinloss, *S-for-Sugar* was the eighth bomber into the attack, over the target at 00:30. Canadian-born Plt Off MacIntyre dropped to 200ft to deliver his quartet of thousand-pounder spherical mines and was engaged by heavy anti-aircraft defences. As the weapons were released, W1048's starboard wing burst into flames. Too low to convert speed into height and try for Sweden, MacIntyre put *S-for-Sugar* down on the frozen surface of Lake Hoklingen, east of Trondheim. It was a brilliant bit of flying, Vic Stevens broke his ankle, but all stumbled away from the wreck. With his injury, Vic became a prisoner of war, the rest of the crew evaded and in 72 hours walked to Sweden. Built by English Electric at Samlesbury in Lancashire, W1048 had been on charge with 35 Squadron 18 days and had a total flying time of 13 hours 'on the clock'. Before 28th April was out, the ice gave way and the Halifax sank to the bottom, 92ft down. *S-for-Sugar* was one of five bombers lost that night; two Halifax IIs from 10 Squadron; another from 35 and a Lancaster I from 97 Squadron. Including MacIntyre's crew, eight men evaded, ten became prisoners of war and 15 were killed. *Tirpitz* was finally sunk by 9 and 617 Squadrons on 12th November 1944.

In 1971 local divers found *S-for-Sugar* and the following September a team from the RAF Sub-Aqua Club carried out a series of dives. It was missing its starboard outer Merlin XX, the area where the bomber has taken the most damage from the flak batteries. Lake Hocklingen was fresh water and the state of preservation was excellent. It was quickly established that by using new techniques such as pneumatic airbags a recovery was very 'do-able'. There was no intact surviving Halifax and the 'crash and smash' specialists from 71 Maintenance Unit, based at Bicester near Oxford were authorised to lend a hand and a Lockheed Hercules C.1 from the Lyneham Wing was also detailed. Coming up with the codename Operation HALIFAX must have taken weeks! Diving started on 19th June 1973 and eight days later the first lift was attempted. As airbags broke violently out of the water, it was obvious something had gone wrong. The weakened starboard outer wing had broken. On the 30th at 14:10, the Halifax came to the surface and was towed to the shore. The errant starboard wing was also recovered. On 25th August 1973 a Royal Corps of Transport landing craft docked at Ipswich and the bomber was loaded on vehicles and moved to Henlow.

S-for-Sugar after beaching on the edge of Lake Hocklingen, June 1973. *KEC*

In July 1977 the forward fuselage was taken to Wyton, Cambs, for restoration by a team of volunteers, led by W/O Patrick W 'Paddy' Porter – a stalwart of many projects, large and small. Paddy is representative of thousands of RAF personnel who have helped RAFM in many ways in their spare time. As well as *S-for-Sugar*, Paddy selflessly contributed to the Yorkshire Air Museum's Halifax recreation, Tony Agar's Mosquito project and Meteor NF.14, all at Elvington; the Battle of Britain Memorial Flight and IWM Duxford Lancasters also gained from his 'I know where...' expertise. Paddy was a Boy Entrant to the RAF at 16, retiring in 1994. Tragically, he died suddenly on 7th November 1996, robbing the preservation movement of an untold potential. The author got to know Paddy from the earliest days on *FlyPast* magazine and the can-do Warrant Officer was a mine of information – historic and practical. Also involved in W1048 was the Rochester-based Medway Aircraft Preservation Society which took on the restoration of the port outer Merlin XX from 1980. A re-assessment of the Halifax project declared that it was far too ambitious to return W1048 to 'as was' standard. The decision was taken to present it as though it were resting on the lakebed in Norway. *S-for-Sugar* was brought to Hendon in 1982 and laid out accordingly. This was a sensible conclusion, but the vista of the partially-restored front turret continues to confuse visitors.

Yorkshire Air Museum at Elvington is home to *Friday the 13th*, an incredible recreation of a Halifax, based on many original or appropriate, elements. This project was completed and unveiled in 1996. In the previous year, *S-for-Sugar* stopped being the only intact surviving Halifax when a Canadian team succeeded in bringing former 644 Squadron special duties Mk.VII NA337 out of the waters of Lake Mjosa in Norway. The Halifax had been dropping supplies to partisans when it force-landed in the lake on 13th April 1945; it is today displayed at Trenton, Ontario.

The late W/O Paddy Porter with the forward fuselage of *S-for-Sugar* at Wyton, 1978 . *KEC*

Hawker Hart Trainer K4972
1935 | Two-seat advanced trainer | One 510hp Rolls-Royce Kestrel X

Chapter 3 profiles Shuttleworth's Hind and sets out, briefly, the importance of Hawker's Kestrel-powered military biplane dynasty. Hendon boasts *two* Harts, one 'flying' in the Milestones hall, and there is an Afghan Hind on show at Cosford. The chosen subject is a great example of how a small organisation can contribute to aviation heritage on a national level.

They could hardly believe their eyes. Following the adage never to leave a stone unturned, members of the Solway Group of Aviation Enthusiasts (SGAE) had heard that the Nelson-Tomlinson School at Wigton, Cumberland, still had a 'biplane' used by the Air Training Corps (ATC) during World War Two. In March 1962 off they went and there it was – in the roof space of an out-building. No engine or undercarriage, but *most* of Hart Trainer K4972. A deal was struck and the airframe was gingerly lifted down on 10th November 1962 and taken to Crosby-on-Eden, Carlisle Airport. Britain's 'stock' of Hawker military biplanes had *doubled*. At that time, nobody, other than a few Afghans, knew that there were Hinds to be found in Kabul (again, refer to Chapter 3). SGAE is now the Solway Aviation Group and runs the excellent Solway Aviation Museum at Carlisle Airport. The Hart was the founder airframe, but wise decisions were made relating to K4972. It was offered to RAFM on 16th October 1963 and gratefully accepted; it travelled to Henlow within days. By early 1968 it was at St Athan, being restored by staff of 4 School of Technical Training. Rolls-Royce pitched in with a Kestrel engine, found in Sheffield; a propeller was held in RAFM stock; and the very badly damaged port lower wing was replaced with one found at an ATC unit in Maidenhead. In 1972 the Hart went on display at Hendon; it was at Cosford 1992-2002, returning to Hendon.

Built by Armstrong Whitworth at Whitley, near Coventry, K4972 was issued to 2 Flying Training School at Digby, Lincs, on 12th November 1935. No.2 FTS re-located to Brize Norton in September 1937, taking K4972 along. It was retired to 24 Maintenance Unit at Tern Hill in June 1938; later being stored at Kirkbride and then Silloth. It was delivered to 1546 Squadron ATC at Wigton on 22nd September 1943 and installed in the roof space. At some point the Kestrel was removed by sawing through the engine-bearers and sold for scrap. Otherwise, it patiently awaited the curious enthusiasts from the Solway group.

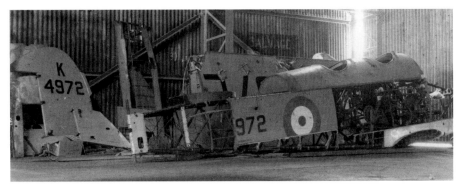

Salvaged from the loft at Wigton, Hart Trainer K4972, dismantled at Crosby-on-Eden, 1963. *MAP*

Hawker Typhoon Ib MN235
1944 | Single-seat fighter | One 2,180hp Napier Sabre IIA

The world's only intact Hawker Typhoon was repatriated to RAFM from a most unlikely location – the USA. Built by Gloster at Hucclecote, MN235 was first flown on 8th February 1944 by Sqn Ldr Alan Smith DFC. Eight days later it was on charge with 51 Maintenance Unit (MU) at Lichfield, for storage but exotic plans were in hand for it. The Typhoon was moved to the packing specialists at 47 MU, Sealand, near Chester, boxed and put on the SS *American Manufacturer*. It was destined for the USAAF's flight test and experimental station at Wright Field, Dayton, Ohio. (Today known as Wright-Patterson Air Force Base, it is still a test centre and

Typhoon I MN235 rolled out at Shawbury at the end of restoration, 14th August 1968. *KEC*

home of the National Museum of the USAF.) Accepted on 6th May 1944, MN235 was for evaluation, although it is not clear what the USAAF sought, unless it wanted to appraise the 24-cylinder Sabre more than the Typhoon. It was allocated the identity T2-491 and the 'buzz-number' 'FE-491' (FE for 'Foreign Evaluation') but these were not worn. An accident when MN235 had only nine hours 'on the clock' put paid to its flying days, but probably saved it for posterity. By July 1944 it was at Freeman Field, Seymour, Indiana, and it is not known if the incident happened in Ohio, or Indiana. Freeman Field was the gathering point for captured *enemy* aircraft; it seems the Typhoon confused its American custodians as to which side it was on!

Freeman Field was slated for closure in 1946 and the aircraft held were dispersed; most, including, MN235, moving to the former Douglas Aircraft plant at Park Ridge, Illinois, for storage. It was allocated to the National Air Museum (which had been created in 1946 as a separate element of the Smithsonian Institution) on 3rd January 1949. The Typhoon stayed where it was, along with a growing cache of aeronautical treasures. By 1952 Douglas was back in business at Park Ridge, the Korean War was raging and museum pieces were of very low priority. The Typhoon survived to enter the Smithsonian's vast storage site at Silver Hill, Suitland, Maryland, by early 1955. In April 1967 a request from RAFM to the Smithsonian for MN235 was approved and Hurricane II LF686 was readied to travel westwards in exchange. The Typhoon was off-loaded at Liverpool docks in January 1968, moving to 27 MU, Shawbury, for restoration in early April. The completed Typhoon was rolled out on 14th August 1968 and on 19th November formally presented to RAFM's Dr John Tanner. It was installed at Hendon during November 1972.

Hawker Tempest TT.5 NV778
1944 | Single-seat high-speed target-tug | One 2,200hp Napier Sabre IID

Two Tempests are on show at Hendon, the only examples on public display in the UK. (A Mk.II and a Mk.V are under restoration to fly in workshops in Lincolnshire and Buckinghamshire respectively.) Former Indian Air Force Mk.II 'PR536' wears the colours of 5 Squadron and represents the longer-serving Bristol Centaurus V radial-powered version. The other 'flies' in the Milestones of Flight gallery and, to the annoyance of some but to the delight of the author, wears the black and yellow stripes of a target-tug. Built at Langley in late 1944, NV778 was issued on 5th January 1945 to Napier, the builders of its awesome powerplant, most probably at the company's airfield of Luton. There is a *possibility* that the Mk.V joined 56 Squadron, at Volkel, Netherlands, in February 1945 but this seems unlikely given that it was still with Napier in August. It was with Hawker – location unconfirmed – for repair by February 1946 and issued to 5 Maintenance Unit (MU) at Kemble on 9th September 1946. By March 1950 it was back at Langley under conversion to TT.5 target-tug status. It was test flown by famous Hawker test pilot Neville Duke (more of him in the next profile) on 9th November 1950. Its second flying career started

Tempest TT.5 NV778 'flying' inside the Milestones hall, September 2012. *Ken Ellis*

on 27th October 1952 when it joined 233 Operational Conversion Unit (OCU) at Pembrey, Wales, which had formed the previous 1st September using single-seat de Havilland Vampire FB.5s and FB.9s to ready pilots for the frontline. Towing 'flags', or 'sleeves', far behind for the Vampires to fire at was NV778's new role. No.233 OCU completed introducing Gloster Meteor F(TT).8s into service during 1955 and NV778 was ferried to 20 MU, Aston Down, on 12th July 1955. (The last-ever flight by an RAF Tempest took place eight days later.)

Hendon's machine was transferred to the Ministry of Supply on 30th November for an unknown purpose, although a number of Tempests were handed on to the Proof and Experimental Establishment (PEE) at Shoeburyness in Essex for use as static ballistics targets. By April 1957 the fuselage of NV778 was noted dumped at North Weald. On 30th September 1958 a Tempest V marked 'SN219' and carrying 33 Squadron codes '5R-F' was displayed during the presentation of 33's standard at Middleton St George – now Durham Tees Valley Airport – as the unit worked up on Gloster Javelin FAW.7s. The remains of NV778 from North Weald, plus a lot of material salvaged from PEE, including the tailplanes and elevators from SN219, had been built up into a display airframe. Placed on the gate at 'Middleton', it was moved to Leeming by September 1963. It was issued to RAFM at Henlow in August 1965 and in June 1968 was in the static at Abingdon for the 50th Anniversary of the RAF before moving to Hendon in 1972. In December 1991 the Tempest was at Cardington for return to TT.5 status; travelling to Cosford on 13th November 2001 and the Conservation Centre. It was back at Hendon on 6th May 2003 and installed in Milestones.

Hawker Hunter F.3 WB188
1951 | Prototype single-seat fighter | One 7,130lb st Rolls-Royce RA7R Avon I On loan to the Tangmere Military Aviation Museum

Rarely does this book profile aircraft not on display in a 'national' but the prototype and World Absolute Air Speed Record holder Hunter is too important to overlook. It also highlights RAFM's superb policy of placing exhibits with other collections where appropriate and where its standards are met. The Hunter is another type that cannot be 'done' through just one profile; the highly capable FGA.9 being the ideal variant to 'book-end' the Hunter's pedigree – and Hendon has one of those – see below.

Steady evolution of the company's knowledge of jets (see the Sea Hawk in Chapter 4) and the introduction of swept-wings (with the P.1052 of 1948 and P.1081 of 1950), Hawker was in a great position to respond to Specification F3/48 seeking a swept-wing day-fighter. Sqn Ldr Neville Duke took the exceptional-looking P.1067 WB188 for its miaden flight from Boscombe Down on 20th July 1951. Testing proceeded so well that five weeks later, he was displaying it at the Farnborough airshow. It was grounded for intensive structural analysis from October, re-appearing in April the following year. Declared as a 'Super Priority' programme, the pace was fast and the second prototype, very close to production standard, was flown by

Duke in May 1952 – by which time the name Hunter had been chosen. On a sortie out of Dunsfold on 24th June Duke was at about 30,000ft and put the pale green WB188 into a shallow dive and watched as the Mach meter went past the all-important '1.0' with no untoward characteristics. In the design office, Sydney Camm was scheming a 'Super' Hunter, the P.1083, with after-burning and greater sweep. As part of this, WB188 was returned to the flight sheds in early December to have a reheated Avon RA.7R installed plus 'wet' wings, to boost endurance. At the same time, it was given 'clam-shell' airbrakes on either side of the rear fuselage; all of these mods giving it the designation F.3. On 13th July 1953, the P.1083 project was axed and morale at Hawker slumped. Three days later, a North American F-86D Sabre took the world speed record to 715.75mph. With this news, everyone bounced back and decided that WB188 was the ideal platform to have a crack for Britain. In late August Duke positioned the needle-nosed, bright red-painted WB188 to the fighter station at Tangmere and started practising over a calibrated course off Rustington, west of Worthing. On 7th September 1953 Duke clinched 727mph and on the 29th took the 100km closed circuit record at 709mph. The 'Super' Hunter may have been killed off but the Hunter was certainly 'super'!

After this stunning achievement, Hawker had no use for WB188 as it was 'non-spec' and production examples were rolling off the line; 43 Squadron becoming operational in July 1954. On 10th November 1954 the one-off F.3 was issued to 1 School of Technical Training (SoTT) at Halton as an instructional airframe; later gravitating to 12 SoTT at Melksham. By 1965 its worth was recognised and it was at the station collection at Colerne, going to St Athan a decade later, and to Cosford by 1986. Approaches from the Tangmere Military Aircraft Museum bore fruit when several low-loaders arrived on 19th September 1992. On board were two airframes with strong Tangmere associations and inter-linked heritage. One was WB188, the other was Gloster Meteor IV Special EE549 which, eight years before the red Hunter, had flown the same course, achieving a record of 615mph. In 1995, RAFM increased its complement of loaned airframes at Tangmere, with the arrival of Swift FR.5 WK281 (profiled below) to illustrate the achievements of Mike Lithgow of

Supermarine. Nineteen days after Neville Duke had taken the world record Lithgow was flying Swift F.4 WK198 in the warm, clear skies of Libya and raised the world record to 737mph. Neville was one of the first to congratulate him! (Swift WK198 did not endure as well as WK281; its battered fuselage is now in the care of the Brooklands Museum.)

Right: Detail of the 'clam-shell' airbrakes installed in the rear fuselage of WB188 prior to the record-breaking flight. *BAe*
Below: Neville Duke flying Hawker P.1067 WB188, 1951. *KEC*

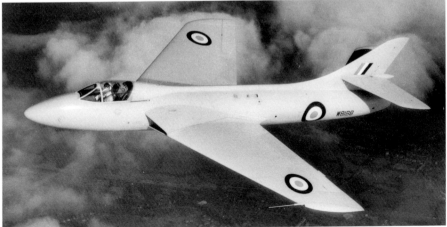

Hawker Hunter FGA.9 XG154

1956 | Single-seat ground attack fighter | One 10,150lb Rolls-Royce Avon 207

Refer to F.3 WB188 above for the beginning of the Hunter story. Built by Armstrong Whitworth as an F.6, XG154 first flew at Bitteswell on 13th June 1956 and was issued to 66 Squadron at Linton-on-Ouse on 27th November. No.66 moved base to Acklington in 1957 and during 1959 XG154 transferred to Horsham St Faith, now Norwich Airport, for conversion to interim FGA.9 standard by a Hawker working party. It was issued to 43 Squadron at Leuchars on 20th June 1960 and transferred with the unit to Nicosia, Cyprus, in June the following year. On 26th February 1963 it joined 8 Squadron at Khormaksar, as part of the Aden Strike Wing (8, 43 and 208 Squadrons), supporting British forces against Yemeni insurgents and in December that year a state of emergency was called. During this time, 8 sent detachments to Muharraq, Bahrain, and XG154 was deployed there in late 1963 and spring of 1964. Operation NUTCRACKER involved pin-point attacks and low-level 'heads down' high-speed runs in the Radfan area until November 1964 when the 'desert' segment of the Aden emergency was won. During this time, XG154 was in action, for example on 25th November Flt Lt Roger Wilkins flew it on a dawn strike. From late 1965, XG154 was in store in the UK, but it returned to the Middle East in August 1966, with 208 at Bahrain; re-locating to Khormaksar in April 1967. By the summer of 1967, Britain was committed to a pull-out from Aden and XG154 returned to 8 Squadron at Muharraq, in early December 1967, but the unit disbanded on the 21st. The Hunter was back in the UK for deep servicing from late 1968, re-joining 208 at Muharraq in August 1969; it returned to the UK permanently in the summer of 1971 and was prepared for a new role. On 17th September 1971 it was issued to 229 Operational Conversion Unit (OCU) at Chivenor, training frontline pilots in weapons, formation flying and tactics. No.229 OCU disbanded on 3rd August 1974 and morphed into the Tactical Weapons Unit, at Brawdy the following month. FGA.9 XG154 transferred, later adopting the squadron markings of 79 Squadron, TWU's 'shadow' unit. On 25th July 1984 the RAF said farewell to the single-seat Hunter and XG154 was part of special flypasts staged at Brawdy and Chivenor. The following day it ferried to St Athan for storage, pending disposal. It was allocated to RAFM on 30th May 1985, moving to Hendon on 17th November 1989. Hendon also has an FR.10 photo-reconnaissance variant, presented by the Sultan of Oman in October 2003.

Heinkel He 111H-20/R1 701152

1944 | Three-crew paratroop transport | Two 1,750hp Junkers Jumo 2113

Never a bomber version of the iconic all-glazed nosed He 111, 701152, factory code 'NT+SL', was built from scratch as a 'H-20/R1 transport capable of taking up to 16 paratroopers. What use, if any, it was put to is unknown but by May 1945, Colonel Harold E Watson had it on his 'shopping list' of significant German types for evaluation in the USA, as Operation LUSTY. The Heinkel was flown to Cherbourg with the intention of it becoming deck cargo on the carrier HMS *Reaper*, but there were many demands on space, and the He 111 was downgraded in importance. The story might have ended there, but pilots from the 56th Fighter Group, flying Republic P-47 Thunderbolts from Boxted, Essex, who had been helping Watson gather his treasures, ferried it to their base on 2nd July 1945. It was painted 'stars n bars' national markings and the code letters 'HV-', denoting its allocation to the 56th's 61st Fighter Squadron. The individual code, at times quoted as 'O' was actually a complex overlay of letters, 'O' for Capt J Ordway, 'C' for Major J Carter and 'W' (inner) for Major Williamson; this trio seeming to regard the He 111 as 'theirs'. The 56th was due to leave for the States in October 1945, so plans were made to 'save' it. It was flown to North Weald on 12th September; moving on to Heston on 14th October. There it gained RAF roundels and was ferried – its last flight – to Farnborough on 3rd November to take part in the extensive German Aircraft Display.

The Heinkel was allocated to the Air Historical Branch (AHB) in May 1946, but this seems to have carried little weight, as it was in Farnborough's scrap area by December. It was whisked away to 47 Maintenance Unit at Sealand by May 1947 and packed for long-term storage. Beyond this it adopted the migratory pattern of most AHB airframes, going from one site to another depending on which the RAF could spare: Stanmore Park, Wroughton, Fulbeck and, by 1960, Biggin Hill. By May 1967 it was at Henlow for possible static use in the film *Battle of Britain* and it very likely was employed for in-cockpit scenes. The Heinkel moved to St Athan in September 1969 and from this point it can be regarded as an RAFM airframe; going to Hendon in May 1978.

Probably at Cherbourg, the Heinkel in 61st Fighter Squadron markings, amid RAF Supermarine Spitfires and Vickers Warwicks. *via Eric Dessouroux*

Junkers Ju 87G-2 'Stuka' 494083
1944 | Two-crew ground-attack I One 1,410hp Junkers Jumo 211

One of only two complete 'Stukas', the other being a Ju 87R-2 in Chicago, 494083 has been in the Battle of Britain hall at Hendon since 1978. Thought to have been built as a Ju 87D-5, it was modified as a 'G-2 with the capability to mount 37mm cannon under wing. It is not known what, if any, operational flying it did. By May 1945 it was to be found at Eggebek in northern Germany and it was allocated for museum purposes, departing on 4th September 1945 by surface transport. It had arrived at 47 Maintenance Unit at Sealand, near Chester, by January 1946 where it was packed for long-term storage. The 'Stuka' followed a similar patter to the Heinkel, above, coming to Henlow, Beds, for use in the film *Battle of Britain*. To this author's amazement, it appears that the Ministry of Defence gave the film crew permission to fly the 'Stuka', but thankfully better sense (mostly fiscal) prevailed. That said, it was dressed up with mock-up dive brakes and other changes, including the removal of the rear gun. By September 1969 it was safely at St Athan and could by then be considered an RAFM airframe. It was given a foretaste of its intended home at Hendon from November 1975 to September 1976 when it took part in the superb 'Wings of the Eagle' exhibition, before moving in permanently in 1978.

Junkers Ju 88R-1 360043
1943 | Three-crew night-fighter | Two 1,730hp BMW 801MA

Coded 'D5+EV', Ju 88R-1 360043 of IV/Nachtjagdgeschwader 3 took off from Kristiansand, Norway, for a fighter sweep over the Skaageraak, the waters between southern Norway and Denmark on 9th May 1943. It was flown by Oberleutnant Heinrich Schmitt with Oberfeldwebel Erich Kantwill as flight engineer and Oberfeldwebel Paul Rosenberger as wireless operator/gunner. At this point there is speculation that Schmitt and/or Rosenberger were sick of the Nazi regime, or even had links with British intelligence. Be that as it may, an hour into the sortie an engine fire was declared and the Junkers plummeted to low level, dropping aircrew life rafts into the sea as it went. Spitfires from 165 Squadron at Peterhead were sent to intercept an incoming 'bogey' which turned out to be 'D5+EV'. The Junkers greeted the fighters with the established 'I surrender' signals – dropping the undercarriage, waggling his wings and firing flares. The Ju 88 headed for Dyce – now Aberdeen Airport – and, despite having pot-shots taken at it by the local defences, touched down safely.

Schmitt and Rosenberger were sweetness and light with their captives, Kantwill was just the opposite. These three were quickly processed as it was realised that they were but minions; still on board the Junkers there was a VIP. That very important package was a Funkgerät (FuG) 202 Liechtenstein BC air intercept radar; the Allies had never had a working version and all the 'how to' documents fall into their hands. On 14th May the Junkers was flown to Farnborough, escorted by Bristol Beaufighters. Oberleutnant Schmitt reportedly offered to do the flying, but this was not taken up. With the British serial number PJ876 and RAF roundels and fin flashes an intensive evaluation of the radar was staged from the 25th amounting to very nearly 67 flying hours. By the spring of 1944 trials to establish the effect of 'Window' radar countermeasures strips on the FuG 202 were complete. The Ju 88 still had more use, without the precious radar, it was issued to 1426 (Enemy Aircraft) Flight at Collyweston, Northants, where it was used to familiarise Allied pilots on the

Ju 88R-1 PJ876 in service with 1426 (EA) Flight, 1944. *MAP*

recognition points of the opposition. Its work more or less done, 1426 Flight was disbanded at Collyweston in January 1945 and the Ju 88 was transferred to the Central Fighter Establishment's Enemy Aircraft Flight at Tangmere. By 1946 the Junkers was at 47 Maintenance Unit at Sealand, for packing and store. Occasionally displayed at special events – for example Horse Guards Parade in London during September 1954 – the Ju 88 was kept at Stanmore Park, Fulbeck, Colerne, and by 1960, was at Biggin Hill. Like other Luftwaffe types, it was moved to Henlow for use by the *Battle of Britain* film crew, but seems to have been shunned by them. It was kept at Henlow, going to St Athan by August 1973 by which time it was firmly RAFM treasure. Restored, it was taken by road to Hendon on 14th August 1978.

Lockheed Hudson IIIA A16-199
1942 | Five-crew maritime reconnaissance | Two 1,200hp Pratt & Whitney R-1830-SIC3-G Twin Wasp

A Hudson had been on RAFM's 'shopping list' from the beginning; it was not to be until 1981 that this was achieved. Built by Lockheed at Burbank, California, for the USAAF as 41-36975, a troop-transport adaptable A-29A, it was shipped directly to Australia in February 1942. It was on the RAF's 'books' as FH174, but when it was assembled for flight test at Laverton, Western Australia, in April 1942 it was given the RAAF serial A16-199. It was issued to 13 Squadron at Hughes, Northern Territories, in June 1942 and immediately put into service attacking Japanese shipping and installations in the former Netherlands East Indies and Timor. On 21st December, during an anti-submarine patrol with Sgt Campbell piloting, the Hudson attacked by Japanese aircraft, a floatplane was fired upon and caught fire, while A16-199 suffered minor damage. In April 1943, the Hudson transferred to 2 Squadron, still based at Hughes. During a sortie off the New Guinea coast on 11th May 1943 A19-166 engaged a Mitsubishi Ki-21 *Sally* bomber and navigator Reg Curtis shot it down, but was wounded in the stomach during the exchange of fire – he was awarded as DFM. With Bristol Beauforts coming on stream, 2 Squadron staged the RAAF's last operational Hudson sortie on 8th April 1944. The following day, A16-199 joined 3 Communications Unit until it was retired to 2 Air Depot at Richmond in August 1944.

Put up for disposal in July 1946 it was acquired, along with ten others, by the Macquire Grove Flying School at Camden, New South Wales. It was civil registered on 18th December 1950 as VH-SMM to Fairfax and Sons, owners of the *Sydney Morning Herald*. *Mike-Mike* was destined to become an aerial paper boy, dropping bundles to outlying settlements. For this it received major surgery, forsaking its Wright Cyclone R-1820s for P&W R-1830s and was given a chute in the lower rear fuselage. This venture did not last long; by May 1952 the Hudson was out of use. It was resurrected in late 1954 by Adastra Airways, for use as an aerial survey platform. On 3rd June 1960 the Hudson hit power cables while flying in the Northern Territories and much of the top section of the flight deck was smashed. It was repaired and the canopy area apparently used Lockheed Lodestar fittings. Re-registered as VH-AGJ in December 1966 it was subjected to a major overhaul and repainted with Adastra Aerial Surveys titling. It was retired and stored at Mascot, New South Wales, by early 1972. The following year it was acquired by Sir William Roberts for a reported A$17,930 for his Strathallan Aircraft Collection, in Scotland. It departed on its epic journey to the UK on 19th April 1973, touching down at Strathallan on 10th May – it was to be its last-ever flight, airframe hours totalling 8,494. By April 1975 it had been painted in 13 Squadron RAAF colours and was placed on the UK civil register as G-EBOX in March 1977. On 14th July 1981 auctioneers Christies staged a sale of some of the collection's airframes and RAFM snapped up the Hudson for £16,000. It was installed at Hendon in October 1981.

Messerschmitt Bf 109E-4/B 4101
1940 | Single-seat fighter-bomber | One 1,050hp Daimler-Benz DB 601A-1

Like Hendon's Junkers Ju 88 – see above – the 'Emil', E-model Bf 109, was an 'aerial delivery'. Within the Milestones hall is a Bf 109G for good measure. Built at Leipzig by Erla Machinenwerk, Bf 109E 4101 was delivered to Jagdgeschwader (JG) 51, part of Luftflotte 2, at Pihen in Northern France on 5th September 1940. It was modified in the field to fighter-bomber status and became *Black 12* of 2/JG 51, based at Wissant, near Calais. On 27th November 1940 on a fighter sweep over Kent, Leutnant Wolfgang Teumer came off the worse in an encounter with Flt Lt George Christie DFC flying a Biggin Hill-based Supermarine Spitfire. Teumer belly-landed the fighter at Manston. The forlorn Bf 109E was taken to the dump run by 49 Maintenance Unit (MU) at Faygate, but it was quickly decided it would be better to rebuild it for tactical evaluation. It was issued to Rolls-Royce at Hucknall on 14th December 1940 and many components from other Bf 109s were used in its resurrection. Painted in RAF camouflage but yellow undersides and with the serial DG200, it made its first flight on 25th February 1941. Rolls-Royce flew it 32 times, evaluating the DB 601's characteristics. A well-known series of images of DG200 flying without a canopy come from this time. Rolls-Royce pilot Harvey Hayworth was tall and could only fly the 'Emil' with the canopy removed. The remainder of its flying life was without this luxury! From Rolls-Royce, DG200 transferred to de Havilland at Hatfield in February 1942 for propeller testing and later that month was at the Aeroplane & Armament Experimental Establishment at Boscombe Down. From April it joined 1426 (Enemy Aircraft) Flight at Duxford – where it was used to familiarise aircrew with the shape and sound of the opposition. No.1426 moved to Collyweston, on 12th April 1943. By September it was decided to retire this Battle of Britain veteran and it went to 52 MU at Pengam Moors, Cardiff, during the summer of 1944. As we have seen with several captured Axis aircraft, a nomadic lifestyle awaited the Bf 109; mostly in store, occasionally displayed at special events. By 1960 it was at Biggin Hill and 'wearing' a 'Galland' canopy from a Bf 109G. It was at St Athan by September 1969 and given a major restoration, including the fitting of a mock-up 'Emil' canopy that had come from the set of the *Battle of Britain* film. It was installed in the Battle of Britain hall at Hendon in May 1978 and *may* become the next major project for the Medway Aircraft Preservation Society.

Messerschmitt Me 262A-2a 112372
1945 | Single-seat fighter | Two 1,980lb st Junkers Jumo 004B

There are things that are *known* about the Luftwaffe twin-jet fighter displayed close to the prototype Gloster Meteor within the Milestones of Flight exhibition at Hendon. There are other elements that remain *unknown*, or perhaps *likely*. It was test flown at Memmingen on 23rd March 1945 and later that month delivered to Jagdgeschwader (JG) 7 'Nowotny'. Hendon's Me 262 is *likely* to be 112372 which was latterly at Twenthe in the Netherlands before coming to Farnborough, Hampshire. Let's return to the known, it was ferried from Farnborough to Brize Norton on 29th June 1945 only to be issued to Royal Aircraft Establishment Aerodynamic Flight and *returned* to Farnborough by September, taking on the RAF serial VK893. It was tested extensively until late November. By 1947 it was part of the Cranwell station museum and remained there until the collection was dispersed in 1960, going to Gaydon. Here it was painted as '110880' *Yellow 7* of JG 7. It was part of the Finningley station museum by late 1971 and was painted as *Red X* of Kampfgeschwader (KG) 51. By 1976 it was at Cosford and late in 1985 it had travelled to St Athan, where it was repainted and returned to Cosford in early 1989. During 2003 it was painted as *Yellow 4* and moved to Hendon on 14th July 2003. Research into the 'middle bit' of this Me 262's history continues.

North American Harvard IIb FE905
1943 | Two-seat advanced trainer | One 550hp Pratt & Whitney R-1340-49 Wasp

Hendon's Harvard has had a varied pedigree, in many ways typical of the cosmopolitan careers of long-serving examples of the 'Pilot Maker'. It was built in 1943 by Noorduyn Aviation at Montreal, for the USAAF as AT-16-ND Texan 42-12392, but was destined to stay in Canada. It was taken on by the Royal Canadian Air Force as

FE905, on 23rd March 1943, serving with 41 Service Flying Training School (SFTS) at Weyburn, Saskatchewan. By late 1943 it was bashing the circuit at 3 Flying Training School, Calgary, Alberta, but was back at Weyburn, this time with 8 SFTS, by mid-1944. It was struck off charge with the RCAF on 27th November 1946 with a mere 74 flying hours to its credit. It was sold to the Danish Government in September 1949 and was handed over to the Royal Danish Air Force as 31-329 in September 1950. Latterly flying from Vaerlose, it was retired on 31st August 1960, by which time it had a much more respectable 1,903 hours 'on the clock'. It was acquired by Norwegian military contractor Fjellfly of Skien, Norway, becoming LN-BNM. Its work was largely target facility flying – acting as a 'sitting duck' for anti-aircraft gun crews (firing blanks!) to learn how to 'train' their weapon correctly. It last flew on 13th September 1968, completing 3,934 hours – Fjellfly got its money's worth out of the AT-16. It was acquired by the Historic Aircraft Museum and shipped to Felixstowe and arrived at Southend Airport in mid-May 1972. HAM was wound down and auctioneers Philips sold most of the content on 10th May 1983. It was 'hammered' to Paul Raymond for £6,000 with the intention of displaying it at either his Whitehall Theatre of War or the London War Museum. Only the former opened to the public, but was short-lived. Prior to the Harvard entering *another* auction, RAFM settled by private treaty with the nightclub impresario and it was delivered to Cardington in May 1985 for restoration. Between 1991 and mid-1994 FE905 was on loan to the Newark Air Museum at Winthorpe, Notts. It moved to Hendon on 5th October 1994.

North American TB-25N Mitchell '34037'
1944 | Five-crew medium bomber | Two 1,700hp Wright Cyclone R-2600-29

Like the Flying Fortress (above), the Mitchell at Hendon serves in place of a former RAF example, but primarily honours USAAF personnel and operations in the European Theatre. Built as B-25J-20-NC at Kansas City, Missouri, 44-29366 was delivered to the USAAF on 18th September 1944. Most USAAF documentation of the 1940s itemises the Base Units tasked with looking after the day-to-day maintenance of a particular aircraft, with precious little on units, roles etc. Accordingly, 44-23966 moved around as follows: Moody Field, Georgia (from September 1944); Turner Field, Georgia (April 1945), Perrin Field, Texas (June 1945 and June 1946); Enid Field, Oklahoma (June 1945 and September 1946); Barksdale Field, Louisiana (December 1946) and Lubbock Field, Texas (October 1949). All of these bases being within Training Command, would indicate the B-25J was used as a crew trainer. An interesting note gives a transfer to the 91st Strategic Reconnaissance Wing at Barksdale – a Strategic Air Command outfit – on 4th October 1949. As it was back on charge at Lubbock six days later, it was either a slip of the pen or a brief assignment. On 4th April 1950 the B-25 was assigned to the 3065th Navigator Training Wing (NTW) at Ellington, at the start of a Texas sojourn as follows: 3500th Pilot Training Wing (PTW – June 1950); 3565th Bombardier Training Wing, Waco (December 1952) and the 3585th PTW, San Marcos. In May 1954 it was with Hayes Aircraft at Birmingham, Alabama, and converted to dedicated crew trainer status as a TB-25N. Then it was back to the tuition grind with the 3545th PTW, San Angelo, Texas, from July 1954, finally returning to Waco in November 1957. It was retired to the famous 'Desert bone-yard' at Davis-Monthan Air Force Base in Arizona during May 1958, bringing to an end 14 years of service.

It was 'surplussed' to Sonora Flying Service of Columbia, California, on 4th January 1960 for $2,000. Civil registered as N9115Z, it was converted to 'fire-bomber' status and flown extensively until 1966. It was acquired by Tallmantz Aviation in 1969 for use in the incredible movie of Joseph Heller's breath-taking novel *Catch-22*. Magnificently directed by Mike Nicholls, the cinematography, led by David Watkin, makes this the best World War Two flying movie ever in the author's opinion. It was not an immediate box office hit when released in 1970, but became a 'cult'. Tallmantz put together an fleet of *seventeen* B-25s, all made to look 'war-weary'; N9115Z wore the name *Hot Pants* at one point and the tail-code '6M' throughout. Filming took place at San Carlos, Sonora, Mexico, January to April 1969. After filming, N9115Z and the others were stored at Orange County, California. Well-known owner/operator David Tallichet bought N9115Z in 1972 and it was displayed alongside one of his aviation-themed diners at Tampa, Florida, by 1977 but its movie days were not over. Tallichet was at the helm when N9115Z, and four others, flew the Atlantic, arriving at Luton on 15th May 1978 for use in director/writer Peter Hyams's *Hanover Street*, starring Harrison Ford and a sizzling Lesley-Anne Down. Most filming took place at Bovingdon with some scenes at Little Rissington. N9115Z wore '151645' and *Marvellous Milly* nose-art for much of the time. Post-film the B-25s were acquired by British 'warbird' dealer Doug Arnold and stored at Blackbushe. RAFM secured N9115Z and it was moved to Hendon on 25th October 1982.

TB-25N 'Marvellous Milly' at Biggin Hill, September 1980. *KEC*

Panavia Tornado GR.1B ZA457
1983 | Two-crew, all-weather tactical strike | Two 15,800lb st Turbo-Union RB199 Mk.103

With respect to the interceptor fighter, or Air Defence Variant, of the Tornado, the 'mud-moving' strike versions, the GR.1 and GR.4, represent one of the most important and RAF capable assets, and will have served for an unprecedented time in the frontline. British prototype P.02 is on show at Cosford, but 'Grib' ZA457 better reflects the extensive career most of the fleet have had. Close by it at Hendon is F.3 ZE887 for comparison. First flown at Warton on 21st June 1983 as a GR.1, ZA457 was issued to the Tornado Operational Evaluation Unit at Boscombe Down on 6th December. Taken on charge by 9 Squadron at Honington on 10th September 1986, ZA457 moved with the unit to Brüggen, West Germany 22 days later. It was briefly with 617 Squadron at Marham during February 1987 but otherwise was loyal to RAF Germany and Brüggen in particular: 9 Squadron (from February 1987 and again from August 1988); 15 Squadron (Laarbruch, from July 1988); 17 Squadron (also July 1988 and again from May 1990). In the first days of January 1991 RAF Germany Tornado GR.1s (ZA457 among them) deployed to Dhahran, Saudi Arabia, as part of Operation GRANBY, the British element of DESERT SHIELD, the response to the invasion of Kuwait by Iraq. Gulf Detachment Tornados at Dhahran took on the names of characters in the wonderful BBC TV historical romp *Blackadder*, and ZA457 took the name *Bob*, after Lord Blackadder's 'man' servant in the 1986 series *Blackadder II*, played brilliantly by Gabrielle Glaister. At dawn on 17th January 1991 DESERT SHIELD gave way to DESERT STORM, and ZA457 took part in 39 sorties, including dropping two JP233 area-denial weapons on Mudaysis airfield on the first day. In 1993 it was ferried to St Athan for conversion to GR.1B (hence 'Grib') anti-shipping strike status, with the capability to carry the Sea Eagle missile. It was with 617 Squadron at Marham in late 1993, moving to the unit's new base at Lossiemouth in September 1994. By December 1998 it was deployed to Ali Al Salem in Kuwait for Operation DESERT FOX, a four-day punitive campaign against Iraqi air defence sites. By 1999 ZA457 was at Lossiemouth with 617 wearing the codes 'AJ-J', in honour of the Lancasters of the 'Dam Busters' raid. As 617 upgraded to GR.4s in 2001, ZA457 moved to Marham and 2 Squadron for its final phase of service. It was retired to St Athan in March 2002 and prepared for exhibition at Hendon; arriving at its new home on 28th July 2003.

Percival Prentice T.1 VS618
1949 | Primary trainer | One 215hp de Havilland Gipsy Queen 30 Mk.2

Prentice *Lima-Kilo* touched down at Cosford on 9th October 2009, completing its last-ever flight and around 3,100 flying hours. It had ticked a long empty box in RAFM's 'shopping list'. As the engine cooled, the UK's population of flying Prentices had been reduced by a third; leaving Classic Air Force's G-APJB and Biggin Hill-based G-APPL. At the time quite a few eyebrows were raised at this; wouldn't one from another museum do?

Prior to October 2009 easily the best Prentice in a UK collection was the Newark Air Museum's VR249, snugly hangared and a valued part of its superb trainer collection. The Midland Air Museum's VS623 is a composite and lives outdoors; the South Yorkshire Aircraft Museum former 'spares ship' G-AOKO is held in deep store. Even if available there would be, at best, conservation work to carry out on any of these. Whereas G-AOLK had a document attesting to its state of health – a Certificate of Airworthiness expiring on 17th September 2010. The purchase of *Lima-Kilo* scored top cost-effective and practicality marks. Besides, turning to the future, G-AOLU and former Shuttleworth G-AOKL (chapter 3) is under restoration to fly in Scotland. It's to highlight this thinking why one of the more unsung RAF trainers has made it to a profile.

Prentice T.1 VS618 was ready for collection at its birthplace, Luton, on 13th May 1949. Five days later, it was taken on charge by what was to turn out to be its only operational unit, 22 Flying Training School at Syerston. With the advent of the Percival Provost T.1 (Chapter 6), the Prentice was withdrawn from use, and VS618 was taken to Cosford for storage on 9th March 1954. It became G-AOLK on 25th April 1956, registered to Freddie Laker's Aviation Traders Ltd. The great entrepreneur had bought 252 of the RAF's 349 Prentices with the intention of refurbishing them and flogging them on as tourers – seating up to six in the type's large cockpit. In a massive undertaken, 150 were ferried to Southend and Stansted for preparation; the balance came by road for spares use. With brand-new US light aircraft available, the Prentice was not a tempting buy and most were scrapped. It was not Freddie's finest hour. *Lima-Kilo* was acquired in turn by two Kent-based operators, Bert Wright in May 1961 and Alan Hilton Smith in January 1971, but by the late 1970s it was based at Southend. Prentice T.1 VS618 arrived at Hendon on 17th August 2010.

Republic P-47D Thunderbolt 'KL216'
1945 I Single-seat fighter-bomber I One 2,300hp Pratt & Whitney R-2800-59 Double Wasp

Ready for acceptance by the USAAF on 8th June 1945, the war in Europe had passed P-47D-40-RA 45-49295 by, and the conflict in the Pacific had 68 days to run. Built at Republic's Evansville, Indiana, plant it was issued to 266th Air Base Unit at Majors Field, Texas, on 2nd July. It seems to have spent most of its time inactive, or used by secondary units, and by early 1950 was in store at Tinker, Oklahoma. Since 1948, it was designated an F-47D, as 'P-for-Pursuit' had been replaced by 'F-for-Fighter'. It was part of a large consignment of F-47Ds shipped via Newark, New Jersey, to Yugoslavia in May 1952. It served with the Yugoslav Air Force as 13064, the with name *Hajduk* (Outlaw) on the cowling early in its new career. Thunderbolts were withdrawn from frontline units during the late 1950s, but some lingered until 1961. Serving as an instructional airframe with a Belgrade technical school, 13064 was later held as a spare with the Yugoslav Aeronautical Museum at Belgrade. It and 13021 (now airworthy in the USA) were acquired by Warbirds of Great Britain and brought to Bitteswell for storage in 1985. RAFM arranged an exchange with Supermarine Spitfire XVI TE356 and 13064 arrived at Cardington in June 1986. Restoration to static display condition was arranged by the Duxford-based The Fighter Collection and it was finished in colours of Thunderbolt II KL216 of 30 Squadron, based in India and Burma, late 1944 to early 1946. It was roaded to Cosford on 6th June 1995 and on 20th May 2003 came to Hendon.

Royal Aircraft Factory FE.2b 'A6526'
1917 I Two-crew bomber I 160hp Beardmore

Dominated by the larger craft in the Bomber Command hall, the FE.2b is nevertheless a very impressive exhibit. Like several other RAFM World War One types, it is a major reconstruction, employing as many original parts as possible. Others that could have been profiled include the BE.2b, or the recently-arrived Dolphin and Snipe, but for sheer scale the FE.2b is compelling. Around April 1976 the nacelle of an FE.2b was presented to RAFM by Richard Garrett Engineering; this was the largest single element of an 'extinct' type and provided the possibility of a resurrection. During 1918 Richard Garrett and Sons of Leiston, Suffolk, was busy with a contract to build FE.2bs. Prior to this the company had produced a large batch of nacelles for Norwich-based Boulton and Paul; it was an unfinished example from this job that was with RAFM. In November 1987 John McKenzie, via his business Aircraft & Weapon Reproductions, was contracted to create an FE.2b based upon the original nacelle and other original parts, at his workshop near Southampton. The Beardmore 'pusher' came from New Zealand. The project was brought to a close in 2007 and finished elements were held in store at Cosford. In April 2008 Guy Black's Retrotec organisation was commissioned to complete the FE.2b. The glorious finished product was delivered to Hendon on 26th May 2009 and unveiled on 1st July.

Short Sunderland MR.5 ML824

1944 I Up to 13-crew, long-range maritime patrol and anti-submarine flying-boat I Four 1,200hp Pratt & Whitney R-1830-900 Twin Wasp

Now bathed in light thanks to the new glass 'wall' at the eastern end of the Battle of Britain hall, Sunderland MR.5 is an imposing and very popular exhibit, not least because it is possible to walk through its cavernous fuselage. It was gently lowered down the slipway at Queen's Island on to the waters of Belfast Lough in June 1944, as a Mk.III. It was taken on charge by the RAF on the last day of the month and immediately handed back to Shorts, to be upgraded to Mk.V status, forsaking the Bristol Pegasus radials for the more practical R-1830s. On 11th November 1945 it was the first Mk.V to be accepted by 201 Squadron at Castle Archdale on Lough Erne, on the west coast of Northern Ireland. During its time with 201, ML824 completed eleven 'ops'; for example, on 2nd April 1945 it dropped a pair of depth charges on a fresh oil slick during a 13-hour sortie. Fifteen days later, the flying-boat was north-bound, heading for 330 (Norwegian) Squadron at Sullom Voe, Shetland Islands, returning to the task of anti-submarine patrols. Maintenance in early May allowed 201's codes 'NS-Z' to be replaced by 'WH-T' for 330. The Norwegians left Sullom Voe in mid-May and moved to their homeland, berthing at Sola, close to Stavanger. An engine fire on 1st July was beyond 330's capability and an fairing was made to allow ML824 to fly on three engines back to the UK. In May 1948 it was in store – afloat – at Wig Bay, near Stranraer. By the summer of 1950 it was back at Belfast, Shorts reconditioned it and it was delivered to Pembroke Dock in West Wales, on 26th October 1951 ready for its new life. Two days later it was off to Brest to join the Aéronavale, the French naval air arm. It served with a variety of units, mostly from Dakar, Senegal, on the West African coast.

Another MR.5, ML797, flew the RAF's last Sunderland sortie on 20th May 1959 at Seletar, Singapore. This machine had been overhauled with the intention of flying it back to the UK for preservation. It seems that while manoeuvring it out to the slip way, it fell off its rear beaching gear and the fuselage was badly distorted. There was nothing for it, ML797 was a write-off and was scrapped on site. At this point preservation pioneer Peter Thomas, having discovered an RAF Sunderland was no longer a possibility, approached the Royal New Zealand Air Force for one; then turned his attentions to the Aéronavale. Peter got a resounding 'Oui!' from France and was offered one of the last two still flying – *at no charge*. The Sunderland Preservation Trust (SPT) was set up and land found at the former flying-boat base at Pembroke Dock. On 24th May 1961, with Capitaine Henri Luthereau at the helm, ML824 unstuck for the last time from the waters of Lanveoc-Pouloc, near Brest, and headed west. Escorted by a pair of St Mawgan-based Avro Shackleton MR.3s the Sunderland made its way around the English and Welsh coastline, alighting before noon and completing a total of 2,900 flying hours. It was brought out of the water the following day and on 2nd June 1962 placed on its own site at 'PD' and opened to the public. By 1967 20,000 people had toured ML824 but the SPT had realised that the long-term for the flying-boat was with an organisation like RAFM and on 11th January 1971 an official hand-over of ML824 was made.

Above: Inside ML824's fuselage, looking aft. *Ken Ellis*

Top: Sunderland V ML824 in service with 330 Squadron – note the Norwegian flag under the cockpit – at Fornebu, Norway, June 1945. *via Björn Hafsten*

Flying ML824 again was out of the question. Based at Bicester in Oxfordshire, 71 Maintenance Unit was charged with moving the monster. No.71 MU's role was 'crash and smash' – the recovery of downed operational aircraft – and transporting the Sunderland was a superb training exercise for its personnel. After four days of preparation, with as much as possible going on low-loaders, the fuselage was placed on to a Royal Corps of Transport landing craft which sailed from Pembroke Dock on 10th March 1971. Unloaded on Dagenham on the Thames the fuselage, on its side, travelled in the early hours of the 21st to Hendon. Using the vacant Grahame-White building (see the beginning of the chapter) the flying-boat was refurbished, re-assembled and in late October put on display outside the museum. In 1978 it was positioned inside the Battle of Britain hall and from 1995, the public were able to inspect its interior.

Cranfield's Hoverfly rotor test-bed, circa 1962. *KEC*

Sikorsky Hoverfly I KK995
1944 | Two-seat general purpose/trainer helicopter | One 185hp Warner R-550-1

Although this pioneering helicopter wears the serial KK995 on its tail, it is much more likely to be KL110. This was built at Stratford, Connecticut for the USAAF as R-4B-SI Hoverfly 43-46596, destined for supply to the RAF. It arrived at Hooton Park, Cheshire, for flight test by Martin Hearn Ltd, on 5th February 1945. It was not until 22nd October that it was issued for service, with the Helicopter Training Flight, part of 43 Operational Training Unit at Andover. On 6th February 1946 it joined the Transport Command Development Unit (TCDU) at Brize Norton. It was detached to the Airborne Forces Experimental Establishment at Beaulieu in the New Forest during the summer of 1947 and used to instruct pilots of the King's Flight. It was transferred to the King's Flight, headquartered at Benson, on 28th August for use ferrying mail between Dyce – now Aberdeen Airport – and Balmoral Castle, near Braemar, until the end of September. This exercise was repeated the following summer, during the Royal family's 'detachment' to Scotland.

The Hoverfly was struck off charge on 26th May 1951 and was sent to the College of Aeronautics at Cranfield for use as a non-flying rotor test-bed. At the same time the gutted and engineless KK995 was also transferred to Cranfield, perhaps for spares use. Some interchange of components certainly took place, and the serial 'KK995' can be found stencilled in several places on the airframe. For most of its time at Cranfield, KL110 was in overall pale grey with no serial; this 'anonymity' and the appearance of 'clues' to KK995 account for the long-term mis-identification. The College officially donated the Hoverfly to RAFM on 14th January 1966 and it was at Henlow by June. Refurbished by personnel from 71 Maintenance Unit at Bicester, it was displayed in the static of the RAF Golden Jubilee celebrations at Abingdon, Oxfordshire, in June 1968. It moved to Hendon during December 1970.

Sopwith Triplane N5912
1917 | Single-seat fighter | One 130hp Clerget 9B

One of only three Triplanes completed by Oakley and Co at Ilford, Essex, in 1917; N5912 and one displayed in Moscow are the only survivors of the breed. By 1918 it was serving with 2 School of Aerial Fighting at Marske, Yorkshire, and seems to have remained on charge well into 1919. As noted in Chapter 2, it was displayed in the Imperial War Museum's Crystal Palace exhibition from 1920 and afterwards was stored in the basement of the Science Museum buildings, in poor conditions, awaiting the creation of a permanent IWM. It was moved to Cardington in the early 1930s and, rejected by IWM, languished in an increasingly derelict state. In 1936 it was spotted by Flt Lt N R Buckle and it and the LVG (see Chapter 3) were rescued and taken to Hendon for a starring role at that year's Air Pageant. With the paddock number '5' on the fin, it was flown by Buckle and took part in a spectacular attack on a barrage balloon. This was so popular that the 'act' was run again at the 1937 event.

With the paddock number '5' on its fin, Sopwith Camel N5912 at the Hendon Air Pageant, 1936. *KEC*

The Triplane was stored throughout the war and by the summer of 1945 was at 5 Maintenance Unit (MU) at Kemble, moving to 76 MU Wroughton for packing for long-term storage in July 1946. In 1950 it was restored by 39 MU, Colerne, ready to appear statically at Farnborough in July 1950 and the *Daily Express* Jubilee display at Hendon a year later. After that, the Triplane was stored at Wroughton and then Fulbeck. In 1961 staff at Hawker Siddeley carried out some restorative work at Dunsfold before returning to storage, this time at Biggin Hill. The Triplane was displayed at celebrations at Yeovilton, Somerset, in May 1964 that included the opening ceremony of the Fleet Air Arm Museum (see Chapter 4). By October 1964 the Triplane was at Henlow and, seemingly, in the mid-1960s was under restoration to *flying* condition. This was amended to static and, upon completion, N5912 was displayed briefly in the Science Museum, South Kensington. It was moved to Hendon on 20th October 1971 and trundled across to the Grahame-White Factory on 17th March 2003.

Supermarine Southampton I N9899
1925 | Five-crew general reconnaissance flying-boat | Two 520hp Napier Lion VA

Whenever the author visits Hendon, a pilgrimage to go and gaze upon the Southampton's hull is essential. After visiting its restoration at Cardington in 1988, I wrote in *FlyPast* declaring it to be "Aviation's *Mary Rose*" and I still feel that way. The story of the survival of this unique reminder of the heyday of wooden-hulled patrol boats is remarkable. Built in the town it took its name from, N9899 was issued to 480 (Coastal Reconnaissance) Flight at Calshot in July 1925; the first of its type to serve with the unit. On 7th September it was on a sortie from Pembroke Dock to Belfast Lough, but suffered an engine failure off Wicklow Head, south of Dublin. It alighted in the Irish Sea and the corvette HMS *Calliope* came to its aid, towing the flying-boat all the way to its destination. It was 20 days before N9899 was back at Calshot. On 23rd November 1928 N9899 and two others were moored off Portland when a gale whipped up; N9899 was torn from its anchorage and wrecked, the other two were damaged. The Napier Lions were salvaged, but the rest was sold off. At least the hull of N9899 was acquired by a Mr Kemp and converted into a houseboat. We now fast-forward to 1951 when it was recorded at Bawdsey Ferry, near Felixstowe. By then it was a 'static'

Southampton I N9899 in its houseboat guise on the River Deben at Bawdsey Ferry, circa 1966. *KEC*

Transformed, the Southampton fuselage arriving at Hendon, 23rd May 1995. *RAF Museum*

houseboat and alongside it was similarly-converted Fairey Atlanta I N119 flying-boat. (This had gone, presumed scrapped, by the mid-1960s.) By 1966 Keith Coombs, it owner, is thought to have been told to move N9899 by the local authority and RAFM was alerted.

In September 1967 a deal was struck and it was sold to the museum for £75 (£1,500 in present-day values). Arriving on the banks of the River Deben on 10th October 1967, a team from 60 Maintenance Unit, Leconfield, specialists at repair and salvage, managed to get the houseboat on a low-loader and it departed to Henlow on the 13th. Tidal conditions, the 'mobile' nature of the mud flats and the water-soaked hull meant that the salvage was a demanding exercise. It speaks volumes of Reginald Joseph Mitchell's design and the craftsmen who built N9899 at Woolston that it stood up to all this treatment. By 1973 N9899 was at Cardington and restoration started in January 1984. By that date, having dried out, it was a *ton* lighter than when it had arrived! It would be impossible to do justice to the incredible devotion needed to turn a neglected houseboat into an aeronautical work of art, but one statistic is unavoidable – 70,000 brass screws had to be replaced! Vital to the resurrection, was the design and construction of a substantial rotatable rig allowing access to the planing bottom or the top of the fuselage. The immaculate fuselage and new tail was delivered to Hendon on 23rd May 1995 and a year later the access gantry was in place; allowing the public to inspect at close quarters an icon of restoration skill.

Supermarine Stranraer 920
1940 | Six-crew general reconnaissance flying-boat | Two 1,200hp Wright Cyclone GR-1820-97

Not far from the magnificent Southampton is another show-stopper; the Supermarine Stranraer. Although originating in 1934, this example was built in 1940, but it 'flies the flag' for the era of giant, all-metal, flying-boats that was crowned by the Short Sunderland. Built by Canadian Vickers at St Hubert, Montreal, Quebec, it was accepted by the Royal Canadian Air Force, as 920, on 28th November 1940 and delivered *by rail*, to 5 (Bomber Reconnaissance) Squadron at Dartmouth, Nova Scotia. As the crow flies, St Hubert to Dartmouth is about 400 miles, or by following the St Lawrence to the Atlantic and approaching from the east – the over-water route –

Stranraer CF-BXO, less tail 'feathers' in store at Vancouver Airport, June 1967. *Roy Bonser*

it's about 570 miles. With an endurance of very nearly 8 hours, these distances were not beyond the 920's capabilities. The clue probably lies in the calendar; it was the dead of winter and a take-off from an ice-bound upstream St Lawrence was impossible. Assembled, 920 was flight tested on 11th January 1941. In September, 5 Squadron started to re-equip with Canadian-built Cansos (Consolidated Catalinas) and on 10th October 920 was transferred to 13 Operational Training Squadron at Patricia Bay on the south end of Vancouver Island, British Columbia – over 2,600 miles to the west! By the summer of 1942 the flying-boat had joined 7 (Bomber Reconnaissance) Squadron, at Prince Rupert, 350 miles up the coast from Patricia Bay. At some point beyond this, 920 moved again, this time southwards to Bella Bella, near Shearwater, on charge with 9 (BR) Squadron.

Stranraer 920 was retired in April 1944 and the following month was sold to the Labrador Mining and Exploration Co, civil registered as CF-BXO for operation by Canadian Pacific Airlines. The flying-boat crossed the length of Canada again, re-acquainting itself with the Gulf of St Lawrence, supporting iron ore extraction, working out of Sept Iles on the St Lawrence. In May 1947 CF-BXO was sold to Queen Charlotte Airlines (QCA), so called from its island base off the coast of British Columbia. Another trans-Canadian epic flight was in order. QCA grew to have a fleet of five Stranraers and the flew daily services up and down the BC coast to outposts, and to Vancouver. In May 1950 *X-ray-Oscar* was given major surgery, with its 810hp Bristol Pegasus Xs replaced by two Wright R-1820s – that's *half* a Flying Fortress, or a third more power! QCA was bought out by Pacific Western Airlines in mid-1955, but the venerable biplane flying-boat service continued. By 1958 CF-BXO was out of use and the following year was acquired by Stranraer Aerial Enterprises for return to airworthiness. It was roaded to Abbotsford, east of Vancouver, for restoration by Aerovive Ltd. On 10th June 1962 CF-BXO was airborne again, having taken off from the *runway* at Abbotsford. With a special trolley under its belly for 'undercarriage', once it gained the 90 knots needed to take-off, the trolley was left to hurtle down the runway until it ground to a halt. Working on charter to Ward Air, if flew out of Yellowknife on the Great Slave Lake in the Northern Territories. It continued with sporadic charters, mostly up and down the BC coast, until its last flight, on 13th August 1966. It was stored at Vancouver Airport by June 1967. It was bought by RAFM and on 4th August 1970 a pair of 53 Squadron Short Belfast C.1s, XR367 and XR371, arrived at Vancouver to take the dismantled CF-BXO to the UK. (Belfast XR371 now dominates the airframes in Cosford's National Cold War Exhibition.) All was secured at Henlow by the 21st. Restored to its RCAF colours, 920 was installed at Hendon in late 1971. It's beaching gear is attached, but famously its wheels lie alongside; the roof trusses of the Historic Hangar are testament to how tight a squeeze the 21ft 9in high Stranraer was!

Spitfire I X4590, supported by some blocks of wood, being assembled – or dismantled – at Horse Guards Parade, London, late 1950s. *KEC*

Supermarine Spitfire I X4590
1940 I Single-seat fighter | One 1,030hp Rolls-Royce Merlin II

Three examples have been picked to profile, as well as Hendon's Mk.I. See Chapter 4 for the Fleet Air Arm Museum's Seafire F.17 and Chapter 8 for the Imperial War Museum's F.24. Built at Woolston, Southampton, X4590 was taken on charge on 22nd September 1940. Seventeen days later it joined 609 (West Riding) Squadron at Middle Wallop. On October 21st Plt Off Hill, flying X4590 was involved in a very low-level chase after a Junkers Ju 88 that had attacked the airfield at Old Sarum, Wiltshire. The Ju 88 was shot down and its four crew were killed; Plt Off Hill claimed a half-share in the 'kill'. No.609 re-located to Warmwell in Dorset on 29th November. As 609 took on Mk.IIs, its Mk.Is – X4590 included – were transferred to 66 Squadron at Exeter. On 7th April 1941 X4590's frontline career came to an end, going to 57 Operational Training Unit (OTU) at Hawarden, near Chester. The Spitfire moved north eastwards on 18th July, to Speke, Liverpool, and 303 (Polish) Squadron. Seven days later it was out of action, a cross-wind landing by a pilot on his first-ever Spitfire flight ended in a collision with a pile of stones. Repaired, X4590 joined 53 OTU at Llandow and was still on charge when it re-located to Kirton-in-Lindsey in early May 1943.

On 16th May 1944 X4590 was at 82 Maintenance Unit (MU) at Lichfield for packing; it is recorded as having 1,036 flying hours 'on the clock'. By August it had moved to 52 MU Pengam Moors, Cardiff, and began the migratory career of Air Historical Branch airframes 'flagged' for future museum use, ending up at Fulbeck by 1958. The following year the Spitfire was in use by its last 'operational' unit, 71 MU based at Bicester. The MU had a fleet of airframes used for recruitment displays all over the country. The Spitfire was regularly popped on a low-loader, trucked to a venue, assembled, dis-assembled, put back on a flat-bed and off again on its travels – no way to treat a Battle of Britain veteran! Salvation was at hand in January 1972 when X4590 went to Henlow, formally 'joining up' with RAFM on 15th November. It was initially displayed at the Finningley station museum, moving to Cosford in 1976 and in 1978 it was installed in the Battle of Britain hall at Hendon.

Swift FR.5 WK281 on show at Hendon, 1991. *Alan Curry*

Supermarine Swift FR.5 WK281
1956 | Single-seat fighter-reconnaissance | One 7,145lb st Rolls-Royce Avon 114 | On loan to the Tangmere Military Aviation Museum

Take a look at the profile of the prototype Hunter, WB188, above for the rationale of why the RAFM's Swift is on 'detachment' at Tangmere. Swift FR.5 WK281 was awaiting collection at South Marston on 31st October 1956 and five days later was issued to 23 Maintenance Unit (MU), Aldergrove, Northern Ireland. It was to be 1959 before it saw service, joining 79 Squadron on 10th April 1959 at Gütersloh, West Germany. No.79 disbanded on the first day of 1961 and on the 20th WK281 was sent to 60 MU at Church Fenton. It was allocated to 14 (Uxbridge) Squadron Air Training Corps and moved to Northolt, where the unit kept it. Its significance was soon noted and it was transferred to the station museum at Colerne on 14th March 1967. It appeared the following year at Abingdon for the 50th anniversary celebrations of the RAF. By 1972 was at Finningley before storage at Swinderby in 1976, then on to station museum at St Athan. By October 1989 it was on show at Hendon, before despatch to Tangmere in 1995.

Westland Lysander III R9125
1940 | Two-crew army co-operation aircraft | One 890hp Bristol Mercury XVA

Lysanders earned fame for agent dropping and collection flights deep into France, although similar exploits in Burma are far less well-known. Built at Yeovil, R9125 was delivered to 225 Squadron at Tilshead, Wiltshire, on 29th September 1940 for coastal patrol and photo-reconnaissance sorties. It was back at Yeovil by September 1941 for conversion to a target-tug. On 24th December 1941 it was issued to the Central Gunnery School (CGS) at Chelveston; the unit having only moved into the airfield 20 days before. So started a life towing 'flags' (also called 'sleeves') at distance behind the aircraft while fighters took shots at the target. On

Wearing the colours of 225 Squadron, Lysander III R9125 in the Battle of Britain hall at Hendon, September 2012. *Ken Ellis*

6th April 1942 CGS re-located to Sutton Bridge, R9125 also making the transition. From 18th June 1942 the Lysander was in Northern Ireland carrying out similar duties with 7 Operational Training Unit at Limavady. On the last day of 1942 R9125 was on charge with the Central Navigation School at Cranage. This unit operated a range of types, mostly twin- and four-engine bombers, but it did have a couple of Lysanders. It is not known if these were used as tugs, or other purposes – teaching 'Special Duties' (SD) pilots to find tiny airstrips in the middle of the night? From 11th February 1944 R9125 was back at Yeovil, this time for conversion to SD standard with a fixed access ladder on the port side, a long-range 150-gallon tank under the forward fuselage, and bench seat in the rear cockpit for 'Joes' (agents). Work complete, it was issued to 161 Squadron at Tempsford on 15th October 1944. No.161 had stopped agent flights early in August, as the Allies advanced towards Germany. Now to turn to the incredible *We Landed by Moonlight* by skilled SD pilot and gifted writer Hugh Verity for R9125's next escapade. "During the third week of November George Turner was flying at Tempsford and on the field at Somersham [north of St Ives] for the RAF Film Unit. The unit was making *School for Danger* for the Central Office of Information. Later called *Now it Can be Told*, its world premiere was not until February 1947. The Lysander used in this film, R9125, is the one survivor now in the RAF Museum at Hendon. It has unfortunately, been converted back to the Army Co-operation style in its exterior appearance in camouflage colours and by the removal of the torpedo-shaped petrol tank and the fixed external ladder. The rear cockpit, however, is still fitted for pick-up passengers and their luggage."

No.161 Squadron disbanded at Tempsford on 2nd June 1945 and on 1st August the OC RAF Tempsford wrote alerting the Air Ministry about the existence of R9125. It worked, on 19th November the Lysander was taken to 76 Maintenance Unit at Wroughton for packing and long-term storage. By 1946, R9125 was at Stanmore Park, later returning to Wroughton and was at Cosford by the spring of 1961. It was issued to Henlow and the RAFM store in September 1967. It regained its 225 Squadron markings at Shawbury during restoration starting in late 1967 ready for display in the static at the RAF's 50th anniversary celebrations at Abingdon in June 1968. It moved to Hendon on 30th November 1971.

Westland Whirlwind HAR.10 XP299

1961 | Three-crew search and rescue helicopter | One 1,050shp Bristol Siddeley Gnome 101

As with the Wessex, see Chapter 4, there was a temptation to include more than one example, but discipline was required. For the Whirlwind the transport and air-sea rescue Mk.10 has been singled out. As with the other Sikorsky-originating designs (in this case the S-55) that Westland took a licence to build, the Whirlwind was so significantly re-engined, re-engineered and re-thought that it deserves a 'Westland' label as the designer. This machine was the first Mk.10 built from scratch, others having been converted, and it had its miaden flight at Yeovil on 28th March 1961. It was issued to the Aeroplane & Armament Experimental Establishment at Boscombe Down on 5th July 1961. It was subjected to intensive handling and performance trials to enable its Controller Aircraft

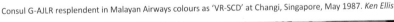

Consul G-AJLR resplendent in Malayan Airways colours as 'VR-SCD' at Changi, Singapore, May 1987. *Ken Ellis*

release, effectively its certificate of airworthiness. This work was completed in April 1962 and XP299 returned to Yeovil for more trials. This was interrupted in September 1964 with an appearance at the Farnborough airshow and in June the following year at the Paris Salon, Le Bourget. After its French break, XP299 was brought up to the latest modification state ready for RAF service. This came on 9th September 1966 at Tern Hill with the Helicopter Wing of the Central Flying School. A new role beckoned on 31st January 1968 when XP299 was despatched to the Queen's Flight at Benson and it was given the lush red with blue trim colours. It was not cleared to carry the Royal Family and was probably used for crew proficiency, filling a gap until the arrival of Wessex HCC.4s in June the following year (one of these is also at Hendon). On 2nd June 1969 XP299 left Royal service and was prepared for use with the Near East Air Force, joining 1563 Flight at Akrotiri, Cyprus, 13 days later. While on Cyprus it transferred to 230 Squadron on 13th April 1970; the unit maintained a detachment supporting United Nations peacekeepers at Nicosia. It was back in the UK by December 1971 and on the 16th joined 22 Squadron at Finningley. No.22 and 202 Squadron operated in the search and rescue role, with detached flights in all corners of the UK and the unofficial mottos: 'Let Twenty-Two Rescue You' and 'Let Two-Oh-Two Rescue You'. Both units continue to do fantastic work, having evolved from Whirlwinds to Wessex to the Sea Kings. The latter will take them through to April 2015 when Bristow Helicopters will civilianise the entire role. Anyway, to return to XP229, in September 1972 it was re-sprayed in the iconic all-over yellow colour scheme. Towards the end of its career, XP299 worked out of Chivenor with 'A' Flight 22 Squadron. It was handed over to the RAFM on 30th November 1981 and flew from Chivenor to Cosford eight days later. It was roaded to Hendon on 10th April 2003.

Former Royal Air Force Museum aircraft

Type	Identity	Built	Arrived#	Notes / *current status, or fate*
AEA Silver Dart replica	–	1982	late 1984	Hendon – *Shipped to Canada spring 1994, Reynolds Collection*
Airspeed Consul	G-AJLR	1940	Jan 1968	Henlow – *Air-freighted to Singapore 4 Nov 1986; Singapore Airlines, Tengah*
Airspeed Oxford I	G-AITF	1942	Mar 1969	Henlow – *Exchanged for Ventura 6130. To South African Air Force Museum Feb 1984*
Armstrong Whitworth Argosy C.1	XN819	1962	Jul 1972	Finningley – *Cockpit at Newark Air Museum*
Auster AOP.9	XR243	1962	Mar 1976	St Athan – *Auctioned 21 Sep 1989, no details*
Avro 504K replica	'H1968'	1968	c1970	St Athan – *Yorkshire Air Museum*
Avro Anson C.19/2	TX226	1946	1964	Colerne – *Spares source Classic Flt, Coventry*
Avro Shackleton MR.2	WL801	1953	7 Jul 1979	Cosford – *Transferred to 2 Sch of Tech Tng and scrapped early 1985*
Avro Shackleton MR.3/3	WR977	1957	Nov 1971	Finningley – *Newark Air Museum*
Avro Shackleton MR.3/3	XF703	1958	23 Sep 1971	Henlow – *Scrapped Sep 1975*
Avro Vulcan B.1	XA900	1957	c 1975	Cosford – *Scrapped 1986*
Avro Vulcan B.1	'XH498	1958	Oct 1967	Finningley – *Scrapped 1970*
Avro Vulcan B.2	XM602	1964	1984	St Athan – *Scrapped on site Oct 1992, cockpit stored in Manchester*
Beagle Basset CC.1	XS770	1965	Oct 1986	Cosford – *Sold, departed 1 Feb 1989 becoming G-HRHI. Scrapped for spares Boscombe Down circa 2010*
Blackburn Beverley C.1	XH124	1957	19 Jun 1968	Hendon – see narrative – *Offered for tender Nov 1989 and scrapped Feb-Mar 1990*
Blackburn Beverley C.1	XL149	1957	Mar 1970	Finningley – *Scrapped Mar 1978. Cockpit at South Yorkshire Aircraft Museum, Doncaster*
Bristol Scout replica	'A1742'	1962	1976	St Athan – *To private owners, on loan to Shuttleworth Collection – Chapter 3*

Type	Identity	Built	Arrived#	Notes / current status, or fate
Bristol Beaufighter I	X7688	1941	1970	Henlow – Forward fuselage and centre section. *To Skysport, Hatch, Beds, 1986, becoming G-DINT. Believed sold in Australia*
Bristol Beaufighter TT.10	RD867	1945	1964	Henlow – *Exchanged in Canada Sep 1969 for Bolingbroke IVT 10001, Canada National Aviation Museum, Rockcliffe*
De Havilland Tiger Moth	NL985	1944	c1976	Finningley – burnt out at Hendon 23rd May 1971. *Registered as G-BWIK 1995 and believed under restoration*
De Havilland Mosquito T.3	TW117	1946	30 May 1963	Hendon – *Exchanged, Royal Norwegian Air Force Museum, 31 Jan 1992, displayed at Bødø*
De Havilland Vampire FB.9	WL505	1951	1969	St Athan – *Became G-FBIX, broken up circa 2010*
De Havilland Vampire T.11	XD506	1954	Sep 1967	Finningley – *Jet Age Museum, Staverton, Glos, stored*
De Havilland Vampire T.11	XD542	1953	1964	Colerne – *Privately owned, Beverley, Yorks*
De Havilland Vampire T.11	XE920	1955	Jun 1972	Henlow – *To Scampton circa 1986, sold as G-VMPR and sold in the USA as N94019 mid-2006*
De Havilland Vampire T.11	XE946	1955	1974	Cardingdon, Henlow – cockpit pod. *To Cranwell Aviation Heritage Centre, 1997*
De Havilland Venom NF.3	WX905	1955	c1968	Henlow – *Tendered Feb 1989, to Newark Air Museum*
De Havilland Venom FB.4	WR539	1956	c1974	Cosford – *Sold Apr 1980, now with de Havilland Aircraft Heritage Centre, London Colney, Herts*
English Electric Canberra B.2	WD935	1951	Mar 1975	St Athan – *Scrapped on site Nov 1989, cockpit at South Yorkshire Aircraft Museum, Doncaster*
English Electric Canberra B.2	WJ573	1953	Sep 1963	Henlow – *Scrapped 1975*
English Electric Canberra B.2	WJ676	1954	1963	Colerne – *Privately owned cockpit, Tyneside*
English Electric Canberra B(I).8	WT346	1956	17 Jun 1962	Colerne – *Royal New Zealand Air Force Museum, Wigram, NZ*

The Nash Collection Farman at the 1936 Hendon Air Pageant. This was exported to New Zealand in December 2012 as part of the exchange that brought the Albatros, RE.8 and Sopwith Snipe in the other direction. *KEC*

Type	Identity	Built	Arrived#	Notes / *current status, or fate*
English Electric P.1B	XA847	1957	1969	Tendered from Hendon Feb 1989. *Private collector, Suffolk*
English Electric Lightning T.5	XM967	1962	9 Jan 1975	Colerne – *Perished on the dump at Kemble, Glos, by 1980*
Farman F.41	F-HMFI	c1913	1964	*Exported to New Zealand late 2012*
FMA Pucará	A-528	c1980	Oct 1982	Cosford – *Departed mid-1985, now with Norfolk and Suffolk Aviation Museum, Flixton*
Gloster Meteor F.4	VT229	1948	1964	Colerne – *Fantasy of Flight, Florida, USA*
Gloster Meteor F.8	WL168	1954	1969	St Athan – *Yorkshire Air Museum*
Gloster Javelin FAW.4	XA549	1954	c1967	Finningley – *Scrapped 1976*
Gloster Javelin FAW.4	XA634	1956	c1964	Colerne – *Displayed RAF Leeming, Yorks*
Gloster Javelin FAW.9R	XH892	1958	c1964	Colerne – *Norfolk and Suffolk Aviation Museum, Flixton*
Handley Page Hastings C.1A	TG527	1948	1966	Henlow – *Scrapped on site late 1969*
Handley Page Hastings C.1	TG536	1948	Jan 1974	Colerne – *Destroyed at RAF Catterick, Yorks, fire school, by 1989*
Handley Page Hastings C.1A	TG605	1949	5 Sep 1967	Finningley – *Scrapped*
Handley Page Victor B.1	XA923	1958	c 1975	Cosford – *Scrapped Mar 1985*
Handley Page Victor K.1A	XH592	1958	Jun 1984	Cosford – *Scrapped Oct 1994. Cockpit with private owner, Bruntingthorpe, Leics*
Handley Page HP.115	XP841	1960	1 Feb 1974	Colerne – *Fleet Air Arm Museum – Chapter 4*
Hanriot HD-1	HD-75	1918	1978	See Chapter 3 for its Shuttleworth era. *Exported to New Zealand late 2012*
Hawker Hurricane II	LF686	1944	1965	Colerne – *exchanged for Typhoon MN235 – National Air and Space Museum, Udvar Hazy Center, Dulles, USA*
Hawker Tempest V	EJ693	1944	1968	Henlow – *Sold 1985. Fantasy of Flight as N7027E under restoration to fly at Wycombe Air Park, Bucks*
Hawker Sea Fury FB.11	VR930	1948	15 Jan 1965	Colerne – *Royal Navy Historic Flight, Yeovilton*
Hawker Sea Fury FB.11	VX653	1949	10 Dec 1975	Hendon – *Exchanged with The Fighter Collection, Duxford Nov 1991, becoming G-BUCM, under restoration to fly*
Hawker Hunter F.1	WT555	1953	c1977	Cosford – *Auctioned 21 Sep 1989, to private owner, London*
Hawker Hunter F.2	WN907	1954	1964	St Athan – *Robertsbridge Aviation Centre, Sussex, cockpit*
Hawker Hunter F.4	XF309	1956	c1966	Finningley – *To HSA May 1973 as G-9-420 and to Kenyan Air Force as Mk.80 805 Dec 1974*
Hawker Hunter F.5	WP185	1955	Oct 1958	Hendon – *To RAF Abingdon by Dec 1989. Private owners, Essex*
Messerschmitt Me 163B-1	191904	1944	c1949	Colerne – *Luftwaffen Museum, Berlin, Germany*
North American Mustang	68-15795	1944	22 Jun 1976	Henlow, ex US Army, remanufactured Cavalier Mustang Mk.2. *Returned to USA 1980, Minneapolis Air National Guard Museum*
Percival Provost T.1	WV499	1953	1971	St Athan – *Registered as G-BZRF, private owner, Somerset*
Percival Provost T.1	XF545	1955	Jun 1967	Finningley – *Private owner, Reading area*

Wearing 5 Squadron colours, Tempest II 'PR536' at Hendon, December 1991. *Alan Curry*

Type	Identity	Built	Arrived#	Notes / current status, or fate
Percival Provost T.1	XF690	1955	Nov 1968	Colerne – *Airworthy as G-MOOS, Somerset owner*
Royal Aircraft Factory BE.2 rep	'6232'	1962	c1969	St Athan – *Yorkshire Air Museum*
Saunders-Roe Skeeter AOP.12	XN341	1960	Dec 1971	St Athan – *Stondon Transport Museum, Beds*
Slingsby Swallow TX.1	XS650	1964	1984	St Athan – *Auctioned 21 Sep 1989, airworthy by 1992*
Sopwith Camel replica	'D3419'	1962	c1969	St Athan – *Montrose Air Station Heritage Centre*
Supermarine Spitfire II	P7350	1940	Jul 1944	Colerne – *Airworthy with the Battle of Britain Memorial Flight, Coningsby*
Supermarine Spitfire IX	MK356	1944	1969	St Athan – *Airworthy with the Battle of Britain Memorial Flight, Coningsby*
Supermarine Spitfire XVI	RW388	1945	Jan 1952	Colerne – *Potteries Museum of and Art Gallery, Stoke-on-Trent*
Supermarine Spitfire XVI	TB382	1944	1974	Henlow – *To RAF Exhibition Flt, Abingdon May 1976; to Battle of Britain Memorial Flt, Coningsby, for spares use Oct 1999*
Supermarine Spitfire XVI	TE184	1945	c1968	Finningley – *Airworthy as G-MKVI, London-based owner*
Supermarine 517	VV106	1948	1964	Colerne – *Fleet Air Arm Museum – Chapter 4*
Vickers Valetta C.1	WD159	1950	2 Sep 1964	Colerne – *Blown up in exercise at Ewyas Garold, Hereford, Dec 1977*
Vickers Varsity T.1	WF408	1952	c1978	Cosford – *To fire dump at Northolt 8 Oct 1992*
Watkins CHW Monoplane	–	1909	1959	St Athan – *National Waterfront Museum, Swansea – Chapter 11*
Westland Dragonfly HR.3	WG725	1951	1966	Colerne – *Museum of Flight, Nowra, Australia*
Westland Whirlwind HCC.12	XR486	1964	1981	St Athan – *Became G-RWWW, The Helicopter Museum*
Wright Flyer replica	–	1966	11 Sep 1966	Finningley – *Yorkshire Air Museum*

Notes: Full details of the following RAF Museum 'out-stations' Colerne, Finningley and St Athan, were given in the companion volume *Lost Aviation Collections of Britain* and details have been abbreviated here. Airframes that were held in the British Airways collection are detailed in Chapter 6. # First taken on by RAF Museum

Royal Air Force Museum aircraft on loan

Type	Identity	Built	Origin	Arrived#	Location
Avro 504K	G-ABAA	1918	UK	1968	Museum of Science and Industry Manchester
Avro Shackleton AEW.2	WR960	1954	UK	Jan 1983	Museum of Science and Industry Manchester – see profile
Avro 707A	WZ736	1953	UK	c1967	Museum of Science and Industry Manchester
Bristol 173 Series 1	XF785	1952	UK	1968	Bristol Aero Collection
Bristol Belvedere HC.1	XG454	1960	UK	1969	Museum of Science and Industry Manchester
De Havilland Comet C.2	XK699	1957	UK	Jun 1967	Lyneham, Wiltshire – to re-locate to Cosford
Dornier Do 24T-3	HD5-1	1939	Germany	30 Jul 1982	Soesterberg, Netherlands
English Electric Canberra B.2	WH725	1953	UK	1971	Imperial War Museum Duxford
English Electric P.1A	WG763	1955	UK	Aug 1963	Museum of Science and Industry Manchester
Fairey Jet Gyrodyne	XJ389	1948	UK	1979	Museum of Berkshire Aviation, Woodley
Folland Gnat F.1	XK740	1957	UK	Jan 1974	Solent Sky, Southampton
Gloster Meteor IV Special	EE549	1946	UK	Apr 1967	Tangmere Military Aviation Museum
Gloster Meteor NF.14	WS838	1954	UK	Feb 1972	Midland Air Museum
Gloster Javelin FAW.9	XH903	1958	UK	Aug 1967	Jet Age Museum
Hafner Rotachute III	P-5	1943	UK	1968	Museum of Army Flying – Chapter 7
Hawker Hurricane II	'BN230'	1944	UK	21 Mar 1985	LF751, Spitfire and Hurricane Memorial Museum, Manston
Hawker P.1052	VX272	1948	UK	1964	Fleet Air arm Museum – Chapter 4
Hawker Hunter F.3	WB188	1951	UK	c1965	Tangmere Military Aviation Museum – see profile
Hawker P.1127	XP831	1960	UK	1972	Science Museum – Chapter 1
McDonnell Phantom FGR.2	XV408	1968	UK	1996	Tangmere Military Aviation Museum
Miles Magister I	'T9707'	1940	UK	1968	T9708, Museum of Army Flying – Chapter 7
Supermarine Spitfire XIV	MT847	1945	UK	1979	Museum of Science and Industry Manchester
Supermarine Spitfire XVI	TB752	1945	UK	Jul 1978	Spitfire and Hurricane Memorial Museum, Manston
Supermarine Spitfire F.24	PK683	1946	UK	Nov 1972	Solent Sky, Southampton
Supermarine Swift FR.5	WK281	1956	UK	14 Mar 1967	Tangmere Military Aviation Museum – see profile
Vickers Valiant B.1	XD816	1956	UK	Aug 1970	Brooklands Museum, cockpit
Westland Dragonfly HR.1	VX595	1949	USA	c1968	Fleet Air Arm Museum – Chapter 4
Yokosuka MXY-7 Ohka 11	997	1945	Japan	c1968	Museum of Science and Industry Manchester

Notes: # First taken on by RAF Museum.

Royal Air Force Museum Hendon aircraft

Type	Identity	Built	Origin	Arrived#	Notes
Airspeed Oxford I	MP425	1943	UK	Mar 1969	see profile
Albatros D.Va	'D7343'	2011	Germany	28 Aug 2012	–
Auster I*	LB264	1942	UK	23 Oct 2002	see profile
Avro 504K	'E449'	1918	UK	Mar 1963	–
Avro Rota I	K4232	1934	UK	14 Jun 1978	–
Avro Anson I	W2068	1939	UK	19 Apr 1996	–
Avro Lancaster I	R5868	1942	UK	Mar 1972	see profile
Avro Vulcan B.2	XL318	1961	UK	1 Jan 1982	–
Blackburn Buccaneer S.2B	XW547	1972	UK	20 Jan 1993	see profile
Blériot XI	164	1910	France	1964	–
Blériot XXVII	433	1911	France	May 1963	–
Boeing B-17G Flying Fortress*	44-83868	1945	USA	13 Oct 1983	see profile
Boulton Paul Defiant I	N1671	1940	UK	23 Jul 1968	see profile
Bristol M.1C replica	'C4994'	1987	UK	Aug 1987	–
Bristol F.2b Fighter	'E2455'	1918	UK	1965	–
Bristol Bulldog IIA*	'K2227'	1930	UK	31 Mar 1999	see profile
Bristol Bolingbroke IVT	'L8756'	1942	UK	25 Apr 1966	see profile
Bristol Beaufort VIII	'DD931'	1944	UK	1991	–
Bristol Beaufighter TF.10	RD253	1944	UK	1965	see profile
Bristol Sycamore HR.12	WV783	1950	UK	1995	–
Bristol Belvedere HC.1*	XG474	1962	UK	7 Aug 1969	see profile
Bücker Bü 131 Jungmann	E3B.521	1956	Germany	23 Jan 1997	CASA-built example
Caudron G.3	'3066'	1916	France	1964	–
Clarke Chanute glider	–	1910	UK	1983	on loan from Science Museum – see Chapter 1
Consolidated Liberator VI	KN751	1945	USA	1 Jul 1974	see profile
Curtiss Kittyhawk IV	'FX760'	1943	USA	29 May 1992	–
De Havilland DH.9A*	F1010	1918	UK	15 Jun 1977	see profile
De Havilland Tiger Moth II	T6296	1941	UK	15 Mar 1972	see profile
De Havilland Mosquito TT.35	TJ138	1945	UK	Jun 1967	see profile
De Havilland Vampire F.3	VT812	1947	UK	9 Jun 1964	–
DH Canada Chipmunk T.10	WP962	1952	Canada	5 May 2000	see profile
EHI EH.101*	ZJ116	1990	UK/Italy	20 Nov 2002	–
English Electric Canberra PR.3	WE139	1953	UK	23 Apr 1969	see profile
English Electric Lightning F.6	XS925	1967	UK	26 Apr 1988	see profile
Eurofighter Typhoon DA2*	ZH588	1994	UK/Ger/It/Sp	22 Jan 2008	see profile
Fairey Battle I	L5343	1939	UK	21 Nov 1972	see profile
Fiat CR-42 Falco*	MM5701	1940	Italy	1968	–
Focke-Wulf Fw 190F-8/U-1	584219	1944	Germany	Sep 1970	–
Fokker D.VII*	8417/18	1918	Germany	Mar 1966	see profile
Gloster Gladiator II	K8042	1937	UK	Nov 1965	see profile
Gloster Gladiator II	N5628	1939	UK	Aug 1968	wreckage
Gloster F9/40 Meteor*	DG202/G	1942	UK	1965	see profile
Gloster Meteor F.8	WH301	1951	UK	17 Feb 1967	–
Handley Page Halifax II	W1048	1942	UK	25 Aug 1973	see profile
Handley Page Victor K.2	XM717	1963	UK	2 Mar 1994	cockpit
Hawker Hart	'J9941'	1935	UK	1972	–
Hawker Hart Trainer	K4972	1935	UK	16 Oct 1963	see profile

Type	Identity	Built	Origin	Arrived#	Notes
Hawker Hurricane replica	'Z3427'	1990	UK	1990	full-scale model 'gate guardian'
Hawker Hurricane I	P2617	1940	UK	May 1972	–
Hawker Hurricane I*	P3175	1940	UK	1978	wreckage
Hawker Typhoon Ib	MN235	1944	UK	19 Nov 1968	see profile
Hawker Tempest II	'PR536'	1946	UK	13 Nov 1991	–
Hawker Tempest TT.5	NV778	1944	UK	Aug 1965	see profile
Hawker Hunter FGA.9	XG154	1956	UK	30 May 1985	see profile
Hawker Hunter FR.10	853	1955	UK	6 Sep 2003	ex XF426
Hawker Siddeley Harrier GR.3	XZ997	1982	UK	4 Dec 1991	–
Heinkel He 111H-20/R1	701152	1944	Germany	Sep 1969	see profile
Heinkel He 162A-2	120227	1944	Germany	1961	–
Hunting Jet Provost T.3A	XM463	1960	UK	1991	'hands-on' exhibit
Hunting Jet Provost T.5A	XW323	1970	UK	1992	–
Junkers Ju 87D-3 'Stuka'	494083	1944	Germany	Sep 1969	see profile
Junkers Ju 88R-1	360043	1943	Germany	Sep 1969	see profile
Lockheed Hudson IIIA	A16-199	1942	USA	14 Jul 1981	see profile
Lockheed-Martin F-35*	–	2010	USA	2011	full-scale model
McDonnell Phantom FGR.2*	XV424	1969	USA	12 Nov 1992	–
Messerschmitt Bf 109E-4/B	4101	1940	Germany	Sep 1969	see profile
Messerschmitt Bf 109G-2	10639	1942	Germany	10 Mar 2002	–
Messerschmitt Bf 110G-4-R6	730301	1944	Germany	Aug 1973	–
Messerschmitt Me 262A-2a	112372	1945	Germany	1972	see profile
North American Harvard IIB	FE905	1943	USA	Mar 1985	see profile
North American TB-25N Mitchell	'34037'	1944	USA	25 Oct 1982	see profile
North American P-51D Mustang*	'413317'	1944	USA	18 Nov 2003	–
Panavia Tornado GR.1	ZA457	1983	UK/Ger/It	28 Jul 2003	see profile
Panavia Tornado F.3*	ZE887	1988	UK/Ger/It	18 Oct 2010	–
Percival Mew Gull replica	'G-AEXF'	2008	UK	17 Apr 2008	–
Percival Prentice T.1	VS618	1949	UK	9 Oct 2009	see profile
Republic Thunderbolt	'KL216'	1945	USA	Jun 1986	see profile
Royal Aircraft Factory BE.2b rep	'687'	1988	UK	Jun 1992	–
Royal Aircraft Factory FE.2b	'A6526'	1917	UK	Apr 1976	see profile
Royal Aircraft Factory RE.8 rep	'A3930'	2011	UK	28 Aug 2012	–
Royal Aircraft Factory SE.5a	F938	1918	UK	Dec 1964	–
Short Sunderland MR.5	ML824	1944	UK	11 Jan 1971	see profile
Sikorsky Hoverfly I	KK995	1944	USA	14 Jun 1966	see profile
Slingsby Grasshopper TX.1	WZ791	1952	UK	8 Aug 1991	–
Slingsby Cadet TX.3	XA302	1952	UK	5 May 2005	–
Sopwith Tabloid replica	'168'	1980	UK	23 Mar 1983	–
Sopwith 1½ Strutter replica	'A8226'	1980	UK	Jan 1981	–
Sopwith Triplane*	N5912	1917	UK	late 1964	see profile
Sopwith Pup	'N5182'	1916	UK	Jun 1982	–
Sopwith F1 Camel	F6314	1918	UK	9 Jan 1964	–
Sopwith 5F1 Dolphin*	'C3988'	1918	UK	Jun 1967	–
Sopwith Snipe replica*	'E6655'	2011	UK	28 Aug 2012	–
Sud Gazelle HCC.4	XW855	1973	France	1 Apr 2003	–
Supermarine Southampton I	N9899	1925	UK	Sep 1967	see profile
Supermarine Stranraer*	920	1940	UK	Jul 1970	see profile
Supermarine Seagull V	A2-4	1935	UK	May 1972	–

Type	Identity	Built	Origin	Arrived#	Notes
Supermarine Spitfire replica	'MH486'	1990	UK	1990	full-scale model 'gate guardian'
Supermarine Spitfire replica	–	–	UK	–	full-scale model
Supermarine Spitfire I	X4590	1940	UK	Jan 1972	see profile
Supermarine Spitfire Vb	BL614	1942	UK	Oct 1972	–
Supermarine Spitfire F.24	PK724	1946	UK	20 Feb 1970	–
Vickers FB.5 Gunbus replica	'2345'	1966	UK	10 Jun 1968	–
Vickers Vimy replica	'F8614'	1969	UK	Dec 1970	–
Westland Wallace II	K6035	1935	UK	Apr 1977	fuselage
Westland Lysander III	R9125	1940	UK	Mar 1961	see profile
Westland Whirlwind HAR.10	XP299	1961	USA	30 Nov 1981	see profile
Westland Wessex HCC.4*	XV732	1969	USA	26 Mar 2002	–

Notes: # First taken on by RAF Museum * illustrated in colour section

Vickers test pilot 'Dizzy' Addicott flying the Vintage Aircraft and Flying Association-built Vimy replica G-AWAU at Brooklands, June 1969. *KEC*

A variety of RAF Museum brochures, from a simple duplicated hand-out on progress pre-1972.

CHAPTER 6

Testing Times – Cold War Containment
Royal Air Force Museum
Cosford, Shropshire

www.rafmuseum.org

When the Duke of Gloucester officially opened Cosford's Visitor Centre on 22nd June 1998 there was an announcement greeted with considerable glee by all of those who had followed the progress of the Shropshire collection since the mid-1970s. Gone was the Aerospace Museum, it had become the Royal Air Force Museum Cosford. Hendon and Cosford were equal partners as Britain's largest aviation museum. Of course, at Cosford staff and volunteers alike had known this for a long time, but the official recognition was very welcome!

Readers diving into this page directly are best to take a look at the previous chapter as the bulk of the history of the Royal Air Force Museum (RAFM from now on) is related there. Cosford's origins lie with the RAF's regional collections, or station museums. As Cosford was also the home of 2 School of Technical Training (SoTT – see below) the collection benefitted from a wealth of skills and manpower, not to mention a supply of former instructional airframes. The collection was established within the hangars at the northern edge of the site, today housing the Test Flight and Warplane exhibitions. From early on, Cosford became the centre for RAFM's impressive gathering of prototypes, experimentals and test-beds. With the recent arrival of the EAP, the forebear of the Eurofighter Typhoon, this policy continues.

Soviet radar designation models, Canberra PR.9 XH171 and Valiant BK.1 XD818 (right) on the 'top floor' of the National Cold War Exhibition, Cosford. *Steve Fletcher-Key Publishing www.flypast.com*

Just like other station museums, Cosford ran largely on a volunteer basis, with custodianship of Air Historical Branch (see Chapter 5) airframes bestowed upon the 'most likely' unit on base; for example 49 Maintenance Unit at Colerne and of course 2 SoTT at Cosford. With such a concentration of historic machines on site, requests from the public to visit were met where-ever was practical. Slowly this developed with the occasional open day, or special event. During the early 1970s Cosford had taken on the name of the Aerospace Museum, with a badge of a pterodactyl – a flying dinosaur. The prime mover for the Aerospace Museum was Flt Lt Derek Eastwood and his efforts, and those of the team he gathered around him, provided the firm foundation on which Cosford became a world-ranking museum. In the 1970s the Aerospace Museum received no grant funding from MoD, or from RAFM; it was known as a 'Unit/Branch Museum' and costs were covered by the Station. Tragically, Derek died in 1983 and his place was taken by Flt Lt Len Woodgate, who had been running the St Athan, Wales' 'out-station'. Vital to the museum, then and now, was to input of volunteers and the support of the Cosford Aerospace Museum Society.

By 1975 the museum was open much more regularly and had produced edition three of its guidebook. That year much effort had been put in to arranging the German missile collection for inspection and in 1985 the rocketry held at Newton moved to Cosford to create a concentration that cannot be equalled anywhere else in Europe. By the late 1970s Hangar 1, on the flight line and alongside the control tower, was fully in use. The site encompassed 170 acres, essentially the boundaries that it occupies today, and there was a small shop and cafe.

As it grew in stature, RAFM Trustees accepted management of the collections at Cosford as a fully-fledged subsidiary of Hendon and the Aerospace Museum opened accordingly on 1st May 1979. John A Francis was appointed as General Manager in 1990 and was to oversee the transitions at Cosford up to the advent of the National Cold War Exhibition. In 1996 Hangar 1 was remodelled in a £154,000 project that included new galleries and an elevated walkway. As noted at the beginning of the chapter, the Visitor Centre was inaugurated in June 1998; this dramatically improved the 'reception' element, with a large car park, a huge and airy lobby area and a restaurant over-looking the airfield.

A view of Hangar 1 in 1979, Liberator in the foreground. *RAF Museum*

Part of the rocket collection in the late 1970s. An 1944 Enzian flak rocket (left) and a Rheintochter III transonic flak rocket. *Roy Bonser*

School for engineers

RAF Cosford celebrates its 75th anniversary during 2013. First up and running was 5 Aircraft Storage Unit, but this was swiftly renamed, becoming 9 Maintenance Unit (MU) on 15th March 1938. Duties of the MU centred on acceptance from manufacturers, preparation for service and storage. The present day 3,700ft Runway 06/24 was in use from 1942 and there have always been grass runways. Spitfires became a major part of 9 MU's work and the assembly and flight test of Airspeed Horsa assault gliders was also carried out at Cosford. No.9 MU closed its doors on 22nd June 1956.A less well known part of Cosford's past is that it served as an extension of the massive Castle Bromwich Aircraft Factory to alleviate Spitfire production problems and help disperse the construction process. Known as No.23 Factory, it created sub-assemblies, knitted them together and carried out flight tests. All this from a purpose-built complex located next to where today the police and air ambulance helicopters operate.

The largest and longest-running RAF presence at Cosford was 2 SoTT which was established on 15th July 1938 with an extensive campus north of the Shrewsbury-Wolverhampton railway line, as well as the hangars on the northern perimeter of the airfield. Many skills have been taught over the decades, centring on engine and airframe qualifications, with nearly 80,000 mechanics of all descriptions being trained during World War Two. From its earliest days, the SoTT had a large selection of instructional airframes and other substantial teaching aids and these became a font for the nascent RAFM. This continues today, with examples being 'flagged' for RAFM and eventually rolling across the apron. No.1 SoTT at Halton disbanded on 9th September 1993 and on 24th November 1994 was reborn when 2 SoTT was redesignated as 1 SoTT. A decade later (1st April 2004) it became the Headquarters Defence College of Aeronautical Engineering (DCAE), with satellite operations for the Army at Aborfield and at Gosport for the Navy. From 1st October 2012 DCAE was renamed the Defence School of Aeronautical Engineering (DSAE). Scheduled to open in 2015 at Lyneham is the Combined Defence Technical Establishment, which was announced on 18th July 2011. Arborfield, and another site at Borden, Hampshire, will be wound down by 2015. Just what will happen to RAF Cosford has yet to be announced but the long-term vision is that all technical training will be centred at Lyneham by 2020.

Flying from the airfield are the Grob Tutor T.1s of the Birmingham University Air Squadron, while 633 Volunteer Gliding School use Grob Vigilant T.1s. Non-flying organisations at Cosford include: 1 Radio School; the RAF School of Physical Training; Defence School of Photography and number of smaller lodger units.

A line-up of 2 School of Technical Training instructional airframes plus some station museum airframes outside Hangar 1, 1972. *Peter Green Collection*

Heavyweights

Within Chapter 1 the thorny problem of preserving airliners was discussed, along with a table examining the UK's present 'population'. From the mid-1970s onwards, the Science Museum at its Wroughton out-station, the Duxford Aviation Society at Duxford and RAFM at Cosford began to collect airliners. Cosford's timeline for this was as follows:

Cosford's airliners

Arrival	Type	Identity	Built	Notes
2 May 1976	Vickers Viscount 701	G-AMOG	1953	ex BA. *To Museum of Flight, East Fortune 17 Aug 2006 – Chapter 10*
31 May 1978	Junkers Ju 52 (CASA 352)	T2B-272	1954	later painted as 'G-AFAP' – see profile
17 Sep 1978	DH Comet 1XB	G-APAS	1953	see profile
6 Oct 1978	Short Belfast C.1	XR371	1967	later painted in HeavyLift colours – see profile
1979	Vickers Viking 1	G-AGRU	1946	ex Soesterberg. *To Brooklands Museum, Surrey 27 Jun 1991*
25 Oct 1979	Vickers VC-10 Srs 1101	G-ARVM	1964	ex BA. *Scrapped, forward fuselage to Brooklands Museum, Surrey, 19 Oct 2006*
Feb 1980	Westland Dragonfly HR.3	'G-AJOV'	1953	on display
12 Jun 1981	Boeing 707-436	G-APFJ	1960	ex British Airtours. *Scrapped, forward fuselage to Museum of Flight, East Fortune (Chapter 10), Apr 2006*
2 Apr 1982	Hawker Siddeley Trident 1C	G-ARPH	1964	ex BA. *Scrapped, cockpit to Museum of Flight, East Fortune (Chapter 10) 2006*
31 May 1984	Bristol Britannia 312F	G-AOVF	1957	displayed outside, in RAF colours as 'XM497'
29 Dec 1992	BAC 111-510ED	G-AVMO	1968	ex BA. *To Museum of Flight, East Fortune (Chapter 10), 9 Sep 2006*
23 May 2000	HP Jetstream 200	G-BBYM	1969	ex British Aerospace. *To Newcastle Aviation Academy 29 Jul 2008*

RAFM came to a co-operative agreement with British Airways in 1980. As well as the supply of retired airliners, BA sent along regular working parties of apprentices, along with tools and materials, to look after the exhibits. It was hoped that this would lead to a 'parallel' air transport museum at some stage. To expand upon this relationship a special annex was opened in May 1984 within the 'top' hangars devoted to the history of BA and its antecedents. To add to this collection, the Spanish-built Junkers was painted in 1938 British Airways colours in October 1985; the Belfast acquired a HeavyLift scheme in the summer of 1982 and the Dragonfly HR.5 took on a 1950 British European Airways livery.

The regularity of the BA working parties became less and less at Cosford and after the 9/11 terrorist attacks in the USA in 2001 BA withdrew all support for the airliner collection. In 2003, BA revealed that Cosford was not going to be on the receiving end of a Concorde, despite the gathering of its former airframes. There was no chance of one flying in, but moving large aircraft by road and re-assembling them was second nature to RAFM. By 2005 it was clear that another difficult decision was required from RAFM Director Dr Michael Fopp (see Chapter 5). It was announced in January 2006 that RAFM and BA were reviewing the status of the airliner collection. With all financial elements of what was to become the National Cold War Exhibition in place, the vista of increasingly weather-beaten airliners on show outside the new building was not a promising one. Without the initial input of the airline, the 'British Airways Collection' was less and less viable and besides, within a decade RAFM faced the advent of ever-larger aircraft within its *direct* acquisition policy. The Brooklands Museum and the National Museum of Flight Scotland took on the airframes (see the table above), in part or in whole, with the blessing of BA. The airline financed what it referred to as the "deconstruction and reconstruction" of the collection and engaged specialists Air Salvage International to undertake the exodus.

The Britannia remained outside, but the 'Cold War' hall allowed the Belfast indoors, and freed up space within Hangar 1 putting the Comet G-APAS, Andover, Argosy and Varsity and others under cover. Retirement dates for RAF aircraft became increasingly difficult to predict in the 1990s and 21st century, either types lingered far longer than anticipated, or had their service lives cut dramatically. A Hercules C.3 arrived in December 2011, although the remainder of the C-130K fleet continues in service as this is written. The Nimrod MR.2s had the rug pulled from under them and then the R.1s succeeded in a life extension in the light of the Libyan uprising. As related in the profile below, the R.1 arrived by road in March 2012. The Britannia, 'Herk', Nimrod and SP-2H Neptune (outside since 1982) are now the only large aircraft outside. This is due to change; Comet C.2 XK699, former 'guardian' at Lyneham, is due to make the trek to Cosford by road. A Vickers VC-10 tanker is also expected before the end of 2013. These represent a great responsibility, in terms of day-to-day conservation and in long-term accommodation planning. RAFM's rationale behind putting an end to the airliner collection was painful, but prescient.

Scaffolding surrounding Belfast C.1 XR371 during its 1988 repaint. *RAF Museum*

Profiled below is the second largest aircraft currently on show in a museum in the UK, the Short Belfast. (The B-52 at Duxford takes the top slot.) It also serves as a 'case study' in the headaches of looking after such giants in the open air. Four years after it flew in, during the summer of 1982 it was decided to paint the Belfast in the colours of civil operator HeavyLift Cargo Airlines, that way 'placing' it within the airliner collection as much as mainstream RAFM 'territory'. The top of the tail on a Belfast is an eye-watering 47ft away and the wing is 2,466 square feet in area. A repaint is a costly exercise in gantries, scaffolding, paint and labour. In 1988 it was decided to put the Belfast back into Air Support Command colours, so another repaint was in order. This was not flippancy, the integrity of the paint scheme, plus a dehumidifying regime within the cavernous fuselage, was the best way to keep the airframe from falling foul of the UK climate. The bill for this exercise came to £18,000 (£36,000 in present-day values) with the Manpower Services Commission, Shorts and – ironically – HeavyLift sponsoring the project. Move on eight years and XR371 needed the same tender, loving care plus the undercarriage was treated to new wheels and tyres. Shorts – actually Bombardier Aerospace Belfast since June 1989 – again helped out and a local firm donated the paint. Contractor Challenge Aviation carried out the work and XR371 took on Transport Command colours and the name *Enceladus*. All of this was to look after the steady erosion of rain, but there can be times when nature turns to direct action. On 4th January 1998 the Belfast became what a member of Cosford's curatorial team called: "Britain's biggest weathercock". Despite an empty weight of around 127,000lb the Belfast was blown 25ft away from its undercarriage plinths in a gale; damage was remarkably slight. Repaint No.4 was carried out by Challenge Aviation again in September 2002 by which time the Cold War hall was well into formulation.

Receipt and despatch

In Chapter 5 the central RAFM storage site, Henlow in Bedfordshire, was outlined. It played a pivotal role in providing a 'collection point' for what became an 'exhibit surge' as the Hendon museum began to take form. Fondly known as the 'Pickle Factory' and it was not until 1990 that Henlow, a repository for everything from airframes to photographs, was completely cleared. Around the same time, the regional collection and workshop facility at St Athan, Wales, began to be vacated. Since 1975 the huge former Shortstown airship works at Cardington, Bedfordshire, had increasingly been the home of RAFM storage and restoration. To clarify, this was not – as often thought – the gargantuan twin airship hangars, but the factory adjacent. Rack upon rack held carefully itemised and catalogued artefacts from: period telephones for use in dioramas; engines of all shapes and powers; the rear fuselage of a World War One biplane, awaiting the moment when

Above: Rolling the fuselage of the Supermarine Southampton at the Cardington workshop, November 1988. *Peter Green*

Left: Just a small section of the artefact stacks at Cardington, 1982. *KEC*

it could become a viable project for resurrection; all the way to airframes under restoration. It is probably wrong to mention one project among many carried out at Cardington, but the Supermarine Southampton fuselage (profiled in Chapter 5) *has* to be one of the most memorable. Throughout these decades, RAFM was a 'tenant' and if the Ministry of Defence (MoD) decided to close a facility, then RAFM was also on the move. MoD was at pains to keep each tenure as long as possible, aware of the massive disruption a 'change of address' presented to the RAFM Restoration and Storage Centre.

As it became clear that the RAF's tenure at Cardington was waning, a new approach was adopted. Much of RAFM's artefact 'stock' was held in 'deep store' – not needing to be directly at hand. It may be a case of a researcher from Hendon's incredible Department of Records and Information Services (glorying in the abbreviation DORIS) needing to inspect an item for potential use in a display; or to help a 'warbird' restorer with a project; or simply to hold for 'eventualities' or trade with another museum. Along with the 'deep store' a well-located workshop was needed, but they need not be co-located. The best site for the workshop boiled down to one option – Cosford. Cardington, and Henlow before it, had acted as a 'receipt and despatch' centre for RAFM – very much the role of the Maintenance Units (MU) and Royal Navy Aircraft Yards that crop up so often in the exhibit profiles in this book. To concentrate staff at two sites would make much more sense and the proximity of a runway was also useful, but not vital. Plans for what would become the Michael Beetham Conservation Centre (MBCC) at Cosford were first announced in May 1996 and is dealt with below. At the same time the search started for the 'deep store', a sort of gigantic 'lock-up'. In the end this was found just 12 miles to the north-east of Cosford – as the crow flies – at 16 MU, Stafford, and administered by the Defence Logistics Organisation. A 60,000 square foot facility was secured within the complex site and the move in began in March 1999 – 160 lorry-loads were needed! RAF Stafford officially closed down on 31st March 2006, the base becoming MoD Stafford with tri-service units in residence. (See also the table 'Royal Air Force Museum aircraft held in store'.)

Plans for the new centre at Cosford were set to come to fruition in 2002, but the official announcement that RAF Cardington would close its doors on 1st January 2000 meant that a temporary home was needed for the workshop. Room was found at Wyton, near Huntingdon, and re-location from Cardington began in June 1999. Meanwhile progress was being made with the Cosford restoration centre which was to be built to the west of the museum site. Sqn Ldr Bruce James, later to be in charge of the MBCC, was the main liaison with MoD, securing a state-of-the-art facility to replace Cardington. Final elements from the 'bolt-hole' at Wyton arrived in the new building in the early weeks of 2002. The centre was opened by MRAF Sir Michael Beetham GCB CBE DFC AFC DL on 13th May 2002 and named in his honour. Sir Michael had been the longest-serving Chairman of Trustees – 15 years – and is President of the very vibrant Friends of the Royal Air Force Museum organisation. A Lancaster pilot with Bomber Command, his post-war service career was a tour-de-force that cannot be done

A view of the MBCC at Cosford during the November 2012 open day: fin of Wellington T.10 MF628 in the left foreground, Hampden TB.1 P1344 in the centre and Kestrel FGA.1 XS695 to the right. *Dean Wright*

Detailed work and constructional drawings of Hampden TB.1 P1344 on show at the MBCC, November 2012. *Dean Wright*

justice to here, but included development and operation of the V-Bombers and becoming Chief of the Air Staff in mid-1977. He was CAS during the Falklands conflict and credited with the concept of the BLACK BUCK raids (see the profile of Victor XH672 below). He became Marshal of the Royal Air Force in October 1982.

Staff at MBCC, and its forebears, have exceptional skills, but represent a finite resource. There had always been an element of on-the-job training but one of the aims of the MBCC was to allow for a more formalised approach to preserving *skills* as well as artefacts. In 2005 RAFM launched its apprentice scheme, centred on MBCC, teaching subjects such as historic aircraft restoration, carpentry, welding and fabrication and machine and bench fitting. The scheme went from strength to strength, so much so that in early 2013 it was extended in conjunction with Barnet and Southgate College based upon motor vehicle repair disciplines allowing students to become registered conservation technicians.

Annual open days at the MBCC attract a huge following of enthusiasts, but otherwise it is not available for public inspection as the vital work needs minimum interruption! On 1st July 2010 a major project rolled through the doors of the MBCC, Wellington T.10 MF628 for return to its status as a post-war crew trainer. As it is not on public gaze, it cannot have an exhibit profile, but a brief 'biography' is essential. When it was installed at Hendon on 26th October 1971, it was the *only* Wellington in the world. Then on 21st September 1985 Wellington N2980 *R-for-Robert* emerged from the waters of Loch Ness and is now at the Brooklands Museum. Built at Squires Gate, Blackpool, as a Mk.X MF628 moved to Boulton Paul's Pendeford factory for conversion to a T.10. It joined 1 Air Navigation School at Hullavington in April 1949, but an accident in December 1951 cut short its training career. It was flying at Hemswell from April 1954 to take part in the filming of *The Dam Busters*. In January 1955 Vickers acquired MF628 from the RAF and presented it to the Royal Aeronautical Society. It was flown to Wisley on 24th January 1955 – the last-ever flight of a 'Wimpey'. By March 1961 it was at Biggin Hill and the following year was presented to the nascent RAFM.

Wellington T.10 MF628 in 1955 after being acquired by Vickers. *KEC*

Two German types also merit mention. Arriving on 20th December 2012 was Focke-Wulf Fw 190A-8/R6 733682 having completed a long-term loan to the Imperial War Museum (IWM) at South Lambeth, London (Chapter 2). As outlined in the table 'Royal Air Force Museum aircraft on loan' in Chapter 5, RAFM has long had a vigorous policy of sharing its airframe stock with other organisations, provided they meet its environmental and curatorial standards. At Hendon, two-seat Fw 190F-8/U1 584219 is currently displayed. The former Lambeth example had been the upper component of a 'Mistel S3B' composite with a Junkers Ju 88H-1. The specially-modified Ju 88 was joined to the Fw 190 by a rig and when close to a high-value target the intention was to point the Junkers, laden with high explosive, in the right direction while the fighter disengaged and flew home. While 733682 made it to the UK in July 1945, the Junkers was scrapped where it was found at Schleswig in northern Germany. As described in Chapter 2, with the remodelling of the IWM in readiness for the centenary of World War One, it was decided to release the fighter back to the care of RAFM. It is being prepared for display and it is planned to put on show perhaps as early as 2013.

A very challenging project is due at MBCC. On 26th August 1940, stricken Dornier Do 17Z-2 1160 '5K+AR' of 7/KG3 carried out a wheels-up landing on the Goodwin Sands, off the coast of Kent; two of its crew survived. The bomber had *probably* been damaged by a Boulton Paul Defiant of 264 Squadron, operating from Hornchurch, Essex. Miraculously, the wreck has endured remarkably well and since 2008, RAFM, in association with Wessex Archaeology, evaluated the possibility of recovery. Salvage started in May 2013 and this incredible project will bring back from extinction a very significant Luftwaffe type. (See also the table Royal Air Force Museum Cosford Michael Beetham Conservation Centre aircraft.)

A Divided World

The author's enthusiasm for the National Cold War Exhibition has already been mentioned in Chapter 4 where his regard for the brilliant Carrier display was confessed. The story of the 'Cold War' from its naming by George Orwell and Churchill's famed speech at Fulton, Missouri, USA, when he coined the phrase 'Iron Curtain' in the 1940s to the collapse of the Berlin Wall in 1989 and the dissolution of the Soviet Union in 1991 is the

Aerial view of the National Cold War Exhibition Hangar, looking south with Hangar 1 behind it. The northern access 'wall' has yet to be closed, and the Valiant provides scale. *RAF Museum*

dominating world political and military epoch of the second half of the 20th Century. The social impact of that varied and mostly conceptual struggle was vast and its influence and legacy on the UK's armed forces, the intelligence community and the global military was immense. Expansion at Cosford had long been considered and by the 1990s it had gelled around the 'Cold War'.

Building a new display around this topic would also free up space at Hendon and elsewhere on the Cosford site, to put other airframes indoors – as mentioned above. The number of aircraft movements required would do justice to a small airport! Sqn Ldr Bruce James started two years before the opening to park aircraft on the airfield in the order in which they would be inserted. Michael Fopp commented: "His ability to move monsters to within an inch of a position was incredible. On one occasion I saw him with huge sheets of the steel with a layer of oil between them, upon which he was turning an aircraft 180-degrees in its own width!"

The ambitious scheme was first announced in December 2003 as a £12 million project planned for the autumn of 2006. In March 2004 a £4.9 million grant from the Heritage Lottery Fund (HLF) was secured. Initially to have been called 'Divided World: Connected World' to emphasize the schism of ideologies and the nature of the building proposed, the name National Cold War Exhibition was eventually settled on. The sheer scope of this undertaking is difficult to convey; fund-raising; architecture and physical presentation; the methods and content by which to tell a complex and challenging era; the restoration, moving and placing of exhibits; coupled with the 'knock-on' effect within the RAFM collection as a whole. The 'Cold War' hall was a quantum leap on from the other impressive achievements at Hendon and Cosford.

When it comes to architecture, HLF always seeks what it calls 'landmark' buildings; the aim being to enhance the local area, the skyline and the region as well as 'contain' the museum, art gallery, exhibition etc. When the 'Cold War' hall was opened for a press preview, the author spoke to a HLF representative, explained his praise for the awesome structure but believed a lot of *FlyPast* readers would be non-plussed. She explained: "This is not an uncommon reaction from die-hards, who would be very happy with the sort of warehouse structure you see at the edge of every town but these really should be addressed as what they are – massive grey slabs. [HLF] is about adventurous architecture that will appeal to and challenge the wider public." The site chosen 'joined' the 'top' hangars with Hangar 1 on the flight line with a tall and futuristic structure affording 75,000 square feet of display area plus a massive zone within the roof in which to 'fly' other aircraft. The land sloped considerably but while this provided more than a few headaches, it allowed for a huge 'step' in the middle,

with which to provide visitors with a sudden vista looking down on the lower floor. Or, for those coming the other way, to look up and see the Vulcan 'taking off' in front of them. The 'step' also permitted the placing a lecture theatre/cinema under the exhibits. Elevated walkways, an observation gallery and generous spacing of exhibits allows for endless vision angles on the aircraft, tanks, missiles and much more. Dotted around the building are 'Silo Theatres', also known as 'Hot Spots', in which visitors can immerse themselves in sub-themes of the 'Cold War', for example the Cuban Missile Crisis. These and the exhibition concept in general was the domain of Neal Potter and the architects were Fielden Clegg Bradley. Her Royal Highness Princess Anne opened the National Cold War Exhibition on 7th February 2007 and it has met wide acclaim ever since. A comment at the time by a member of RAFM staff summed it all up brilliantly: "How are we going to top this?"

Vladimir Ilyich Lenin embracing capitalism in the Cold War hall! *Steve Fletcher-Key Publishing www.flypast.com*

'Hanging' each exhibit was a painstaking task in the Cold War hall, late 2006. Centre is Lightning F.1 XG337 having successfully 'rotated', but yet to have been winched to height. On the left is a Thor ICBM, with Vulcan B.2 XM598 behind and to the right Hunter T.7A XL568. *RAF Museum*

Armstrong Whitworth Argosy C.1 XP411
1962 | Four-crew medium range tactical transport | Four 2,470hp Rolls-Royce Dart 101

Given that the Argosy's role was to fetch and carry loads, that its twin-boom layout resembled handles and its Dart turboprops had a distinctive whine, the affectionate nickname 'Whistling Wheelbarrow' becomes obvious. First flown from Bitteswell on 6th April 1962 XP411 was issued to 105 Squadron at Benson on 1st June. Fifteen days later, it flew eastwards to Khormaksar, Aden, working in support of British Army units fighting insurgent forces, including air drops of supplies. On 11th November 1965 Rhodesia unilaterally declared independence from the Commonwealth and 105 Squadron was involved in the British government's initial response. Deploying to Francistown in Bechuanaland (now Botswana), 105's Argosies ferried equipment for ground forces and in December flew gear into Ndola and Lusaka in Zambia. No military action was taken. With withdrawal from Aden announced, 105 re-located to Muharraq, Bahrain, in August 1967 and disbanded there on 20th January 1968. By the end of the month XP411 was back at Benson, operating in a 'pool' for 114 and 267 Squadrons. Next came service with 70 Squadron at Akrotiri, Cyprus, from 7th July 1970, XP411 having the name *Excalibur* applied under the cockpit. With the advent of the Lockheed Hercules C.1 in RAF service, XP411 was retired to 27 Maintenance Unit (MU), Shawbury, on 16th December 1970. By March 1974 it was at 23 MU at Aldergrove, Northern Ireland, to be prepared for trials for the projected Argosy T.2 crew trainer conversion. As such it was given red and white 'trainer' colours and several sources quote it as a 'T.1', but this is thought not to have been an official designation. It was despatched to 6 Flying Training School at Finningley for evaluation. The T.2 programme was ditched as a cost-saving exercise and XP411 was retired to 2 School of Technical Training at Cosford on 22nd May 1975 and transferred to the museum in April 1988.

Avro Lincoln B.2/4A RF398
1945 | Seven-crew heavy bomber | Four 1,680hp Packard-built Rolls-Royce Merlin 68A

Built by Armstrong Whitworth, RF398 first flew at Baginton (now Coventry Airport) on 11th September 1945. It spent the next 13 years in storage or undergoing modifications to keep it up to date with Bomber Command specifications; ending up at 'Phase 4A' status with Mk.IV H2S radar. It was issued to the Bomber Command

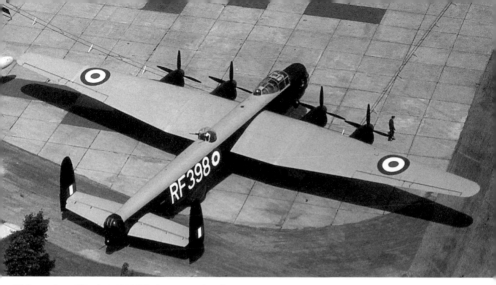

Bird's eye view of Lincoln B.2 RF398 in the static at Abingdon, June 1968. *Roy Bonser*

Bombing School (BCBS) at Lindholme on 27th November 1957, having missed all of the Lincoln's frontline era with the RAF. BCBS retired its Lincolns in October 1960, but RF398 avoided the axe and was delivered to the Central Signals Establishment (CSE) at Watton on 27th July 1961. CSE was renamed as 151 Squadron on the first day of 1962, its Lincolns soldiering on until 12th March 1963 when a trio, including RF398, flew a 'farewell' sortie. Completing 1,043 flying hours when it touched down at Henlow, RF398 was flown for the last time on 30th April 1963. Repainted and restored, RF398 was moved by road to Abingdon on 2nd May 1968 in readiness for the 50th anniversary celebrations of the RAF in June. Afterwards it was trucked to Cosford.

Avro 707C WZ744
1953 | Two-seat delta-wing research test-bed | One 3,600lb st Rolls-Royce Derwent 8

As part of the Vulcan development programme, it was determined that a series of scaled-down deltas would help explore wing shape and low speed handling before the mighty V-Bomber flew. (Turn to Chapter 10 for a profile of Vulcan B.2 XM597.) The Avro 707 was roughly a one-third scale version and five were built, the first getting airborne on 4th September 1949. The Type 707C was the only two-seater and WZ744, constructed in Manchester, was assembled at Bracebridge Heath and trundled the short distance down the A15 to Waddington, where it first flew on 1st July 1953. Its contribution to the Vulcan programme was minimal, the prototype of the huge deta having soared into the skies on 30th August the year before. The little delta was not built in vain, it spent a very useful life investigating and refining powered flying controls. At the Farnborough airshow in September 1953, WZ744 was part of a formation that stopped everyone in their tracks: the two prototype Vulcans (VX770 and VX777) with 707As WD280 and WZ736 and 707B VX790. (WD280 is extant in Australia; WZ736 is at the Museum of Science and Industry, Manchester.) On 12th January 1956 WZ744 joined the Royal Aircraft Establishment at Farnborough, serving on until it was retired on 7th June 1966. It was taken by road to the station museum at Colerne on 17th April 1967; later moving to Finningley, before settling on Cosford in April 1973.

BAC TSR-2 XR220
1964 | Two-crew prototype strike/reconnaissance | Two 30,610lb st Rolls-Royce Olympus 320

Even today, hackles rise when the TSR-2 is discussed. The product of a forced marriage of English Electric and Vickers, it was axed on 6th April 1965, the prototype having flown 192 days previously. Let's not debate the merits of the machine, or of the decision, although in terms of programme terminations since that time it was a lot 'cleaner' than, for example, Nimrod AEW.3 or the Nimrod MRA.4. The second of nine development aircraft, XR220 was built at Brooklands and taken by road to the Aeroplane & Armament Experimental Establishment at Boscombe Down on 9th September 1964. The low-loader jack-knifed on the apron and the fuselage fell off, requiring repair by a working party from BAC at Warton. The prototype TSR-2, XR219, first flew at Boscombe on 27th September 1964. With repairs complete, XR220 started ground-running on 22th February 1965. The ministerial axe fell on the very day that it was planned to fly XR220. The one and only 'flyer', XR219, became a static ballistics target at the Proof and Experimental Establishment, Shoeburyness, on 14th August. The fourth airframe, XR222, was presented to the College of Aeronautics at Cranfield and now is at the Imperial War Museum, Duxford – see Chapter 8. Everything else, including the jigs, was scrapped; a lot of it going to Coley's scrapyard at Hounslow. All that is but XR220, which had a stay of execution... Rolls-Royce needed it for ground-running tests in readiness for the Concorde supersonic airliner programme and a series of trials were staged at Boscombe Down. These were completed in February 1966 and the engines were removed in October. On 20th June 1967 XR220 was delivered to Henlow and on 4th May 1975 arrived at Cosford.

Bristol 188 XF926
1963 | Single-seat high speed research aircraft | Two 10,000lb st de Havilland Gyron Junior DGJ.10

Built at Filton, Bristol, to requirement ER.143D seeking an experimental type that could achieve sustained speeds beyond Mach 2, the Bristol 188 proved well short of this. The flying careers of the two completed was relatively short. Test pilot Godfrey Auty took XF923 into the air for the first time, from Boscombe Down on 14th April 1962. Cosford's example, XF926, was flown by Auty from Filton on 29th April 1963 using the engines that had originally powered XF923. As well as Auty and J Williamson from Bristol, Lt Cdr Paul Millet of the Royal Aircraft Establishment flew XF926. On its 47th sortie, XF926 managed Mach 1.88, the highest speed achieved by the entire project. It was flown just four more times, its last sortie on 12th January 1964 bringing its total time in the air to just 26 hours, 11 minutes. Both 188s were trucked to the Proof and Experimental Establishment at Shoeburyness in April 1966 to become static ballistics targets. The folly of this was eventually realised and on 3rd September 1972 arrived at Cosford.

British Aerospace EAP ZF534
1985 | Single seat proof-of-concept technology demonstrator | Two 27,500lb st Turbo-Union RB.199R Mk.104D

Having paved the way, the SEPECAT Jaguar ACT (see below) allowed British Aerospace to create a technology demonstrator with which to prove advanced fly-by-wire control and canard format pathfinding for the Eurofighter. With *some* involvement from Aeritalia and Germany's MBB, the Experimental Aircraft Programme (EAP) was a wholly British Aerospace-led project, with major input from other elements of UK industry. Rolled out at Warton on 27th October 1985, systems testing of a such a complex device took many months. Test pilot Dave Eagles took it on its inaugural flight on 8th August 1986, ZF534 'clocked' Mach 1.1 during the 67-minute sortie. Confidence was such that it was demonstrated at the Farnborough airshow the following month. EAP ZF534 was retired on 1st May 1991, its 259th and last excursion; completing 191 hours 21 minutes of flying time. It moved to Loughborough University's Department of Aeronautical and Automotive Engineering on 27th June 1996 taking up the space previously occupied by the Jaguar ACT, which had travelled to Cosford. Replaced by Hawk 200 ZH200 at Loughborough, the EAP travelled to Cosford on 27th March 2012. Turn to Chapter 5 for the profile of the UK Eurofighter Typhoon prototype.

British Aerospace Harrier GR.9A ZG477
1990 | Single-seat V/STOL strike/reconnaissance | One 21,750lb st Rolls-Royce Pegasus 107

Even the weather was dismal on 15th December 2010 and the RAF was paying off the incredible Harrier, with an unseemly haste. This had been brought about by the announcement the previous 12th October that under the Strategic Defence and Security Review Joint Force Harrier was no more. Later on most of the Harriers were to be transferred to Arizona for spares consumption by the US Marine Corps. Since the 'big-wing' GR.5, the Harrier had been a combined programme with McDonnell Douglas of the USA and the two talents had created an awesome strike weapon, which evolved to its final UK iteration, the GR.9A. (See chapter 1 for the P.1127 and Chapter 4 for the Sea Harrier.) Built as a GR.7, ZG477 first flew at Dunsfold on 3rd September 1990 and was taken on charge two days later. It served initially with 4 Squadron at Gütersloh and for just a few days was based in *West* Germany as the country re-united on 3rd October. It transferred to 3 Squadron at Laarbruch in 1992, but by the spring of 1993 it had returned to No.4. During 1993-1994 the RAF Harrier units, 1, 3 and 4

EAP ZF534 dazzling the crowds at the 1986 Farnborough airshow. *Alan Curry*

Squadrons provided crews and aircraft at Incirlik, Turkey, policing the 'no-fly' zone of northern Iraqi airspace under Operation WARDEN. From the spring of 1999 the force was required for the interminably complex and woefully brutal politics of the Balkans, deployed to Gioia Del Colle in the 'heel' of Italy as part of Operation ALLIED FORCE. Harriers, including ZG477, were tasked to fly across the Adriatic Sea against Serbian forces during the Yugoslav Civil War until the campaign wound down in late June 1999. On 1st April 2000 Joint Force Harrier, the combined Fleet Air Arm and RAF operation of GR.7s and GR.9s was established at Cottesmore. By 2003 ZG477 had been upgraded to GR.7A status; in 2004 it became a GR.9A. During its time at 'Rutland International', Cottesmore, ZG477 flew with 3 Squadron, the Naval Strike Wing, 4 and finally 1 Squadron. From June 2008 ZG477 was deployed to Kandahar, Afghanistan, as part of Operation HERRICK, on round-the-clock readiness for strikes using laser- or GPS-guided weapons or recce sorties. The Harriers were back at Cottesmore in July 2009 and in November 2010, ZG477 was transferred to 1 Squadron – the very first frontline Harrier unit – for what would be a sorrowful series of flights. On 19th November ZG477 was deployed with three others on HMS *Ark Royal* – also facing the axe – for its final cruise. Five days later, ZG477, flown by Lt Cdr James Blackmore, was the last to depart from the vessel's ski-jump. Then came the dismal 15th December and ZG477 was part of a 16-aircraft final 'thrash'. It was placed in 'overseen' storage at Cottesmore, and while it was ground-run, in the end it was not flown again and made the road journey to Cosford on 19th December 2011.

De Havilland Devon C.2/2 VP952
1947 | 8-9 seat communications aircraft | Two 400hp de Havilland Gipsy Queen 175

The Devon was the military version of the Dove light transport, and VP952 served as the prototype. Built as a C.1, it was notified as awaiting collection – ready for the RAF to take it on – at its birthplace, Hatfield, on 24th July 1947. Ahead of it was an incredible career, nobody could have envisaged that it would retired 37 years later. During that time, VP952 served with several units, the most exotic being the Headquarters Allied Air Forces Central Europe, at Fountainbleau, France, from September to November 1953. It has a strong link with Hendon, its first 'comms' unit being the Station Flight there from 8th February 1949. It joined the Hendon-based Metropolitan Communications Squadron in November 1955 and was on charge when the airfield formally closed on 4th November 1957, very likely taking part in the farewell flypast (see Chapter 5). Throughout its career, VP952 was upgraded and it was despatched to de Havilland at Hawarden, near Chester, on 25th September 1970 where it was re-engined with Gipsy Queen 175s and given the enlarged cockpit glazing; emerging as a C.2 Phase 2 (or C.2/2). Since June 1968 VP952 had been part of the Western Communications Squadron, at Andover, Hampshire, and in February 1969 the unit was renamed as 21 Squadron. After the engine upgrade, VP952 returned to duties at Andover. On 29th May 1974 it joined its last unit, 207 Squadron at Northolt. The Devon bowed out of RAF operational service on 30th June 1984 when 207 Squadron disbanded. Five days later VP952 made its last flight when it was ferried to the station museum at St Athan. Touching down, it completed its 13,234th landing and a flying life of 8,626 hours. This venerable servant was moved to Cosford in February 1986.

De Havilland Comet 1XB G-APAS
1953 | Modified airliner, research and experimental test-bed | Four 5,500lb st de Havilland Ghost 50 Mk.4

The world's first jet airliner to operate regular commercial services deserves more than one profile. Mk.4 G-APDB with the Duxford Aviation Society (Chapter 8) illustrates the later development of the type. As these words hit the word processor, Cosford was readying for the arrival, by road, of the former Lyneham 'gate guardian' Comet C.2 XK699. Built for Air France as Mk.1A F-BGNZ, it was delivered from Hatfield to Le Bourget, Paris, on 22nd July 1953, entering service on 8th September. Fitted out for 44 passengers, *November-Zulu* worked routes to Rome and on to Beirut and also to Cairo, Algiers and Casablanca. On 10th January 1954 BOAC Comet 1 G-ALYP was lost over the Mediterranean and the entire fleet was grounded. Wearing the 'B Condition' (or 'trade plate') markings G-5-23, F-BGNZ was ferried to Hatfield on 18th February 1954 for modifications intended to put it back in service. On the day it test flew, 8th April 1954, BOAC lost G-ALYY and F-BGNZ's days as a civilian were over. As G-5-23 it was flown to the de Havilland factory at Hawarden, near Chester, to be upgraded to Mk.1XB. Ghost 50 Mk.2 turbojets were replaced with Mk.4s and the cabin windows were altered from square to round. Civil registered as G-APAS on 30th January 1958 it was handed over to de Havilland's propellers division at Hatfield for used as a test-bed. A jet being used by a *propeller* outfit was not as odd as it first appears as missiles were an increasing part of its task, which was later to take on the title Hawker Siddeley Dynamics. The civil identity was short-lived, the Comet becoming XM823 in May 1958. It was frequently grounded for long periods as special equipment – mostly to do with infra-red seekers – was installed, or removed, and it was involved in detachments to the USA. Its last flight took place on 8th April 1968, going to Shawbury, as it was deemed it could not use the relatively short Cosford runway. At Shawbury it was painted in spurious British Overseas Airways Corporation colours so that it could play a role in the developing British Airways Museum. It was trucked to Cosford on 17th September 1978 and in early December 2006 was rolled into Hangar 1.

Comet 1XB XM823 sizzling past the tower at Hatfield. *Hawker Siddeley Dynamics*

English Electric Canberra PR.9 XH171

1960 | Two-crew, long-range high-altitude reconnaissance | Two 11,250lb st Rolls-Royce Avon 206

For the early iteration of the Canberra, PR.3 WE139 is profiled in Chapter 5. Short Brothers and Harland at Sydenham, Belfast, was given design authority to create the final reconnaissance version of the Canberra. Cut backs resulted in only 23 PR.9s being built, but they gave exceptional service. Taken on charge by 58 Squadron at Wyton on 5th September 1960, XH171 adopted the standard pattern for many Canberras – service interrupted by sometimes lengthy sessions with contractors for systems upgrades. On 9th October 1963 XH171 was at Luqa, Malta, with 39 Squadron, transferring to 13 Squadron on 28th September 1970. It re-joined 39 on 10th March 1976 by which time the unit was resident at Wyton. Retired to 2 School of Technical Training at Cosford on 13th July 1982, it transferred to the Aerospace Museum early in 1992. Having been prepared for suspension, it was moved into the Cold War hall in May 2006 and carefully put into its 'flying' pose.

Fieseler Fi 156C-7 Storch 475081

1944 | Two-crew observation and communications | One 240hp Argus As 10C-3

In Chapter 4 Lt Cdr Eric Brown's pioneering landing of a Vampire on a carrier is recorded; Cosford's Storch has also flown from a 'flat-top', courtesy of the same pilot. Although lacking the appeal of a Focke-Wulf or a Messerschmitt, along with the Junkers Ju 52 (see later), the Storch is an incredibly important type, not just in terms of Luftwaffe history but of aviation in general. While other Axis types have been left out of the profiles, it would be a crime to ignore the Fi 156. Built by Mraz at Chocen in Czechoslovakia 475081 was captured at Flensburg, near the Danish border. It was one of three flown to the Royal Aircraft Establishment (RAE), Farnborough, on 5th September 1945 and initially flew with the Air Ministry identification number 101, taking on the RAF serial VP546 in May 1946. It was used extensively by RAE's Aerodynamics Flight, initially to assess the type itself and its full-span leading edge slats. Beyond that, its slow-flying capabilities made it ideal for aerial photography, glider towing and its ability to get in and out of *very* small fields was most useful. On 28th May 1946, Eric Brown and VP546 had an appointment with HMS *Triumph*. In *Wings on My Sleeve*, he describes the sortie: "I was given a German Fieseler Storch, that remarkable slow-flying plane. To baptize it thoroughly, I took it to sea and landed it aboard the carrier *Triumph*. They put the barrier up for us, as the Storch had no arrester hook, but it was not needed. To the astonishment of the 'goofers' the little plane landed and came to a stop right on the aft lift... We paid our way while we were on board by using the Storch's incredible gift of hovering to photograph the approach path to a carrier, something that had not been properly done before..." By 1955 a lack of spares grounded VP546 and it was offered for disposal. No.1 School of Technical Training at Halton took it on, arriving on 3rd August 1956, but it was not suitable as an instructional airframe. The Air Historical Branch intervened and it moved through a series of venues, joining the station collection at St Athan by June 1973, finally arriving at Cosford on 6th April 1989.

Fábrica Militar de Aviones Pucará A-515

1978 | Two-crew light strike / close-support | Two 978shp Turboméca Astazou XVIG

A more graphic portrayal of the Argentine forces that faced Operation CORPORATE, the liberation of the Falkland Islands in 1982, would be a Douglas A-4 Skyhawk or a Dassault Super Etendard. Other than wreckage, such assets were not available for return to the UK as spoils of war. The FMA Pucará, which first appeared in November 1974, was by far the most interesting type fielded by Argentina; an indigenous twin-turboprop perhaps best compared with the role of the North American OV-10 Bronco. Built at Cordoba in about 1978, by early 1982 it was with the Fuerza Aerea Argentina's Group 3 de Ataque at Santa Fe. Deployed to Stanley on the Falklands in mid-May 1982, A-515 took part in the last Pucará strike of the conflict on 10th June 1982, one of three detailed to attack British gun emplacements on East Falkland. On the 14th the surrender of Argentine forces was accepted and, other than a few bullet holes, A-515 was found to be in airworthy condition. On 10th July it was airlifted by RAF Boeing Chinook on to the *Atlantic Causeway* and shipped to the UK. It was issued to the Aeroplane & Armament Experimental Establishment at Boscombe Down for evaluation and air-to-air combat comparison. Marked as ZD485, it took to the air on 28th April 1983. It made its last flight, to Cosford, on 9th September.

Folland Gnat T.1 XR977
1964 | Two-seat advanced trainer | One 4,230lb st Bristol Siddeley Orpheus 100

Also at Cosford is a single-seat Gnat F.1 lightweight fighter which was not taken up by the RAF but, licenced-produced in India where it was known as the Ajeet, it proved itself as a potent warplane. With the RAF the Gnat is forever linked with the RAF Aerobatic Team, the 'Red Arrows'. First flown at Hamble, Hampshire, on 1st January 1964, XR977 was issued to 4 Flying Training School at Valley, Anglesey, on 11th February. On 12th April 1976 it transferred to the 'Red Arrows' at Kemble, Glos. It took part in the final 'Red Arrows' Gnat display, over its old home of Valley, on 16th September 1979; the team were then to work up on the Hawker Siddeley Hawk for the 1980 season and the 'Reds' still fly this type. The last flight for XR977 came on 5th October 1979 when it joined 2 School of Technical Training at Cosford. It transferred to the Aerospace Museum in 1982.

General Dynamics F-111F 74-0177
1975 | Two-crew all-weather strike | Two 25,000lb st Pratt & Whitney TF30-P-100

The swing-wing F-111 is important to UK aviation history as well as its place in world provenance. The type equipped two large USAF Wings in the UK, the 20th at Upper Heyford, with F-111Es (and EF-111 Ravens of the 42nd Electronic Countermeasures Squadron) and the 48th at Lakenheath, with F-models. Upper Heyford was the first with the sophisticated strike bombers, from 1970 with Lakenheath coming on stream seven years later. With the Berlin Wall down and the Soviet Union a thing of the past, the 'Swingers' departed, in 1993 and 1992 respectively. Known affectionately as the 'Aardvark' – because of its long nose – the F-111 never received an official name. Perhaps uniquely, the type was retrospectively named Aardvark by the US Department of Defense after it had left service. Built at Fort Worth, Texas, 74-0177 was delivered to the 366th Tactical Fighter Wing (TFW) at Mountain Home, Idaho, on 6th October 1975. It joined the 48th TFW at Lakenheath on 29th June 1977 and by 1981 was assigned to the constituent 492nd Tactical Fighter Squadron. On 14th April 1986 74-0177 took part in Operation EL DORADO CANYON, raiding targets in Libya. Lakenheath was eerily quiet on 25th August 1990; the 48th TFW had deployed en masse to Taif in Saudi Arabia in response to the Iraqi invasion of Kuwait. On 17th January 1991 Operation DESERT STORM was launched and between then and 28th February, the F-111Fs of the 48th took part in over 4,000 missions. The 48th returned its F-111s to the USA in 1992, taking on McDonnell Douglas F-15E Strike Eagles – its current equipment. Stateside 74-0177 served with the 27th TFW at Cannon, New Mexico, from the summer of 1993. It was retired to the famous 'desert boneyard' at Davis-Monthan in Arizona in October 1995. In June 2005 it was allocated to RAFM and on 9th July 2005 it was airborne again – inside the capacious hold of a Lockheed C-5A Galaxy transport bound for Mildenhall in Suffolk. The Aardvark was delivered by road to Cosford on 3rd November 2005 and installed in the Cold War hall.

Handley Page Victor K.2 XH672
1960 | Five-crew air-to-air tanker | Four 19,750lb st Rolls-Royce Conway Mk.201

Victor B.2 XH672 first thundered down the runway of its birthplace, Radlett, Herts, on 6th April 1960, in the hands of Peter Baker AFC. The following day 'Johnnie' Allam took it for a shake-down and was to spend much time at the helm during its time at Radlett. It was to be five years before XH672 joined a squadron, the time in between mostly spent on automatic pilot, automatic landing system and testing a reconnaissance system either from Radlett, or at the Aeroplane & Armament Experimental Establishment at Boscombe Down. During 1961 the V-Bomber was fitted with a long cylindrical pod under the port wing in the position normally occupied by the 'slipper' fuel tank; the starboard 'slipper' was retained. This was a device codenamed RED NECK, sideways-looking airborne radar. Cancelled in February 1962, RED NECK was intended for the strategic reconnaissance version of the Victor, the SR.2; and that was XH672's next tasking. In July 1962 was rolled back into the factory for conversion to SR.2 status and Johnny Allam took the honours of the test flight in the new guise on 10th July 1965. It was issued to 543 Squadron at Wyton on 13th August.

The role was set to change again in 1974. Converting Mk.2s to tankers had been devised by Handley Page, but the company collapsed in 1970 and the contract was eventually taken on by Hawker Siddeley. On 20th March 1974 XH672 touched down at Woodford, near Manchester, to await its turn for transformation. On 14th April 1978 Charles (later Sir Charles) Masefield carried out the test flight, XH672 being the final aircraft in the programme. Taken on charge by 57 Squadron at Marham on 24th May 1978, it commenced the busy, long-ranging life of a tanker. Chapter 10 details the exploits of Vulcan B.2 XM597 and the deltas spring to mind whenever the BLACK BUCK raids on the Falklands Islands are mentioned. Vulcan men are the first to explain that without the skills of the Victor crews, the incredible venture would have been a pipedream. Flying non-stop to Wideawake airfield on Ascension on 23rd April 1982, XH672 was ready to take its part in Operation CORPORATE. Eleven Victors did a stream take-off, imagine the noise, on the 30th forming up the complex 'relay' that was to allow BLACK BUCK 1, Vulcan B.2 XM607, to fly to Stanley and bomb the runway. The same exercise was repeated so that BLACK BUCK 1 could come home to Wideawake. Same again on May 3, Vulcan XM607 again making the long run south and returning with a little help from XH672. (Vulcan XM607 is displayed at Waddington.) When not 'tanking' for BLACK BUCKS, XH672 and the rest of the Victor force were 'riding shotgun' for Sea Harriers or Harriers transitting to HMS *Hermes* or Nimrod recce flights. Back at Marham in mid-June, XH672 was off to St Athan for a well-deserved major overhaul by the end of the month. No.57 Squadron disbanded on 30th June 1986 and two days later XH672 joined the other K.2 unit, 55 Squadron, also at Marham. From August 1990 all of the Marham tankers were busy as thirsty RAF assets streamed eastwards during the build-up of forces to the gulf, following the Iraqi invasion of Kuwait. For XH672 a second war was looming. Deployed to Muharraq, Bahrain, XH672 adopted the nose-art *Maid Marion* and completed 52 tanking sorties during Operation GRANBY, the British element of the Coalition Operation DESERT STORM. With the conflict over, demands on the Victor fleet were still intense with 'no-fly' zones to be patrolled and RAF fighters to be topped-up. On 15th October 1993, hard-working 55 Squadron was disbanded. As a veteran of the BLACK BUCK raids and the highest-sortie GRANBY Victor tanker, XH672 had been requested for RAFM. Cosford's runway was too 'tight' for a Victor and XH672 was flown to nearby Shawbury on 30th November 1993, making the last-ever intentional flight by the crescent-winged wonder. Four crew members and a passenger climbed down; the latter was former Handley Page test pilot Johnny Allam, who had got to know it 33 years before. Dismantled, XH672 made the journey to Cosford early in the New Year and was installed into the Cold War hall in May 2006.

Victor K.2 XH672 with the brake 'chute deployed as it comes to a stop on its last-ever flight, Shawbury 30th November 1993. *RAF Museum*

Hawker Siddeley Andover E.3A XS639
1967 | Three-crew general duties transport | Two 3,245hp Rolls-Royce Dart Mk.201C

Adapted from the successful civil Avro 748 twin-turboprop airliner/transport, the Andover was aimed at replacing in part the RAF's venerable Handley Page Hastings and Vickers Valettas. A converted 748, with widened centre section and 'beaver-door' tail, served as the prototype, making its first flight from Woodford, near Manchester, on 21st December 1963. To help with loading via the tail ramp, the Andover also had 'kneeling' undercarriage, allowing the aircraft to 'sit' lower when parked. As well as the tactical airlifter C.1s, the RAF also ordered conventional HS.748s as Andover CC.2s for the Queen's Flight and VIP use. Built at

Woodford, XS639 was taken on charge by 46 Squadron at Abingdon, Oxfordshire, on 1st May 1967 and in September 1970 the unit re-located to Thorney Island on the Hampshire coast. No.46 disbanded on 29th August 1975 and XS639 joined the VIP communications unit, 32 Squadron at Northolt briefly during November and December 1975. During 1976 XS639 was one of eight Andovers allocated to replace the Argosy E.1 used by 115 Squadron for airways flight-checking and calibration. Three machines, including XS639, did not receive the full kit of the E.3s and, designated E.3As, were used for training, light transport and other duties. It was issued to 115 at Brize Norton on 27th September 1976, moving with the unit to Benson on 4th January 1983. No.115 disbanded in October 1993 and its task was handed on to contractor Hunting Aviation and a quartet of E.3s re-located to East Midlands Airport, near Derby. The E.3As, including XS639, were taken on by 32 Squadron at Northolt. Upon retirement XS639 was ferried to Cosford on 13th July 1994.

Hawker Siddeley Nimrod R.1 XV249
1970 | Signals/electronic reconnaissance platform | Four 12,160lb st Rolls-Royce Spey 250

No.4 Spey suffered a major mechanical failure half an hour into a post-maintenance air test out of Kinloss on 16th May 1995. A turbine blade punctured one of the fuel tanks, No.3's fire warning lights burst into life and panels were observed falling from the starboard wing. Then explosions and fire were both felt and seen and the hydraulics packed up. Nimrod R.1 XW666, affectionately known as 'Damien' to the crews of 51 Squadron, was 4½ miles off the Moray coast and its captain, Flt Lt Art Stacey, decided that there was only one option, ditching the 'spy' jet. The Nimrod bounced twice on hitting the forbidding waters of the Moray Firth, the rear fuselage fractured and sank, but the rest floated and all seven crew took to the dinghies. A Sea King from Lossiemouth whisked them to safety. Art Stacey was awarded the AFC for his skilful handling of the incident and another member of the crew received a Queen's Commendation for bravery in the air. (The salvaged cockpit of 'Damien' is on show at the South Yorkshire Aircraft Museum, Doncaster.)

Until that moment, 51 Squadron had a trio of Nimrod R.1 'snoopers', in great demand. Five weeks after the loss of XW666, British Aerospace at the Nimrod's birthplace, Woodford, near Manchester, was given a contract to create a replacement R.1 from one of the stored MR.2s at Kinloss. (There cannot have been many instances in RAF history whereby an aircraft was modified and received a 'mark number' *smaller* than the one it started with: ie MR.2 to R.1.) Quickly given a major service, XV249 was ferried to Woodford on 23rd October 1995 and removal of all the maritime reconnaissance and anti-submarine warfare gear took much of the following year. It was ferried to Waddington on 19th December 1996 for installation of the mission equipment. On 10th January 1997 Project ANNEKA commenced; so named in honour of Anneka Rice famed in those days for high-pressure tasks against the clock in TV programmes such as *Treasure Hunt* and *Challenge Anneka*. The inspiration clearly worked; XV249 took to the air as a fully-fledged R.1 on 2nd April 1997 and 26 days later was signed off as operational and joined 51 Squadron.

So began XV249's second life; the first started at Woodford on 22nd December 1970 with its maiden flight as a MR.1. It was issued to 206 Squadron at Kinloss on 2nd February 1971. The Nimrod moved to Luqa, Malta, and 203 Squadron on 15th May 1977. Its time in the sun was fleeting, 203 disbanded on the last day of 1977. On 9th January XV249 was back at Kinloss, joining the 'pool' of aircraft in the Nimrod Wing. It was back at Woodford on 5th December 1983 to start the comprehensive upgrade to MR.2 status which was completed on 26th March 1985 when it returned to Kinloss. Defence cuts dictated a slim-down of the MR.2 fleet and XV249 was placed in 'deep store' at Kinloss on 7th September 1992 – there to await resurrection as an R.1.

On 12th October 2010 the Strategic Defence and Security Review wielded the not unexpected axe on the Nimrod MRA.4 programme, but also terminated the MR.2 fleet. At Waddington, 51 Squadron was down to a pair of R.1s, XV249 and XW665 with retirement slated for March 2011. The pair was given a stay of execution as Coalition Forces engaged the Gaddafi regime in Libya in support of revolutionary forces under Operation UNIFIED PROTECTOR. The Nimrods flew communications intelligence-gathering sorties from Akrotiri, Cyprus, XV249 returning to Waddington on 23rd May 2011, leaving XW664 to the last missions. On 28th June the Nimrod R.1 was formally retired, with XV249 making a ceremonial flypast. On 29th July XV249 carried out the last-ever Nimrod flight, positioning to Cotswold Airport (the former RAF Kemble) bringing its total flying hours to 18,488. Resident contractor Air Salvage International prepared it for the road journey to Cosford which took place in March 2012. The re-assembled airframe was formally unveiled on 28th September 2012.

Hunting Jet Provost T.1 XD674
1954 | Basic trainer | One 1,750lb st Armstrong Siddeley Viper ASV.5

Plt Off R T Foster went solo in a jet on 17th October 1955 at 2 Flying Training School (FTS), Hullavington. It was a great personal achievement for Foster and a moment of world aviation history. The Pilot Officer was the first to go what was called 'all-through' training; 2 FTS was trialling the new Jet Provost in the hope that the RAF could start its students on jets. This alone secured the Jet Provost a place in the exhibit profiles; but its production at Luton and later at Warton, running from 1955 to 1982 is impressive. To expand on the story of the 'JP', the pugnacious Strikemaster is featured in Chapter 8. Using much of the airframe of the piston-powered Provost T.1 (WV562 is on show at Cosford), Hunting developed the Jet Provost and XD674, the prototype, was first flown at Luton by Dick Wheldon on 26th June 1954. This machine spent its time with Hunting on development work, with Armstrong Siddeley at its test airfield at Bitteswell and with the Aeroplane & Armament Experimental Establishment at Boscombe Down, while other T.1s went to 2 FTS for comparative trials on the flying syllabus. Its test and trials life over, on 4th June 1957 was issued back to Hunting for potential issue to RAF service. By then the much-refined T.3 had been ordered in quantity and effort to bring XD674 to anything like this specification would be impractical. It joined to 71 Maintenance Unit at Bicester on 23rd April 1958 for spares recovery. By 1966 it was with the station museum at Finningley and via Swinderby and St Athan, came to Cosford in 1985.

Jet Provost T.1 XD674 during an early air test, 1954. *Hunting Aircraft*

Hunting 126/50 XN714
1963 | Single-seat jet-flap research platform | One 4,000lb st Bristol Siddeley Orpheus 805

The last aircraft to be designed and built by Hunting at Luton, the H.126 was a very sophisticated research platform for jet-flap technology. Envisaged at first as a propulsion system, jet-flaps bled air out of the trailing edge of the wings to either replace a conventional jet exhaust, or complement it. In May 1959 a contract was issued to Hunting to build a pair of H.126s, although the second was never completed. The H.126 was propelled via two outlets low down on each side of the fuselage, a rear exhaust and through two ducts under each wing. It was rolled out at Luton in August 1962 then trucked to the Royal Aircraft Establishment (RAE) at Thurleigh and flown there on 26th March 1963 in the hands of Hunting test pilot Stanley Oliver. Testing by RAE was interrupted in October 1964 for a visit to the blower tunnel at the Aeroplane & Armament Experimental Establishment, Boscombe Down, and in June 1965 XN714 was displayed at the Paris Salon, Le Bourget, France. On 9th November 1967, XN714 flew for the last time, completing just under 142 flying hours. America's National Aeronautics and Space Administration expressed an interest in evaluating the H.126 in the huge wind tunnel at Ames, California. On 3rd April 1969 XN714 was airborne again but this time as cargo inside 53 Squadron Short Belfast C.1 XR366. It was returned to the UK by May 1970 and was stored, still in its transit casing, at Holme-on-Spalding Moor and then at Thurleigh until it was delivered by road to Cosford on 30th April 1974.

The unmarked Hunter 126 during roll-out at Luton, August 1962. *Hunting Aircraft*

Junkers Ju 52 (CASA 352L) 'G-AFAP'
1954 | Three-crew paratroop and general purpose transport | Three 775hp ENMSA B.4 'Beta'

The Junkers Ju 52 is more than a famous Luftwaffe paratroop transport. It started off as large single-engined 'bushplane' but in April 1931 a tri-motor version was flown and it became a 'staple' of airlines in Europe and elsewhere. The emerging Luftwaffe began to acquire large numbers and the type was tried out during the Spanish Civil War, initially as a transport then as a bomber. Its rugged capabilities facilitated German airborne forces warfare and 'Tante Jus' were the backbone of Luftwaffe supply operations. Close to 5,000 were built, including examples by Amiot in France and others assembled in Hungary. Post-war, Ju 52s worked hard as interim transports with many air forces and airlines, including British European Airways (BEA). Post-war Amiot produced another 400 as AAC.1 Toucans at Colombes and Spain produced 170 from June 1945. All of this makes the Ju 52 an important airframe for RAFM and had one been 'flagged' for preservation from 1945, there is every chance it would be where the CASA is now.

Construcciones Aeronauticas SA (CASA) of Getafe, Madrid, Spain, built the Cosford example as CASA 352A T2-272 for the Ejercito del Air (the Spanish Air Force) in 1954 and it commenced service with the Escuela de Paracaidistas at Alcantarilla in January 1955. In the Summer of 1958 it was back at Getafe being reworked with ENMSA engines as a CASA 352L and its serial was changed to T2B-272. It was next issued to Ala de Transport 36 at Gando on the Canary Isles on 8th February 1961. The unit was renamed on 1st April 1965 as Ala Mixta 46. In 1968 it was back on the mainland and re-joined the parachute school at Alccantarilla. T2B-272 was retired to Cuatro Vientos, Madrid, in December 1972 and RAFM bought it at an auction staged by the Spanish Air Ministry on 3rd June 1977. Don Bullock of 'warbird' specialists Euroworld ferried it to the UK and the Junkers touched down at Cosford on 22nd May 1978. In October 1985 it was repainted in 1938 British Airways colours as 'G-AFAP' to take its place in the airliner collection. The original G-AFAP was at Oslo's Fornebu Airport on 9th April 1940 and was captured by invading German forces. (*That* British Airways became part of British Overseas Airways Corporation in late 1940. BOAC and BEA merged into the present BA in 1972.)

Lockheed Hercules C.3 XV202
1967 | Five-crew tactical transport | Four 4,910hp Allison T56-A-15

The 'Herk' is a legend within the RAF, let alone the global phenomena it became, in constant production since 1955. The second-generation, 'J-Models' now in RAF service (C.4s and C.5s) will ultimately be replaced by the Airbus Military A400 Atlas. Built at Marietta, Georgia, with the 'paperwork' USAF serial 66-8552, C-130K Hercules C.1 XV202 was delivered to Marshall of Cambridge at Teversham on 17th August 1967 for service preparation. By October 1967 it was at Changi, Singapore, with 48 Squadron. No.48 returned to the UK in September 1971, becoming part of the Lyneham Transport Wing (LTW). C.1 XV202 had presaged this, arriving at Lyneham in February, but by December 1971 had moved to Thorney Island to join 242 Operational Conversion Unit (OCU). Thorney closed in late 1975 and XV202 and the OCU relocated to Lyneham where its aircraft were pooled with LTW. During 1981 XV202 was one of the first C.1s to be 'stretched' to C.3 status by Marshall at Teversham. From 1986 the C.3 fleet was fitted with in-flight refuelling probes over the cockpit. The last Hercules vacated Lyneham in July 2011 with the fleet moving to Brize Norton, XV202 nominally being on charge with 47 Squadron. The stay was short for XV202 as it was ferried to Cosford on 12th August 2011.

Mikoyan-Gurevich MiG-15bis *Fagot* 1120
1955 | Single-seat fighter | One 5,952lb Klimov VK-1

In terms of which aircraft to illustrate the opposite side of the 'Iron Curtain' during the 'Cold War', the MiG-15 is essential. Its combat debut came in the skies of Korea, engaging United Nations forces and forcing Western strategists to rethink. (See the Sea Fury entry in Chapter 4 for a *Fagot* shoot-down.) Cosford's example was built in Poland as an SBLim-2 in 1955 and was part of batch of 14 acquired by Andy MacGill of LBA Systems and imported into the UK in October 1986, being initially stored in Middlesborough. Mr MacGill donated 1120 to RAFM on 29th October 1986 and the following month it was put on show at Hendon, attracting great interest as the first of its breed on permanent show in Britain. It migrated to the Imperial War Museum at South Lambeth 1989 to 1992 before going back to Hendon in 1995. It moved to Cosford on 1st August 2001 and in May 2006 was placed inside the National Cold War Exhibition.

Mitsubishi Ki-46-III Dinah 5439
1944 | Two-crew reconnaissance aircraft | Two 1,500hp Mitsubishi Ha-112-II

Surviving Japanese World War Two aircraft are rare and knowledge of their operational use, if any, is thin on the ground. This is the case with Cosford's shapely *Dinah*. What *is* known is that by early 1946 it was at Seletar, Singapore, for crating by 390 Maintenance Unit. A total of 64 Japanese types had been selected by March 1946 for return to the UK for evaluation, but space restrictions on vessels was restricted as tens of thousands of personnel were in need of repatriation. The number of airframes to be shipped to the UK was reduced to a quartet, for museum purposes. These comprised the *Dinah*, the Mitsubishi A6M 'Zero' that is now held by the Imperial War Museum (Chapter 2), a Kyushu K9W1 *Cypress* and it is *believed* the Kawasaki Ki-100, also held at Cosford. (The *Cypress* was a licence-built Bücker Jungmann which ended its days on the dump at Wroughton, Wiltshire, in the late 1950s.)

After arrival at Portsmouth in August 1946, the *Dinah* moved around various storage sites and by 1963 was at Biggin Hill, later moving to Henlow. By 1970 it was at St Athan and extensively restored between 1975 and 1981. During this, RAF roundels were found under the paint and the lettering 'ATAIU-SEA' on the fuselage. This stood for Air Technical Air Intelligence Unit, South East Asia, which had been formed in India in 1943 and by 1946 was based in Singapore. Further 'digging' revealed an etched-on badge of the 81st Sentai on the tail wheel doors, and an element of this unit was known to have flown Ki-46-IIIs in Burma in 1944. During March 1989 the *Dinah* moved to Cosford. From 1992 a further restoration was initiated, with the fuselage going to the RAFM workshop at Cardington while the wings were sub-contracted to Trent Aero at East Midlands Airport, near Derby. Mitsubishi Heavy Industries of Tokyo contributed considerably to the costs of this project, which was completed in 1993 when the aircraft returned to Cosford.

The Mitsubishi Ki-46 after completion of its restoration, 1993. *RAF Museum*

North American Sabre F.4 XB812
1953 | Single-seat interceptor | One 5,200lb st General Electric J-47-GE-13

Sabres had a brief frontline career with the RAF, acting as 'stop-gaps' in West Germany from 1953 to 1956 until the arrival of the Hawker Hunter. As such it could be declared a 'minor' type but, like the MiG-15 above, its impact on world aviation history was far wider. Built under licence by Canadair at Cartierville, Montreal, as CL-13 Mk.4 19666, the equivalent of the USAF's F-86E, XB812 first flew on 16th April 1953. It was issued to 112 Squadron at Brüggen, West Germany, on 29th January 1954, transferred to 93 Squadron at Jever on 11th May 1954. It was retired to 33 Maintenance Unit at Lyneham on 1st June 1955, bringing its brief RAF career to an end. It was transferred to Aviation Traders at Stansted three months later for refurbishing because the Sabres, all US-financed, were destined for use with other air arms under the Mutual Defense Assistance Program. In July 1956 XB412 was bound for the Italian Air Force as MM19666 and it is known to have served from Pratica di Mare. By 1976 it was in use as an instructional airframe with a college in Rome where it was 'discovered' by the Duxford-based The Fighter Collection which arranged for its acquisition and restoration in exchange for Spitfire V EP120, a former gate guardian (see Chapter 5). Finished in the colours of 93 Squadron, it was delivered to Hendon on 31st January 1994, moving to Cosford in January 2006. It is now dramatically posed within the Cold War hall.

Saunders-Roe SR.53 XD145
1956 | Single-seat, mixed-power experimental interceptor | One 1,640lb st Armstrong Siddeley Viper 101 turbojet and one 7,000lb st de Havilland Spectre rocket

Providing solid-propellant rocket boost to interceptors – referred to as mixed-power – seemed in the 1950s to be a practical method of taking interceptors to great height in the shortest possible time, after which they could patrol or fight using conventional 'air-breathing' turbojets. In late 1952 Saunders-Roe (or Saro for short) were contracted to build three prototypes, later cut to two. The project was beset with challenges and delays and the first example, XD145, started engine runs at the Aeroplane & Armament Experimental Establishment, Boscombe Down, in January 1957. The infamous Defence White Paper of April 1957 announced that only the English Electric P.1 (the Lightning's precursor,

The Saro SR.53 mixed-power interceptor; the lower jet pipe contained the Spectre rocket motor. *Saro*

see Chapters 5 and 8) would be allowed to survive as a fighter project and predicted that it would be the last RAF interceptor to carry an organic pilot. Saro had been working on a more powerful, radar-equipped, design, the SR.177 and this project was wound down. On 16th May 1957 Sqn Ldr John Booth took XD145 into the air for its maiden flight. Since the previous month, the SR.53 was a pure research programme and not a precursor to a new interceptor. Tragedy struck the programme on 5th June 1958 when John Booth was killed in the second SR.53, XD151, which suffered a take-off over-run at Boscombe Down. On 23rd February 1958 Lt Cdr Peter 'Sheepy' Lamb DFC took XD145 back into the air and the following month was appointed as Saro's new chief test pilot. The delta was last flown on 20th October 1959; its 46th sortie with flying time totalling just under 18 hours. In December 1960 XD145 was trucked to Westcott, Bucks, the home of the Rocket Propulsion Establishment, for static testing. By the summer of 1969 it had moved to Henlow. A team at Brize Norton restored the SR.53 during a three-year project starting in November 1978 and it was delivered to Cosford on 2nd March 1982.

SEPECAT* Jaguar GR.1(mod) XX765
1975 | Single-seat experimental flight control test-bed | Two 7,305lb st Rolls-Royce/Turboméca RT 172 Adour 104

Presently, RAFM does not have an operational Jaguar on display, although it has a wealth of choice in the machines serving as instructional airframes at the Defence School of Aeronautical Engineering, also resident at Cosford. This machine saw brief frontline service, but entered aviation history books in another manner. First flown at Warton on 13th June 1975 as a GR.1 it was issued to 14 Squadron at Brüggen, West Germany, on 2nd July. This seems to have been only to fill a shortfall as on 3rd December is was at Lossiemouth with 226 Operational Conversion Unit. Seven months later XX765 was in store at Abingdon. It was ferried back to Warton on 4th August 1978 where British Aerospace (BAe) undertook a complex rebuild to turn it into the ACT – Active Control Technology – demonstrator. ACT is perhaps best known as fly-by-wire, no physical linkage from the pilot's controls to the ailerons, elevators, rudder and flaps, all being moved by digitally-controlled actuators. The Jaguar was destined to be the world's first aircraft to fly with a digital quadruplex control system with no physical back-up. Such systems would allow future fighter designs to be inherently unstable, allowing regimes that could not be obtained with 'conventional' controls. From the ACT Jaguar, BAe could take the leap to the EAP (see above) and from there to the incredible Typhoon (Chapter 5). Test pilot Chris Yeo was at the controls when XX765 first flew in this new form on 20th October 1981. BAe, the Aeroplane & Armament Experimental Establishment at Boscombe Down and the Royal Aircraft Establishment, were both involved in testing this pioneer. Its job done, XX765 was retired in November 1984. In January 1991 the Jaguar was delivered by road to Loughborough University's Department of Aeronautical and Automotive Engineering, for use as a teaching aid. It departed to Warton on 13th September 1999, having been replaced by the EAP at Loughborough. At Warton it was returned to its striking red/white/blue 'test' colour scheme, known as 'Raspberry Ripple', from the previous dark green. The ACT arrived at Cosford on 10th November 1999.

(* The Jaguar was a joint programme by the British Aircraft Corporation – later BAe – and the French Breguet. Between them, they formed Société Européenne de Production de l'Avion d'Ecole de Combat et d'Appui Tactique to manage the undertaking. Roughly translated as European company building a trainer and strike aircraft, the French version stuck, but rolled off the tongue much better as SEPECAT!)

Jaguar XX765 with enlarged forward strakes (behind the cockpit) and 'ACT' titling on the fin. *BAe*

Short SB.5 WG768
1952 | Single-seat low-speed swept-wing research | One 4,850lb st Bristol Siddeley Orpheus

English Electric's P.1 supersonic interceptor programme, which blossomed as the Lightning, faced plenty of design challenges and Short Brothers and Harland at Sydenham, Belfast, responded to a requirement for a simple, fixed-undercarriage, jet to test out the proposed highly swept wing configuration in the low speed regime. It was also to help determine if the P.1 should have a low-set tailplane or a 'T-tail'. The sweep of the main wings could be changed, but only after 'surgery' on the ground – this was not a variable geometry ('swing-wing') aircraft in the sense of designs like the General Dynamics F-111 or the Panavia Tornado. Tom Brooke-Smith took WG768 on its maiden flight from Boscombe Down on 2nd December 1952. At this point it was in 'T-tail' configuration and with 50-degrees of sweep. On 29th June 1953 it was flown with 60-degrees of slope and the following month Roland Beamont, the English Electric chief test pilot, sampled it. The next metamorphosis was tested in January 1954, when WG768 started flying with the low-set tailplane. To achieve this swop-over, the SB.5 was designed to have two rear fuselages, and the 'T-tail' is on show alongside WG768 at Cosford. On 4th August 1954 Roland Beamont took P.1 WG760 into the air for the first time. (This machine is also displayed at Cosford.) The SB.5 was transferred to the Royal Aircraft Establishment (RAE) at Thurleigh, Bedford, on 20th September 1955 to continue aerodynamic research. It was returned to Shorts at Sydenham in April 1958 for a major rebuild with the Rolls-Royce Derwent 8 replaced by an Orpheus – the only major criticism of the SB.5 was that it was underpowered. It returned to the air on 18th October 1960 and continued trials with the RAE's Aero Flight. On 1st December 1965 it joined the varied fleet of the Empire Test Pilots School at Boscombe Down. It made its last flight on 7th March 1968 to the station museum at Finningley, Yorks. It arrived at Cosford in 1974.

The SB.5 in T-tail configuration and minus cockpit canopy. *Short Brothers and Harland*

Short Belfast C.1 XR371
1967 | Six-crew strategic airlifter | Four 5,730hp Rolls-Royce Tyne 101

Walking around the National Cold War Exhibition at Cosford, visitors tend to have problems at times taking in the building's scale. An effective way to appreciate it is to take a walk around the Belfast; then take the lift to the observation gallery and look down! From that aspect, the 158ft 9½in wingspan giant still seems huge, but the edifice that contains it and all the other treasures takes on Cathedral-like dimensions. The last of a production run of just ten, XR371 had its maiden flight at Sydenham, Belfast, on 14th June 1967 and 20 days later it joined 53 Squadron at Brize Norton, Oxfordshire. No.53 was the only unit to fly the mammoth airlifter; Belfasts worked hard and flew vast distances, often carrying aircraft or other bulky loads. Carrying the name *Enceladus* underneath the cockpit from 1969, XR371 had its share on interesting cargo. See the profile of the Supermarine Stranraer in Chapter 5 for a case of an exhibit being flown by an aircraft also destined to become an exhibit! As part of defence cuts, the entire Belfast fleet was axed in August 1976 and 53 Squadron disbanded on 14th September 1976. All of the fleet were parked up at 5 Maintenance Unit, Kemble. Ironically, HeavyLift Cargo Airlines (HCA) went on to operate several Belfasts as civilian aircraft, often picking up Ministry of Defence contracts! Rolls-Royce also acquired some of the redundant airlifters (including XR371), ferrying them to Hucknall, to remove their Tyne turboprops which had considerable resale value then scrapping the airframes. Rolls-Royce donated XR371 to RAFM and it was flown to Cosford on 6th October 1978, with its Tynes being taken out on site. The huge airlifter was positioned inside the Cold War hall during 2006.

Vickers Varsity T.1 WL679
1953 | Six-crew advanced aircrew trainer | Two 1,950lhp Bristol Hercules 264

Built at Hurn, Bournemouth, WL679 first flew on 9th September 1953. Unlike the bulk of the fleet of 163, WL679 was destined for a life of test and trials and not pounding the circuit, practise bombing or navigation exercises. It was issued to the Royal Aircraft Establishment (RAE) at Farnborough on 14th January 1954 and was used by the Radio Flight on a wide range of trials. It moved to Pershore on 29th August 1968 where its large fuselage and long endurance made it very suitable for the work of the Royal Radar Establishment. It was back with RAE on 13th July 1973 but at Thurleigh, Bedford, not Farnborough, flying with the Blind Landing Experimental Unit (BLEU). To ready it for BLEU, the Varsity was flown to West Malling, where Short Brothers and Harland had a 'special fit' workshop and operated Ministry of Defence aircraft on contact via the Shorts Flying Unit (SFU). At 'Malling, WL679 was fitted with a low-light television system for evaluation as a landing aid. It was flown by SFU in this mode from its Kent base infrequently until the spring of 1977 when it re-joined the RAE at Farnborough. In 1988 RAE was modernised slightly, with the word 'Aircraft' being dropped and 'Aerospace' inserted. More drastic renaming occurred in 1991 when the iconic initials RAE gave way to the Defence Research Establishment. This rebranding largely passed WL679 by; as the last Varsity flying it was long in the tooth and was retired on 2nd August 1991. On 27th July 1992 it made its last flight, transitting to Cosford.

Vickers Valiant BK.1 XD818
1956 | Five-crew strategic bomber with tanker capability | Four 10,500lb Rolls-Royce Avon 204

Once again in the overall white that it wore on roll-out in 1956, Valiant XD818 is displayed amid other artefacts within the National Cold War Exhibition. Arranged on special handling trollies or cradles are examples of Britain's early air-droppable nuclear weapons – chilling reminders of the purpose of the V-Bombers. First flown at Brooklands on 4th September 1956, XD818 had been selected as one of eight B.1s to try out Britain's nuclear arsenal. Extensive modifications were installed, including enhanced navigation and communications systems, data recording devices and screens, shutters and seals to increase crew survivability after detonation. (Vickers referred to this as Modification 2154, which downplays the sheer extent of the work required.) After flight trials at Wisley, XD818 was delivered to Wittering for 49 Squadron, under the command of Wg Cdr Kenneth Hubbard. On 3rd March 1957, with Hubbard as captain, XD818 set out from Wittering westwards across the Atlantic and North America via Honolulu, Hawaii, to the British territory of Christmas Island, just over 300 miles off the coast of Java, Indonesia. The island had been administered by Singapore, but sovereignty was transferred to Australia in 1957. The first of four 49 Squadron Valiants, XD818, touched down on 12th March – Operation GRAPPLE was about to start. Three days later, 49 had a complement of seven Valiants on the island. The drops were to take place adjacent to an atoll 400 miles south west of Christmas Island with the weapons set to air-burst. Training got underway with the release of 100lb conventional practise bombs to determine the margin of error. On 3rd May the ante was upped when XD822 released a 10,000lb high-explosive bomb; XD818 doing likewise on the 11th. Captained by Hubbard, co-piloted by Fg Off R L Beeson, XD818 climbed to 35,000ft on 15th May and released a thermonuclear fusion bomb codenamed SHORT GRANITE at 11:38 local. The Valiant turned away in a carefully-devised manoeuvre and about 150 seconds after release the crew, shrouded in darkness flying on instruments, felt very little turbulence as the shock wave billowed outwards. This was the first-ever release of a nuclear weapon from a British aircraft. Hubbard and all of his crew received the Air Force Cross for their skills. The intention was that SHORT GRANITE unleash one megaton of explosive power but due to a 'trigger' problem, the yield turned out to be in the region of 0.3mt; a statistic that caused politicians a lot of grief as the trials were to demonstrate that the UK was in the 'big league'. Two more nuclear weapons were dropped during GRAPPLE, on 31st May and 19th June. The Valiants (including XD818 each time) returned to Christmas Island for GRAPPLE X (November-December 1957), GRAPPLE Y (March to April 1958) and GRAPPLE Z (July to September 1958). For these, XD818 did not take part in the drops, but flew as 'grandstand' (observer and chase-plane). The fifth drop of a 'nuke' took place on 28th April 1958 with Sqn Ldr R M Bates at the helm of XD825 when a BLUE DANUBE bomb containing a GREEN GRANITE warhead achieved a strategically-satisfying yield of 3mt. During this drop, XD818 was one of three other Valiants airborne.

With the end of the tests, XD818 was brought up to operational Bomber Command 'spec' by Vickers at Hurn, Bournemouth, from November 1959 to January 1960. No.49 Squadron moved to Marham on 26th June 1961 and XD818's life was one of crew training, exercises and long-ranging deployments. In July 1961 it was again at Hurn, this time for conversion to BK.1 status, with the ability to become a single-point in-flight refuelling tanker. During night exercises on 6th May 1964 148 Squadron Valiant B.1 WZ363 crashed near Market Rasen, killing all five crew. As investigations unfolded, it was clear that the Valiant fleet was suffering from fatigue problems and on 11th December, all were grounded. In a ceremony at Marham on 25th May 1965 XD818 was unveiled as 'gate guardian' with the intention that it would join RAFM in due course. With the advent of the Bomber Command Hall at Hendon, the massive task of dismantling, moving, re-assembling and painting in white 'anti-flash' colours was achieved during 1982. The process was repeated in August 2005 when XD818 was roaded to Cosford to meet up with Vulcan B.2 XM598 and Victor K.2 XH672 and the exhibits in the Cold War hall.

Very likely at Wisley, Valiant B.1 XD818 in Operation GRAPPLE configuration, 1956. *BAC*

Royal Air Force Museum Cosford aircraft

Type	Identity	Built	Origin	Arrived#	Notes
Armstrong Whitworth Argosy C.1	XP411	1962	UK	Apr 1988	see profile
Auster C4	WE600	1951	UK	c Oct 1964	–
Avro Anson C.19	TX214	1946	UK	29 Aug 1963	–
Avro York C.1	TS798	1945	UK	16 May 1972	–
Avro Lincoln B.2/4A*	RF398	1945	UK	30 Apr 1963	see profile
Avro Vulcan B.2	XM598	1963	UK	20 Jan 1983	–
Avro 707C	WZ744	1953	UK	17 Apr 1967	see profile
BAC TSR-2	XR220	1964	UK	20 Jun 1967	see profile
Blackburn Buccaneer S.1	'XN972'	1963	UK	Jul 1995	XN962, cockpit
Bristol Sycamore HR.14	XJ918	1956	UK	1983	–
Bristol Britannia 312F	'XM497'	1957	UK	2 May 1984	G-AOVF
Bristol 188*	XF926	1963	UK	3 Sep 1972	see profile
British Aerospace EAP	ZF534	1985	UK	27 Mar 2012	see profile
British Aerospace Harrier GR.9A*	ZG477	1990	UK/USA	19 Dec 2011	see profile
Comper Swift	G-ACGL	1933	UK	3 Nov 2011	–
Consolidated PBY-6A Catalina	L-866	1945	USA	29 May 1974	–
De Havilland Mosquito TT.35	TA639	1945	UK	5 Jul 1967	–
De Havilland Devon C.2/2	VP952	1947	UK	5 Jul 1984	see profile
De Havilland Comet 1XB*	G-APAS	1953	UK	17 Sep 1978	see profile
De Havilland Venom FB.54	J-1704	1956	UK	8 Jun 1979	–
DH Canada Chipmunk T.10	WP912	1952	Canada	14 Dec 1976	–
Douglas Dakota C.4*	KN645	1944	USA	1 May 1974	–
English Electric Canberra PR.9	XH171	1960	UK	Jan 1992	see profile
English Electric P.1A	WG760	1954	UK	Jan 1986	–
English Electric Lightning F.1	XG337	1959	UK	Oct 1983	–
Fairchild Argus II	'FS628'	1943	USA	Feb 1973	G-AIZE
Fairey FD.2	WG777	1956	UK	8 Sep 1967	–
Fieseler Fi 156C-7 Storch	475081	1944	Germany	Jun 1973	see profile
FMA Pucará*	A-515	c1978	Argentina	9 Sep 1983	see profile
Focke-Achgelis Fa 330A-1	–	1943	Germany	Sep 1967	–
Folland Gnat F.1	XK724	1956	UK	14 Aug 1985	–
Folland Gnat T.1	XR977	1964	UK	1982	see profile
General Dynamics F-111F	74-0177	197	USA	3 Nov 2005	see profile
Gloster Meteor T.7(mod)	WA634	1949	UK	Aug 1974	ejection seat test-bed
Gloster Meteor F.8(mod)	WK935	1953	UK	12 Jan 1965	–
Gloster Meteor NF.14	WS843	1954	UK	13 Mar 1967	–
Gloster Javelin FAW.1	XA564	1954	UK	Sep 1975	–
Handley Page Hastings T.5	TG511	1948	UK	16 Aug 1977	–
Handley Page Victor K.2	XH672	1960	UK	30 Nov 1993	see profile
Handley Page Jetstream T.1	XX496	1975	UK	22 Mar 2004	–
Hawker Cygnet	G-EBMB	1924	UK	1968	–
Hawker Hind (Afghan)	–	1937	UK	20 Jan 1968	–
Hawker Hurricane II	LF738	1944	UK	8 Feb 1984	–
Hawker Hunter F.6A	XG225	1956	UK	1988	–
Hawker Hunter T.7A	XL568	1958	UK	12 Feb 2002	–
Hawker Siddeley Dominie T.1*	XS709	1964	UK	11 Feb 2011	–
Hawker Siddeley Andover E.3A*	XS639	1967	UK	13 Jul 1994	see profile
Hawker Siddeley Nimrod R.1	XV249	1970	UK	11 Mar 2012	see profile

Type	Identity	Built	Origin	Arrived#	Notes
Hunting Jet Provost T.1*	XD674	1954	UK	1966	see profile
Hunting Jet Provost T.3	XM351	1958	UK	Jun 1996	–
Hunting 126/50	XN714	1963	UK	30 Apr 1974	see profile
Junkers Ju 52 (CASA 352L)*	'G-AFAP'	1954	Germany	3 Jun 1977	see profile
Lockheed SP-2H Neptune	204	1961	USA	22 Jul 1982	–
Lockheed Hercules C.3*	XV202	1967	USA	15 Aug 2011	see profile
Messerschmitt Me 163B-1a	191614	1944	Germany	1975	–
Messerschmitt Me 410A-1/U2	420430	1943	Germany	1961	–
Mignet HM.14 'Flying Flea'	G-AEEH	1936	France	1966	–
Mikoyan-Gurevich MiG-15bis	1120	1955	USSR	29 Oct 1986	see profile
Mikoyan-Gurevich MiG-21PF	503	c1966	USSR	18 Oct 2006	–
Mitsubishi Ki 46 Dinah	5439	c1944	Japan	1963	see profile
North American P-51D Mustang	'413573'	1944	USA	1991	–
North American Sabre F.4	XB812	1953	USA	30 Jan 1994	see profile
Panavia Tornado P.02	XX946	1974	UK/Ger/It	16 Nov 1994	–
Percival Provost T.1	WV562	1954	UK	Sep 1979	–
Percival Pembroke C.1	WV746	1955	UK	13 Apr 1987	–
Saunders-Roe SR.53	XD145	1956	UK	May 1969	see profile
Scottish Aviation Pioneer CC.1	XL703	1956	UK	1 Oct 1968	–
Scottish Av Twin Pioneer CC.1	XL993	1958	UK	Feb 1979	–
Scottish Aviation Bulldog T.1*	XX654	1974	UK	1993	–
SEPECAT Jaguar GR.1(mod)	XX765	1975	UK	25 Jun 1996	see profile
Short SB.5	WG768	1952	UK	7 Mar 1968	see profile
Short Belfast C.1*	XR371	1967	UK	6 Oct 1978	see profile
Sikorsky MH-53M Pave Low*	68-8284	1968	USA	17 Dec 2008	–
Supermarine Spitfire I	K9942	1939	UK	9 Nov 1971	–
Supermarine Spitfire PR.XIX	PM651	1945	UK	Dec 1989	–
Vickers Varsity T.1	WL679	1953	UK	27 Jul 1992	see profile
Vickers Valiant BK.1*	XD818	1956	UK	Apr 1982	see profile
Westland Dragonfly HR.3	'G-AJOV'	1953	USA	Feb 1980	WP495
Westland Wessex HC.2	XR525	1964	USA	13 May 2004	–

Notes: # First taken on by RAF Museum * illustrated in colour section

Gnat T.1 XR977 in Hangar 1, 2009 with (left to right) York C.1 TS798, Dragonfly HR.5 'G-AJOV', Anson C.19 TX214, Auster C4 WE600 and Hastings T.5 TG511. *Ken Ellis*

Royal Air Force Museum Cosford Michael Beetham Conservation Centre aircraft

Type	Identity	Built	Origin	Notes
Bristol Brigand TF.1	RH746	1946	UK	fuselage
De Havilland Vampire T.11	XD515	1954	UK	–
Handley Page Hampden TB.I	P1344	1942	UK	–
Hawker Siddeley Kestrel FGA.1	XS695	1965	UK	–
Kawasaki Ki-100-1b*	16336	c1944	Japan	–
LVG C.VI	7198/18	1918	UK	see also Chapter 3
Vickers Wellington T.10	MF628	1944	UK	see narrative

* – illustrated in the colour section

Royal Air Force Museum aircraft held in store

Type	Identity	Built	Origin	Notes
Boulton Paul Sea Balliol T.21	WL732	1954	UK	Cosford
Bristol Sycamore HR.14	XL824	1957	UK	Stafford
De Havilland DH.60GM Moth	G-AAMX	1929	UK	Stafford
De Havilland Dragon Rapide	G-AHED	1946	UK	Stafford
De Havilland Vampire FB.5	WA346	1951	UK	Cosford
De Havilland Vampire FB.6	J-1172	1952	UK	Stafford
Elliotts of Newbury Eton TX.1	WP270	1951	UK	Stafford
Fairchild Cornell II	–	1944	USA	Stafford
Fairey Swordfish IV	HS503	1943	UK	Stafford
Hawker Hunter F.1	WT619	1954	UK	Stafford
Hawker P.1121	–	1958	UK	Fuselage, Cosford
Lockheed Ventura II	6130	1942	USA	Cosford
McDonnell Phantom FGR.2	XT903	1968	USA	Nose, Cosford
Miles Hawk Major	DG590	1935	UK	Stafford
Miles Mohawk	G-AEKW	1936	UK	Stafford
Morane BB	A301	1916	France	Stafford
Percival Proctor III	Z7197	1940	UK	Stafford
Republic F-84F Thunderstreak	'6771'	1952	USA	Cosford
Santos-Dumont Demoiselle rep	–	1964	France	Stafford
Saunders-Roe Skeeter AOP.12	XM555	1959	UK	Stafford
Slingsby Sedbergh TX.1	VX275	1952	UK	Stafford
Slingsby Sedbergh TX.1	XN185	1956	UK	Stafford
Slingsby Prefect TX.1	WE982	1950	UK	Cosford
Vickers Valetta C.2	VX573	1950	UK	Cosford

Sikorsky MH-53M 68-8284 arrived at Cosford, courtesy of a 99 Squadron Globemaster, 17th December 2008. *RAF Museum*

A variety of Cosford brochures.

CHAPTER 7

Silent Wings, Rotors and Inflatables
Museum of Army Flying
Middle Wallop, Hampshire
www.armyflying.com

On the top floor of the Museum of Army Flying (MoAF) is the 'Apache Cafe' offering everything from a cup of coffee to a hot meal. While tucking in, visitors get a panoramic view of the airfield at Middle Wallop and the comings and goings of the resident helicopters: Bell 212s, Gazelles, Lynxes, Squirrels and the formidable Apache gunship that the eatery takes its name from. There might also be the sight of an Army Air Corps Historic Flight aircraft leaving, or returning, on airshow duty. Middle Wallop is the Army Air Corps (AAC) Centre and it is not surprising that it should also be the venue of a museum telling the somewhat unsung story of Army aviation since the first steps were taken in the late 1860s. What was originally known as the Army Air Corps Museum, was set up in March 1968. In those days it was a by-appointment venue for non-military visitors; the present-day MoAF opened its doors to the public in November 1974. As explained in the introduction, in the true sense of the term, Middle Wallop is not a 'national' museum; but as it flies the flag for a very significant *national* force, its place is well earned in this book.

Above: 'Flying Mattress' XK776 displaying to the incredulous press at White Waltham on 21st May 1957. The wing is the 'Puffin' variant. *KEC*

While visitors look out on the airfield, few may realise that Middle Wallop itself has had a varied past, including a valiant role in the Battle of Britain and even as a Royal Naval Air Station. Intended as a bomber station, the airfield was ready for business in April 1940, initially with Airspeed Oxford trainers, but in May 1940 the Hurricanes of 601 Squadron arrived and fighters in a variety of forms became the norm for the rest of the war. (Among these was 609 Squadron and one of its Spitfires was X4590, on show today at Hendon, see Chapter 5.) On 14th and 15th August the airfield took a pasting from Junkers Ju 88s with civilian and military personnel killed, a hangar destroyed and several Blenheims and Spitfires written off. Blenheims and, from late 1940, Beaufighters of 604 Squadron turned the Hampshire airfield into a night-fighter centre of excellence, with the combination of Sqn Ldr John Cunningham and Sgt C F Rawnsley receiving much press attention. Mosquitos and Mustangs were also based until August 1943 when 'Wallop became USAAF Station 449. Photo-recce configured Mustangs, designated F-6s, of the Ninth Air Force's 67th Tactical Reconnaissance Group, arrived to capture on film every last inch of Normandy's roads, railways and defensive installations. The 67th moved with the invasion forces into France in July 1944. Middle Wallop briefly hosted the Fleet Air Arm from February 1945, the station becoming HMS *Flycatcher*. Grumman Wildcats and Supermarine Walruses of 700 Squadron graced the circuit until April 1946. Then RAF returned with Spitfire XVIs, among other types. In January 1948 the airfield's enduring role arrived in the form of Austers for Air Observation Post training which was formalised with the Light Aircraft School in 1952. The clatter of rotor blades became regular in March 1955 when the Sycamores and Whirlwinds of the Joint Experimental Helicopter Unit descended upon Middle Wallop. On 1st September 1957 the AAC was established and 'Wallop became its headquarters, a role that continues to the present day.

The hangars and main camp at Middle Wallop in the early 1980s, looking north. The A343 can be seen to the left and the present-day MoAF would be located bottom left. Of the five main hangars, the one to the rear on the right has a different colour roof: it was this one that was wrecked in the air raids of August 1940. *AAC*

Origins of 'Eyes for the Guns'

As this story of Army aviation is far less known than that of the RAF or Royal Navy, some background is important here. I am grateful to MoAF's superb web-site for much of what follows. In the 1860s and 1870s, Captains Grover and Beaumont of the Royal Engineers carried out experiments at their own expense using balloons for military purposes. The British Army appointed Captains Templer and Lee to undertake the construction and trials of a balloon called *Pioneer* in 1878. The first air unit of the British Army, the Balloon Section and Depot, was formed in 1890 and in 1905 it became the Balloon Company, under Lt-Col Capper.

Operations were not confined to balloons; man-lifting kites, pioneered by Samuel Cody, were added in 1906. (More on Cody in Chapter 1.) The first Army airship, Dirigible No.1 *Nulli Secundus*, appeared at the Balloon Factory at Farnborough in 1907 with Capper at the controls and Cody assisting. (A replica of *Nulli Secundus* – which means second to none – is displayed in Milestones of Flight at the RAF Museum Hendon – see Chapter 5.) Cody's name was becoming synonymous with Army aviation; his British Army Aeroplane No.1 featuring heavily in Chapter 1.

In 1911 an Air Battalion was formed within the Royal Engineers at Farnborough. On 13th May 1912 the Royal Flying Corps was established, followed by the Royal Naval Air Service on 1st July 1914 – see Chapter 4. Both of these absorbed the air role of the Royal Engineers. The Royal Air Force came into being on 1st April 1918, combining the RFC and RNAS into an independent service.

After the Armistice, the RAF maintained some dedicated Army Co-operation squadrons and the Old Sarum-based School of Army Co-operation perfected tactics. SAC included Army officers seconded as pilots, some becoming unit commanders. Some of these officers pioneered the use of light aircraft for artillery fire control – 'eyes for the guns' – leading to the Air Observation Post (AOP) units. No.651 Squadron was the first to go to war; in North Africa in November 1942, moving to Sicily and then Italy. Fifteen AOP squadrons were formed during the war; three of which were Canadian and one had mainly Polish personnel.

Gliders to Apaches

Successful German use of airborne forces – combinations of transport-borne paratroopers and soldiers conveyed by assault gliders – galvanised Winston Churchill to issue a directive that Britain should have a similar capability. RAF doubts that it could provide sufficient aircraft and personnel *and* meet all its other tasks gave rise to three specialist regiments: Glider Pilot, Parachute and Special Air Service. This trio formed the basis of the first iteration of the Army Air Corps (AAC). Volunteer Army pilots started to train on impressed civilian sailplanes from September 1940. At the same time requirements for assault gliders were being formulated, leading to the Hotspur, Horsa and Hamilcar. The American Waco Hadrian was also adopted in large numbers. All four of these types, plus a Slingsby Kirby Kite representing the original hotchpotch of trainers, are on show at Middle Wallop – an incredible achievement. (See the profiles below for the life and times of the Horsa and Hamilcar.)

The original AAC was disbanded in 1950 and the era of assault gliders was soon gone forever. Members of the Glider Pilot Regiment transferred to the RAF Light Liaison Flights. During the Korean conflict, 1950-1953, the US Army made comprehensive use of helicopters and this was noticed by the British. On 1st April 1955 the Joint Experimental Helicopter Unit was established at Middle Wallop and one of its first machines was Sycamore HR.14 XG502 which is today on show at MoAF – see the profile below. The present-day AAC was established on 1st September 1957 from the remaining AOP units and surviving elements of the Glider Pilot Regiment. At this stage, support helicopters were supplied by the RAF, but the first steps to independent operation were made in 1958 with light observation Saunders-Roe Skeeters. With the advent of the Scout, the AAC started to embrace the helicopter as an offensive asset with wire-guided missiles and fixed and pintle-mounted machine-guns. The Skeeter gave way to the Sioux and then to the turboshaft-powered Gazelle. The Scout was replaced by the very capable Lynx (and the AAC is in the early stages of adopting its second-generation development, the Wildcat) and the formidable McDonnell Douglas Apache from 2000.

Temporary 'digs' to commanding view

Supported entirely by volunteers and donations, what was essentially a non-public station museum was initiated at Middle Wallop in March 1968. Courtesy of the Camp Commandant, what had been the NAAFI within Stockwell Hall was converted to take the ever-growing archives, collections of memorabilia and airframes. This was the Army Air Corps Museum and its three 'founder' airframes were an Airspeed Horsa fuselage, Auster AOP.9 WZ721 and Skeeter AOP.12 XL813 – all three are still on show. The Horsa, one of two previously used as changing rooms at Abingdon jail, was a 'walk-in' exhibit with displays inside on the Glider Pilot Regiment. As is often the case, the material available far outstripped the capacity of the building. This was partially relieved in 1971 when the former station cinema was converted as the museum's new home.

Throughout this time, the Army Air Corps Museum was available to the public on a prior-arrangement basis but plans were afoot to establish a purpose-built structure with complete ease of access on what was a fully operationally base. In readiness for this and to reflect the much wider story of Army aviation, including the balloon, kite and airship origins, the name was changed to the Museum of Army Flying in August 1974. Three months later, MoAF opened up to the public on a regular basis although in those days there were occasional restrictions on how many days in the week it could be available as it was entirely staffed by volunteers. Visitors had the privilege of parking in the Officers' Mess car park, in the western camp, crossing the A343 Andover road, to view the collection.

It was the A343 that provided the key to where the new MoAF could be sited. Plans were drawn up for an impressive building adjacent to the main road a short distance south west of the main camp and very close to the control tower and operational aprons. With access off the road straight into a car park, the museum was in a self-contained, secure, location. As related at the beginning of the chapter, the cafe was innovatively located on the top floor, over-looking the activity on the airfield. As well as a main exhibition hall, there were other display areas, conference facilities, offices, archives, a shop and a workshop. The 16,000 square foot building was opened on 2nd July 1984 to great acclaim. On 31st August 2007 Sir George Young MP cut the ground for the museum's three-phase extension programme. The first element expanded the internal space by 9,688 square feet and opened to the public on 17th April the following year. A new archive and a lecture hall/theatre soon followed. Long before the other services get to their aviation centenaries, from 1978 the Museum of Army Flying at Middle Wallop has been basking in a series of '100ths' when the first Army static balloon, appropriately called *Pioneer*, was inaugurated.

General view of the main display hall, Prospector in the foreground. *Ken Ellis*

Former Museum of Army Flying aircraft*

Type	Identity	Built	Arrived	Notes, *current status or fate*
Airco DH.2 replica	'5984'	1977	May 1985	*Disposed of 1999, to private owner in Rugby, Warks*
Auster AOP.9	XP277	1961	3 Mar 1982	*Shipped to Fort Rucker, Alabama, USA 3 Jun 1982 in exchange for the Cessna L-19*
Auster AOP.9	XP281	1961	Mar 1970	*Direct to Imperial War Museum, Duxford, on loan Mar 1970. Due to re-locate*
Bell Sioux AH.1	XT131	1965	1979	*Transferred to AAC Historic Aircraft Flt*
De Havilland Tiger Moth	N6985	1939	1987	*ex G-AHMN. Held with AAC Historic Aircraft Flt, but not airworthy*
FMA Pucará	ZD486	c1980	15 Feb 1984	ex Argentine Air Force. *Scrapped Mar 1997*
FMA Pucará	A-528	c1980	16 May 1985	ex Argentine Air Force. To North East Aircraft Museum, Sunderland, 1993. *To Norfolk and Suffolk Av Museum, 24 Jul 1994, on loan*
Hafner R.II	–	1932	1983	On loan. *To The Helicopter Museum, Weston-super-Mare, Mar 2000*
Saunders-Roe Skeeter AOP.12	XL738	1958	Aug 1981	*Privately owned, stored in S Yorks.*
Saunders-Roe Skeeter AOP.12	XL770	1958	17 Dec 1985	*To Hall of Aviation, now Solent Sky, Southampton, 1989*
Saunders-Roe P.531/2	XR493	1959	1976	*ex G-APVM. To instructional airframe at Middle Wallop 8040M*
Sud Gazelle 03	XW276	1970	Oct 1981	*To Newark Air Museum, Notts, on loan*

Note: * The table does not include aircraft that were briefly held by the museum as potential exhibits, or awaiting exchange with other museums and organisations.

Airspeed Horsa II 'KJ351'
1944 | Medium-sized assault glider

There are many delights within MoAF, but perhaps the greatest of all is the unprecedented collection of World War Two assault gliders, vividly portraying the brief era when massive aerial armadas were towed into battle as the Allies invaded France and pushed eastwards. By their very nature, these expendable wooden creations have not stood the passage of time well and those at Middle Wallop include a degree of composite construction and recreation of missing elements. The most numerous British assault glider was the Airspeed Horsa, designed from the outset for maximum capacity, ease of flying in the hands of the men of the Glider Pilot Regiment and the ability to be built at furniture factories. Three substantial sections of Horsa are displayed at Middle Wallop; all Mk.IIs.

Towed behind an Armstrong Whitworth Whitley, the prototype took to the air at the Great West Aerodrome – now swallowed within London's Heathrow Airport – on 12th September 1941. This was just less than ten months after the specification had been issued. Total Horsa production amounted to 3,792 units, split roughly evenly between the Mk.I troop-carrier (25 men) and the Mk.II which featured a detachable cockpit section allowing Jeeps, light artillery pieces and other equipment to be rapidly loaded on and off. First major campaign for Horsas was Sicily when 27 were towed out to North Africa from the UK, then over to the Mediterranean island on 10th July 1943. Over 250 Horsas were used in June 1944 for D-Day; including examples crewed and operated by the USAAF. For Arnhem in September 1944 the first wave on the 17th comprised a staggering 320 Horsas, followed by another 296 next day. The final airborne glider assault using the type was the crossing of the Rhine on 24th March 1945.

The largest Horsa set-piece at Middle Wallop is centred on a superbly-created Horsa II fuselage and centre section. This is based upon Harris Lebus of Tottenham-built TL569 which was one of two discovered by the Historic Aircraft Preservation Society in 1969 in use as changing rooms at the sports field within Abingdon jail. (This has also been quoted as TL726. This Mk.II was issued to 6 Maintenance Unit at Brize Norton on 14th September 1945 and was declared surplus there on 5th July 1950. Other parts came from the Newark Air Museum, sections of 8569M from the RAF Museum and Austin-built Mk.I LH208 acquired locally.

A line-up of Horsas awaiting launch for D-Day at Cottesmore, Rutland, June 1944. *KEC*

The superbly restored, composite, Horsa, displayed at MoAF. *Terry Dann*

Auster AOP.9 WZ721
1955 | Two/three seat air observation post/liaison I 180hp Blackburn Bombardier 203

Turn to Chapter 5 for the early days of the military Auster. The AOP.9 was the last of the 'eyes for the guns' to enter production. Test flown at Rearsby on 10th October 1955, WZ721 was issued to 652 Squadron at Detmold in West Germany on 13th January 1956. It was flying from Middle Wallop in February 1960, probably with 6 Flight. It departed 'Wallop on 15th September 1960 bound for the Far East routing via Lyon, Salon, Malta, Idris, Cairo, Khartoum, Asmara, Jiwani, Rangoon and onwards, arriving at Kuala Lumpur in Malaysia on 9th October. In 125 flying hours, it had flown 9,600 miles. This was not the standard way of delivering an Auster half-way around the world; they normally went by sea or as air freight. While in the Far East, it served with the following Flights: 11 (from 1961), 7 (1962), 14 (1962) and then 16 from late 1962. By 1964 WZ721 carried the name *Dragon* on the cowling and was flying with 4 Royal Tank Regiment's Air Squadron, including time detached to Kuching, Sarawak. It was retired in September 1966 when Sioux helicopters came on stream and was shipped to the UK in May 1967, carrying stencilling that it was destined for the Imperial War Museum. In 1968 it became a 'founder member' of the Middle Wallop museum and remains on display.

Bell Sioux AH.1 XT108 and Bell 47G-4A G-AXKS
1964 and 1969 | Two/three seat light helicopter | One 260hp Lycoming TVO-435-A1A

To replace the underpowered Saunders-Roe Skeeter the AAC selected the well-known and robust Bell 47, the prototype of which first flew on 8th December 1945. A licence arrangement was concluded with Agusta of Gallerate, Italy, for production by Westland at Hayes, Middlesex. The first 50, including MoAF's example XT108, were built by Agusta and delivered in 1964-1965. The first Westland-built one took to the air in March 1965 and production of 206 further AH.1s was completed in 1968. (The RAF received 15 HT.2s pure trainer versions.) The AAC ran a very popular display Sioux team, the 'Blue Eagles', between 1968 and 1976. Sioux XT108 served for the vast majority of its time with the Development and Trials Flight at Middle Wallop, joining the museum in June 1984. As well as the 'pure' Army Sioux, Westland also built 16 Bell 47G-4A trainers for Bristow Helicopters in 1969. Civil-registered, these spent their entire time training AAC pilots under contract at Middle Wallop. MoAF's example, G-AXKS, was handed over by Alan Bristow on 22nd April 1982. The Sioux gave way to the French-designed Sud Gazelle turbine-powered helicopter in 1984.

Bristol Sycamore HR.14 XG502
1955 | Four/five seat general purpose helicopter | One 550hp Alvis Leonides

As will be seen under the references for the Hafner Rotachute and 'Flying Jeep' below, Austrian-born Raoul Hafner joined Bristol at Filton in late 1944. He went on to create the Sycamore, the first British-designed helicopter to enter series production and fly with the UK military. The prototype had its maiden flight on 27th July 1947. It is fitting that MoAF has a Sycamore on show, to highlight the evolution of Hafner's rotorcraft thinking. (Beyond the Sycamore came the twin-rotor Belvedere, featured in Chapter 5.)

Built at Filton HR.14 XG502 first took to the air on 24th February 1955 and was issued to the Joint Experimental Helicopter Unit at Middle Wallop on the last day of March, ready for the unit's official establishment the following day. As the title implied, JEHU was a multi-service outfit, designed to perfect the use of helicopters between the Army, Navy and RAF and refine tactics. JEHU was not all theory, in October 1956 JEHU crews and six of its Sycamores (including XG502 and XG523, the latter preserved at the Norfolk and Suffolk Aviation Museum) embarked upon the carrier HMS *Ocean*, bound for Malta as part of Operation MUSKETEER, the Anglo-French re-possession of the Egypt's Suez Canal Zone. As well as the Sycamores, JEHU had Westland Whirlwind HAR.2s on *Ocean* and, under the command of Lt Col J F T Scott, on 6th November 1956 both types began ferrying personnel of 45 Commando to Port Said; the Sycamores carrying three fully-armed commandos on each sortie. Joint-force operations from a carrier using helicopters had become a reality for Britain.

After this 'limelight', XG502 retuned to duties at 'Wallop until JEHU was disbanded in 1959. On 1st May 1959 the Sycamore transferred to the Transport Command Communications Flight at Upavon. An accident in October 1960 put paid to XG502's time at Upavon and it returned to Bristol for repair. Its next tasking was with 118 Squadron at Aldergrove, Belfast, from 29th November 1961. This was short-lived, as 118 disbanded on 31st August 1962. Four days later XG502 was on charge with 72 Squadron at Odiham, but this too was brief, transferring on 30th October to the Central Flying School at Little Rissington, staying there until 28th February 1963. After a short spell at 15 Maintenance Unit, Wroughton (now the Science Museum's out-station) XG502 joined the Metropolitan Communications Squadron at Northolt to the west of London, on 13th December 1963. MCS provided wide-ranging 'taxi' services using a variety of types. On 3rd February 1969 MCS was re-titled as 32 Squadron, its role and base remaining unchanged. The Sycamores had handed over to Westland Whirlwind HC.10s by September 1971 and XG502 was once more sent to Wroughton (by then a Royal Naval Aircraft Yard handling helicopters for all three services). It was struck off charge on 29th August 1972 and transferred to the Army Air Corps Museum at Middle Wallop. It was camouflaged to represent the Sycamores of the 106 Light Liaison Flight and JEHU.

Sycamore HR.14 XG502 of 32 Squadron alighting at the RAF specialist radio facility at Medmenham, Bucks, in the late 1960s. *KEC*

General Aircraft Hamilcar I TK777
1944 | Heavy assault glider

The forward fuselage of Hamilcar I TK777 is a 'walk-through' exhibit at MoAF and provides a glimpse of the largest assault glider used operationally by the Allies. With a wing span of 110ft and the ability to carry a 7-ton Tetrarch light tank, the all-wood Hamilcar was an awesome creation. The prototype was towed into the air behind a Halifax bomber at Snaith in Yorkshire on 27th March 1942. General Aircraft built another 22 and another 390 were created by sub-contractors including furniture manufacturers. Seventy of these lumbering monsters arrived in the fields of Normandy after D-Day and 28 were used at Arnhem. A powered version, the Mk.X, was created for use in the Pacific theatre, getting airborne in February 1945, but did not see action.

The Middle Wallop Hamilcar is based upon sections of TK718 and TK777, both salvaged from a field near Christian Malford close to Lyneham. Additional sections came from NX836. All of these were built by the Birmingham Railway Carriage and Wagon Company which assembled its Hamilcars at Henlow. Elements of TK718 also comprise the impressive forward fuselage displayed at the Tank Museum, Bovington, which also includes a Tetrarch tank.

Early trials of a Rotachute; it is mounted on a fixed rig on the back of a speeding lorry. *KEC*

To pave the way for the massive Hamilcar cargo-carrying assault glider, General Aircraft built a half-scale test-bed, the GAL.50, which first flew on 15th November 1941. Although a Hamilcar does not appear to have been ear-marked for preservation, the more space-efficient GAL.50 DP226 was. It was stored at Stanmore Park, Middlesex, until at least 1958 when it was offered for sale and the trail went cold. *KEC*

Hafner AFEE 10/42 Rotabuggy replica 'B-415'
1982 | Towed rotorcraft adaptation of a Willys 5 cwt Jeep

Understandably, the prospect of a Jeep with helicopter-like rotor blades, stops a lot of visitors to Middle Wallop in their tracks; especially when they read that it was planned to lead to a rotor-borne Valentine tank! This incredible device was the brainchild of Austrian-born Raoul Hafner whose first full-sized helicopter, the R.I, had its maiden flight in Vienna in 1930, but was not a success. The improved R.II appeared in 1931 and the following year Hafner re-located to Great Britain, bringing the R.II with him. (This survives at The Helicopter Museum and was for a while displayed at MoAF – see the table 'Former Museum of Army Flying Aircraft'.) The AR.III Gyroplane of 1937 was in the classic Cierva mould, but it pioneered the cyclic and collective control system adopted by helicopters.

With the onset of war, Hafner worked with the oddly-named Central Landing Establishment based at Ringway, now Manchester Airport. CLE developed airborne forces equipment, with parachutes dominating, in readiness for the invasion of Europe. During January 1942 CLE became the Airborne Forces Experimental Establishment (AFEE) and that July moved to Sherburn-in-Elmet. Hafner turned his experience to the creation of a one-man fully steerable rotorcraft 'parachute'. Using bicycle frame construction techniques, a very simple twin-blade rotor and a simple plywood tail section, he came up with the Rotachute, weighing at just 48lb unladen. The first was towed into the air at Ringway on 2nd February 1942, fluttering back to earth under full control. MoAF's example is on loan from the RAF Museum.

From the Rotachute concept, the Rotabuggy emerged. By installing a rotor pylon on which to mount a large 46ft 8in 'free-wheeling' two-blade rotor, adding a simple box-like rear fuselage with fins for an element of directional control, a means of towing a Willys 5 cwt Jeep behind an aircraft to a battle zone was created. Once it had landed – on its own wheels – the rotors and fuselage could be discarded and the Jeep and its crew could go to war. As can be seen elsewhere in this chapter, assault gliders were envisaged as an efficient way of getting troops and vehicles into combat. Hafner argued that a Horsa cost £2,450 (£134,750 in present-day values) to transport a Jeep on what more than likely was a one-way trip for the glider. But with a Rotabuggy, the job could be done for as little as £500.

Engineering specialists R Malcolm Ltd created the Rotabuggy at Slough. (R Malcolm Ltd, perhaps most famous for the development of 'Malcolm Hood', clear-vision sliding canopies for early Spitfires and Mustangs, became ML Aviation in late 1943 – see the profile on the ML Utility below for more.) Officially designated AFEE 10/42, the unique vehicle-rotorcraft crossbreed was also known as the 'Malcolm Blitz Buggy'. The amazing contraption, numbered B-415, was first flown under tow by a Bentley, no less, at Sherburn on 27th November 1943. An Armstrong Whitworth Whitley towed the Rotabuggy aloft on 30th January 1944 and on 11th September a brave pilot let go the tow line and free-flew for the first and only time. Around 60 flights were carried out, but it needed a very skilled pilot and the plan was that quickly-trained Army drivers would fly them in action. By then D-Day had been and gone and the Rotabuggy and any ideas of towing an airborne tank into battle had subsided. Hafner envisaged a Handley Page Halifax bomber towing a 37-ton Valentine tank fitted Rotabuggy-like modifications – for this job a 152ft rotor would have been needed. In a far-sighted move, Bristol Aircraft offered Hafner the chance to start up a helicopter department in late 1944. He went on to design the first British helicopter to enter production, the Sycamore – see above – and the twin-rotor Belvedere, featured in Chapter 5.

It was members of the Wessex Aviation Society who came up with the idea of recreating the 'Flying Jeep' for MoAF. The museum supplied a set of Westland Whirlwind rotor blades and a Jeep was found by browsing through *Exchange and Mart*. Construction was carried out at the WAS workshop at Stapehill, Dorset, with Dave Tizzard as project officer. The visitor-arresting rotorcraft made its debut at Middle Wallop in July 1982 and was presented to MoAF in 1985.

Above: The Rotabuggy, or 'Flying Jeep' at AFEE Sherburn, 1944. Note the Horsa assault glider behind. *ML Aviation*

Left: Scout AH.1 XP847 is displayed complete with armament of four SS.11 wire-guided anti-tank missiles. *Terry Dann*

ML Utility Mk.1 XK776
1957 | Experimental inflatable wing aircraft I One 38hp Walter Mikron III

On 1st September 1954 a curious craft clawed its way into the air at Twinwood Farm, near Bedford. Powered by a McCulloch OQ-90 'pusher' mounted in a bath-like fuselage suspended under a swept-back wing, it was not so much this configuration that aroused interest, but that the wing was *inflatable*. This was the brainchild of the Research and Development Establishment, under the guidance of Dan Perkins. R&DE was based at Cardington, home of the gigantic pre-war airship sheds. This machine was taken to the Royal Aircraft Establishment (RAE) at Farnborough for further trials and in 1955 it was decided to use it as the basis of a development programme. The ability to have the fuselage become a container for the deflated wing and for it to be towed on its own undercarriage behind a vehicle was part of the design's remit. Downed aircrew rescue and clandestine missions were expected to be potential applications.

ML Aviation at White Waltham was given a contract for three aircraft, Mk.1 XK776, Mk.2 XK781 and a rebuilt version of the R&DE prototype, XK784. In 1940 the gifted chief designer for Fairey, Marcel Jules Odilion Lobelle, left the company and entered into a partnership with Ronald Malcolm of R Malcolm Ltd. The aim was to expand the activities of 'Ronnie's' sub-contracting concern into design and production; the new company was named ML Aviation after Marcel Lobelle. R Malcolm Ltd had been the main contractor on the AFEE Rotabuggy – see above. ML went on to such things as ejection seats, remotely piloted aircraft, control systems, weapons technology, becoming part of the Cobham Group in 1997.

ML set about re-engineering the first example and in January 1956 it was back with RAE. Mk.1 XK776 began test flying at White Waltham in early 1957 and on 21st May was demonstrated to the press there. Officially designated ML Utility Mk.1, it was also referred to as the 'Inflatable Wing Mk.1'. Needless to say, the press had other ideas, calling it the 'Air Jeep' and even 'Flying Mattress'. A dozen different wings, originating with R&DE, were created for the programme. These were given a variety of far-from-scientific sounding names, eg 'Bunty' 'Puffin' and 'Randy', to help identify them. The name was stitched on to the leading edge, near the centre-line, of each wing. After inflation on the ground by a compressor, the wing was 'topped up' once airborne by a household vacuum cleaner, powered by the on-board electrics.

On 25th June 1957 XK776 was delivered by road to the Aeroplane & Armament Experimental Establishment (A&AEE) at Boscombe Down for evaluation, officially going on charge on 6th September. The craft became known as the 'Delta Durex' at A&AEE! The Mk.1 was demonstrated to the Army at Bulford Camp on Salisbury Plain in October 1957. Later that month, on the 25th, XK776 suffered structural failure of the rear struts and Flt Lt Geoff R K Fletcher brought it down for a 'dead-stick' landing. After a final evaluation in February 1958 (see below) the whole project was terminated on 28th March 1958. The first machine, XK784, was scrapped, but substantial elements of XK781 survived and are held by the RAF Museum at its storage facility at Stafford, Staffs.

AAC wanted to try out the ML Utility for its own purposes and XK776 was transferred to Middle Wallop on 16th August 1960. These were brief and XK776 was put into store at Cardington. In July 1969 XK776 was displayed statically at an airshow at Middle Wallop and in April 1977 it was inflated to take part in Cardington's 60th anniversary celebrations. In July 1982, along with the 'Clouy', 'Delta' and 'Gadfly' wings it was delivered to Middle Wallop and presented to MoAF.

Westland Scout AH.1 XP847
1961 | Five-seat general duties helicopter | One 685 shp Bristol Siddeley Nimbus 102

During the June 1982 Falklands conflict, AAC Scouts gave exceptional service and were involved in successful Nord SS.11 wire-guided rocket attacks against Argentine targets. One of the three Scouts on show at MoAF, XP847, is displayed carrying four SS.11s. The second production Scout, XP847 was built at Hayes in 1967 and spent all of its life in trials with Westland and service acceptance flying with the Aeroplane & Armament Experimental Establishment at Boscombe Down. This work included radio assessments (March 1964), instrument ergonomics (September 1966) and operational reliability testing (August 1967). In May 1970 the helicopter was used for trials of BAC Swingfire wire-guided anti-tank missiles. These initially involved inert jettison trials, followed by live firings. By the late 1970s, XP847 had been retired and was in use as an instructional airframe with the Air Engineering Training Wing at Stockwell Hall, Middle Wallop. It was transferred to MoAF in 1984. The navalised version was known as the Wasp and is detailed in Chapter 4.

Record-breaking Lynx AH.1 XX153 at Middle Wallop. *MoAF*

Westland Lynx AH.1 DB XX153
1972 | Utility/battlefield helicopter | Two 900 shp Rolls-Royce Gem 2

First flown on 21st March 1971, the Westland Lynx utility/battlefield and anti-submarine helicopter family has been in continuous production at Yeovil, ever since. From July 2000 the company has been known as AgustaWestland and the latest iteration of the Lynx is the AW159 Wildcat. The naval story can be picked up in Chapter 4. MoAF has two Lynx on display; AH.7 XZ675, which first flew on 5th November 1981, joined the collection in November 2011. The AH.7 represents the ultimate development of the short-fuselage, skid-equipped, utility Lynx which works alongside the AAC's AH.9/AH.9A wheeled undercarriage models. With respect to 'youngster' XZ675, it is early example XX153 that steals the limelight.

The Lynx programme, the first British aircraft to be designed with metric measurements, had great pace to it. Just over a year after the prototype had flown, Westland had the first near-production standard model in the air. Designated Lynx AH.1 DB Utility, XX153 took to the air at Yeovil on 12th April 1972. (DB – development batch.) With this machine Westland was determined to prove how advanced this new helicopter was. On 29th June 1972 test pilot Roy Moxam set a new world speed record in class E.1 of 199.92mph and 1st July he and XX153 sizzled around a 100km closed-circuit to clinch another record at 197.91mph. Again with Moxam at the controls, XX153 was the first helicopter to be rolled routinely, courtesy of its semi-rigid main rotor. Roy stopped the crowd in its track at the September 1972 Farnborough airshow by casually rolling the helicopter. Despite these claims to fame, when XX153's useful development career was at an end it was issued to the Proof and Experimental Establishment at Foulness; potentially to end up as a static ballistics target. Thankfully, this was not the end and it moved in mid-1995 to the AAC base at Wattisham, becoming instructional airframe 9320M. It was at Wattisham that XX153's provenance was recognised and it was roaded to Yeovil for restoration by AgustaWestland apprentices for MoAF. Returned to its record-breaking configuration, XX153 was delivered to Middle Wallop on 28th October 2003.

Museum of Army Flying aircraft*

Type	Identity	Built	Origin	Arrived	Notes
Airspeed Horsa II	'KJ351'	1945	UK	1968	see profile, also a fuselage and a cockpit
Auster 5	TJ569	1945	UK	Oct 1981	G-AKOW
Auster AOP.6	WJ358	1952	UK	Jul 1980	G-ARYD
Auster AOP.9	WZ721	1955	UK	1969	see profile
Bell 47G-4A*	G-AXKS	1963	USA	22 Apr 1982	see profile
Bell Sioux AH.1	XT108	1964	USA	Jun 1984	see profile
Bell UH-1H Iroquois	AE-409	1972	USA	Jul 1982	–
Bell AH-1F Cobra	70-15990	1970	USA	2003	–
Bristol Sycamore HR.14	XG502	1955	UK	1982	see profile
Cessna L-19A Bird Dog	111989	1951	USA	1982	–
DH Canada Chipmunk T.10	WG432	1951	Canada	1997	–
DH Canada Beaver AL.1	XP821	1961	Canada	2 Oct 1985	–
DH Canada Beaver AL.1	XP822	1961	Canada	15 May 1993	–
Edgar Percival Prospector*	'XM819'	1959	UK	14 May 1981	composite
GAL Hotspur II replica	'HH268'	1995	UK	13 Dec 2001	–
GAL Hamilcar I*	TK777	1944	UK	20 Jan 1984	see profile
Hafner Rotachute III	P-5	1943	UK	1983	–
Hafner AFEE 10/42 replica	'B-415'	1982	UK	Jul 1982	see profile
Miles Magister I	'T9707'	1940	UK	Jun 1999	T9708, ex G-AKKR
ML Utility Mk.1	XK776	1957	UK	Jul 1982	see profile
Saunders-Roe Skeeter AOP.12*	XL813	1959	UK	23 Jan 1968	–
Slingsby Kirby Kite	'G285'	1936	UK	1989	–
Sopwith Pup	'N5195'	1916	UK	1985	–
Sud Alouette AH.2	XR232	1960	France	May 1992	–
Sud Gazelle AH.1	ZA737	1980	France	Dec 1999	–
Waco CG-4A Hadrian*	'243809'	1944	USA	1985	fuselage
Westland Scout AH.1	XP847	1961	UK	1984	see profile
Westland Scout AH.1	XP910	1963	UK	2002	–
Westland Scout AH.1	XV127	1967	UK	1995	–
Westland Lynx AH.1	XX153	1972	UK	28 Oct 2003	see profile
Westland Lynx AH.7	XZ675	1981	UK	7 Aug 2011	–

Note: * – illustrated in the colour section

A variety of Museum of Army Flying brochures.

CHAPTER 8

Place of Pilgrimage
Imperial War Museum
Duxford, Cambs

www.iwm.org.uk

M ost parents adjust to the idea that their offspring will be bigger than them. Chapter 2 outlined the origins and growth of the 'father' organisation, the Imperial War Museum South Lambeth. From 1978, the public were allowed in on a regular basis to an airfield near Cambridge that rapidly grew to be a brand in its own right, known purely and simply as 'Duxford'.

On the last day of March 1961 the Hawker Hunter F.6s of 65 Squadron were paid off and the unit disbanded at Duxford. The sound of jets lasted until the middle of July when the Gloster Javelin FAW.9s of 64 Squadron decamped to nearby Waterbeach. The days of RAF Duxford were dwindling. The station closed in 1968, but immediately burst into life again for the filming of *Battle of Britain* – of which more anon. From 1969 increasing elements of the site became available for occupation or development. The Imperial War

'Oregon's Britannia', P-47D Thunderbolt '226413' on show inside the American Air Museum. *Ken Ellis*

Museum had for some time been looking for a large object store and from 1970 started to move material in to Duxford; Auster AOP.9 XP281, presented by the Army Air Corps, arrived in March. At the same time the East Anglian Aviation Society (EAAS) was developing a presence with Miles Magister N3788 as an early restoration project. Airliners were an early theme, with Dakota G-ANAF on site by 1972 and a real coup in the shape of de Havilland Comet 4 G-APDB which flew in on 12th February 1974, a gift from Dan-Air. During that year, EAAS established the incredible Tower Museum at nearby Bassingbourn and by 1975 centred its operations there. The Duxford Aviation Society (DAS) took on the mantle, more of that shortly.

The 1970s were the formative years of the UK's 'warbird' era and Duxford was in the vanguard. A taste of what was to come was supplied by the Yesterday's Air Force former Indian Air Force B-24J Liberator N94459 which interrupted its ferry flight from Poona to the USA at Duxford on 28th October 1973. Volunteers toiled to transform it into '250551' *Delectable Doris* of the Hethel-based 566th Bomb Squadron, 389th Bomb Group. The stop-over was a long one and the workmanship impressive. The B-24 departed for Prestwick and the USA on 11th September 1975. Any museum has its share of volunteers and Duxford has been blessed with such vital input over the last 40-plus years. Restoration projects both short and epic; display projects; manning the flight-line walk; or archiving images; all of these are many, many more tasks have been and are the domain of people giving of their skills and time, functioning for the IWM, or through DAS or other operators on site. In the exhibit profiles that follow there could be many names mentioned, but this would become an unwieldy, if not impossible, task. Their work shines out as tributes to all of them – you know who you are!

From now on in this chapter, 'Imperial War Museum' spelt full-out refers to South Lambeth; when abbreviated as IWM it denotes Duxford. In February 1976 IWM cemented its presence at Duxford by taking on the entire site, including the domestic area to the north of the Royston Road. The airfield remained owned by Cambridge Country Council, with IWM operating it; the 'flying field' was transferred to IWM in 2008. A couple of open days and airshows were staged in the early years but 1978 was the pivotal one when a huge amount of work gelled and Duxford was opened up. In that year Ted Inman was appointed as Director and he was to steer the increasingly complex site through refinement and expansion for the next 22 years; Ted retired on 11th June 2004.

In April 1978 the sixth edition of *Wrecks & Relics* was published and looking through its pages provides a 'snapshot' of the nascent Duxford. New for IWM were the former Canadian Boeing 'Stearman' and Grumman Avenger, arriving road in November the previous year. Grabbing all the attention was the former Skyfame Collection which had mostly arrived that spring – see below. DAS were basking in BAC/Sud Concorde 101 G-AXDN which had touched down on 20th August 1977. Also resident as an 'associate' DAS aircraft was 1945-built Auster J/1 G-AGTO owned by Mike Barnett and David Miller. In 2013 *Tango-Oscar* was still in the hands of these two and resident! A pair of Beagle prototypes were in temporary storage; 206X G-ARRM and Pup 200 G-AVDF. Michael Russell had established the Russavia Collection of light aircraft, with BAC Drone G-AEDB, DH Tiger Moth G-APMM and a series of classic gliders, among others. Sandy Topen had moved some of his 1950s jets on to the airfield, including Gloster Meteor NF.14 WS760.

Line-up at Duxford in 1978, exemplifying the variety of 'agencies' on the site. Left to right: IWM SAAB Draken and P-51D Mustang (see Chapter 1), DAS Concorde 101 G-AXDN, Shuttleworth Collection Spitfire V (see Chapter 3) and an Haydon-Baillie Collection Silver Star. *KEC*

'Warbirds' were dominated by Boeing B-17G Fortress G-BEDF *Sally B* which had flown in from Biggin Hill on 16th March 1975 and in 2013 continues to display as the IWM 'flagship'. Robs Lamplough was flying his North American Harvard II G-BBHK and had salvaged a quartet of North American P-51D Mustangs and a pair of Supermarine Spitfire IXs from Israel and had set up a workshop to restore them. All of the Duxford community was mourning the death of Ormond Haydon-Baillie in a Mustang in West Germany on 3rd July 1977. He had brought to Duxford his pair of airworthy Canadair-built T-33 jets and Hawker Sea Fury FB.11 G-AGHB. Also sitting in one of the hangars was a pair of Fairchild-built Bolingbroke IVTs; which were to inspire Graham Warner to return one of them to flying condition. In a co-operative arrangement with the Shuttleworth Collection, volunteers had completed Spitfire V AR501 and it first flew at Duxford on 27th June 1975, followed by Sea Hurricane Z7015 on 16th September the same year. Work had started on Spitfire PR.XI PL983, but this was sold before completion – see Chapter 3 for more. All of this was before well-known operators such as the Aircraft Restoration Company, British Aerial Museum, Historic Flying, Old Flying Machine Company, Plane Sailing, The Fighter Collection and others became established. Now, hopefully for a gentle let down... Perhaps more famous than the static aircraft at Duxford, all of the 'warbird' operators are independent while having a loan agreement with IWM; as such these are beyond the scope of this book. Besides, a full and proper study of Duxford's 'warbirds' and the personalities behind them is a book in its own right. That said, some of the early pioneers (Haydon-Baillie, British Aerial Museum and the Vintage Aircraft Team) are featured in the companion volume *Lost Aviation Collections of Britain*.

Duxford in 1918, looking toward the east. Construction of the 'Belfast Truss' hangars is still in process on the airfield site, while the North Site is a hotchpotch of wooden buildings. *KEC*

Fighting the Battle of Britain – twice

Any condensed history of Duxford is going to raise hackles somewhere in the readership; it has a spectacular legacy. Construction started in 1917 and the station officially opened on 1st March 1918. By then 119 and 129 Squadrons were resident, the latter operating DH.9s, an example of which 'flies' within AirSpace today. It was 1919 before the airfield was properly ready and its three Double General Service Sheds (also known as 'Belfast Truss' hangars) and a single-bay example were functioning along with a host of canvas examples along Royston

A Sopwith Dolphin outside one of the yet-to-be-completed hangars at Duxford. *KEC*

road. The north site was composed completely of wooden buildings. Duxford was put into care and maintenance in June 1919, but in April 1920 it re-opened as 2 Flying Training School with Avro 504s, Bristol F.2bs and DH.9As. From 1922 its career as a fighter station was established with 19 and 29 Squadrons flying Sopwith Snipes, soon replaced by Gloster Grebes. In 1923 the Station Headquarters (SHQ) building was constructed and it was heavily modified in 1933. During the mid-1930s the North Site took on the appearance that it still has in the 21st Century.

In August 1938 the station had the honour of introducing the Spitfire I into RAF service, with 19 Squadron. Spitfires of 66 Squadron pounced on a Luftwaffe Heinkel He 111 off the Norfolk coast on 11th January 1940 and it was later discovered to have been written off – Duxford's first 'kill'. The station was in the thick of the Battle of Britain and there can be no better way of getting the 'feel' of this than to visit the 'Ops Room' which was been lovingly brought back in time and 'frozen' at 08:30 hours on 31st August 1940 when Dornier Do 17Zs of KG2 were detailed to deliver a powerful blow to the airfield. The raid was fought off, by a combination of anti-aircraft fire and the exploits of 19 Squadron. Three of 19's Spitfires fell that day; Fg Off F N Brinsden safely taking to the silk; Fg Off J B Coward doing likewise but had to have a leg amputated; Plt Off R A C Aeberhardt perished in R6912 on landing at nearby Fowlmere. In April 1943 the USAAF 78th Fighter Group arrived at Duxford, which was quickly renamed 'Duckpond' by Americans bemused by the weather and the antiquity of the facilities. Initially operating Republic P-47 Thunderbolts, the 78th later flew P-51Ds. By August 1945 the Americans had gone and RAF returned. No.66 Squadron was back in September 1946 with Spitfires but by early 1947 had converted to Meteor F.3s. The runway was extended in the summer of 1948 and jets dominated until the disbanding of 65 Squadron and the departure of 64 Squadron in 1961, as outlined at the beginning of the chapter.

During 1968, a small air force had been gathered at the Bedfordshire airfield of Henlow – home to the RAF Museum's expanding store and workshops. This impressive collection of Hawker Hurricanes, Spitfires and Merlin-engined, Spanish-built Messerschmitt Bf 109s and Heinkel He 111s had been assembled by Gp Capt T G 'Hamish' Mahaddie for director Guy Hamilton's film *Battle of Britain*, based on the book *The Narrow Margin* by Derek Wood and Derek Dempster. Much of the filming was staged at Duxford and was to have a lasting impact on the airfield. For what is only seconds in the film, the pyrotechnic wizards were allowed to demolish the single-bay 'Belfast Truss' hangar. The author has always regarded this as an act of needless vandalism. Another change to the Duxford scenery had far more practicality to it and indeed has eased access on a day-to-day basis and especially during airshows – the M11 motorway. Built during 1975 to 1980, at Duxford, the highway severed the eastern end of the airfield, reducing the usable runway length and causing a great furore at the time. It was far from the end of the world and to quote from Michael J F Bowyer's seminal *Action Stations Revisited – Eastern England*: "That the M11 was able to hack its way through the runway was regrettable, but many of the nicest aeroplanes dislike long runways". On 8th October 1983 the largest type so far preserved in a UK museum – the B-52 Stratofortress – didn't have its style cramped by the motorway!

Duxford's recreated 'Ops' Room, as it was on the morning of 31st August 1940. *Ken Ellis*

Station HQ, a Bailey Bridge and tanks

The north site, the SHQ and all of the other period buildings, took a long time for IWM to assimilate; offering the museum and others a unique opportunity to turn historic artefacts into working institutions. Archives, offices and much more are now to be found within these structures and the SHQ was massively refurbished for special events and conferences. Having the A505 Royston to Newmarket road cutting right through the entire site was not conducive to safety for staff, or the public. To solve this, another 'living' exhibit was installed. For many visitors to Duxford during an airshow, the climb up the slope to the Bailey Bridge provides a commanding view of some of the delights that will perform later in the day. There is a small wooden building on the North Site that probably very few people give a second thought to. This is a classic example of how IWM facilitates other organisations and how to preserve more unsung elements of British aviation heritage. This is the former de Havilland Stag headquarters building, relocated by BAE Systems in 2007, and used by de Havilland Support Ltd. Originally at the first de Havilland aerodrome and factory, Stag Lane, Edgware, it was the office in which the famous company was incorporated in September 1920. After the closure of Stag Lane it was re-erected in the 1930s at the new Hatfield production line and airfield. It was moved no less than *three* times during its tenure at Hatfield.

The airfield site has boasted many exhibitions over the decades, some temporary, others more long-term. In terms of size, the building at the far western end is a reminder that the Imperial War Museum has a vast remit, of which aviation is just one facet. This is the Land Warfare Hall which contains a world class selection of armoured fighting vehicles and opened in September 1992. With its role as a Battle of Britain station, a major display on the subject had long been planned. On 16th June 2000 a permanent exhibition was opened in Hangar 4, centred around Bf 109E-3 1190 which force-landed on 30th September 1940 and former Soviet Hurricane IIb 'Z2315' plus a huge amount of supportive material. Within AirSpace is Airborne Assault, the Museum of the Parachute Regiment and Airborne Forces which opened in 2005. This includes the majority of the former Airborne Forces Museum at Aldershot.

Saving Skyfame

Established at Gloucester's Staverton aerodrome in August 1963 by Peter Thomas, his family and friends, the Skyfame Museum was a pioneer in the history of British aircraft preservation. Peter had cut his teeth in saving a Sunderland for the UK in 1961 – see Chapter 5. The museum at Staverton staged regular flying displays and boasted over 20 aircraft at its height. Skyfame closed the hangar doors for the last time on 2nd January 1978 and negotiations with the IWM resulted in the biggest museum rescue ever staged in the UK. Work started on the mass departure on 25th January with the first whole airframe – Sycamore G-48/1 – leaving on 5th February. A brilliantly co-ordinated to-ing and fro-ing of articulated trucks made for a very smooth operation. By 1980 most of the airframes were assembled and on show at Duxford. Initially on loan, title to the majority transferred to IWM by 1988.

Airliners and vital support

As recounted earlier, the East Anglian Aviation Society had centred its activities on the Tower Museum at Bassingbourn by 1975. Stepping into the breach was the Duxford Aviation Society which was formed on 6th April 1975 and by July had 562 members and has continued to grow. EAAS had been donated de Havilland Comet 4 G-APDB and DAS kept up the airliner theme, with the support and encouragement of IWM. The formative year was a busy one, DAS members playing a major part in the two-day airshow that year, staged on 28/29th June. On the first day of the show, DAS highlighted its intention to preserve important examples of British airliners with the airborne delivery of Bristol Britannia G-AOVT. This was the start of what is now known as the British Airliner Collection. As related in Chapters 1 and 6 the preservation of airliners in the UK has been a somewhat ad hoc process and is fraught with problems; not least the sheer size of the subject matter! There is much more to DAS than airliners, there is also an active Military Vehicle Section and DAS members contribute to almost every aspect of activity at Duxford.

There can have been no finer tribute to DAS than the gifting of pre-production BAC/Sud Concorde 101 G-AXDN by the Department of Transport; it was the only example of the supersonic transport donated to a volunteer group. *Delta-November* became the fourth member of the DAS fleet on 20th August 1977 – see the table 'Duxford Aviation Society – British Airliner Collection'. Moved under cover into Hangar 1, the 'Superhangar', in 1999 G-AXDN remained in the warm and dry until 2005 when the restructuring work to turn the building in the AirSpace hall required it to be emptied – see below. Since it was first opened to the public in March 1978 it is estimated that more than 4 million visitors have walked through *Delta-November*.

In late 2000 DAS was awarded a Heritage Lottery Fund (HLF) grant of £314,000 to restore five of its collection – Ambassador, Comet, Concorde, Hermes and York. The monies allowed more interpretive displays and better access for those of restricted mobility. DAS volunteers strive to have a selection of airliners available for internal inspection and the ability to install lifts for access was a great boon. The fuselage of the Handley Page Hermes, acquired from Gatwick in 1981, is a unique artefact from the immediate post-war era of large piston-engined airliners. Its interior was always basic and it has been turned into a 'display hall' with cabinets and it stands alongside Concorde 101 within AirSpace.

Developing the east and the west

Duxford must have seemed vast to Director Ted Inman and his staff in the late 1970s. The site offered the ability for expansion, although the listed status of the World War One and later period buildings, meant that the skyline in the 'middle' could not be radically altered; that left the east (the M11 end) and the west. The collection of airframes, engines, vehicles, even small warships and submarines, grew at an incredible pace in the 1970s and 1980s, far out-stripping covered accommodation. By the early 1980s, land on the eastern edge was allocated for the creation of what is really called Hangar 1, but to almost everybody is known as the 'Superhangar', offering an additional 70,000 square feet of display space. The table 'Expansion Timeline – Major Building Projects' provides an overview of the incredible construction projects undertaken in the UK. Taking the title 'Home of the British Aircraft Collection', the 'Superhangar' was exactly that, a no-frills huge space with wide access doors, allowing easy changing of exhibits care of a large apron and from there on to the taxiways. A grant of 'just' £1.3 million highlighted the economic nature of this structure. The first aircraft, the Vulcan, was rolled into the cavernous space on 9th December 1985.

Duxford Aviation Society – British Airliner Collection

Arrived	Type	Identity	Built	Origin	Notes
1975	De Havilland Comet 4	G-APDB	1958	UK	see profile [1]
28 Jun 1975	Bristol Britannia 312*	G-AOVT	1958	UK	see profile
21 Feb 1976	Vickers Viscount 701*	G-ALWF	1952	UK	see profile [2]
20 Aug 1977	BAC/Sud Concorde 101	G-AXDN	1968	UK/France	–
15 Apr 1980	Vickers Super VC-10	G-ASGC	1964	UK	see profile
11 Jan 1981	Handley Page Hermes 4	G-ALDG	1950	UK	fuselage
13 Jun 1982	Hawker Siddeley Trident 2E	G-AVFB	1967	UK	see profile
Feb 1984	De Havilland Dove 6	G-ALFU	1949	UK	[3]
7 Jul 1985	Handley Page Herald 201	G-APWJ	1963	UK	see profile
23 May 1986	Avro York	G-ANTK	1945	UK	see profile
16 Oct 1986	Airspeed Ambassador*	G-ALZO	1952	UK	see profile
29 Oct 1992	BAC 111-510ED	G-AVMU	1968	UK	see profile

Notes: * – illustrated in the colour section. [1] Donated to East Anglian Aviation Society, flew in 12th February 1974; transferred to DAS on its establishment, 1975. [2] On loan from the Viscount Preservation Trust, signed over to DAS in December 2011. [3] Donated to IWM in 1973, transferred to DAS in February 1984.

With the 'Superhangar' up and running, thoughts turned to another display hall, this one to reflect the US heritage of Duxford and the East of England in general. IWM had all the credentials to tell the story of US air power in the UK from World War One to the present day. In July 1995, HLF cleared an award of £6.5 million out of an estimated £11 million required for the American Air Museum in Britain (AAM). IWM had for a long time fostered strong links with veteran organisations in the USA and a large fund-raising operation was set into being to generate lots of dollars to meet the difference in funding; this was achieved by a good margin.

Take a look at Chapter 6 for comments about the 'landmark' nature that HLF was looking for from the early 1990s; that's certainly what Sir Norman Foster provided at the west end of Duxford. Her Majesty Queen Elizabeth II opened the AAM at Duxford on August 1, 1997. Set on two levels, there are moments when visitors suddenly grasp that among all the aircraft and supporting exhibits is a B-52 Stratofortress, its 185ft wingspan emphasizing the size of the building. Two walls on the lower floor carry the names of 28,000 airmen lost in action. Around the outside of the curved walls is another form of remembrance – 52 glass panels entitled 'Counting the Cost', conceived by sculptor Renato Niemis. These carry outlines of the 7,031 US aircraft – fighters and bombers – lost in action during World War Two.

Expansion Timeline – Major Building Projects

1978	Battle of Britain Hall	Royal Air Force Museum, Hendon
1980	Concorde Museum, later including Leading Edge	Fleet Air Arm Museum, Yeovilton
1983	Bomber Command Hall	Royal Air Force Museum, Hendon
1985	'Superhangar'	Imperial War Museum, Duxford
1997	American Air Museum	Imperial War Museum, Duxford
1999	Cobham Hall, storage and archive facility	Fleet Air Arm Museum, Yeovilton
2002	Michael Beetham Conservation Centre	Royal Air Force Museum, Cosford
2003	Grahame-White Factory – 2011 Watch Tower added	Royal Air Force Museum, Hendon
2003	Milestones of Flight	Royal Air Force Museum, Hendon
2007	National Cold War Exhibition	Royal Air Force Museum, Cosford
2007	AirSpace – major reconstruction of 'Superhangar'	Imperial War Museum, Duxford

Not long after the opening, an impassioned (is there any *other* sort?) *FlyPast* reader wrote in to the editorial office and called the AAM, the "Black Hole", because "the aircraft are so densely packed that even light cannot escape from that dreadful building" and it certainly has developed a 'love it or loathe it' image. A major spin-off was that it freed up space elsewhere within the IWM complex for more exhibits to go under

The delicate task of 'hanging' aircraft within the AAM. The Avenger getting ready of 'flight' with the T-33, TB-29, B-52 and U-2 behind. *IWM*

cover. AAM eventually revealed a major impracticality; the impossibility of most airframes to move without extensive surgery to the structure. In 2011 it was announced that a major refurbishment of the building would take place in 2014, including the removal of the otherwise fixed glass 'wall'. Inspection of the B-17G *Mary Alice* had shown popped rivets and corrosion that could not wait until the major reshuffle. During March 2010 a complex, time-consuming, 'eye of the needle' operation started to take the bomber to Hangar 5 for restoration. With just 2½ inches to spare, the fuselage and wings went through the 9ft 4in 'main' door in the glass wall; all of this was only possible because the B-17 was the closest airframe to the 'exit'.

By 2000 more thoughts had been given to the 'Superhangar' (Hangar 1) because it had the potential to evolve and grow. The scheme was to 'stretch' the building forwards, towards the flight line, and expand both sides, increasing the display space by 40%. There would also be an education centre, a 'hands-on' learning area and – at the flight line end – a capacious conservation centre. At the same time, the beams in the structure were to be 'beefed up' to allow for a number of aircraft to be 'flown' in the otherwise dead space of the already tall building. This would allow for a significant number of airframes previously displayed outside to come indoors to what was inevitably called the 'Super-Superhangar'. Space freed in the other hangars allowed still more aircraft to come off the flight line. As related earlier, the contents of the 'Superhangar' had been referred to as the 'Home of the British Aircraft Collection' and for the new creation – to be called AirSpace – this theme was extended. BAE Systems saw it as a 'shop window' for its heritage and came to an agreement with IWM to sponsor the new project to the tune of £5 million, including some serious hardware – including a Strikemaster, Jaguar and Tornado and, later, a prototype Typhoon. HLF joined in during September 2001 with £9 million for the £19.3 million enterprise and the East of England Development Agency also pledged its support. Richard Ashton became Director IWM in November 2004 and was pitched straight into the challenging logistics of preparing airframes for AirSpace, planning the 'chess game' of aircraft across the site that would be required in the re-shuffle the expanded building allowed; plus myriad other elements

Balconies on three sides allow incredible access to the 'upper' levels of AirSpace; in the foreground the DAS Dove and Comet 4. *Ken Ellis*

including overseeing the exceptional 'learning zone' on the balcony of the 'west' wing. AirSpace was opened in a phased manner from the summer of 2007 and within it are 30 significant airframes in a spacious and thoughtfully laid out manner. Among them are the following large exhibits: Comet 4, Concorde 101, Hastings C.1A, Lancaster X, Sunderland MR.5 and a Vulcan B.2 – emphasizing the scale of this enormous undertaking.

Airspeed Ambassador G-ALZO
1952 | Medium-range airliner | Two 2,625hp Bristol Centaurus 661

With a dismal production run of 23, there could be an argument that the sole surviving Ambassador only has rarity on its side as an argument for preservation. Christchurch-based Airspeed had been a de Havilland company since 1940, but traded under its own name. De Havilland was seeking additional production capacity and a gifted design house and it is likely the Ambassador would have been the last new type to carry the Airspeed label no matter how well it sold. British European Airways (BEA) became the only customer, calling the type the 'Elizabethan', and it proved to be a very workmanlike airliner, well regarded by passengers. BEA took delivery of G-ALZO *Christopher Marlowe* at Heathrow Airport on 25th November 1952. Upon retirement *Zulu-Oscar* was one of two that joined the Royal Jordanian Air Force, as 108, from 20th May 1960 on VIP duties. Replaced by Heralds (see below) in early 1963, G-ALZO and 'Y were traded in to Handley Page but quickly snapped up by Dan-Air which along with BEA was most associated with the type.

On 26th September 1971 G-ALZO embarked on its last revenue-earning flight, from Gatwick to Jersey and return. On the 29th *Zulu-Oscar* flew a 'Champagne Charter' to Reims for airline employees and friends and then positioned to Dan-Air's engineering base at Lasham. From there the ultimate Ambassador flight was staged early in October when a Rolls-Royce Spey was flown out to Zagreb, Yugoslavia, to a stranded BAC 111. Returning to Lasham, it joined three others (G-ALZR, G-AMAE and 'H) awaiting the scrap man's torch. By late 1972 G-ALZO was the sole survivor and it was passed on to the Dan-Air Preservation Group. In 1985 the Ambassador and York G-ANTK (see below) were donated to the Duxford Aviation Society. A team from DAS, eight stalwarts appropriately calling themselves 'The Elizabethans', dismantled G-ALZO over a four-day period and signed the hull and painted on the legend 'Moved Faster than Epsom Salts'! *Zulu-Oscar* departed for Duxford on 16th October 1986 and in 2013 it was nearing the end of an epic restoration.

Avro Anson I N4877
1938 | Three-crew general reconnaissance aircraft | Two 350hp Armstrong Siddeley Cheetah IX

It was impossible to choose a single example of the 'Faithful Annie' to profile; so as well as IWM's Mk.I turn to Chapter 3 for the Avro Nineteen at Shuttleworth. N4877 and the Hastings, below, were once part of the pioneering Skyfame Collection which is detailed in the narrative above. Built in 1938 and test flown from Woodford, Anson I N4877 was issued to 26 Maintenance Unit (MU) at Cardington on 17th November and was not released for active service until 2nd May 1940 when it joined 3 Ferry Pilots Pool, part of the Air Transport Auxiliary (ATA), based at the organisation's headquarters at White Waltham. ATA pilots were civilians delivering aircraft from manufacturers to MUs, or ferrying them from one unit to another and N4877 acted as a 'taxi' dropping off, or picking up ATA personnel. The men and women of this quite small organisation provided a unique contribution during World War Two. With the occasional interruption for repairs, N4877 served ATA until an accident put it out of action in late 1943. It was not declared as repaired until 25th March 1946 and the following month the Anson was taken on charge by the School of Flying Control at Watchfield. The unit was renamed as the School of Air Traffic Control in November 1946.

Retirement came on 14th March 1950 and it was acquired by Air Navigation and Trading Ltd at Squires Gate, Blackpool, taking on the civilian registration G-AMDA on 20th July 1950. In July 1955 it joined the fleet of Derby Aviation at Burnaston and was used for aerial survey work; including time trailing a magnetometer probe on a cable with associate company Canadian Aero Services. Later in its career, the Anson served with the London School of Flying at Elstree (which had been owned by Derby Aviation since 1952) and it was there that it was ferried to Staverton to become a founder member of the Skyfame Collection in late 1963. As related above, Skyfame closed in 1978 with most of the airframes going to Duxford in an epic logistics exercise. It is displayed within AirSpace, in the colours of 500 Squadron.

Anson I G-AMDA of the London School of Flying on a rare sortie out of Elstree, September 1962. *Stuart Howe*

Avro York G-ANTK
1945 | Five-crew long-range military transport / airliner | Four 1,280hp Rolls-Royce Merlin 24

In an incredible adaptation, Avro grafted an entirely new and capacious fuselage on to the wings and tail of a Lancaster to create the York which became a loyal transport for the RAF and a hard-working post-war airliner and later freighter. Built as York I MW232 at Avro's factory at Yeadon (now Leeds-Bradford Airport) it joined 242 Squadron on 7th January 1946 at Merryfield, moving to Oakington in May. On 5th June 1947 the York relocated to Lyneham, joining 511 Squadron. From June 1948 to May 1949, MW232 and much of the York fleet, were to be found in West Germany flying intensively along the narrow air corridors to airfields in the Western sectors of Berlin during the Airlift. MW232 was the centre of publicity when it carried the 100,000th ton of supplies into the besieged city. Thus the York became an early 'Cold War Warrior'; the only other survivor, the RAF Museum's TS798, is displayed within Cosford's exhibition dedicated to the ideological conflict. By May 1950 MW232 was with Avro for major work, reportedly in preparation for a two-month stint with Fairey Aviation for flight refuelling trials, but so far nothing has been unearthed of this.

Placed into long term store, MW232 was acquired by Dan-Air in July 1954, registered as G-ANTK, and worked hard for its living flying out of Blackbushe and later Gatwick. Services included MoD contracts to and from the rocket trials site at Woomera in Australia. The last of its fleet of six freighters, Dan-Air retired *Tango-Kilo* on 30th April 1964 to its engineering base at Lasham. That October it was donated to the Lasham Air Scouts for use as a bunkhouse. On 7th May 1974, its significance was recognised and the Air Scouts received Comet 4 G-APDK instead and the nascent Dan-Air Preservation Group took care of the York, until it folded in 1982. The Duxford Aviation Society had been eyeing the York for some time and on 23rd May 1986 it arrived at its new home. It had been dismantled and loaded by a team calling themselves 'The Yorkies', who were soon to come back for the Ambassador – see above. After a major, long-term, restoration G-ANTK was installed into AirSpace in 2007.

York G-ANTK in use as a bunkhouse at Lasham, April 1969. *Sam Tyler*

BAC 111-510ED G-AVMU
1968 | 97-109-seat short-/medium-range airliner | Two 12,000lb st Rolls-Royce Spey 512-14E

Two Weybridge products, the Viscount and the BAC 111, championed British production runs until the advent of Airbus and the eventual eroding of Boeing's pre-dominance. The Duxford Aviation Society has examples of both of these game-changers in its collection. *Mike-Uniform* first flew at Hurn (now Bournemouth Airport) on 29th January 1969 and was delivered to British European Airways (BEA) on 19th March, being based at the airline's 111 'hub', Birmingham Airport. BEA and British Overseas Airways Corporation morphed into British Airways in April 1974 and, as *Mike-Uniform* was repainted, it gained the name *County of Dorset* on the nose. As BA5383, G-AVMU carried out its last revenue flight on 16th October 1992, from Dusseldorf to Birmingham; positioning to Hurn for storage on the 29th. Donated to the Duxford Aviation Society it touched down at its new home on 4th March 1993, completing 45,541 landings and 40,280 flying hours.

BAC Strikemaster Mk.80 1133
1976 | Two-crew light strike and weapons trainer | One 3,410lb st Bristol Siddeley Viper 535

After the cancellation of TSR-2 in April 1965 (see Chapter 6) the Jet Provost T.5 for the RAF and the 'beefed up' Strikemaster light strike version are regarded by many within the then newly-created British Aircraft Corporation as helping to keep the wolf from the door at Warton. The Jet Provost is another type that requires at least two exhibit profiles; turn to Chapter 6 for the prototype.

Wearing the 'B Condition' (or 'trade-plate') identity G-27-297, Strikemaster 1133 took to the air for the first time at Warton in 1976, one of the last of an order of 45 for the Royal Saudi Air Force, deliveries of which had commenced in 1967. It was placed on the UK civil register as G-BESY in April 1977, perhaps for demonstration purposes, before being ferried to its new home as 1133 in July. Laid up by 1996, the aircraft was selected for the BAE Systems-supported AirSpace hall and was brought back to Warton, where it was prepared for display. Delivered by road to Duxford on 22nd March 2000, it was handed over in an official ceremony on 13th April. It was installed within AirSpace in 2007.

Boeing TB-29A Superfortress 461748
1945 | Ten-crew long-range bomber | Four 2,200hp Wright Cyclone R-3350

With its own B-17G Flying Fortress, the airworthy *Sally B* operated by B-17 Preservation and the B-52 (see below), Duxford offers a concentration of Boeing 'heavies' unrivalled outside of the USA. The B-29's place in history was assured with the dropping of the two atomic bombs on Hiroshima and Nagasaki in August 1945. B-29s made very few visits to the UK during World War Two, but beyond 1945 deployments by Strategic Air Command to Britain were frequent and included the much-improved B-50 model, including tankers. The RAF used B-29s, under the designation Washington B.1, to bolster Bomber Command from 1950 with the last examples leaving service in 1958.

B-29A 44-61748 was built at Renton, Washington State, and was accepted by the USAAF on 25th May 1945. It spent its time in 'limbo', some of it at the famous Davis-Monthan 'boneyard' in Arizona. In March 1952 it joined the 307th Bomb Group operating from Kadena on Okinawa for combat missions over Korea. It was with the 307th that it got the name *Hawg Wild* and it clocked up 105 missions. It returned to Davis-Monthan after hostilities finished in October 1954 and in 1955 was modified to TB-29A crew trainer status. By November 1956 it was with the Naval Ordnance Test Station at China Lake, California, with target-towing gear under the rear fuselage. In due course *Hawg Wild* was retired and became a range target at China Lake, thankfully during this time the only damage it received was to a wing tip. IWM had long been looking for a B-29 for Duxford and this one had nothing but good vibes coming out of it. Aero Services were contracted to work on the bomber and return it flying condition – by far the most cost-effective way of bringing it to the UK. A team of six mechanics toiled at China Lake for nearly a year. In September 1979 it was registered as G-BHDK in readiness for its ferry flight – gear down – from China Lake to Aero Services' facility at Tucson, Arizona, in November 1979. Another three months preparation was needed before the big day arrived. It was reported at the time the cost of resurrecting the B-29 came to around £40,000 – about £280,000 in present-day values. Crewed by pilots Skip Creiger and Don Davies, Henry Raimey as navigator and Jack Kern flight engineer, *Delta-Kilo* departed Tucson on 17th February 1980. The routing was: Flint, Michigan; Loring, Maine; Gander, Newfoundland; Sondestrom Fjord, Greenland (seven-day layover because of extreme weather); Keflavik, Iceland; touching down at Mildenhall on 1st March. The following day the B-29 arrived at Duxford, the only one of its type to have been preserved in Europe.

Boeing B-52D Stratofortress 60689
1957 | Six-crew strategic bomber | Eight 12,100lb st Pratt & Whitney J57-P-19W

It must have been an awesome sight, Brize Norton 16th January 1957 and B-52B *City of Turlock* of the 93rd Bomb Wing was inbound – the first visit by the eight-engined giant to the UK. From then on Stratofortresses became fairly regular visitors. In February 1991 the massive bombers used Fairford as the lift-off point for raids into Iraq during Operation DESERT STORM. B-52s were back at Fairford in anger in 1999 for strikes against targets within the former Yugoslavia and in 2003 Iraq was again the destination during Operation IRAQI FREEDOM. A B-52 for IWM was a 'must' and in October 1983 the US Department of Defense presented a Vietnam-veteran B-52D to the UK with Duxford determined as its destination. Built by Boeing at Wichita, Kansas, 56-0689 was delivered to the USAF on 11th October 1957.

Like most B-52s, it had a complex history, joining a wide range of Bomb Wings (BW) across the USA and with regular deployments to South East Asia. These are best presented in table form:

Oct 1957	28th BW, Ellsworth, South Dakota
Feb 1960	95th BW, Biggs, Texas
Jun 1964	494th BW, Sheppard, Texas
Apr 1966	509th BW, Pease, New Hampshire
Jul 1966	91st BW, Glasgow, Montana
Sep 1966	91st BW – deployed to Andersen, Guam
Jul 1967	99th BW, Westover, Massachusetts, with deployments to Guam and U-Tapao, Thailand
Apr 1968	306th BW, McCoy, Florida
Jun 1969	Andersen, used in 'pool' by 454th and then 509th BW
Jan 1969	U-Tapao, used in 'pool'
Sep 1969	99th BW – deployed at U-Tapao
Aug 1970	99th BW, Westover
Nov 1971	99th BW – deployed at U-Tapao
Sep 1972	96th BW – deployed at Andersen
Nov 1972	7th BW, Carswell, Texas
Dec 1972	99th BW – deployed at Andersen
Jul 1973	7th BW, Carswell – with deployments to Andersen and U-Tapao
Mar 1975	96th BW, Dyess, Texas -with deployments to Andersen and U-Tapao
Oct 1982	7th BW, Carswell

During its time 56-0689 had taken part in 200 combat missions over Vietnam, including the ROLLING THUNDER (1964 to 1968); LINEBACKER I (May to October 1972) and LINEBACKER II (December 1972) campaigns. A 7th BW crew brought the B-52D across from Texas, dropping into the USAF base at Mildenhall to allow for a ground-based 'look-see' at the runway at Duxford – the M11 motorway having brought the length down to 4,930ft. On 8th October 1983 it made a long, flat approach from the east to Runway 24 and comfortably came to a stop. The largest aircraft preserved in the UK had arrived.

Bristol F.2b E2581
1918 | Two-crew fighter | One 275hp Rolls-Royce Falcon III

The Bristol F.2b was an important fighter, first introduced in 1917 it provided a combination of reliability, good performance and the ability to deal out – and take – punishment. Production wound down dramatically in 1919, but it was so well-suited to Army co-operation, or 'air policing', and later training, that it stayed in production until 1927. The last were withdrawn from RAF service in 1932. Built by Bristol, E2581 was issued to 39 Squadron on 20th September 1918 at Hounslow. Its frontline service was brief, it joined 1 Communications Squadron at Hendon on 22nd November, by which time the Armistice had been in force eleven days. It was back at Hounslow on 11th December, with the South Eastern Area Headquarters Flight. It didn't stray far, going on 30th April 1919 to 30 Training Depot Station at Northolt for service with its subsidiary unit 2 Group Communications Flight. It was withdrawn from use on 22nd April 1920 and, as seen in Chapter 2, took part in the IWM's exhibition at Crystal Palace. Stored afterwards, most likely in the Science Museum building, it was on show at South Lambeth from 1936. It came to Duxford in 1984 and was restored.

Bristol Britannia 312 G-AOVT
1958 | Long range airliner | Four 4,120hp Bristol Proteus 755

Victor-Tango was the last Series 312 'Whispering Giant' to be delivered to British Overseas Airways Corporation. It first took to the skies on 17th December 1958 and was delivered from Filton to Heathrow on New Year's Day 1959. It joined the Liverpool-based British Eagle International Airlines from September 1963, named originally *Enterprise*, and later as *Ajax*. The Britannia started work with the fleet of Monarch Airlines at Luton on 18th August 1968. It carried out the last all-passenger service in Europe by a Britannia, flying from Lisbon, Portugal, to Luton on 14th October 1974 for Monarch. After this, *Victor-Tango* was stripped out for freight operations and leased to Invicta International Airlines and based at Manston, from 13th December 1974. Its last commercial flight came on 10th March 1975 from Tripoli, Libya, to Manston. Presented to the Duxford Aviation Society, it was flown from Luton on 29th June 1975, arriving in the middle of an airshow in real style! With this *Victor-Tango* clocked up 10,760 landings and 35,739 flying hours.

Bristol F.2b E2581, one of the aircraft displayed at the Imperial War Museum's Crystal Palace Exhibition in the early 1920s. *Ken Ellis*

De Havilland Comet 4 G-APDB
1958 | Long-range airliner | Four 10,500lb st Rolls-Royce Avon 524

Two Comet 4s facing one another, ready to roll down two runways – with the Atlantic Ocean in between. *Delta-Bravo* was about to enter the history books, on 4th October 1958, by operating the first scheduled service by a jet airliner from New York to London, taking just 6 hours, 11 minutes to do it. Coming the other way was G-APDC and as the two passed each other in mid-ocean they exchanged pleasantries over the radio. Just 22 days later US airline Pan American put its Boeing 707s into service on the New York to Paris route.

Delta-Bravo first flew at Hatfield on 27th July 1958 and was delivered to British Overseas Airways Corporation at Heathrow on 12th September prior to a ceremony of hand-over, with *Delta-Charlie*, 19 days later. Phased out in favour of 707s in 1965, G-APDB was sold to Malaysian Singapore Airlines as 9M-AOB on 11th September. Prolific UK Comet operator Dan-Air bought 9M-AOB and, re-registered as G-APDB, it arrived at the airline's engineering base at Lasham on 16th September 1969. It last revenue-earning service took place on 12th November 1973, routing Alicante, Spain, to Tees-side. Ever mindful of the need to preserve airliners, management at Dan-Air decided that *Delta-Bravo* should be donated to the East Anglian Aviation Society. It touched down on 12th February 1974, completing 15,733 landings and 36,269 hours. In 1975 the Duxford Aviation Society was established and ownership was transferred; the Comet becoming the founder-member of what became the British Airliner Collection. See also Chapter 6 for the story of an early Comet survivor, Mk.1X G-APAS.

Douglas C-47A Skytrain 315509
1944 | Four-crew parachute and general duties transport | Two 1,200hp Pratt & Whitey R-1830-92

Wearing the markings it carried while flying towards the D-Day beachhead, Skytrain 315509 is the only World War Two combat veteran inside the American Air Museum. A Dakotas could have been chosen for an exhibit profile, but this pedigree alone makes the IWM example stand out. Built by Douglas at its Long Beach, California, factory as C-47A 43-15509, it was accepted by the USAAF on 4th April 1944 and assigned for operations with the Ninth Air Force in the UK on 28th May. Upon arrival, it joined the 37th Troop Carrier Squadron (TCS), part of the 316th Troop Carrier Group (TCG) at Cottesmore. On the night of 5th June 1944, the C-47A was part of a massed launch, dropping US paratroops near St Mere Eglise early on the morning of D-Day. For Operation MARKET, 315509 took US paratroopers to drop zone 'N' on 17th September 1944. The following day it was towing a Waco CG-4 bound for Landing Zone 'T' near Groesbeek, but the tow rope severed over the Channel – the personnel in the glider were rescued. On 9th October 1944, the C-47A moved a short distance south to Spanhoe to the 315th TCG, and its 34th TCS. From this Northamptonshire airfield,

C-47 Skytrains at Cottesmore, lined-up ready for an airborne 'op', possibly Operation VARSITY. To the left are aircraft from the 37th Troop Carrier Squadron with which the Duxford example served 1944-1945. *KEC*

315509 took part in Operation VARSITY, the Rhine Crossing, on 24th March 1945, carrying British airborne troops and returned with light flak damage to both wings. The 315th redeployed to Amiens in France on 6th April 1945 and by the end of the following month, returned to the USA.

Skytrain 315509 was disposed of via Canadair of Montreal, Canada, on 11th October 1945 and on 10th December it was sold to AB Aerotransport, Swedish Airlines, becoming SE-BBH *Vraken*. In 1948 it joined the combined fleet of Scandinavian Airlines Systems and was renamed *Helge Viking*. By 1953 the C-47A was in the USA, registered as N9985F briefly before becoming N51V with Piedmont Aviation. Retired from airline use in 1962, it was time for a second period of military service, on 5th May 1962 'enlisting' with the Ejercito del Aire Espanol, the Spanish Air Force, as T3-29. In 1977 the C-47A was withdrawn from use and put into store at Cuatro Vientos, Madrid. Mike Woodley, managing director of Aces High, acquired T3-29 and registered it as G-BHUB on 30th April 1980. Painted as 'G-AGIV' and with 'Ruskin Air Services' titling, it took part in the filming of the ITV series *Airline* at Duxford and elsewhere. Screened in 1982, *Airline* was the story of Jack Ruskin, played by Roy Marsden, and his struggles to operate a small business using Dakotas. In 1981 IWM acquired 315509 and it was painted in 316th TCG colours.

English Electric Lightning F.1 XM135
1959 | Single-seat interceptor | Two 11,250lb st Rolls-Royce Avon 210

It was a 'rogue' and beginning to frustrate the personnel of 33 Maintenance Unit (MU) at Lyneham. Lightning F.1 XM135 had arrived on 13th January 1965 and was due to enter service with the Target Facilities Flight (TFF) at Leuchars, but an electrical fault was defeating all efforts to cure it. Wg Cdr Walter Holden was the Commanding Officer of 33 MU and an engineer. Writing in the Spitfire Flying Club's journal, Wg Cdr Holden described the nature of the 'glitch' on XM135: "...on the initial few yards of a take-off run, the inverter, supplying power to the primary flight instruments, would cut out and the stand-by inverter would have to cut in, clearly an unsatisfactory state of affairs." The 'techies' had placed a web of wires within the cockpit, so that a pilot could wind up XM135, let it trundle along as if for take-off, and by throwing temporary switches, isolate parts of the circuits until the problem was tracked down. This might take several runs, but it *would* work. The wiring required the removal of the canopy. Wg Cdr Holden had learned to fly on de Havilland Tiger Moths of his University Air Squadron and also had time on DHC Chipmunks and Airspeed Oxfords. He'd flown in a couple of jets, including a Gloster Javelin T.3, but only as a passenger. With the MU slated for closure, pilots for test flights were brought in from other units and there were none available for quite some time. With his piloting knowledge and a briefing on start-up procedure from his trusted ground crew, the 'boss' decided to run the tests himself. Towed out to the disused Runway 36, the Avons were fired up and the first test went well. On the second run the reheat locked in and XM135 thundered down the runway. Ahead a fuel bowser was crossing the runway and a de Havilland Comet transport was rolling for take-off down Runway 25. The 'Wingco' was strapped in, the Martin-Baker ejection seat had all the pins in and was safe, the undercarriage was likewise secured by the external locks and he was climbing at around 250 knots. Gathering his wits, the reheat 'gate' was found and the throttle brought down to less severe speeds. In the back of his head, Holden remembered that a Lightning came over 'the numbers' at about 150 knots. Having ascertained that the Comet was safely out of the circuit – he had no radio – he familiarised himself with the controls and elected to make an approach on the active runway – 25. Too high, too fast, he went around again and while his second approach taught him much, a go-round was prudent. Not liking the look of the approach to 25, there being a valley in front of it, Holden went for the nominally downwind end, 07. He touched down, but being used to 'tail-draggers', bumped the rear end, pulled the brake 'chute and came to a halt! It's not known if he put 12 minute as pilot-in-command in his logbook!

Tim Ferguson took XM135 for its first-ever flight, from Samlesbury on 14th November 1959. It was delivered on 25th May 1960 to the Air Fighting Development Squadron, temporarily 'bolt-holed' at Leconfield, but normally resident at Coltishall. On 29th February 1963 it joined 74 Squadron, at Coltishall, transferring on 30th July 1964 to 226 Operational Conversion Unit, also based at the Norfolk airfield. The history then pauses for its sojourn at Lyneham, as related above. Cured of its electrical problems, XM135 finally got to the TFF at Leuchars on 20th September 1966. It was brought to 60 MU at Leconfield on 29th June 1971 for a major overhaul but was retained for pilot currency flying and carried '60 MU Flagship' lettering below the canopy. Allocated to IWM, it was flown to Duxford on 20th November 1974, bringing its total flying time to 1,343 hours. Take of look at Chapter 5 for the career of an F.6 version.

Lighting F.1 XM135 in 74 Squadron colours, awaiting its turn to move across to AirSpace, 2006. *Ken Ellis*

Fairchild A-10 Thunderbolt II
1979 | Single-seat ground-attack fighter | Two 9,055lb st General Electric TF-34

While deserving its nickname of 'Warthog', the A-10 remains a very potent strike weapon, its huge seven-barrel GAU-8/A 30mm rotary cannon giving it exceptional fire power. The first A-10s arrived at Bentwaters for the 81st Tactical Fighter Wing (TFW) in August 1978 and the last one left the UK in March 1993 – as such the A-10 was an important UK-based American aircraft. Fairchild acquired Republic in 1965, hence the A-10 took on the name Thunderbolt II, in deference to the World War Two P-47 (an example of which is underneath the A-10 in the American Air Museum). Built at Hagerstown, Maryland, 77-0259 was issued to the 81st TFW at Bentwaters on 26th March 1979, being allocated to the constituent 510th Tactical Fighter Squadron (TFS). From 19th August 1981 it served with the Air National Guard (ANG), starting with the 176th TFS, 128th TFW at Truax, Wisconsin. Then it was off to Willow Grove, Pennsylvania, and the 103rd Tactical Air Support Squadron, 111th Tactical Air Support Group. By 1990 it had reverted to the Wisconsin ANG at Truax and in July that year the 176th deployed to Sculthorpe in Norfolk under Exercise CORONET LARIAT. It was exchanged with the 81st TFW and re-acquainted itself with Bentwaters. This was only brief, for the 'Warthog' was issued to the 509th TFS which was based with the 10th TFW at Alconbury. While the Bentwaters and Woodbridge A-10s were deployed to Saudi Arabia for DESERT STORM, much of 509th remained at Alconbury, including 77-0259. With the de-activation of the Alconbury A-10s, 77-0259 was presented to IWM and flew into Duxford on 6th February 1992. A 10th TFW fact sheet released at the time put a price tag of $8.7 million on the 'Warthog'.

Fairey Gannet ECM.6 XG797
1957 | Three-crew electronic countermeasures platform | One 3,035hp Armstrong Siddeley Double Mamba 101

Turn to Chapter 4 for the much-developed, airborne early warning version of the Gannet, the AEW.3. IWM's Gannet was built at Hayes as an AS.4 sub-hunter and taken to Ringway (now Manchester Airport) for flight-testing; having its maiden flight on 8th March 1957. It was issued to 810 Squadron at Culdrose on 1st May 1959, before moving to the operational trials unit 700 Squadron at Yeovilton on 30th August 1960. During this time it was deployed for a while in 1961 to the Indian Navy carrier, *Vikrant*. Its role was to change considerably when it was moved to Lee-on-Solent in December 1963 for conversion to ECM.6 status. Work complete, it was taken on charge by 831 Squadron at Watton on 17th May 1965. Its time with 831 was brief, the unit disbanding and the role was discontinued on 16th May 1966. Its final bought of service came with the Headquarters Flight of 849 Squadron – the Gannet AEW.3 unit – at Brawdy from 10th July 1967. It was retired to Arbroath on 7th August 1968, becoming an instructional airframe with a total flying time of 794 hours. It was delivered by road to Duxford on 21st May 1972.

Gloster Javelin FAW.9 XH897
1958 | Two-crew all-weather interceptor | Two 11,000lb st Bristol Siddeley Sapphire 210

Any Javelin is good-looking, but the Duxford example is the best of them all! Completed at Hucclecote in December 1958 as an FAW.7, XH897 served with 25 Squadron at Waterbeach from 12th March 1959. From April 1960 it was converted to FAW.9 status at Hucclecote. It next served with 33 Squadron at Middleton St George, from 3rd January 1961 and then joined 5 Squadron at Geilenkirchen, West Germany, on 21st November 1962. Briefly retired to 27 Maintenance Unit at Shawbury in October 1963, it moved to the test fleet of Bristol Siddeley Engines at Filton on 20th July 1965. From 1st April 1968 it was taken on charge by 'A' Squadron of the Aeroplane & Armament Experimental Establishment at Boscombe Down. Up to August 1968 all of this had been done in camouflage, but then that XH897 took on the superb red-and-white colour scheme. It served on a variety of trials at Boscombe until 24th January 1975 when it was ferried to Duxford, the last flight of the type.

Handley Page Hastings C.1A TG528
1948 | Long-range transport / paratroop aircraft | Four 1,650hp Bristol Hercules 102

Hastings took over the transport role from Avro Yorks (see above) for the first time in September 1948. The type served on until the late 1960s when it was replaced by the Armstrong Whitworth Argosy and Lockheed Hercules (see Chapter 6) but crew trainer versions served on for another decade. IWM's example was one of

Javelin FAW.9 XH897 on the Duxford apron in 1982 – 64 Squadron examples parked on this hardstanding in 1961. Behind is the Saro SR.A/1 TG263 of the Skyfame Collection, later handed on to Solent Sky at Southampton. *Ken Ellis*

the first off the production line at Radlett and was issued to 47 Squadron at Dishforth on 12th October 1948 as a C.1. (It was later upgraded to C.1A status with additional fuel tanks.) Twenty-one days after TG528 joined 47, it and much of the unit, settled in at Schleswigland in Northern Germany to take part in the Berlin Airlift. This astounding operation, supplying the beleaguered capital with all of its needs by air, came to a halt on 12th May 1949. In July TG528 had settled at Topcliffe, 47's new base from the following month. Like many of the breed, TG528 had a long and varied history, alternating repairs and modifications with a variety of units. On 3rd July 1953 TG528 was at Lyneham and operating in a 'pool' with 53 and 99 Squadrons. From 5th April 1956 the transport was back at Dishforth, this time in the training role with 242 Operational Conversion Unit until October 1963. It was used in the tactical transport role from 2nd July 1964 when TG528 was issued to the 'pool' of 24 and 36 Squadrons at Colerne. In July 1967, 36 Squadron made the leap to the Hercules C.1 and moved to Lyneham, leaving 24 to soldier on, ready for its turn with the 'Herk' in January 1968. Knowing that 24 was due to re-equip, the Skyfame Museum approached the RAF about taking on a Hastings. Bill Betteridge, John Fairey, Peter Swettenham and the Skyfame Supporters Society stumped up for TG528 and the transport flew into Staverton on January 24, 1968. As explained at the beginning of this chapter, like most of the collection, TG528 was moved to Duxford following the closure of Skyfame, arriving on 1st April 1979. The transport has had two restorations in its time, the latest one in 2006 in readiness for its installation in AirSpace.

Shortly after its arrival at Staverton, crowds queue to hazard the ladder and have a view inside Hastings C.1A TG268, 1968. *KEC*

Handley Page Herald 201 G-APWJ
1963 | Short/medium-range airliner | Two 1,910hp Rolls-Royce Dart 527

Starting off as a four-engined piston-powered airliner in 1958, the Herald adopted two of the spectacularly successful Rolls-Royce Dart turboprops in 1958, but the production run only amounted to 50 units when the line was wound up in the summer of 1968. *Whisky-Juliet* was the tenth built from scratch with Darts, flying from Radlett for the first time on 29th May 1963. It was delivered to Jersey on 13th June for the Channel Island division of British United Airways. In July 1970 the airline was restructured as British Island Airways, with G-APWJ continuing to be based either at Jersey or Blackpool. It was transferred to Air UK at Norwich Airport on 15th May 1980; its last services being flown in June 1985. It was donated to the Duxford Aviation Society and arrived at its new home on 7th July 1985 – a 30-minute 'hop' from Norwich.

Hawker Siddeley Trident 2E G-AVFB
1967 | Medium-range airliner | Three 11,930lb st Rolls-Royce Spey 512/5W

As can been seen above, IWM's C-47 Skytrain came home with bullet holes in it in March 1945. In May 1977 a Trident landed at London's Heathrow Airport, not a remarkable thing in itself, but G-AVFB had several bullet holes carefully patched up. It disappeared into the vast British Airways (BA) engineering base for a long period, to lick its wounds. Built for British European Airways (BEA), *Fox-Bravo* had its maiden flight from Hatfield on 2nd November 1967 and was delivered to Heathrow on 6th June 1968. It was leased to associate airline Cyprus Airways as 5B-DAC from March 1972 and was acquired by the company in June of the following year. On 20th July 1974 Turkish armed forces invaded Cyprus with airborne forces in helicopters, Douglas C-47s and Transall C-160s and an amphibious assault. This was in response to a Greek nationalist coup five days previously. At Nicosia Airport, there was a series of fire-fights and Trident 5B-DAC was one of the casualties, although a minor one. On 15th August 1974 the so-called 'Attila' line was drawn across the island and this demarcation remains to the present day. The previous April, BEA and British Overseas Airways Corporation had merged into BA. In 1977 a team of BA engineers were very surprised at how good 5B-DAC was and BA acquired the airframe on 12th May 1977. The patched-up tri-jet was flown back to Heathrow for a full refurbish. Painted in BA colours it plied the airways until its final revenue-earning service, from London to Manchester on 27th March 1982. Donated to the Duxford Aviation Society, *Fox-Bravo* arrived during an airshow on 13th June 1982 and gave a display before touching down. It had completed 11,726 landings and 21,642 flying hours. In 1990 G-AVFB was repainted into the original BEA colours it wore on delivery in 1968.

Lockheed U-2CT 66692
1956 | Single-seat strategic reconnaissance platform | One 17,000lb st Pratt & Whitney J75-P-13B

One of the iconic aircraft of the 'Cold War', the designation 'U-2' became a household name with the shooting down of Gary Powers in a Central Intelligence Agency (CIA) operated example in May 1960 and the disturbing images of Soviet missiles being assembled on Cuba brought back by one of the long-winged 'snoopers' in October 1962. The Americans took little time in deploying U-2s to the UK. The prototype made its first flight in 1955 and in April the following year two were operating from Lakenheath under the auspices of the CIA, but apparently with the 1st Weather Reconnaissance Squadron. Visits since have been sporadic but from 1982 until 1993 Alconbury was home to the 9th Reconnaissance Wing, operating U-2Rs and the TR-1 battlefield surveillance version. U-2Rs and TR-1s were still on the active list with the USAF in 2013.

Duxford's U-2C was completed at Lockheed's Bakersfield, California, facility and first flew in October 1956 at Groom Lake, Nevada. It was flown in a Douglas C-124 Globemaster II to Giebelstadt, West Germany, the following month and began over-flights of the USSR. By June 1958 it was at Atsugi in Japan taking a close look at the *other* end of Soviet territory. In December 1960 it was handed on by the CIA to the USAF, joining the 4080th Strategic Reconnaissance Wing at Laughlin, Texas, and was then converted by Lockheed to a U-2F. The CIA was back in charge of 56-6692 in June 1964 with missions out of Taoyuan, Taiwan, until 1966. For the next six years it was mostly operating out of Edwards, California, on evaluation work; by 1968 with the 6515th Test Squadron. Lockheed brought it back to U-2C standard in August 1974 and in January 1976 it was turned into a two-seater by removing the camera bay behind the pilot and putting in another, raised, cockpit. In this guise it served with the 100th Strategic Reconnaissance Wing (SRW) at Davis-Monthan, Arizona, and then the 9th SRW at Beale, California. It had its last flight on 28th December 1987 and it was freighted to Alconbury on 22nd February 1988 for battle damage repair training. It was decided that this was a poor fate for such a vital airframe and it was donated to IWM. Work was carried out at Alconbury to return it to single-seat U-2C guise. It was delivered by road on 26th June 1992 and now 'flies' within the AAM.

Lockheed SR-71A Blackbird 17962
1966 | Two-crew, high-speed strategic reconnaissance platform | Two 35,200lb st Pratt & Whitney J-58

Like the U-2, above, the SR-71 is emblematic of the 'Cold War'. Only 32 were built, but the type held a fascination for decades, at first cloaked in secrecy then, thanks to the occasional airshow appearance and record-breaking flights, an 'open' and awesome flying machine. Duxford's example, 64-17962 first took to the air on 29th April 1966 and was issued to the following month to the 9th Strategic Reconnaissance Wing (SRW) at Beale, California. Crewed by Robert Helt and Larry Elliott, 64-17962 was used to establish a world altitude record of 85,068ft on 28th July 1976. It first deployed to Mildenhall on 6th September 1976 and the 9th SRW set up Detachment 4 at the Suffolk base to look after Blackbird operations from the UK. By July 1990 64-17962 was the last SR-71A in use and it was ferried from Kadena, Japan, to Beale. After this, Lockheed's plant at Palmdale, California, was used for the long-term store of the Blackbird fleet until they were dispersed to museums. Gifted to IWM, 64-17962 was carefully dismantled and shipped to the UK, arriving at Duxford on 5th April 2001. It was officially handed over on 11th June 2001.

McDonnell Douglas F-15A Eagle 76-0020
1976 | Single-seat interceptor | Two 25,000lb st Pratt & Whitney F100-PW-100

Since February 1992 the USAF has stationed F-15 Eagles at Lakenheath, with the 48th Tactical Fighter Wing (TFW). In 2013, the 48th was still flying a mixed fleet of F-15C, 'D and 'E variants from the Suffolk base. The AAM's 'gate guardian' was built at St Louis, Missouri, in 1976 and was issued to the 36th TFW at Bitburg, West Germany, in July 1977. By December 1981 it was back Stateside, serving with the 60th Tactical Fighter Squadron of the 33rd TFW at Eglin, Florida. Beyond this, it is known to have flown with the 5th Fighter Interceptor Squadron (FIS) from Minot, North Dakota. Its last unit was the Massachusetts Air National Guard, the 101st FIS, 102nd Fighter Interceptor Wing at Otis. It was retired to the 'desert bone-yard' at Davis-Monthan, Arizona, on 25th October 1993. It arrived at Duxford in April 2001.

North American F-100D Super Sabre 42165
1956 | Single-seat fighter-bomber | one 16,950lb st Pratt & Whitney J57-P-21A

Denmark and France flew F-100s and these machines were occasional visitors to the UK. From the middle of 1957 through to the spring of 1972 the mighty Super Sabre was a very common sight in British skies; flown by the 20th Tactical Fighter Wing (TFW) from Wethersfield and then Alconbury and with the 48th TFW at Lakenheath. Duxford's example was built at Inglewood, California, and accepted for service by the USAF on 26th May 1956. It was taken on by the 48th TFW in 1957, the unit then based at Chaumont, France. In March 1959 the F-100D was transferred under the Mutual Defense Assistance Program to the Armée de l'Air, the French Air Force. It served initially from Reims and, from December 1965, at Toul. At the end of its operational life it was returned to the USAF, flying to Sculthorpe in Norfolk on 24th November 1975. It was dismantled and moved to Duxford on 17th May 1976. For the opening of the AAM it was restored and given a Vietnam era colour scheme and the markings of the 35th TFW.

Royal Aircraft Establishment RE.8 F3556
1918 | Two-crew artillery observation and general reconnaissance | One 150hp RAF 4A

Entering service in 1916, the RE.8 embodied everything that had been learnt from the BE.2 (see Chapter 2) and warfare above the trenches producing a reliable, stable platform acting as 'eyes for the guns'. There is a chance that RE.8 F3556 has no more than two hours flying time 'on the clock'; certainly it never attained double figures. Built by the Daimler Motor Company in Coventry, it was taken on charge at 1 Aircraft Acceptance Park (AAP) at Radford to the north of the city on 25th October 1918. Test flown for half an hour six days later, it was crated and despatched to France. Its arrival date was what became known as Armistice Day, 11th November 1918, and although RE.8s served on in limited numbers until late 1920, this was not to be F3556's destiny, apparently staying in its crate. Testing by Daimler and the one documented assessment flight at 1 AAP became the extent of its aviating. On New Year's Day 1919, the RE.8 had the wording *A Paddy Bird from Ceylon* painted on the port side of the nose. This name had previously been applied to British and Colonial-built BE.2c 4073 which had been presented by the people of Ceylon (now Sri Lanka). By mid-January F3556 was back at 1 AAP, moving on to Tadcaster, Yorks where it may have been intended for use with the resident 38 Training Depot Station. On 20th February 1920 it was sent south by rail, ready to take part in the Imperial War Museum's exhibition at the Crystal Palace (see Chapter 2) and afterwards going to Cardington for storage. By 1936 it was on show, suspended from the roof structure, at South Lambeth. It came to Duxford in 1974 where it was restored and today is displayed in AirSpace.

Supermarine Spitfire F.24 VN485
1947 | Single-seat fighter | One 2,050hp Rolls-Royce Griffon 85

The third 'Spitfire' to be profiled; the others being Mk.I X4590 at Hendon (Chapter 5) and Seafire F.17 SX137 at Yeovilton (Chapter 4). Sqn Ldr John Derry first flew VN485 at South Marston on 27th August 1947 and Flt Lt Tarkowski ferried it to 9 Maintenance Unit at Cosford nine days later. It did not emerge again until 30th June 1949 when it was flown to Renfrew and from there it was loaded on the carrier HMS *Ocean*, arriving at Seletar, Singapore, on 25th August 1949. On 3rd October 1950 it was taken on charge by 80 Squadron at Kai Tak, Hong Kong. In December 1951 the unit started to re-equip with de Havilland Hornet F.3s and F.4s. This was not the end of VN485's career; it was destined to join another air arm. On the last day of May 1952 it was transferred to the Royal Hong Kong Auxiliary Air Force (RHKAAF), also based at Kai Tak. RHKAAF used a mixture of PR.19s and F.24s and on 21st April 1955 the small air arm staged the last official Spitfire sortie – a formation of PR.19s PS852 and PS854 and F.24s VN318 and VN485. The year before, on 1st April, 81 Squadron at Seletar has flown Spitfire PR.19 PS888, carrying the legend *The Last!* on its nose, as the last-ever RAF operational sortie. The quartet flying at Kai Tak on 21st April 1955 represented the last operational Spitfire flight by a UK-controlled unit. With 241 hours, 20 minutes, 'on the clock' VN485 was initially stored and then, from September 1956, was put on static display. It was repatriated in July 1989, coming to the UK courtesy of a Cathay Pacific Boeing 747 and the Spitfire arrived at Duxford on 18th July 1989. It was put through a thorough restoration programme and was rolled-out on 10th November 2004.

Spitfire F.24 VN485 in April 1990, not long after its arrival from Hong Kong. *Peter Green*

Vickers Viscount 701 G-ALWF
1952 | Medium-range airliner | Four 1,547hp Rolls-Royce Dart 506

A massive success, the Viscount transformed the post-war prospects of Vickers, providing it with a cash-cow for a decade up to 1962 when the last of 445 was delivered. As the world's first turboprop airliner, it changed the face of medium-haul services. *Whisky-Fox* was the second production example, and is the oldest survivor. It first took to the air at Brooklands on 3rd December 1952 and was delivered to British European Airways as *Sir John Franklin* on 2nd February 1953. Replaced by the bigger 800 Series Viscounts, G-ALWF was sold on to Channel Airways of Southend in August 1963. It was leased to Liverpool-based British Eagle International Airlines from 18th November 1964 as *City of Exeter*. Its final operator was Cambrian Airways from Christmas Eve 1971 and it was based at Cardiff's Rhoose Airport. In the early 1970s Paul St John Turner entered into negotiations with Cambrian to preserve *Whisky-Fox* and, as these crystalized, he started the task of finding a venue for it. He came to an agreement with the management at Liverpool Airport, Speke; G-ALWF had flown services there frequently. The Viscount Preservation Trust (VPT) was formed to acquire the airliner and look after it. Its final flight came on 12th April 1972, departing Cardiff, picking up VIPs at Heathrow and then touching down at Liverpool. With this, *Whisky-Fox* completed 28,299 flying hours and 25,398 landings. In a unique arrangement, Paul St John Turner gathered a team of enthusiasts – many from the Merseyside Aviation Society, original publishers of *Wrecks & Relics* – to develop a supporting display and open up the Viscount to the public. Housed inside the art-deco Hangar 1, G-ALWF was officially opened on 5th December 1972. Visitor figures each weekend were good, but eventually security considerations – Liverpool having services to both Northern Ireland and Ireland – brought an end to public access to the airliner. The Duxford Aviation Society stepped in with a rescue plan, *Whisky-Fox* would be its third airliner and the first to be dismantled and moved by road. From 11th October 1975 to 15th February 1976 a DAS team drove up most weekends and worked in the teeth of a Scouse winter in the open air to prepare the Viscount for its journey. The fuselage departed on 21st February 1976 and then DAS volunteers turned to the long job of re-assembly and restoration. The airliner remained the property of VPT until ownership was formally transferred to DAS in December 2011. In 1986 G-ALWF was returned to its 1952 livery and put through a painstaking refurbishment in 1992. This important machine had been intended for display within AirSpace, but demands on floor space dictated otherwise. As this book was published *Whisky-Fox* was well into its 37th year outdoors.

Viscount 701 G-ALWF at Isle of Man Airport, Ronaldsway, 1971. *KEC*

Vickers Super VC-10 G-ASGC
1964 | Long-range airliner | Four 22,500lb st Rolls-Royce Conway 550

As this book was readied for press, the plan was that the RAF would retire the last of venerable VC-10 tankers by the end of 2013; with one destined for the RAF Museum at Cosford. This will bring to an end the service life of an incredibly well regarded airliner and military transport, and its second era as a hard-working tanker. For a long time the VC-10's passenger appeal with launch customer British Overseas Airways Corporation (BOAC) was legendry; First Class passengers often expressing their distain when seeing they had been put on a 707! By the time this was established, the VC-10 was already on the road to a grim production run of 54; a classic example of relying on the launch customer's specification to lower, or destroy, broader market appeal. *Golf-Charlie* climbed into the sky from the short runway at Brooklands on New Year's Day 1965, destined for the Vickers flight test airfield at Wisley, three miles to the south-west. It was delivered to BOAC on 30th April 1965 at Heathrow. From April 1966 BOAC entered a co-operative venture with Cunard and *Golf-Charlie* wore BOAC-Cunard lettering behind the cockpit. This 'marriage' was dissolved in October 1966, but on 1st April 1974 BOAC and British European Airways combined to form British Airways and G-ASGC faced another colour scheme change. Its last revenue-earning flight was Amsterdam-London on 22nd October 1979. *Golf-Charlie* became the Duxford Aviation Society's fifth airliner on 15th April 1980 when it performed its 16,415th and last landing, completing a flying time of 54,623 hours.

Selection of Duxford leaflets, airshow souvenirs and a fund-raising pamphlet for the AAM.

Former Imperial War Museum Duxford aircraft and examples on loan

Type	Identity	Built	Arrived	Notes / current status, or fate
BAe Sea Harrier FA.2	ZA175	1981	Jul 2004	Delivered directly to Norfolk and Suffolk Aviation Museum, on loan
Bristol Sycamore III	G-48/1	1951	1978	Skyfame – *to Int Helicopter Museum, Weston-super-Mare*
Consolidated B-24D Liberator	251457	1942	Feb 1996	Forward fuselage. *To the Mighty Eighth Air Force Museum, Savannah, Georgia, USA Apr 2008*
Convair VT-29B Samaritan	17899	1951	1975	*Broken up on site Aug 1998*
Dassault Mystère IVA	57	c1955	18 Mar 1979	*Roaded to Mildenhall 21 Jan 2007, airfreighted to USA for USAF Museum*
De Havilland Mosquito T.3	TV959	1945	1989	Exchanged with The Fighter Collection for Hurricane; *Exported to the USA Jun 2003*
De Havilland Comet C.2R	XK695	1956	10 Jan 1975	Broken up Oct 1992, *fuselage to Newton*
Fairey Firefly I	Z2033	1944	1978	Skyfame – *To Fleet Air Arm Museum 25 Jul 2000 – Chapter 4*
Fieseler Fi 156 Storch	–	c1946	1984	French-built MS.502. *To private owner, Germany, 8 Oct 2012*
Gloster Meteor F.4	VT260	1948	Dec 1993	Exchanged for F-86A Sabre. *Exported to Chino, USA, Aug 1997*
Gloster Meteor NF.11	WD686	1952	1974	*To Muckleburgh Collection, Norfolk, early 1991*
Hawker Tempest II	LA607	1943	1978	Skyfame – Sold in USA by Skyfame 1984. *Fantasy of Flight, Florida, as N607LA*
Hawker Hunter F.2	WN904	1954	11 May 1974	To 'gate guardian' Waterbeach 1989. *Displayed at Sywell Aviation Museum, Northampton*
Messerschmitt Me 163B	191660	1944	Oct 1976	Exchanged for DH.9. *To USA May 2005*
Mikoyan-Gurevich MiG-15*bis*	3794	c1953	Sep 193	Norfolk and Suffolk Aviation Museum (Czech-built Letov S-103) on loan
Mil Mi-24 *Hind-D*	96+21	c1980	Apr 1996	On loan – *to USA 21 Sep 2012, Pima Air and Space Museum, Arizona*
North American F-86A Sabre	0242	1948	26 Jun 1996	Midland Air Museum, on loan
Republic F-105D Thunderchief	91822	1959	Apr 2001	*To Krakow, Poland 17 Jun 2010*
SAAB J35A Draken	35075	c1970	1 Jun 1977	Dumfries and Galloway Aviation Museum – on loan
Saunders-Roe SR.A/1	TG263	1947	1978	Skyfame – *To Solent Sky, Southampton, late 1993*
Short Sherpa	G-48-1	1953	1978	Skyfame – To Medway A/c Pres Soc, Rochester 10 Mar 1993. *Ulster Aviation Collection – Chapter 9*
SPAD S.XIII	N4727V	1918	12 Feb 1982	*Sold in France 23 Jan 1995*
Vickers Varsity T.1	WF425	1952	1974	*Scrapped October 1993*
Vickers Varsity T.1	WJ945	1953	26 Oct 1974	Originally privately operated as G-BEDV; presented to IWM. *To Classic Air Force, Newquay Jan 2013*
Westland Dragonfly HR.3	WG752	1952	Dec 1985	*To the Aviodome, Netherlands, 28 Aug 1991*
Westland Whirlwind HAS.7	XG577	1957	13 Jun 1974	To the 'gate' at Waterbeach by Nov 1986, returning Sep 1989. *To Leconfield Oct 1990, rescue training*

Imperial War Museum Duxford aircraft

Type	Identity	Built	Origin	Arrived#	Notes
Airspeed Oxford I	V3388	1940	UK	1978	–
Auster AOP.9	XP281	1961	UK	10 Mar 1970	R
Avro Anson I	N4877	1938	UK	1978	see profile
Avro Lancaster X	KB889	1944	UK	14 May 1986	–
Avro Shackleton MR.3/3	XF708	1959	UK	22 Aug 1972	–
Avro Vulcan B.2	XJ824	1961	UK	13 Mar 1982	–
Avro Canada CF-100 Canuck 4B	18393	1955	Canada	29 Mar 1975	–
BAC TSR-2	XR222	1964	UK	21 Mar 1978	–
BAC Strikemaster Mk.80A	1133	1976	UK	22 Mar 2000	see profile
BAe Harrier GR.9A*	ZD461	1989	UK/USA	14 Mar 2012	destined for South Lambeth
Bell UH-1H Iroquois	72-21605	1972	USA	15 Jul 1997	–
Blackburn Buccaneer S.2B	XV865	1968	UK	21 Jan 1999	–
Boeing PT-17 Kaydet*	'217786'	1944	USA	Nov 1977	–
Boeing B-17G Flying Fortress	483735	1945	USA	1975	–
Boeing TB-29A Superfortress*	461748	1945	USA	2 Mar 1980	see profile
Boeing B-52D Stratofortress	60689	1957	USA	8 Oct 1983	see profile
Bristol F.2b Fighter	E2581	1918	UK	16 Dec 1922	see profile
Bristol Bolingbroke IVT	10038	1942	UK	1974	stored
Cierva C.30A	HM580	1934	UK	1978	–
Consolidate B-24M Liberator	'450493'	1944	USA	29 Jun 1999	–
De Havilland DH.9	D5649	1917	UK	19 Apr 2007	–
De Havilland Tiger Moth	'N6635'	c1942	UK	5 Mar 2002	–
De Havilland Mosquito TT.35	TA719	1945	UK	1978	–
De Havilland Vampire T.11	WZ590	1953	UK	4 May 1973	–
De Havilland Sea Vampire T.22	XG743	1954	UK	15 Jun 1972	R
De Havilland Sea Venom FAW.21	XG613	1956	UK	1971	R
De Havilland Sea Vixen FAW.2	XS576	1964	UK	17 Mar 1972	–
Douglas C-47A Skytrain*	315509	1944	USA	Jul 1980	see profile
English Electric Canberra B.2*	WH725	1953	UK	1972	–
English Electric Lightning F.1	XM135	1959	UK	11 Nov 1974	see profile
Eurofighter Typhoon DA4	ZH590	1997	UK/Ger/It/Sp	22 Apr 2009	–
Fairchild A-10A Thunderbolt II*	77-0259	1977	USA	6 Feb 1992	see profile
Fairey Swordfish III	NF370	1944	UK	30 Jun 1952	–
Fairey Gannet ECM.6*	XG797	1957	UK	21 May 1972	see profile
FMA Pucará	A-549	c1981	Argentina	Oct 1983	–
Focke-Achgelis Fa 330A-1	100143	1943	Germany	16 Jan 1977	–
General Dynamics F-111E	67-0120	1967	USA	19 Oct 1993	–
Gloster Meteor F.8	WK991	1953	UK	10 Dec 1963	–
Gloster Javelin FAW.9	XH897	1958	UK	24 Jan 1975	see profile
Grumman TBM-3E Avenger	'46214'	1944	USA	1977	R
Handley Page Hastings C.1A	TG528	1947	UK	1 Apr 1979	see profile
Handley Page Victor B.1A(K2P)	XH648	1959	UK	2 Jun 1976	–
Hawker Hurricane FSM	'P2954'	2000	UK	Oct 2000	'gate'
Hawker Hurricane IIb	'Z2315'	1941	UK	Sep 1997	–
Hawker Sea Hawk FB.5	WM969	1954	UK	20 Jan 1977	–
Hawker Hunter F.6A	XE627	1956	UK	14 Nov 1986	–
Hawker Siddeley Harrier GR.3	XZ133	1976	UK	2 Sep 1993	–
Heinkel He 111	B2I-27	c1950	Germany	2002	(Spanish-built CASA 2-111)
Junkers Ju 52/3m	6316	c1946	Germany	May 1974	R (French-built Amiot AA.1 Toucan)

Type	Identity	Built	Origin	Arrived#	Notes
Lockheed T-33A	14286	1951	USA	8 Apr 1979	–
Lockheed U-2CT	66692	1956	USA	26 Jun 1992	see profile
Lockheed SR-71A Blackbird	117962	1966	USA	5 Apr 2001	see profile
McDonnell F-4J(UK) Phantom	155529	c1967	USA	Jul 1991	–
McDonnell Douglas F-15A Eagle	76-0020	1976	USA	Apr 2001	see profile
Messerschmitt Bf 109E-3*	1190	1940	Germany	17 Mar 1998	–
Mikoyan-Gurevich MiG-21PF	501	c1970	USSR	Nov 1997	–
Miles Magister I	G-AFBS	1939	UK	1978	–
Mitsubishi A6M3 *Zeke*	3685	c1943	Japan	1986	stored
North American AT-6C Texan	–	1942	USA	1988	R
North American B-25J Mitchell	31171	1944	USA	Oct 1976	–
North American Mustang FSM	'463209'	1991	USA	1996	–
North American F-100D	42165	1956	USA	17 May 1976	–
Panavia Tornado GR.1B	ZA465	1983	UK/Ger/It	25 Oct 2001	–
Percival Proctor III	LZ766	1944	UK	1978	–
Pilcher Hawk replica	–	1930	UK	Nov 2004	–
Republic P-47D Thunderbolt*	'226413'	1945	USA	Nov 1985	–
Royal Aircraft Factory RE.8	F3556	1918	UK	20 Feb 1920	see profile
Schweizer TG-3A	252983	1945	USA	Aug 1996	R
SEPECAT Jaguar GR.1A	XX108	1972	UK/France	29 Oct 2003	–
Short Sunderland MR.5	ML796	1944	UK	9 Jul 1976	–
Slingsby Cadet TX.3	XN239	1959	UK	1986	R
SPAD XIII replica	'S4513'	1978	France	17 Jun 1996	–
Supermarine Spitfire FSM	'X4178'	2006	UK	Aug 2006	'gate'
Supermarine Spitfire F.24	VN485	1947	UK	18 Jul 1989	see profile
Westland Lysander	'V9673'	1940	UK	1991	–
Westland Whirlwind HAS.7	XK936	1957	UK	28 Oct 1975	–
Westland Wessex HAS.1	XS863	1965	UK	8 Oct 1981	–
Westland Wasp HAS.1	XS567	1964	UK	Aug 1992	–
Westland Sea King HAS.6	XV712	1972	UK	27 May 2010	–
Westland Lynx AH.7	XZ194	1978	UK	Apr 2013	–
Yokosuka MXY-7 Ohka 11		1945	Japan	Apr 2011	–

Notes: * – illustrated in the colour section. # With the IWM, either at Lambeth or Duxford. R – Airframes highlighted in the review of 2010 for *probable* disposal. See also the separate table on the airliner collection of the Duxford Aviation Society. See Chapter 1 for details of former Lambeth airframes expected to stay at Duxford.

TSR-2 XR222 at the College of Aeronautics, Cranfield, 1970. *KEC*

CHAPTER 9

NORTHERN IRELAND
Ulster Folk and Transport Museum
Cultra Manor, Holywood
www.nmni.com/uftm

With sweeping views of Belfast Lough and the rolling countryside of Ballymena and Larne the 170 acres of Cultra Manor, Holywood, occupied by the Ulster Folk and Transport Museum, straddles the A2 Belfast-Bangor road. The folk element was set up in 1958 as an off-shoot of the Belfast Municipal Museum with important buildings removed from their original location and re-assembled brick-by-brick within the new landscape. As this was developing, it was becoming clear that the Belfast Transport Museum was desperately short of space and so the dual theme of social and transport heritage was adopted.

Fully opened in 1976, the site has been expanding and evolving ever since. On the Lough-side the incredible railway and land transport halls were unveiled in 1995. With assistance from Bombardier Aerospace, the 'Flight Experience' gallery opened in 2001 and has proved to be very popular. (In October 1989 Shorts became a part of the Canadian Bombardier organisation.) Space restrictions have meant that the aviation element is not extensive, although the exhibition is to the highest standards. This does not constitute a 'national' aviation collection but the world renown of the Cultra Manor site gives it enhanced status.

Above: Three Short Sealands in late 1951. In the foreground are the two for Yugoslavia, with the company demonstrator, G-AKLV, in the background. Closest to the camera, YU-CFK is preserved at Belgrade. *Short Brothers and Harland*

Short Sealand 1 G-AKLW
1951 | Six to eight seat general purpose amphibian | Two 340hp DH Gipsy Queen 70-3

At the rear of the 'X2 Flight Experience Gallery' is a large smoked-glass window that is well worth peering through. This is the museum's large object conservation and restoration workshop, established in 2001. Within is the only amphibian to enter post-1945 series production in the UK; the Short Sealand. So named to emphasize its ability to operate from water or runways, it was devised by Shorts to meet the needs of 'developing' nations. Despite being vigorously marketed, it was expensive when compared to war surplus Consolidated Catalinas and the like. The prototype first flew at Sydenham, Belfast, on 22nd January 1948 and 24 others were built, with the last being delivered in 1954.

Holywood's example was completed as G-AKLW in late 1951 to the order of His Excellency Abboun Ahmed Pasha of Egypt's Khedivial Mail Line shipping line. Equipped with six luxurious seats, named *Nadia* and registered SU-AHY, it started its delivery flight from Sydenham on 23rd February 1952. When the Khedivial fleet was nationalised in 1961, *Hotel-Yankee* was gifted to the Saudi Arabian Air Force for air-sea rescue work. By 1968 it was derelict at Jeddah and acquired by a US collector who shipped it westwards. It was donated to the Bradley Air Museum (renamed the New England Air Museum in 1984) at Windsor Locks, Connecticut.

During the mid-1980s British pilot and restorer, Nick Grace, began negotiations to bring the Sealand home to Northern Ireland. This involved a three-cornered exchange finalised in August 1986 when G-AKLW arrived and Spitfire XVI TE184 left the museum for Trent Aero's workshop at East Midlands Airport, Leicestershire. (Much later it was appreciated that TE184 was on Ministry of Defence charge, technically on loan from the RAF Museum, but by then it was a case of shutting the stable door after the horse had bolted!) As G-MXVI, the Spitfire took to the air again on 23rd November 1990 and is presently based in Germany. As its part of the deal, New England received Hawker Tempest II MW810 on 1st July 1986. This was previously with Warbirds of Great Britain and the Indian Air Force before that.) The largest airframe at Holywood, the Sealand was stored until the workshop was created. Two other Sealands survive, both in museums; one in India, one in the former Yugoslavia.

Short SC.1 XG905
1957 | Single-seat vertical take-off research aircraft | Five 2,130lb st Rolls-Royce RB.108

With the success of the Thrust Measuring Rig – nicknamed the 'Flying Bedstead' and displayed at the Science Museum, see Chapter 1 – Rolls-Royce started development of a purpose-built lift jet engine. This was the RB.108 which boasted a thrust-to-weight ratio of 8:1 and showed great promise. Experimental Research requirement ER.143T was issued and Shorts at Sydenham were awarded a contract for SC.1s XG900 and XG905 – the former

Short SC.1 XG905 hovering clear of the special rig built at Sydenham on 2nd June 1958. The massive structure was made from Bailey Bridge sections and known as the 'Goal Post'. *Short Brothers and Harland*

is also at the Science Museum. The format was a rotund delta with four RB.108s mounted behind the cockpit; these could tilt 35-degrees forwards or backwards to provide some directional thrust as well as lift. In the tail was another RB.108 mounted 30-degrees downwards from the horizontal, providing propulsion.

Chief test pilot Tom Brooke-Smith piloted XG900 on its maiden, conventional, flight from Boscombe Down on 2nd April 1957. At this point, it was only fitted with the propulsion RB.108; XG905 was to be the first with the full five powerplants. Ground-running of XG905 commenced on 3rd September 1957 with Tom Brooke-Smith at the controls. Its first tethered flights were made using a huge rig, called the 'Goal Post', at Sydenham on 23rd May 1958. The tethers were discarded on 25th October. Moved to the Royal Aircraft Establishment at Thurleigh, XG905 carried out the inaugural transition from vertical to horizontal flight, and back again, on 6th April 1960. Brooke-Smith demonstrated this publically the Farnborough airshow that September.

With J R Green at the controls over Sydenham on 2nd October 1963, disaster occurred. The triply redundant auto-stabilization system failed and the SC.1 rolled upside-down and crashed, killing its pilot. At Thurleigh XG900 was grounded as the circumstances were investigated. During rebuild XG905 was upgraded with a head-up display, data link and a completely rethought control system. It began flying again on 17th June 1966 and was issued to Thurleigh for use by the Blind Landing Experimental Unit. Its trials life over, it was moved to Sydenham and put into store in April 1971, transferring to the Ulster Folk and Transport Museum on 20th May 1974.

Ulster Folk and Transport Museum aircraft

Type	Identity	Built	Origin	Arrived	Notes
Ferguson Monoplane replica	–	1973	UK	4th May 1976	–
McCandless M-4 gyroplane	G-ATXX	1968	UK	1987	–
Short Sealand	G-AKLW	1951	UK	Aug 1986	see profile
Short SC.1*	XG905	1957	UK	20 May 1974	see profile
Short 330 Sherpa	G-BKMW	1982	UK	2000	cockpit

Notes: Does not include aircraft in deep store and unavailable for public inspection. * – illustrated in the colour section

Stirling bombers under assembly in June 1942 in the hangar that is now home to the UAC. *Ulster Aviation Society*

Ulster Aviation Collection
Maze Long Kesh Regeneration Site, near Lisburn

www.ulsteraviationsociety.org

Rules are made to be broken, or at least bent a little, and the author has decided to include a nascent museum that has long since punched above its weight. Founded in 1968, the Ulster Aviation Society, has been amassing airframes, artefacts and archives and is consolidating its activities on the former wartime airfield at Long Kesh. This is not a 'national' in the accepted sense of the term, but it its well on the way! When Short-built Canberra PR.9 XH131 was unveiled at the former Long Kesh airfield on 23rd September 2011, the opportunity was taken to emphasize that the collection was the largest in *all* of Ireland and had been so for two decades. The Canberra was the nineteenth airframe, but since the figure has gone beyond 20.

UAC's founding body is the vibrant Ulster Aviation Society, established in 1968. Previously dispersed, the collection settled at the former USAAF airfield at Langford Lodge on the eastern shore of Lough Neagh in 1991. For a variety of reasons this arrangement had to come to an end in 2005 and the offer of a new home at Long Kesh pushed all the buttons. From 1971 Long Kesh gained notoriety as the Maze prison with 'H-blocks', forbidding perimeter walls and observation towers. The prison closed in September 2000 and the site is under regeneration. During a frenetic period in 2006, UAC moved in, including all 29,000lb of its HS Buccaneer. If the status of the UAC needed further reinforcement, on 27th May 2009 the Dublin Government handed over a former Irish Air Corps Sud Alouette III helicopter; the only example to be preserved beyond the borders of Ireland. At present the collection is available for viewing by prior arrangement only but the medium-term plan is to open on a regular basis.

The tail-less Short Sherpa and its aero-isoclinic wing. *Short Brothers*

Short Sherpa G-14-1
1953 | Single-seat research aircraft | Two 352lb st Turboméca Palas

On August 10, 1951 the first of two Short Sperrin four-engined bombers had its maiden flight. The Sperrin was intended as 'insurance' for the V-Bomber programme that resulted in production contracts for the Valiant, Victor and Vulcan. Shorts had hoped that an advanced version might attract interest and investigated the 'aero-isoclinic' (AI) wing concept of Professor Geoffrey T R Hill. A pioneer of tail-less layouts, Hill is best remembered for his Pterodactyls – see Chapter 1 for his Mk.I of 1928 at the Science Museum. The AI format allowed great controllability for a radically swept, high-speed wing. Rotating wing-tip 'controllers' acted as ailerons and prevented tip-stalls at low speed – a major cause for concern with swept-wing types at the time. The wing also did away with the need for horizontal tail surfaces.

Shorts built an all-wood glider, the SB.1 G-14-1, as a one-third scale aerodynamic version of the proposed bomber. It was towed into the air for the first time on July 14, 1951. Ninety-one days later, on its fourth flight, the SB.1 was badly damaged while being tugged aloft. Test pilot Tom Brooke-Smith was injured and put out of action until early 1952. The Hill wing was intact and an all-metal replacement fuselage was designed. The new machine, designated SB.4 and named Sherpa, was powered by a pair of Turboméca Palas turbojets. Brooke-Smith took the new version aloft on October 4, 1953. (Sherpa stood for Short and Harland Experimental Research Prototype Aircraft.) Nothing came of the AI venture, but the SB.4 helped build knowledge of 'all-flying' control surfaces.

The Sherpa moved to the College of Aeronautics at Cranfield for further evaluation from April 1957 as G-36-1. In 1964 the then grounded test-bed was handed on to Bristol College of Advanced Technology. To get it there, the one-piece wing was cut in half and the institute eventually tested the starboard specimen to destruction. The engineless fuselage and half a wing was handed on to the Skyfame Museum at Staverton in May 1966.

When Skyfame closed in 1978 the Imperial War Museum (IWM) at Duxford carried out one of the most ambitious museum 'rescues' on record, taking the vast majority of Skyfame on. Included was the Sherpa; though at *some* point in the late 1970s its precious wing was lost. In terms of the IWM's acquisitions policy, the SB.4 was an 'orphan' but despite this Duxford stuck with the oddity and in 1993 commissioned the Medway Aircraft Preservation Society (MAPS) to restore it. Thanks to sleuthing by the Ulster Aviation Collecton's Paul McMaster, the original Palas turbojets, complete with jet pipes and logbooks, were discovered at Sydenham and delivered to MAPS at its Rochester, Kent, workshop in July 2002. Recognising its relevance in Northern Ireland, the Sherpa was delivered on 16th July 2008 into the care of the UAC. During mid-2011 the IWM reviewed what could be called its 'B-list' airframes and decided to dispose of the Sherpa and in October the following year ownership was transferred to UAC. Among its many artefacts, UAC has a museum-standard cutaway model of the AI wing and under Fred and John May a replica wing is currently being built.

Second prototype Shorts 330 G-BDBS in 1976. *Shorts*

Short 330 G-BDBS
1976 | Prototype 30-seat airliner | Two 1,198shp Pratt & Whitney Canada PT6A-45R

In 1963 Shorts flew the prototype of a twin turboprop utility transport, the Skyvan, and this transformed the company's prospects, turning it into a commercial aircraft manufacturer. When the last one rolled off the line in 1986 at Sydenham, 153 Skyvans had been produced. By then Shorts had used the wing and box-section fuselage of the Skyvan to create a dynasty of commuter airliners. The first Shorts SD3-30 (later Shorts 330) 30-seater appeared on 22nd August 1974 and was followed by the second example, initially G-14-3001 later G-BDBS, on 8th January 1976. *Bravo-Sierra* was used for development and demonstration work and was finally retired in the early 1990s. It was donated to the Ulster Aviation Society and made its last flight – suspended under a RAF Chinook helicopter – from Sydenham to Langford Lodge on 7th April 1993. It moved to Long Kesh by road in 2006.

In 1981 a stretched version of the 330, with 36 seats and the former's twin tails replaced by a raked single fin, appeared as the Shorts 360. Including the C-23 Sherpa military freighter for the US Air Force, production of 330s and 360s amounted to 321 units with the last example being delivered in 1998. Skyvans, 330s and 360s remain in use worldwide. A Skyvan would be a great addition to the Ulster Aviation Collection, but as the type is in a niche market and a rarity in UK skies, this may be difficult to achieve.

Ulster Aviation Collection aircraft

Type	Identity	Built	Origin	Arrived	Notes
Aero Composites Sea Hawker	EI-BUO	1987	USA	1998	–
Air & Space 18A Gyroplane	EI-CNG	1966	USA	17 Nov 2012	–
Chargus Cyclone hang-glider	–	1979	USA	Nov 1994	–
Clutton FRED II	G-BNZR	1991	UK	2010	–
De Havilland Vampire T.11	WZ549	1953	UK	Oct 1991	–
EMBRAER Tucano	G-BTUC	1986	Brazil	Jan 2001	–
English Electric Canberra PR.9*	XH131	1959	UK	13 Dec 2010	–
Eurowing Goldwing microlight	G-MJWS	1983	UK	2001	–
Fairchild Argus II	G-AJSN	1943	USA	Jul 2011	–
Fairey Gannet AS.4	XA460	1956	UK	29 Dec 2011	–
Grumman Wildcat V	JV482	1944	USA	30 Apr 1984	–
Hawker Sea Hawk FB.3	WN108	1954	UK	Oct 1991	–
Hawker Siddeley Buccaneer S.2B*	XV361	1968	UK	18 Apr 1994	–
Hunting Jet Provost T.3A	XM414	1960	UK	23 Dec 2004	–
Robinson R22 Beta	G-RENT	1988	USA	28 Feb 2003	–
Rogallo hang-glider	–	c1980	USA	Feb 2000	–
Short SB.4 Sherpa	G-14-1	1953	UK	16 Jul 2008	see profile
Short 330	G-BDBS	1976	UK	7 Apr 1993	see profile
Sud Alouette III	202	1972	France	27 May 2009	–
Team Hi-Max 1700	G-MZHM	1997	USA	13 Sep 2007	–
Westland Wessex HC.2	XR517	1964	UK	3 Dec 2005	–

Note: * – illustrated in the colour section

CHAPTER 10

SCOTLAND
National Museum of Flight Scotland
East Fortune Aerodrome
and
National Museum of Scotland, Edinburgh
www.nms.ac.uk/flight

While the rest of the UK has yet to achieve what can be *really* called a dedicated national museum of *all* flight, Scotland has long since basked in one. Like the Science Museum, the National Museum of Flight Scotland can trace its roots to the Prince Albert-inspired Great Exhibition of 1851. It was not greenhouse maestro Joseph Paxton's Crystal Palace that provided the impetus, but the public's incredible response to all things industrial and mechanical. Four years later in Edinburgh the Industrial Museum of Scotland was established, changing its name and remit in 1864 to the Edinburgh Museum of Science and Art. In 1904 it became the Royal Scottish Museum (RSM), remaining so until 'rebranding' as the National Museum of Scotland (NSM) in 1995.

Above: Concorde G-BOAA on board the barge 'Terra Marique' sailing past the 'London Eye' on its way to East Fortune, 13th April 2004. *Duncan Cubitt-Key Publishing www.flypast.com*

As outlined in the profile below, the Royal Aeronautical Society was given Percy Sinclair Pilcher's Hawk glider and in 1909 it was presented *on loan* to the RSM. This was the first complete fixed-wing aircraft to be placed with a UK museum but the first to be *given* lock, stock and barrel, was the Cody at the Science Museum (Chapter 1). During the 1920s a collection of aero engines was established, including a four-cylinder Wright of 1910, presented by Orville Wright. In 1968 a Slingsby Gull sailplane was acquired to 'fly' alongside the Pilcher, highlighting the advances in design over the 42 years separating them.

An exhibit in its own right

In 1971 RSM was allocated Spitfire XVI TE462 and plans were made to install it within the Hall of Power in Chambers Street, Edinburgh. Delivery was pressing and temporary storage was needed and part of a hangar at East Fortune airfield was offered by the Department of the Environment. The Spitfire arrived on 19th February 1971 – what was to become the Museum of Flight (MoF) had received its first airframe. DoE's need for the hangar waned and RSM put a 'bid' in for what was then seen as a large objects store, just in time for an influx of Fleet Air Arm types: Sea Hawk, Sea Vampire, Sea Venom and the cockpit of a Buccaneer S.1. The importance of East Fortune (EF) *itself* was considered and the idea of an aviation museum was given serious consideration.

In September 1915 a detachment of the Royal Naval Air Service detached to EF from Dundee to bolster defence of the approaches to the Firth of Forth. The airfield was officially commissioned as an RNAS station in August the following year. Avro 504s and other types were used but EF was also a major base for coastal patrol airships. Initially these were non-rigid 'blimps' but from the summer of 1917 much more sophisticated rigid airships were based in giant hangars protected by enormous windbreaks. From 1st April 1918 the airfield became an RAF station, specialising in torpedo attack training using types such as Sopwith Cuckoos and 1½ Strutters.

With a crew of 30, captained by RAF Major G H Scott, the 643ft long airship R34 lifted off from EF at 13:42 hours on 2nd July 1919. It headed west and 108 hours, 12 minutes later it arrived at Roosevelt Field, Mineola, New York, completing the first east-west Atlantic crossing. (Seventeen days previously Alcock and Brown had crossed that ocean west to east in the Vickers Vimy now at the Science Museum, see Chapter 1.) Built at Inchinnan, near Glasgow, the R34 had five 250hp Sunbeam Maori engines, and it and its Armstrong Whitworth-built sister R33, were based at EF at some time during their careers. R34 departed the USA on 10th July and, taking advantage of the prevailing winds, alighted at Pulham, Norfolk, on the 13th, completing the first two-way crossing of the Atlantic. There is a memorial commemorating this incredible voyage at EF.

Spitfire XVI TE462, East Fortune's 'founder' airframe, inside Hangar 4 in the early 1990s. Behind is the Sheila Scott Piper Comanche. *KEC*

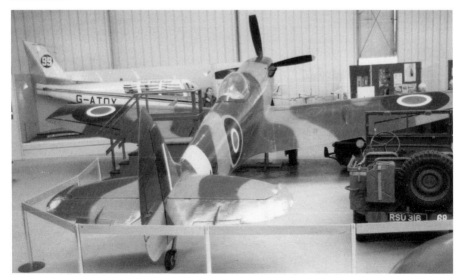

The airfield closed early in 1920, the domestic site on the northern perimeter becoming a hospital. Reactivated in the summer of 1940, by the end of the year the airfield had gained the classic three-runway layout along with the present-day hangars and outbuildings. No.60 Operational Training Unit arrived in June 1941 readying night-fighter crews for action, eventually standardising on twin-engined Bristol Blenheims and Beaufighters. From late 1942 the role changed to Coastal Command strike attack training with 132 OTU with Beaufighters, Beauforts and Mosquitos as the main equipment. By the end of 1945 all of this activity was over and EF fell silent. In 1950 it was proposed for use by the Americans and during 1960-1961 served as a temporary Edinburgh Airport while runway work closed Turnhouse, to the west of the city. By the 1980s the extreme westerly section of the east-west runway was used by microlights and this remains so, functioning as a self-contained airfield. By the mid-1990s much of the site had gained 'listed' status and was owned by NMS.

Vital and varied support

From the arrival of the Spitfire in February 1971 expansion was rapid and volunteers from the Aircraft Preservation Society of Scotland (APSS) pitched in. It had been APSS members that had championed the idea that EF became an aviation museum. Aircraft were accepted on loan, with the Northern Aircraft Preservation Society supplying a Dragon Rapide and a BA Swallow and a Scottish owner an airworthy SAAB Safir light aircraft (see the table 'Former Museum of Flight and APSS Aircraft'). The Rapide was particularly appropriate as it served with Northern and Scottish Airways from Renfrew from 1936 and later with Allied Airways from Dyce, Aberdeen. (The Rapide is now at the Museum of Science and Industry, Manchester, on loan from The Aeroplane Collection as NAPS was renamed in the early 1970s.)

Formed in 1973, APSS acquired aircraft of its own which were kept at EF in the early days. (From 2000 the 'A' in APSS was changed from 'Aircraft' to 'Aviation'.) Along the way, APSS has evolved to become a much-valued support structure for the MoF across a wide variety of activities from research, manning and planning special events and fund-raising to the restoration of exhibits, airframes and even buildings. Among the APSS airframes, the Miles Monarch was the subject of an eleven-year restoration. Over 30 aircraft and 15 engines belonging to MoF have been restored over the years, an early project being the Slingsby Gull; recent ones including the Anson and the Beaufighter.

An unusual project during the late 1990s was a Slingsby T.53 two-seat all-metal high-performance sailplane. This was returned to flying condition and is group-operated by APSS members from Portmoak, the home of the Scottish Gliding Union. Since April 2001 the APSS workshop has been dominated by the construction of an airworthy replica of a Sopwith 1½ Strutter, a type flown by 208 Training Depot Station at EF in 1918.

Opening up and expanding

A less-than-complete airframe at EF may not look much at first glance, but is has great Scottish provenance. In association with marine craft specialist Saro, Edgar Percival designed and built a three-engined all-wooden mailplane, the A.24, at Cowes in 1932. Percival transferred the design rights to Saro who in turn trusted development to another Cowes-based concern, Spartan Aircraft. Re-thought as a six-passenger airliner and re-named Cruiser, 16 were built in three series with the last one being delivered in May 1935.

EF's survivor was the first Cruiser III, G-ACYK, joining Spartan Air Lines at Cowes in April 1935. The company was absorbed into British Airways (the first airline to have that name) a year later and the tri-motor was sold on to Northern and Scottish Airways at Renfrew, Glasgow, in August 1936. On 14th January 1938 the Cruiser impacted on the Hill of Stake, near Largs, thankfully without fatality. Some elements were salvaged, others were removed as time went by. The metal cockpit and cabin structure remained as a waypoint for walkers for a long time. It was salvaged with the help of a Fleet Air Arm Westland Sea King helicopter on 25th July 1973 and moved to EF.

During 1974-1975 a major refurbishment of the somewhat basic museum accommodation was carried out with a workshop, offices, reception area and a lecture theatre installed. Now officially called the Museum of Flight, and with Don Storer as Keeper of the Department of Transport, it was opened to the public for a fortnight from 7th July 1975. Open periods and school visits were extended as the years went by and a second hangar was taken over in 1976. By 1991 MoF was open all week April to September and in 1999 it opened on a daily basis.

When the Strathallan Aircraft Collection slimmed down its exhibits at an auction in June 1981, the opportunity was taken to acquire five of the lots, four arriving by road (Bolingbroke, Dragon, Puss Moth and Tiger Moth) while two flew in, the Cygnet and Provost. The Bolingbroke, a Canadian-built Blenheim IV, added

Spartan Cruiser II G-ACYK, circa 1935. *KEC*

a type that was common at EF during World War Two. The runway proved its worth again with the arrival of a former Dan-Air Comet 4 in September 1981 and the Falklands campaign Vulcan in April 1984.

Throughout the 1990s magic was being worked inside Hangar 4, with Bob Major and then Adam Smith overseeing its transformation from 'formal' exhibits-in-a-hangar to an interpretive, multi-layered tribute to all aspects of aviation. On the floor was an impressive sweep of types from Dragon and Puss Moth to Spitfire, Twin Pioneer and Bulldog. Suspended above were sailplanes, hang-gliders, homebuilds and microlights – most built in Scotland or with a strong Scottish provenance. This was a superb spectacle and influenced other collections and curators in its day. The impending arrival of Concorde in the spring of 2004 dictated the end of this and the hangar was gutted; much of the iconic sport and light aviation collection destined to disappear into long-term storage. Not one hang-glider or sailplane is presently on show...

For 2000, MoF embarked on a challenging 'outreach' programme, the 'Festival of Flight' under the directorship of Dawn Kemp, later to take on the mantle of Curator. A series of events across Scotland was

A view of Hangar 4 in 2001. 'Flying' in the foreground is Scottish-built Eurowing Goldwing G-MBPM, behind it a hang-glider and the Slingsby Gull. On the ground are, left to right: Miles M.18, Monarch G-AFJU, the Pilcher Hawk, GAL Cygnet and the Kay Gyroplane. *Ken Ellis*

Beaufighter TF.10 BF-10 in open store at Alverca in Portugal, circa 1977. *Peter Green Collection*

staged, with help from the Heritage Lottery Fund, culminating in an expanded version of the annual airshow at East Fortune in July. The millennium was a busy year and swift action secured another important type that served at EF during World War Two, a Bristol Beaufighter. A former Portuguese and RAF TF.X, in store near Pretoria since 1983, was put up for sale by the South African Air Force Museum. The Beaufighter was available at US $250,000 and was attracting considerable interest from 'warbird' owners and restorers. With NMS pledging £90,000 MoF Curator Adam Smith secured the deal and commenced a frantic three days finding the balance from public donations, which willingly flowed in. Unloaded at Tilbury docks, the dismantled torpedo-bomber arrived at its new home in early December 2000. Restoration started in 2001, but was dropped with the advent of Concorde. Since then, work had re-commenced and those that forked out the £100,000 of public funding – including the author – patiently await the 'roll-out' of 'their' Beaufighter.

Supersonic ambitions

Drive through the entrance to East Fortune and a sign declares your arrival at the 'Home of Scotland's Concorde'. The story of Scotland's *Alpha-Alpha* includes the most ambitious relocation of the supersonic airliner to date. The first Concorde to be delivered to British Airways, G-BOAA was first flown at Filton on 5th November 1975 and joined the airline on 14th January the following year. A week later, BA and Air France staged a simultaneous entry into commercial service from Heathrow and Charles de Gaulle airports. At Paris, F-BVFA blasted off for Rio de Janeiro, Brazil, and in London *Alpha-Alpha* screamed off eastwards to Bahrain. With the retirement of the BA fleet on 24th October 2003, thought was given to what-went-where; the fleet was to be presented on permanent loan to several organisations. MoF's collecting policy meant that it had the pre-dominant rationale for a Concorde, but the size and state of the runways at EF precluded an airborne 'delivery'. At Heathrow, a pair of Series 102s had been withdrawn earlier and held as spares 'Christmas Trees' for the rest of the fleet: G-BOAA last flown 12th August 2000 and G-BOAB touching down for the last time three days later. It was decided to keep *Alpha-Bravo* at Heathrow for potential display, perhaps at Terminal 5 when it eventually opened up in March 2008. (This machine continues to linger at Heathrow; its long-term future far from mapped-out.)

Moving *Alpha-Alpha* to Scotland was an epic of logistics. With the fin, rudder, undercarriage, outer wings, engines and nacelles removed, G-BOAA was taken on a 38-wheel low-loader out of Heathrow and taken to Isleworth on 3rd April 2004. Roads were closed off, lamp posts, overhead cables and road signs were taken down as it passed. At Isleworth it was rolled on to the specialist transport barge *Terra Marique* and on the 13th it sailed down the Thames, pausing for the all-important photo-opportunity alongside the 'Eye' and the Houses of Parliament, before turning left at Essex and heading for the power station at Torness on the Lothian coast. On the 17th, *Alpha-Alpha* came ashore and in the early hours of the following day trundled westwards down the A1 Great North Road. Meanwhile the Royal Engineer's 53 Field (Air Support) Squadron had prepared a cross-country route of just over a mile to Hangar 4 at EF. *Alpha-Alpha* was tucked into the hangar on 19th April.

The journey north was estimated to have cost £2 million, but this almost certainly did not taken into account all of the 'ancillaries'; police presence, removal of street 'furniture', road-closure 'paperwork' etc. Re-assembly of G-BOAA and the re-generation of Hangar 4 started immediately. Early in 2004 announcements about the forthcoming 'Concorde Experience' exhibition made it obvious that *Alpha-Alpha* was not just going to dominate the hangar, but be the *only* airframe in there. This brought the following comment from the author in the 19th Edition of *Wrecks & Relics* (April 2004): "Other exhibits will be redistributed... Some will be going into 'deep store', others leaving [altogether]. The opportunity to contrast the Pilcher alongside the Concorde is an incredible prospect – testament to the amazing variety of exhibits the museum boasts. Not content with ignoring this perfect possibility, the iconic Pilcher is now in deep store." Patricia Ferguson, Minister of Tourism, Culture and Sport, officially opened the 'Concorde Experience' on 15th March 2005. *Wrecks & Relics 20* (April 2006) noted: "The supporting display ...is well put together but the over-riding image, for at least the compiler, is the huge waste of space within the rest of the hangar. A number of relevant and contrasting airframes could have been here, adding to the so-called 'visitor experience'." But things were to change, led by circumstances in Shropshire...

As outlined in Chapter 6, in 2006 British Airways declared it was to finance what it liked to call the "deconstruction and reconstruction" of the airliner collection previously held at the RAF Museum Cosford. MoF grasped the nettle and four airframes were bound for Scotland: BAC One-Eleven 'bus stop' jet; Rolls-Royce Conway-engined Boeing 707 forward fuselage; Hawker Siddeley Trident 1 cockpit section and four-turboprop Vickers Viscount 701. By incredible co-incidence, One-Eleven G-AVMO was Christened *Lothian Region* in 1974; it still carries that name. All but *Mike-Oscar* were accommodated indoors, the twin-jet joining the Comet 4 and Vulcan outside. The One-Eleven had been on external display at Cosford for 14 years, so it's now been 21 years in the cold; the Comet having clocked 32 and the Vulcan 29 years exposed to the elements. At the same time as Concorde made its appearance, NMS was talking of a plan to house *all* of the airliners, and probably the Vulcan, in a purpose-built exhibition hall to the east of the present site, so as not to infringe on the period buildings. Heritage Lottery Funding would be vital and it was anticipated that this phase could not be launched until 2009, at the earliest.

In April 2009 two new interactive displays were launched as part of a £2 million development. 'Fortunes of War' dealing with the airfield's history and 'Fantastic Flight' unwrapping the secrets of how aircraft fly, aimed at kids of all ages! Not content with this, on 1st April 2010 the 'Jet Age' exhibition was unveiled with the newly-refurbished and impressive-looking Boeing 707 forward fuselage in gleaming BOAC colours and the Trident 1 cockpit joining Concorde, along with an airport fire engine and evocative ephemera such as baggage trollies to set the scene. As with Concorde, visitors can sit inside the 707 and so compare 'jet set' transport of the early 1960s with the days of the 'champagne set' and sonic bangs!

Concorde G-BOAA featured heavily in British Airways publicity. *British Airways*

Former Museum of Flight and APSS Aircraft

Type	Identity	Built	Arrived	Notes, *current status or fate*
Air and Space 18A gyroplane	G-BVWL	1966	Oct 2004	*To The Helicopter Museum, Weston-super-Mare, 21 Nov 2007*
Auster AOP.5	'TJ398'	c1944	1974	APSS – Disposed of by Apr 2006. *Private owner, South Shields, Northumberland*
BA Swallow 2	G-AEVZ	1937	1974	Northern A/c Pres Soc loan. *To Hamble 17 Sep 1983 for restoration to fly; sold in Spain 2001*
BAC 221	WG774	1954	15 Jan 1975	FAA Museum loan, *returned to Yeovilton 1980, see Chapter 4.*
Bensen B.8M gyroplane	G-ARTJ	1962	15 Nov 1980	APSS – *Returned to Cupar 1995, stored at Leven, Scotland*
Brantly B.2B	G-AXSR	1967	7 Apr 1979	APSS – Disposed of during 1995. *Sold in the USA Jun 2002*
Brantly B.2B	G-ATFG	1965	1987	APSS – *To The Helicopter Museum, Weston-super-Mare, 21 Jan 2004*
Bristol Beaufighter	–	c1941	11 Dec 2000	RAF Museum loan, cockpit. Ex Hendon, Duxford, Hendon, Cranfield. *Returned to RAF Museum Hendon 17 Dec 2004*
De Havilland Dragon Rapide	G-ADAH	1935	1974	Northern A/c Pres Soc loan. *To Museum of Science and Industry, Manchester 7 Apr 1989*
De Havilland Sea Vampire T.22	XA109	1953	1972	*Departed mid-2010, at Montrose Air Station Heritage Centre, Montrose, Scotland*
Mignet HM.14 'Flying Flea'	–	1936	1977	TAC loan. *To Museum of Science and Industry, Manchester, 20 Jan 1998*
Miles Monarch	G-AFJU	1938	14 Nov 1983	APSS – *Disposed of 2007, under restoration to fly*
Rolls-Royce TMR	XJ314	1953	3 Jun 1987	Science Museum loan. *To FAA Museum Yeovilton 21 Feb 1989. At the Science Museum, London, see Chapter 1*
SAAB Safir	G-ANOK	1954	1974	On loan. *To Strathallan Aircraft Collection, 1985. Stored at Yarrow, Scotland*
Sopwith Camel replica	'B5577'	c1968	26 Nov 2002	*To Montrose Air Station Heritage Centre, Montrose, Scotland, mid-2006*
Westland Whirlwind HAS.7	XG594	1957	Aug 1991	Fleet Air Arm Museum loan. Returned to Yeovilton 11 Dec 2003, *stored at the Fleet Air Arm Museum, Chapter 4*

Avro Vulcan B.2 XM597
1963 : Five-crew long heavy range bomber | Four 20,000lb st Bristol Olympus 301

Vulcans have paid many overseas trips on 'flag waving' sorties or long-ranging exercises, but the visit of XM597 to Galeas Air Base, Rio de Janeiro, Brazil, on June 2, 1982 was by far the most momentous, hitting the headlines the world over. Four Vulcans, pooled under the aegis of Waddington-based 44 Squadron, arrived at Wideawake airfield, Ascension Island: XM597 (27th May 1982), XM598 (29th April), XM607 (29th April, now displayed at RAF Waddington) and XM612 (14th May, now at the City of Norwich Aviation Museum, Norwich Airport).

First sortie for XM597 was *Black Buck 4* of 28/29th May with it slotted as the 'Primary' with XM598 as the reserve. Argentinian radar sites around Port Stanley were the target, with both underwing pylons toting 'twin-packs' of AGM-54A Shrike anti-radiation missiles. Crew was captain Sqn Ldr Neil McDougall; co-pilot Fg Off Chris Lackham; radar nav plotter Flt Lt Dave Castle; nav plotter Flt Lt Barry Smith; air electronics officer (AEO) Flt Lt Rod Trevaskus and air-to-air refuelling instructor (AARI) Flt Lt Brian Gardner. The AARI was from the Victor tanker

Tornado F.3 ZE934, joined the collection in September 2005 having previously served at Leuchars. *Ken Ellis*

force and swopped with the co-pilot when a top-up was due, advising and guiding the Captain; Vulcan crews had long since stopped training on in-flight refuelling (IFR). *Black Buck 4* aborted when a Handley Page Victor K.2 tanker went unserviceable when the entire 'circus' was a long way towards the tiny South Atlantic target.

The whole raid, same crews, same aircraft, was rescheduled as *Black Buck 5* for the night of 30th/31st May 30. The crew was to time the arrival to co-incide with a Harrier strike so that the Argentinians would be forced to use their radar, allowing *Black Buck 5's* AEO to get a 'fix' so that the Shrikes could do their work. Three AGM-54As were launched, but damage assessment could not be undertaken. The same combo of crew and aircraft was put together for the night of 2nd/3rd, as *Black Buck 6*. This was another four-up Shrike mission, but this time with a low-level profile followed by a sharp pull-up in the hope of tempting the radar stations to 'illuminate' the delta. Two Shrikes were fired and it is thought one damaged the principal radar site.

The hook-up with the Victor after the raid ended in disaster, the IFR probe fractured. Without a hope of continuing to the next tanker, XM597 set course for Rio, the only possible diversion airfield that didn't involve Argentina. Naturally, it would have been of great help to the Brazilians if the aircraft were not armed, so the remaining Shrikes were jettisoned. One refused to go and caused many diplomatic red faces when *Black Buck 6* landed at Galeas with virtually dry tanks – probably not enough for a 'go-around'. Crew and aircraft were 'held' for a week then released; minus the errant missile and on the strict proviso that XM597 was not to be used on operations again. For this Vulcan the war was over! It arrived at Ascension on 10th June and was back at Waddington 72-hours later.

Vulcan B.2 XM597 with Blue Steel stand-off missile at East Fortune, looking north. In the background is the Law, the distinctive hill that acts as a landmark for the town of North Berwick. *Ken Ellis*

A close up of Vulcan XM597's nose, showing 'raid markings' for the two Falklands Shrike sorties and a Brazilian flag to denote its impromptu visit there. *Ken Ellis*

When XM597 undertook the *Black Buck* raids it had been in service with the RAF for 18 years, ten months. It first flew at Woodford on 12th July 1963 and was taken on charge by 12 Squadron at Coningsby on 28th August. From 21st December 1964 XM597 was on charge with the Cottesmore Wing (a pool of 9, 12 and 35 Squadrons) at the Rutland base. On 18th April 1967 it moved over to its last 'home', Waddington, and that station's Vulcan wing, then comprising 44, 50 and 101 Squadrons (with 9 Squadron joining from January 1975). Briefly detached to the Aeroplane & Armament Experimental Establishment at Boscombe Down for trials of a revised radar warning receiver, XM597 was back at Waddington by 12th February 1973. On 12th April 1984 the V-Bomber was ferried north to its new home in Scotland.

Britten-Norman Islander G-BELF
1977 | Passenger/utility light aircraft | Two 260hp Lycoming O-540-E4C5

With 1,250-plus built, the Islander is Europe's most successful light commercial aircraft. In continuous production since April 1967, Islanders are in service in 120 countries. All of this adds up to the type being exceptionally important and with the launch customer being Scottish airline Loganair it is not surprising that MoF has an example. John Britten and Desmond Norman combined their talents in 1949 and produced the one-off BN-1 G-ALZE two years later – this machine is presently on show at Solent Sky in Southampton. The pair spent much of the 1950s developing aerial spraying techniques and hovercraft. Design of the BN-2 Islander started in 1963 and on 13th June 1965 both men were at the helm of the prototype, flying from Britten-Norman's base at Bembridge on the Isle of Wight. From August 1969 a production agreement with IRMA in Romania meant that all airframes were built there in basic form, coming to Bembridge for customisation. The first three-engined and enlarged Trislander flew in September 1970, entering limited production. From 1971 the Islander was offered in military guise as the Defender and in 1980 the first turboprop version was flown. Headquartered at Daedalus Airfield (the former Fleet Air arm Lee-on-Solent base) since 2011, the Britten-Norman Group now largely caters for the security and surveillance market.

East Fortune's Islander first flew at Bucharest, Romania, as G-BELF on 18th August 1977, arriving at Bembridge on 5th September. It was fitted out for its customer, Atlas Air Services of West Germany, which

One of many East Fortune coups, Islander G-BELF. *Ken Ellis*

operated it as D-IBRA. It was restored to the UK register in October 1987, joining Coventry-based Atlantic Air Transport. From 1991 it served with a succession of skydiving outfits, in Sussex, Dundee and Lancashire. In mid-2004 it was acquired by Cormack (Air Services) Ltd at Cumbernauld in Scotland and re-registered as G-HEBZ. Proprietor George Cormack donated the Islander to the museum and it was handed over on 7th July 2005. Painted in the colours of the Scottish Air Ambulance service, it is the only intact Islander preserved in the UK.

De Havilland Dragon VH-SNB
1942 | Six/eight passenger and utility | Two 130hp DH Gipsy Major I

In many ways, the Britten-Norman Islander (above) is a modern interpretation of the ground-breaking Dragon biplane that first appeared on 12th November 1932. The last of 115 came off the line in 1936, the type still finding a market despite the advent of the later DH.89 Dragon Rapide. An urgent requirement for a radio and navigator trainer for the Royal Australian Air Force (RAAF) brought a surprising return for the Dragon. Car manufacturer Holden was already building the Gipsy Major engine and the more simplistic DH.84 could be built faster than the DH.89. De Havilland Australia at Bankstown, New South Wales, produced 87 DH.84As within a year from September 1942.

In the 1930s Dragons were operated by Aberdeen Airways, Highland Airways, Midland and Scottish Air Ferries, Northern and Scottish Airways and Scottish Motor Traction; the type helped to open up the highlands and islands of Scotland to air travel and introduced air mail and air ambulance flights. With this background, it is not surprising that a Dragon should have been high on MoF's 'hit list'. Sir William Roberts wanted a Dragon for his Strathallan Aircraft Collection at Auchterarder and acquired an Australian-built example in 1973 from New South Wales (NSW). This was auctioned off on 14th June 1981, being 'hammered' for £7,000 and moving to EF. Built as a DH.84A at Bankstown for the RAAF as A34-13 it was first issued to 2 Air Depot at Point Cook, Victoria, on 25th October 1942. It was modified for ambulance duties and taken on charge by 6 Communications Flight at Batchelor, Northern Territories, on 22nd May 1943. It was retired into storage in July 1945 and transferred to the Commonwealth Department of Health with the civil registration VH-ASK in mid-1946 and worked for the Royal Flying Doctor Service until January 1954. By the late 1950s it had been re-registered as VH-SNB and it went through a series of private owners until it was out of use at Camden, NSW, in the early 1970s.

Gloster Meteor NF.14 G-ARCX
1953 | Two-crew night/all-weather fighter | Two 3,600lb st Rolls-Royce Derwent 8

Laid down as NF.11 WM261 in March 1953, East Fortune's Meteor was completed as the NF.14 prototype and first flew at Bitteswell on 15th July 1953. It was despatched to the Aeroplane & Armament Experimental Establishment at Boscombe Down for trials 13 days later. There, it was initially placed in front of the huge blower unit – to assess the blown-Perspex canopy for open cockpit and jettison trials – before staging an airborne assessment of the new arrangement. It returned to AWA for further development work then moved to Warton for use by English Electric on the Lightning's Ferranti AIRPASS (Airborne Interception Radar and Pilot Attack Sight System). Sold to Ferranti on 6th September 1960 and civilian registered as G-ARCX it was ferried to the company's operating base at Turnhouse, now Edinburgh Airport. It was converted to act as a radar test-bed, initially with the AIRPASS II system and made its first flight in its new guise on 21st January1963. *Charlie-X-ray* was retired in February 1969 with a total flying time of just 364 hours 30 minutes and stored at Turnhouse. Ferranti presented it to MoF in 1973 and it arrived at EF in August 1975. With its overall off-white colour scheme and red fuselage stripe, the Meteor was frequently referred to at Turnhouse as 'Mentadent', after the pioneering two-colour toothpaste of the time!

Pilcher Hawk
1896 | One-man hang-glider

The honour of being the first complete aircraft to be presented to a British museum belongs to Percy Sinclair Pilcher's Hawk glider; the oldest heavier-than-air craft in the UK. It was placed on loan to the RSM in Edinburgh in August 1909. This pre-dates the Cody at the Science Museum (Chapter 1) by 28 months, but as the latter was donated, the author sticks to his guns that No.304 is the UK's first whole flying machine in full-blown museum care! Irrespective of this, the Hawk is elemental to the history of flight in the UK and one of the oldest fixed-wing aircraft in the world. As will be seen below, while it was built in Glasgow, all of the Hawk's flying took place in England, but its time in 'captivity' has been largely Scottish. Who knows, depending on Scotland's whims when it comes to the independence referendum in the autumn of 2014, the less-than-United Kingdom may have a claim on it coming south o' the border!

Percy Sinclair Pilcher was born in Bath in 1867 and joined the Royal Navy at 13 but after six years pulled out to study engineering. He became an assistant lecturer in naval architecture at Glasgow University. Fascinated by flight, he built his first glider, the Bat, in 1895. In modern-day terminology, Pilcher's designs would be called hang-gliders, with the pilot influencing flight by shifting his weight and 'hanging' within the structure, with his legs also acting as 'undercarriage'. Prior to trials with the Bat, Pilcher travelled to Berlin to watch the Prussian, Otto Lilienthal, the first person in history to make sustained, fixed-wing flights. Pilcher's initial glides in the Bat took place at Cardross, west of Dumbarton, in June 1985. These launches were the first true fixed-wing flights in the UK.

Yorkshireman Sir George Cayley's glider of 1849 had a ten-year old on board and then his coachman went aloft in 1853 – both were certainly flying in a fixed-wing device, but they could never be termed 'pilots', they were passengers. This is not to erode Cayley's place in aviation history. He was the father of flight, determining the dynamics involved and defining the format of fixed-wing aircraft, inspiring the 'second generation' of pioneers, including Pilcher. While Percy might have been 'along for the ride' in the early glides, he was *piloting* his creation and his knowledge of how to control his progress increased with each launch. The Bat was followed by the Beetle later in 1895, featuring cruciform tail surfaces, and early the following year with the Gull, with a much larger wing area.

Pilcher's fourth device was the Hawk, designed and built in Glasgow over the winter of 1895-1896 with help from Percy's sister, Ella. In the new year Percy moved to Kent to help US-born Hiram Stevens Maxim (Sir Hiram from 1901) who had made a fortune from inventing the machine-gun that carried his name. Maxim was hurling money at achieving powered flight with his huge 104ft-span, steam-powered and ultimately aborted biplane. (Elements of this survive with the Science Museum, see Chapter 1.) Pilcher first tested the Hawk at Eynsford, Kent, in the summer of 1896 and during the spring of 1897 carried out to some excursions with the use of a tow-line. On 19th July 1897 a flight of 250 yards was achieved. In 1897 Pilcher was presented with a Lilienthal glider which had been acquired from Germany in March 1895 by T J Bennett. Pilcher did not fly it and it is believed that Bennett didn't either. This craft is today held in store by the Science Museum – see Chapter 1.

While demonstrating the Hawk in the grounds of Lard Braye's estate at Stanford Hall, near Rugby, on 30th September 1899, Pilcher reached about 30 to 40ft under tow from horses when a structural failure brought the craft plummeting to the ground. Percy Pilcher died from his injuries on 2nd October; he was just 32 and the second man to perish in a fixed-wing aircraft accident. (The first was his inspiration, Lilienthal, who crashed on 10th August 1986 and died 36 hours later.)

At the time of his death, Pilcher was working on a powered triplane using a pusher-configured 4hp oil engine of his own design. A team from Cranfield University's College of Aeronautics faculty and Bill Brooks of Mainair Sports built a modern-day version for a TV film in 2003 to see if the design could fly. Powered by a 8hp two-stroke powerchute engine, it was flown by Bill Brooks on 29th August 2003 and seven days later succeeded in a flight of a quarter of a mile. This exercise in 'what if' thinking was presented to the Shuttleworth Collection (Chapter 3) and today 'flies' within the main hangar block at Old Warden.

The Hawk was presented to the Royal Aeronautical Society (RAeS) in early 1900 and shown at the Crystal Palace. In January 1901 it was put into the care of RAeS member E P Frost as it had become dilapidated and in December 1906 it was moved to Alexandra Palace, but not unpacked from its crate. It was repaired in 1909 by Thomas Wigston Kingslake, Clarke and Company of Kingston-on-Thames (the Clarke Chanute-type biplane glider of 1910 is part of the RAF Museum collection – see Chapter 5) and it went on show at Olympia on 6th July 1909. In August 1909 it was presented on loan to RSM and displayed. After 18th March 1911 it was lent to the Scottish National Exhibition at Glasgow and on 5th November 1911 it was damaged when a building collapsed in a gale. Repairs were instigated by RSM and completed on 24th January 1912.

In January and February 1913 the Pilcher, the Clarke Chanute and the Bennett/Pilcher Lilienthal (see above) were exhibited at the Science Museum at its first aeronautically-themed exhibition. It was back at RSM by March. Around October/November 1913 it was shown by the RAeS at the Ghent Exhibition, returning to RSM on 16th January 1914. The Hawk was given to RSM on a permanent basis on 24th March 1920 and was suspended from the ceiling of the Machinery Hall at Chambers Street, Edinburgh. It was stored during the war years in a dismantled state, during which time the fabric rotted, and it remained out of sight until 1961. On 17th March that year, the Hawk was taken to Old Warden and restored by the Shuttleworth Collection, under the guidance of Leonard 'Jacko' Jackson. It was returned to Edinburgh and put on display from 12th November 1963. In 1993 it was transferred to EF and put on show in Hangar 4, amid hang-gliders, gliders and aircraft of later eras. With the coming of Concorde, the Hawk was put into store and its centenary of joining the RSM and its successor organisation was completely passed by. Plans are that this incredibly important exhibit will again be on public view, in Chambers Street, in 2013 or 2014.

The Pilcher Hawk at Glasgow, prior to gaining tail surfaces, 1896. *via Don Storer*

Scottish Aviation Twin Pioneer Series 3 G-BBVF
1959 | Civil/military short take-off and landing utility transport | Two 640hp Alvis Leonides

Based at Prestwick, near Ayr, Scottish Aviation Ltd (SAL) had found a niche market with its single-engined Pioneer and followed it up with a twin-engined design. Built for the RAF as Twin Pioneer CC.1 XM961, SAL was ready to hand this machine over at Prestwick on 14th January 1959. It was ferried out to Kenya via Benson, going on charge with 21 Squadron at Eastleigh, on 1st June. Its time in East Africa was short, joining 230 Squadron at Odiham on 23rd September 1960. No.230 was the last RAF unit to operate the 'Twin Pin' and by April 1962 it was busy converting to Westland Whirlwind HAR.10 helicopters. There was still a need to keep pilots current on the big 'taildragger' twin and after a spell of modifications – perhaps upgrade to CC.2 status – at Prestwick, XM261 was put on charge with the Station Flight at Odiham from July 1963. It was finally retired on 13th July 1967, going to 27 Maintenance Unit at Shawbury. Turn-around here was swift and 16 days later it moved to 1 School of Technical Training at Halton, becoming a ground instructional airframe.

Its flying days were not over as aerial photography specialist Flight One, based at Staverton was looking to expand its fleet of civilian 'Twin Pins'. A deal was struck for XM961 in July 1973 and it was registered as G-BBVF in December 1973. After modification to an aerial camera platform, *Victor-Fox* entered service in May 1974. On 30th September 1981 G-BBVF was ferried to Shobdon, near Hereford, for storage, clocking up a total of 3,549 flying hours. Sadly, *Victor-Fox* was damaged in a gale on 11th March 1982 and its flying days were definitely over. MoF had been looking for a suitable Twin Pioneer for a long time and a deal was reached. Curator David N Brown decamped to Herefordshire and undertook much of the initial dismantling almost single-handed; G-BBVF moved to EF in September 1982.

Scottish Aviation Bulldog 104 G-AXIG
1971 | Primary trainer | One 200hp Lycoming IO-360-A1B6

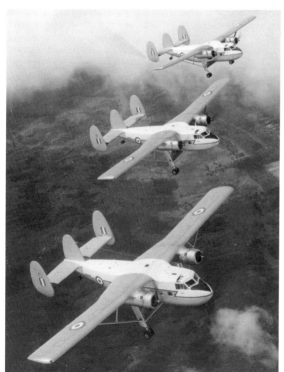

NMS boasts two examples of the most produced aircraft in Scotland – the Bulldog. As the Pup civilian trainer/tourer became a success Beagle Aircraft decided to create a trainer version with an eye on the RAF's need to replace the venerable de Havilland Canada Chipmunk. The prototype Bulldog, G-AXEH, first flew at Shoreham, Sussex, on 19th May 1969 and was vigorously marketed. Launch customer was the Swedish Defence Ministry and early in 1970 *Echo-Hotel* was in Sweden undertaking trials, including ski undercarriage. Beagle collapsed in 1970 and the company was put into liquidation. In June 1970 Scottish Aviation Ltd (SAL) secured the design rights to the Bulldog and continued development. *Echo-Hotel* moved to Prestwick and became a demonstrator. It was presented by British Aerospace (which absorbed SAL in 1977) and flown to EF on 23rd December 1984.

Twin Pioneer XM961 in the foreground of a formation of 21 Squadron examples, Kenya, 1959. *KEC*

Bulldog G-AXIG in Swedish colours during 1971. *Scottish Aviation*

The second prototype was started at Shoreham but came north to Prestwick for completion. As G-AXIG, it had its maiden flight on 14th February 1971. It became a hard-working demonstrator until it was replaced by Series 120 G-ASAL in 1974. By that time the factory at Prestwick was meeting its largest order for 130 Bulldog T.1s for the RAF. The Bulldog found considerable favour in the export market and the last of 320 was delivered to Botswana in 1982. Bulldogs were phased out of RAF service in 2001 and the type has since become a very popular private aircraft. SAL disposed of *India-Golf* in November 1973 but it returned to Scottish skies in 1997 when it was acquired by Angus Alan Douglas Hamilton. During this time, it carried Swedish camouflage and yellow roundels with a red heraldic lion; these markings were described by Angus as those of the "Scottish Republican Air Force"! Angus – the 15th Duke of Hamilton – was well versed with the Bulldog, having been a test pilot for SAL, and he test flew G-AXIG in 1971. Angus died, aged 71, on 5th June 2010 and *India-Golf* was presented to NMS. On 23rd February 2011 the Bulldog made a short hop from its base at the airstrip at Dirleton to EF, for its last-ever flight. In July it was mounted in 'flying' pose within NMS in Chambers Street, Edinburgh.

A selection of Museum of Flight publications. *KEC*

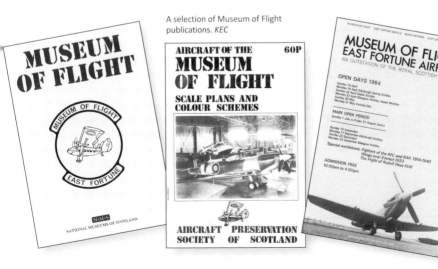

National Museum of Scotland aircraft

Type	Identity	Built	Origin	Arrived	Notes
Kay Gyroplane	G-ACVA	1935	UK	mid-2009	at East Fortune from 1998
Pilcher Hawk*	–	1896	UK	due	see profile
Scottish Aviation Bulldog 104	G-AXIG	1971	UK	Jul 2011	see profile
Weir W-2	W-2	1934	UK	late 2005	–

National Museum of Flight Scotland aircraft

Type	Identity	Built	Origin	Arrived	Notes
Air & Space 18A gyroplane	G-BVWK	1965	USA	Oct 2004	–
Avro Anson C.19	VM360	1947	UK	Aug 1977	–
Avro Vulcan B.2	XM597	1963	UK	12 Apr 1984	see profile
BAC 111-510ED	G-AVMO	1968	UK	9 Sep 2006	–
BAC/Sud Concorde 102*	G-BOAA	1975	UK / France	19 Apr 2004	see narrative
Beagle Bulldog Srs 1	G-AXEH	1969	UK	23 Dec 1984	–
Beech E.18S	G-ASUG	1956	USA	1976	–
Boeing 707-436	G-APFJ	1960	USA	Apr 2006	fuselage
Bristol Bolingbroke IVT	9940	1942	UK	8 Aug 1981	–
Bristol Beaufighter TF.10	BF-10	1944	UK	9 Dec 2000	ex RAF RD220
Britten-Norman BN-2A Islander	G-BELF	1977	UK	7 Jul 2005	see profile
De Havilland Puss Moth	VH-UQB	1930	UK	1981	–
De Havilland Tiger Moth	G-AOEL	1940	UK	1980	–
De Havilland Dragon I	VH-SNB	1942	UK	1981	see profile
De Havilland Dove 6	G-ANOV	1954	UK	Oct 1978	–
De Havilland Comet 4C*	G-BDIX	1962	UK	30 Sep 1981	–
De Havilland Sea Venom FAW.22	WW145	1955	UK	1972	–
Druine Turbulent	G-AVPC	1973	France	Apr 2003	–
English Electric Canberra B.5	VX185	1952	UK	Oct 1997	cockpit
English Electric Lightning F.2A*	XN776	1962	UK	8 May 1982	–
General Aircraft Cygnet II*	G-AGBN	1941	UK	11 Aug 1981	–
Gloster Meteor Mk.14	G-ARCX	1953	UK	Aug 1975	see profile
Handley Page Jetstream 1	G-BBBV	1969	UK	May 1994	fuselage
Handley Page Jetstream 3100	G-JSSD	1969	UK	Feb 1996	–
Hawker Sea Hawk F.2	WF259	1954	UK	10 Jul 1972	–
Hawker Siddeley Trident 1C	G-ARPH	1964	UK	2006	cockpit
Hawker Siddeley Buccaneer S.2B	XT288	1966	UK	Jul 1994	–
Hawker Siddeley Harrier GR.1*	XV277	1966	UK	Apr 2000	–
Hawker Siddeley Nimrod MR.2	XV241	1970	UK	10 Feb 2011	fuselage
Ikarus C42 microlight	G-SJEN	2004	Germany	Jul 2011	–
McDonnell F-4S Phantom II	155848	1968	USA	13 May 1999	–
Messerschmitt Me 163B Komet	191659	1944	Germany	1976	–
Mikoyan-Gurevich MiG-15bis	3677	1953	USSR	Dec 1993	Czech-built Letov S-103
Miles M.18-2	G-AHKY	1940	UK	1991	–
Morane-Saulnier Criquet	G-BIRW	1947	Germany	9 Nov 1982	–
Panavia Tornado F.3	ZE934	1989	UK/Ger/It	13 Sep 2005	–
Percival Provost T.1	WV493	1953	UK	11 Aug 1981	–
Piper Comanche 260B*	G-ATOY	1966	USA	1979	–
Saro Skeeter AOP.12	XL762	1958	UK	1 Nov 1975	–
Scottish Aviation Twin Pioneer 2*	G-BBVF	1959	UK	19 Aug 1982	see profile
SEPECAT Jaguar GR.1A	XZ119	1976	UK / France	27 Apr 2009	–

Type	Identity	Built	Origin	Arrived	Notes
Spartan Cruiser III	G-ACYK	1935	UK	1973	gutted fuselage, see narrative
Supermarine Spitfire XVI	TE462	1945	UK	19 Feb 1971	–
Vickers Viscount 701	G-AMOG	1953	UK	17 Aug 2006	–

Note: * – Illustrated in the colour sections.

National Museum of Flight Scotland aircraft in 'deep store'

Type	Identity	Built	Origin	Arrived	Notes
Airwave Magic Kiss hang-glider	–	1989	UK	2005	–
Albatros ASG.21 hang-glider	–	1977	Germany	1995	–
Birdman Moonraker hang-glider	–	1977	USA	1987	–
Blackburn Buccaneer S.1	XK533	1961	UK	1972	cockpit
Catto CA-16 microlight	–	1981	USA	1983	–
Chargus 18/50 hang-glider	–	1975	USA	from new	–
Dragonfly 2 man-powered aircraft	G-BDFU	1981	UK	1981	–
Electra Floater hang-glider	–	1979	USA	1995	–
Eurowing Goldwing	G-MBPM	1980	UK	Apr 1999	–
Firebird Sierra hang-glider	–	c1983	USA	2002	–
Goldmarque Gyr	–	c1982	UK	2002	–
Hiway Cloudbase hang-glider	–	1979	UK	1995	–
Hiway Super Scorpion microlight	G-MBJX	1982	UK	1998	–
Mikoyan-Gurevich MiG-15UTI	3309	1953	USSR	Dec 1993	Polish-built WSK SBLim-2
Schleicher Rhönlerche II glider	591	1956	Germany	1987	–
Scotkites Cirrus III hang-glider	–	1982	UK	1987	–
Slingsby Gull I glider	BED	1938	UK	1968	–
Slingsby Cadet TX.2 glider	TS291	1944	UK	1980	–
Slingsby Grasshopper TX.1 glider	XA228	1953	UK	Jun 2000	–
Slingsby T.21A glider	BJV	1949	UK	28 May 1982	–
Solar Tri-Flyer / Typhoon micro	G-MMLI	1984	UK	1998	–
Southdown Sigma II hang-glider	–	1980	UK	1987	–
Waco CG-4A Hadrian assault glider	–	1944	USA	1980	nose section

Museum of Flight publications. *KEC*

CHAPTER 11

WALES
National Waterfront Museum, Swansea

Although Wales has a diverse aeronautical heritage it has never had a 'national' aviation collection. Presently within the Principality there are four museums with aeronautical content, all with varying degrees of merit but none of these constitute a national 'flag-waver'. Bizarrely, the National Waterfront Museum at Swansea houses the Watkins CHW, arguably the jewel in the aviation crown of Wales. Because of the status of the Watkins, its provenance is profiled.

Watkins CHW Monoplane
1909 | Single-seat monoplane | One 40hp Watkins

Charles Horace Watkins of Maendy, Cardiff, seems to have kept himself to himself with a great degree of success. Despite designing and building his own aeroplane, including its three-cylinder engine and some remarkable devices to help him fly it, there is not one independent source to vouch for him. Wg Cdr Paul Brindley, curator of the aircraft collection at RAF St Athan, near Barry, spent a lot of time with Mr Watkins and wrote extensively on his findings. Try as he might, Paul could not pin it down to a definitive chronology. Be this as it may, the CHW is certainly the most precious indigenous Welsh aviation artefact and at the very least is now 100 years old.

Above: The Watkins CHW Monoplane during a rare moment outside of the 'museum' hangars at St Athan, Wales, in early 1974. *KEC*

Watkins was born in 1885 and trained as a motor engineer. He built the monoplane at Mynachdy Farm from as early as 1907 and to at least 1909, he claimed. Watkins said that the project cost about £300 which would be in the region of £33,000 in present-day values. The monoplane took its designer's initials – CHW – as its designation but it was more often referred to by its affectionate name, *Robin Goch* (Red Robin) because of the red dope with which its flying surfaces were covered. When asked why there was no newspaper reports to back up his exploits, Watkins explained that he never saw the need to alert the 'media' and that when he made his early flights, large crowds came to the farm, breaking fences and disturbing hedges in their attempts to get a better view. His answer to this was to aviate close to dusk or just after dawn. Watkins said that he made his first 'hop' in 1909 and was making cross-countries, including flying over Cardiff's dockland, by the following year. (Memo: Cody first got properly airborne on 16th October 1908 and Roe likewise on 13th July 1909 – see Chapter 1.) Watkins flew *Robin Goch* extensively until a cylinder cracked in 1916 – the onset of war not deterring him – and he put the monoplane into store. Watkins also claimed to have worked for A V Roe up to the outbreak of World War One but, again, this cannot be substantiated.

Control of the wings was initially by wing-warping, but Watkins found this unsatisfactory. He then devised what he called 'ballast boxes' where sand could be moved into 'collectors' within the wing and the weight would alter the aerofoil shape. The remains of this system could be seen at St Athan, but Watkins abandoned this for what he called 'flaps', acting as ailerons. The CHW had an incredible 'autoland' system, very likely to help Watkins when flying beyond dusk or around dawn. From the cockpit trailed two wires, each with a weight at the end. The longest was 12ft and as this dragged along the ground it would trigger an indicator in the cockpit, warning the pilot. The second wire was six feet long and when its weight came into contact with terra firma it cut the engine, ready for what would later be called a flare and a touch-down.

Robin Goch came out of hibernation in 1943 and was displayed prominently at Cardiff's 'Wings for Victory' exhibition and this appears to be the first time it made the newspapers. Immediately post-war Watkins offered the monoplane to Cardiff's Welsh Museum, but he was not happy with the plans to show it and the CHW remained a recluse. When approached by an officer from RAF St Athan in 1959, Watkins decided to let it be kept at the base and it moved there in 1961. It was re-assembled in 1962 with the help of its creator and a careful restoration was initiated. Charles Horace Watkins, Welsh aviation pioneer, died in 1976. With the winding down of the St Athan collection, the CHW moved to the National Museum and Gallery of Wales in Cardiff in January 1998 and in 2007 it was installed in the National Waterfront Museum at Swansea.

LOCAL TREASURE

As mentioned in the Introduction, the UK basks in a large number of aviation museums all containing their own particular delights and a goodly number of highly-significant aircraft. Their story, particularly the 'amateur' pioneers of the 1960s, deserves telling in its write. One day, perhaps...

The briefest of details follow for museums holding airframes and open to the public, without prior permission, *at least* at weekends. For those that hunger for more, then the latest edition of *Wrecks & Relics* will provide the gen!

ENGLAND

BEDFORDSHIRE

Stondon Transport Museum, Lower Stondon, near Hitchin | **www.transportmuseum.co.uk**
306th Bomb Group Museum, Thurleigh, Bedford | **www.306bg.co.uk**

BERKSHIRE

Museum of Berkshire Aviation, Woodley, Reading | **www.museumofberkshireaviation.co.uk**
REME Museum of Technology, Arborfield, near Reading | **www.rememuseum.org.uk**

CHESHIRE

RAF Burtonwood Heritage Centre, Burtonwood, west of Warrington | **www.burtonwoodbase.org**

CORNWALL

Classic Air Force, Cornwall Newquay Airport, St Mawgan | **www.classicairforce.com**
Davidstow Airfield and Cornwall At War Museum, Davidstow Moor, near Camelford | **www.cornwallatwarmuseum.co.uk**
Davidstow Moor RAF Memorial Museum, Davidstow Moor, near Camelford | **www.davidstowmemorialmuseum.co.uk**
The Flambards Experience, Helston, north of Culdrose | **www.flambards.co.uk**
Land's End, south west of Penzance | **www.landsend-landmark.co.uk**
National Maritime Museum, Falmouth | **www.nmmc.co.uk**

CUMBRIA

Lakeland Motor Museum, Blackbarrow, near Ulverston | **www.lakelandmotormuseum.co.uk**
Solway Aviation Museum, Carlisle Airport | **www.solway-aviation-museum.co.uk**

DERBYSHIRE

Derby Industrial Museum, Derby | **www.derby.gov.uk**

DEVON

Cobbaton Combat Collection, near South Molton | **www.cobbatoncombat.co.uk**

DORSET

Bournemouth Aviation Museum, Bournemouth Airport | **www.aviation-museum.co.uk**
Tank Museum, near Wool, west of Wareham | **www.tankmuseum.co.uk**

ESSEX

Boxted Airfield Historical Group Museum, north of Colchester | **www.boxted-airfield.com**

East Essex Aviation Museum and Museum of the 1940s, Clacton on Sea |
www.eastessexaviationsociety.org

North Weald Airfield Museum, North Weald Aerodrome, east of Harlow |
www.northwealdairfieldmuseum.com

Purfleet Heritage and Military Centre, Purfleet, west of the Dartford Bridge | **www.purfleet-heritage.com**

Stow Maries – A Place in History, near South Woodham Ferrers | **www.stowmaries.com**

GLOUCESTERSHIRE

Bristol's City Museum and Art Gallery, Bristol | **www.bristol-city.gov.uk/museums**

Jet Age Museum, Gloucestershire Airport, Staverton | **www.jetagemuseum.org**

M Shed, Bristol | **www.mshed.org**

Wellington Aviation Museum, Moreton-in-Marsh | **www.wellingtonaviation.org**

HAMPSHIRE

Calshot Castle and Heritage Area, south east of Fawley | **www.calshot.com/castle.html**

Solent Sky, Southampton | **www.spitfireonline.co.uk**

HERTFORDSHIRE

De Havilland Aircraft Heritage Centre, London Colney, near St Albans | **www.dehavillandmuseum.co.uk**

KENT

Brenzett Aeronautical Museum Trust, Brenzett, near New Romney | **www.brenzettaero.co.uk**

Dover Museum, Dover | **www.doverc.co.uk**

The Historic Dockyard Chatham, Chatham, east of Rochester | **www.thedockyard.co.uk**

Kent Battle of Britain Museum, Hawkinge, north of Folkestone | **www.kbobm.org**

Lashenden Air Warfare Museum, Lashenden Aerodrome, Headcorn |
www.lashendenairwarfaremuseum.co.uk

National Battle of Britain Memorial, Capel le Ferne, near Folkestone | **www.battleofbritainmemorial.org**

RAF Manston History Museum, Kent Airport, Manston | **www.rafmanston.co.uk**

Royal Engineers Museum and Library, Chatham | **www.re-museum.org.uk**

Shoreham Aircraft Museum, Shoreham, north of Sevenoaks | **www.shoreham-aircraft-museum.co.uk**

Spitfire and Hurricane Memorial Museum, Kent Airport, Manston | **www.spitfiremuseum.org.uk**

LEICESTERSHIRE

Charnwood Museum, Loughborough | **www.leics.gov.uk/museums**

East Midlands Airport Aeropark, Castle Donington | **www.eastmidlandsaeropark.org**

Lutterworth Museum, Lutterworth | **www.lutterworthmuseum.com**

Snibston Discovery Park, Coalville | **www.leics.gov.uk/museums/snibston**

LINCOLNSHIRE

Battle of Britain Memorial Flight, RAF Coningsby, near Woodhall Spa | **www.raf.mod.uk/bbmf**

Cranwell Aviation Heritage Centre, south of RAF Cranwell, near Sleaford | **www.heartoflincs.com**

Lincolnshire Aviation Heritage Centre, East Kirkby, near Spilsby | **www.lincsaviation.co.uk**

Metheringham Airfield Visitor Centre, Metheringham, near Woodhall Spa |
www.metheringhamairfield.com

LINCOLNSHIRE continued...

North Coates Heritage Collection, North Coates Aerodrome, near Humberston | **www.northcoatesflyingclub.co.uk**

Thorpe Camp Visitor Centre, near Woodhall Spa | **www.thorpecamp.org.uk**

GREATER LONDON

Firepower – The Royal Artillery Museum, Woolwich | **www.firepower.org.uk**

GREATER MANCHESTER

Museum of Science and Industry, Manchester | **www.mosi.org.uk**

Runway Visitor Park, Manchester Airport | **www.manchesterairport.co.uk/manweb.nsf/content/concordeviewingpark**

WEST MIDLANDS

Thinktank – Millennium Discovery Centre, Birmingham | **www.thinktank.ac**

NORFOLK

City of Norwich Aviation Museum, Norwich Airport | **www.cnam.co.uk**

Fenland and West Norfolk Aviation Museum, West Walton Highway, near Wisbech| **http://fawnaps.webs.com**

RAF Air Defence Radar Museum, Neatishead, near Hoveton | **www.radarmuseum.co.uk**

Muckleburgh Collection, Weybourne | **www.muckleburgh.co.uk**

100th Bomb Group Memorial Museum, Thorpe Abbotts, near Dickleburgh | **www.100bgmus.org.uk**

NORTHAMPTONSHIRE

'Carpetbagger' Aviation Museum, Harrington, near Market Harborough | **www.harringtonmuseum.org.uk**

Sywell Aviation Museum, Sywell Aerodrome, Northampton | **www.sywellaerodrome.co.uk/museum.php**

NORTHUMBERLAND and TYNESIDE

Bamburgh Castle Aviation Artefacts Museum, Bamburgh, near Seahouses | **www.bamburghcastle.com**

North East Aircraft Museum, Usworth, Sunderland | **www.neam.org.uk**

NOTTINGHAMSHIRE

Newark Air Museum, Newark Showground, Winthorpe | **www.newarkairmuseum.org**

SOMERSET

The Helicopter Museum, Weston-super-Mare | **www.helicoptermuseum.co.uk**

STAFFORDSHIRE

The Potteries Museum and Art Gallery, Stoke-on-Trent | **www.stokemuseums.org.uk**

SUFFOLK

Norfolk and Suffolk Aviation Museum, Flixton, near Bungay | **www.aviationmuseum.net**

Parham Airfield Museum, Framlingham, near Woodbridge | **www.parhamairfieldmuseum.co.uk**

SURREY

Brooklands Museum, Brooklands, south of Weybridge | **www.brooklandsmuseum.com**

Gatwick Aviation Museum, Charlwood, near Gatwick Airport | **www.gatwick-aviation-museum.co.uk**

EAST SUSSEX

Newhaven Fort, east of Brighton | **www.newhavenfort.org.uk**

WEST SUSSEX

Shoreham Airport Visitor Centre, Shoreham Airport | **www.visitorcentre.info**
Tangmere Military Aviation Museum, Tangmere Airfield, east of Chichester | **www.tangmere-museum.org.uk**
Wings World War Two Remembrance Museum, Balcombe, south of Crawley | **www.wingsmuseum.co.uk**

WARWICKSHIRE

Midland Air Museum, Coventry Airport | **www.midlandairmuseum.co.uk**
Wellesbourne Wartime Museum, Wellesbourne Mountford Aerodrome | **www.xm655.com**

WILTSHIRE

Boscombe Down Aviation Collection, Old Sarum Aerodrome, near Salisbury
|**www.boscombedownaviationcollection.co.uk**

EAST YORKSHIRE

Fort Paull Armouries, Paull, near Hedon | **www.fortpaull.com**
Streetlife Museum of Transport, Hull | **www.hullcc.gov.uk**

NORTH YORKSHIRE

Eden Camp Modern History Theme Museum, Malton, near York | **www.edencamp.co.uk**
Yorkshire Air Museum and Allied Air Forces Memorial, Elvington, near York |
www.yorkshireairmuseum.org

SOUTH YORKSHIRE

Doncaster Museum and Art Gallery, Doncaster | **www.doncaster.gov.uk/museums**
South Yorkshire Aircraft Museum, Doncaster Lakeside Leisure Park |
www.southyorkshireaircraftmuseum.org.uk

ISLE OF MAN

Manx Aviation and Military Museum, Isle of Man Airport | **www.maps.iofm.net**

SCOTLAND

Dumfries and Galloway Aviation Museum, Dumfries | **www.dumfriesaviationmuseum.com**
Highland Aviation Museum, Dalcross Industrial Estate, Inverness | **www.highlandaviationmuseum.org.uk**
Kelvingrove Art Gallery and Museum, Glasgow | **www.glasgowmuseums.com**
Montrose Air Station Heritage Centre, Montrose | **www.rafmontrose.org.uk**

WALES

Caernarfon Airport Airworld Museum, Caernarfon Aerodrome | **www.airworldmuseum.co.uk**
Carew Control Tower Group, Carew Cheriton, near Pembroke | **www.carewcheritoncontroltower.co.uk**
Pembroke Dock Flying-Boat Visitor Centre, Pembroke Dock, Pembroke | **www.sunderlandtrust.org.uk**

BIBLIOGRAPHY

Books and DVDs

Action Stations Revisited, Vol 1 Eastern England and *Volume 2 Central England and London Area*, Michael J F Bowyer, Crécy Publishing, Manchester, 2000 and 2004

Aeronautics – Handbook of the Collections Illustrating Heavier-than-Air Craft, M J B Davy, Science Museum, HMSO, London, 1929

Aeroplanes of the Royal Flying Corps (Military Wing), Jack M Bruce, Putnam, London, 1982

Aircraft of the Royal Air Force since 1918, Owen Thetford, Putnam Aeronautical Books, London, ninth edition, 1995

Air Wars and Aircraft – Air Combat 1945 to the Present, Victor Lintham, Arms & Armour, London, 1989

American Air Museum Duxford – A Tribute to American Air Power, Roger A Freeman, Midland Publishing, Hinckley, 2001

Armstrong Whitworth Aircraft since 1913, Oliver Tapper, Putnam, London, second edition, 1978

Aviation in Leicestershire and Rutland, Roy Bonser, Midland Publishing, Hinckley, 2001

Avro Aircraft since 1908, A J Jackson, Putnam, London, second edition, 1990

Avro Lancaster – The Definitive Record, Harry Holmes, Airlife, Shrewsbury, 2001

Avro's Maritime Heavyweight – The Shackleton, Chris Ashworth, Aston, Bourne End, 1990

Bases: The Encyclopaedia of Airfields and Military Flying Units in Britain since 1912, DVD, Air-Britain, Tonbridge, 2012

Blackburn Aircraft since 1909, A J Jackson, Putnam, London, second edition, 1989

Bristol Aircraft since 1910, C H Barnes, Putnam, London, third edition, 1988

Britain's First Warplanes, Jack M Bruce, Arms and Armour, Poole, 1987

British Aircraft 1809-1914, Peter Lewis, Putnam, London, 1962

British Aviation – The Great War and Armistice, Harald Penrose, Putnam, London, 1969

British Aviation – The Adventuring Years 1920-1929, Harald Penrose, Putnam, London, 1973

British Aviation – Ominous Skies 1935-1939, Harald Penrose, HMSO, London, 1980

British Civil Aircraft since 1919, Volumes 1, 2 and 3, A J Jackson, Putnam & Co, London, second Editions, 1973, 1973 and 1974 respectively

British Civil Aircraft Registers 1919 to 1999, Michael Austen, Air-Britain, Tunbridge Wells, 1999

British Experimental Jet Aircraft, Barrie Hygate, Argus Books, Hemel Hempstead, 1990

British Homebuilt Aircraft, Ken Ellis, Merseyside Aviation Society, Liverpool, second edition, 1979

British Museum Aircraft, Ken Ellis and Phil Butler, Merseyside Aviation Society, Liverpool, 1977

British Naval Aircraft since 1912, Owen Thetford, Putnam, London, revised ed 1971

British Research and Development Aircraft – 70 Years at the Leading Edge, Ray Sturtivant, Haynes Publishing, Sparkford, 1990

British Test Pilots, Geoffrey Dorman, Forbes Robertson, London, 1950

Building Aeroplanes for 'Those Magnificent Men', Air Cdre Allen Wheeler CBE, G T Foulis & Co, London, 1965

Canada's National Aviation Museum: Its History and Collections, K M Molson, National Museum of Science and Technology, Ottawa, 1988

Category Five – A Catalogue of RAF Aircraft Losses 1954-2009, Colin Cummings, Nimbus, Yelvertoft, 2009

Cierva Autogiros – The Development of Rotary-Wing Flight, Peter W Brooks, Smithsonian Institution, Washington DC, USA, 1988

Cold War Years – Flight Testing at Boscombe Down 1945-1975, Tim Mason, Hikoki, Ottringham, 2001

De Havilland Biplane Transports, Paul Hayes and Bernard King, Gatwick Aviation Society/Aviation Classics, Coulsdon, 2003

English Electric Aircraft and Their Predecessors, Stephen Ransom and Robert Fairclough, Putnam, London, 1987

English Electric Canberra, Ken Delve, Peter Green, John Clemons, Midland Counties Publications, Earl Shilton, 1992

English Electric Lightning – Birth of a Legend, and *English Electric Lightning – The Lightning Force*, Stewart A Scott, GMS Enterprises, Peterborough, 2000 and 2004

Eurofighter 2000 – Europe's Fighter for the New Millennium, Hugh Harkins, Aerofax, Earl Shilton, 1997

Fairey Aircraft since 1915, H A Taylor, Putnam & Co, London, 1974

Falklands: The Air War, Rodney Burden, Michael Draper, Douglas Rough, Colin Smith, David Wilton, Arms & Armour, London 1986

Fleet Air Arm Aircraft 1939 to 1945, Ray Sturtivant with Mick Burrow, Air-Britain, Tunbridge Wells, 1995

Fleet Air Arm Fixed-Wing Aircraft since 1946, Ray Sturtivant, Air-Britain, Tunbridge Wells, 2004

Fleet Air Arm Helicopters since 1943, Lee Howard, Mick Burrow and Eric Myall, Air-Britain, Tunbridge Wells, 2011

Force for Freedom – The USAF in the UK since 1948, Michael J F Bowyer, Patrick Stephens, Sparkford, 1994

Gloster Aircraft since 1917, Derek N James, Putnam, London, second edition, 1987

Hawker Hunter – Biography of a Thoroughbred, Francis K Mason, Patrick Stephens, Bar Hill, 1981

Hawker Hurricane R4118, Peter Vacher, Grub Street, London, 2005

Helicopters and Autogyros of the World, Paul Lambermont with Anthony Pirie, Cassell, London, 2nd Edition, 1970

Hendon Aerodrome – A History, David Oliver, Airlife, Shrewsbury, 1994

High Stakes – Britain's Air Arms in Action 1945-1990, Vic Flintham, Pen & Sword, Barnsloey, 2009

History of Aircraft Piston Engines, Herschel Smith, Sunflower University Press, Manhattan, Kansas, USA, 1981

History of British Aviation 1908-1914, R Dallas Brett, Air Research/Kristall Productions, amalgamated edition 1987

Hunter One – The Jet Heritage Story, Mike Phipp with Eric Hayward, Amberley Publishing, Stroud, 2009

In Uniform – Britain's Airworthy Warbirds, Ken Ellis, Merseyside Aviation Society, Liverpool, 1983

Japanese Aircraft of the Pacific War, René J Francillon, Putnam, London, 1979

Junkers Ju 52 – Aircraft and Legend, Heinz J Nowarra, Haynes, Sparkford, 1986

K File – The Royal Air Force of the 1930s, James J Halley MBE, Air-Britain, Tunbridge Wells, 1995

Lost Aviation Collections of Britain, Ken Ellis, Crécy Publishing, Manchester, 2011

Meteor, Bryan Philpott, Patrick Stephens, Wellingborough, 1986

Miles Aircraft – The Early Years, Peter Amos, Air-Britain, Tonbridge, 2009

ML Aviation – A Secret World, Graham Carter, Keyham Books, Chippenham, 2006

Nimrod R.1 – History, Mystery and Gratitude, Royal Air Force Air Media Centre, High Wycombe, 2011

On the Wings of a Gull – Percival and Hunting Aircraft, David W Gearing, Air-Britain, Tonbridge, 2012

One-Eleven Story, Richard J Church, Air-Britain, Tonbridge, 1994

Prelude to the Harrier: P.1127, H C H Merewether obe, HPM Pubications, Beirut, 1998

RAF Flying Training and Support Units since 1912, Ray Sturtivant with John Hamlin, Air-Britain, Staplefield, 2007

RAF Squadrons, Wg Cdr C G Jefford MBE, Airlife, Shrewsbury, 1988

Register of 'Anonymous' Aircraft – British Aviation Preservation Council Register, Ken Ellis, Flying Flea Archive, Rutland, 2004

Royal Aircraft Factory, Paul R Hare, Putnam, London, 1990

Royal Navy Aircraft, Serials and Units 1911-1919, Ray Sturtivant and Gordon Page, Air-Britain, Tonbridge, 1992

Schneider Trophy Races, Ralph Barker, Airlife, Shrewsbury, 1981

Secret Years – Flight Testing at Boscombe Down 1939-1945, 2nd edition, Tim Mason, Crécy Publishing, Manchester, 2010

Shorts Aircraft since 1900, C H Barnes, Putnam, London, 1967

Richard Shuttleworth – An Illustrated Biography, Kevin Desmond, Jane's Publishing, London, 1982

Shuttleworth Collection of Historic Aeroplanes, Cars, Cycles, Carriages and Fire Engines, Wg Cdr T E Guttery MBE, Shuttleworth Collection, Old Warden, second edition 1969

Shuttleworth Collection – Official Guide, David Ogilvy, Airlife, Shrewsbury, 1982

Slide Rule – The Autobiography of an Engineer, Nevil Shute, Readers Union, London, 1956

Sopwith Aircraft 1912-1920, H F King MBE, Putnam, London, 1980

Supermarine Aircraft since 1914, C F Andrews and E B Morgan, Putnam, London, 1981

Survivors, Roy Blewett, Gatwick Aviation Society with Aviation Classics, Croydon, 2012

Taking Flight – Inventing the Aerial Age from Antiquity through the First World War, Richard P Hallion, Oxford University Press Inc, New York, USA, 2003

Time Capsule Fighter – Corsair KD431, David Morris, Sutton Publishing, Stroud, 2006
US Military Aircraft Designations and Serials since 1909, John M Andrade, Midland Counties, Earl Shilton, 1979
Vampire LZ551/G, Sqn Ldr M J Biggs, Society of Friends of the Fleet Air Arm Museum, Yeovilton, 1993
Very Special Lancaster, F E Dymond, Pitkin Pictorials, London, 1976
Veteran and Vintage Aircraft, Leslie Hunt, self-published, Leigh-on-Sea, 1965; also the 1968, 1970 and
      1974 editions
Vickers Valiant – First of the V-Bombers, Eric B Morgan, Aerofax, Hinckley, 2002
Vulcan: Last of the V-Bombers, Duncan Cubitt with Ken Ellis, Osprey, London, 1993
*War Prizes – An Illustrated Survey of German, Italian and Japanese Aircraft Brought to Allied Countries during
      and after the Second World War*, Phil Butler, Midland Counties Publishing, Earl Shilton, 1994
Warbirds Directory, 4th Edition in print and CD, Geoff Goodall, Derek McPhail (publisher), New Gisborne,
      Australia, 2008
We Landed by Moonlight, Hugh Verity, Airdata Publications, Manchester, 1995
Westland Aircraft since 1915, Derek N James, Putnam, London, 1991
Wings on My Sleeve, Capt Eric Brown, Weidenfeld & Nicolson, London, 2006
Wings over Ireland – The Story of the Irish Air Corps, Donal MacCarron, Midland Publishing, Earl Shilton, 1996
Wings over Suez, Brian Cull with David Nicolle and Shlomo Aloni, Grub Street, London, 1996
World War One Survivors, Ray Rimell, Aston Publications, Bourne End, 1990

and, of course...
Wrecks & Relics, all 23 editions: 1st and 2nd editions by D J Stephens, published in 1961 by the
      Merseyside Group of Aviation Enthusiasts, Liverpool and in 1962 by the Merseyside Society of
      Aviation Enthusiasts, Liverpool. 3rd edition by S G Jones, published by MSAE in 1968. 4th edition
      onwards by Ken Ellis; published 1974 and each 'even' year thereon. Publishers were as follows: 4th
      by MSAE, 5th to 10th by Merseyside Aviation Society, Liverpool. 11th to 13th Midland Counties
      Publications, Earl Shilton. 14th to 20th Midland Publishing, Earl Shilton. 21st onwards by Crécy
      Publishing Ltd, Manchester.

Magazines

British Roundel, published by Roundel Research 1997 to 2006
Control Column, published initially by the Northern Aircraft Preservation Society, then by Neville Franklin,
      1963 to 1988
Northern Aeronews, published by the Merseyside Group of Aviation Enthusiasts; in the early 1960s renamed
      Flypast, the MGAE becoming the Merseyside Society of Aviation Enthusiasts and then the Merseyside
      Aviation Society, 1956 to 1985
Prop-Swing, the journal of the Shuttleworth Veteran Aeroplane Society
Roundel, journal of the British Aviation Research Group, 1976 to 1996
Vintage Aircraft, published by Gordon Riley, 1976 to 1982

and, of course...
FlyPast, published by Key Publishing from 1981, Britain's top-selling aviation monthly – **www.flypast.com**

INDEX

Don't trust your mind
It's not always listening

Katie Melua
The Flood, 2010

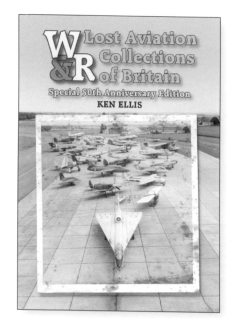